Voices from the House Divided

The United States Civil War as Personal Experience

Voices from the House Divided

The United States Civil War as Personal Experience

Glenn M. Linden
Southern Methodist University

Thomas J. Pressly
University of Washington

McGraw-Hill, Inc.

New York   St. Louis   San Francisco   Auckland   Bogotá   Caracas
Lisbon   London   Madrid   Mexico City   Milan   Montreal   New Delhi
San Juan   Singapore   Sydney   Tokyo   Toronto

This book was set in Palatino by Ruttle, Shaw & Wetherill, Inc.
The editors were Peter Labella and Joseph F. Murphy;
the production supervisor was Annette Mayeski.
The cover was designed by Rafael Hernandez.
R. R. Donnelley & Sons Company was printer and binder.

VOICES FROM THE HOUSE DIVIDED
The United States Civil War as Personal Experience

This book is printed on recycled, acid-free paper containing 10% postconsumer waste.

1 2 3 4 5 6 7 8 9 0   DOC   DOC   9 0 9 8 7 6 5 4

ISBN 0-07-037934-3

Library of Congress Cataloging-in-Publication Data

Voices from the house divided: the United States Civil War as personal experience / Glenn M. Linden, Thomas J. Pressly.
p.   cm.
Includes bibliographical references and index.
ISBN 0-07-037934-3
1. United States—History—Civil War, 1861–1865—Sources.
2. United States—History—Civil War, 1861–1865—Personal narratives.   I. Linden, Glenn M., (date).   II. Pressly, Thomas.
E464.V63   1995
973.7'8—dc20   94-26795

About the Editors

GLENN M. LINDEN is Associate Professor of History at Southern Methodist University. He received his Ph.D. from the University of Washington. He has taught at a number of universities. He is the author of several textbooks, numerous articles, and a book on the Civil War, *Politics or Principle: Congressional Voting on the Civil War Amendments and Pro-Negro Measures, 1837–1869*. He has been active in a number of historical associations, including the American Historical Association, the Southern Historical Association, and the Organization of American Historians.

THOMAS J. PRESSLY is Professor of History, Emeritus, at the University of Washington. He received his Ph.D. from Harvard. He has taught at Princeton and Johns Hopkins and has been in the Department of History at the University of Washington since 1949. He is the author of *Americans Interpret Their Civil War* (1954) and coeditor of *American Political Behavior* (1974) and the *Diary of George Templeton Strong* (1988). A former Ford Foundation Faculty Fellow and Center for Advanced Study in Behavioral Sciences Fellow, he has centered his research on nineteenth-century United States history, particularly the Civil War and Reconstruction, and comparative history.

For
Virginia Linden and Cameron Pressly

Contents

Preface

The recent television series on the Civil War directed by Ken Burns has demonstrated once again the tremendous effectiveness of diaries, letters, and other first-hand accounts in the study of history. These accounts add an important dimension to our understanding of the Civil War years. Contemporary sources are more interesting to most readers than historical monographs or textbooks. The personal sources allow the reader to "discover" the past, and to discover an enlarged past: what wives and husbands wrote to each other, what blacks wrote about whites and what whites wrote about blacks, what soldiers thought about the war, what civilians thought about the war. Readers thus become, to some extent, their own historians.

Many collections of historical sources have been published, but typically they contain brief excerpts from many sources. Unfortunately, the reader does not get to know the authors of these many sources, since there is only a little to read by the author of each account. Our approach is to limit our sources to twenty individuals who left diaries, letters, or other writings. Then we follow these individuals through the years 1861 to 1865. We have found in our teaching over several decades that through this method students come to "know" the historical authors and to experience the past vicariously through their writings. One of our primary goals is that readers of this book will come to know Mary Chesnut, Frederick Douglass, and the other individuals of the 1860s almost as well as they know their own acquaintances in the 1990s. Accordingly, we have included, wherever possible, photographs or portraits of these twenty individuals of the 1860s who make up our "Cast of Characters."

Our Cast of Characters includes both women and men, both wives and their husbands, both blacks and whites, both Southerners and Northerners, both supporters of war and opponents of war, both leaders and followers—all in the attempt to imitate in some small degree the diversity of the "real world" of the 1860s. The words "imitate in some small degree" indicate our realization that the twenty individuals on whom this book is primarily focused cannot possibly reflect the entire range of individuals, of conditions, and of attitudes among the more than thirty-one million persons counted in the United States census of 1860. That difficulty in reflecting the totality of the world of the 1860s has confronted all historical accounts of the Civil War. We have sought to provide some voice for two groups in the population whose members left relatively few personal records and whose own words are frequently not heard in historical accounts: the slaves and those Confederate whites who did not own slaves.

The approximately four million slaves constituted between 10 and 15 percent of the entire population in the census of 1860. One member of our Cast of Characters, Frederick Douglass, was born a slave in Maryland and spent the first twenty-one years of his life there. A second individual in the Cast of Characters, Thomas M. Chester, was the son of a woman who had been a slave. But Chester's mother had escaped from slavery nine years before his birth, and he was born free in Pennsylvania. So also, Frederick Douglass had escaped from slavery in 1838; by the time the fighting broke out in 1861, Douglass had lived more years as a free black in nonslave-holding states than he had lived in slavery. Most of the other persons in the Cast of Characters, whether Northern free blacks, or Northern whites, or Southern white slaveowners, described slaves and slavery in their wartime writings, but we have not found diaries written by slaves themselves during the war years. What has survived, primarily in the records of the Union army, are single letters and other fragmentary and miscellaneous writings from the years 1861 through 1865 by slaves or newly emancipated freedpeople. Many of these writings are now being published in the collection entitled *Freedom: A Documentary History of Emancipation, 1861–1867*, and we have included selections by slaves from that work.

Approximately two thirds of the households of white Confederates did not own slaves, but those households left comparatively few diaries, collections of letters, or other personal accounts written during the war years. We have, however, been able to include in our Cast of Characters one white Confederate couple from Alabama who did not own slaves, John and Mariah Cotton. The Cottons were married in 1850, and their surviving wartime letters to each other show that while they owned no slaves, they did rent a slave and may have attempted to purchase him.

Whatever the difficulties involved in trying to represent in this volume (or in any volume) the totality of the experiences of all the individuals in the Civil War, we think that the virtues of our approach compensate for its unavoidable limitations. Seeing the events of the 1860s primarily through the eyes of twenty individuals can often provide a more immediate, more specific, and more lasting understanding of past occurrences than is conveyed in impersonal and generalized descriptions of entire societies. Until those who study the past can "feel," can "sense," the complex and subtle textures and nuances of life, as those textures and nuances were sensed by individuals in the 1860s, the understanding of the world of the 1860s by later students and scholars will to that extent be diminished.

We have arranged the personal accounts chronologically since that allows us to remain faithful to the manner in which the authors of the accounts experienced their world. We think also that the chronological organization will, in addition, help guard against the pitfalls of "hindsight." The historian David Potter, in one of his most illuminating phrases, described hindsight as "the historian's chief asset and his main liability." The liability of hindsight consists in its distortion and oversimplification of the past by, among other things, failing to provide understanding and appreciation of how individuals who lived in the period under study perceived their situations at the time. To reduce the liability of hindsight, the opinions and actions of individuals in April, 1865, need to be compared with the opinions and actions of the same individuals in 1861 and 1862. Even more, analyses of the Civil War expressed in the 1990s need to be compared with analyses current during the actual years of war.

Within the chronological framework, we have arranged the personal selections thematically around the prevailing military situation. The Civil War was clearly "more than battles." Some who hold this view cite the Emancipation Proclamation of 1862 and analogous Congressional legislation against slavery during the war as the really important actions that make unnecessary much attention to military events. Yet, whether the Emancipation Proclamation or the Congressional legislation against slavery were to have any substantial effect depended above all upon the success of the Union military forces. If the Union armed forces lost the military struggle against the Confederate forces (i.e., lost the war), would the Emancipation Proclamation or the Congressional legislation have freed many, or any, slaves?

Moreover, once the armed hostilities began at Fort Sumter in April, 1861, the course of those hostilities increasingly set the patterns for much that happened in both the Union and the Confederacy. The raising, supplying, and transporting of armies and navies affected, directly or indirectly, the lives of most individual Unionists and Confederates, whether they wished it or not. Conversely, the perception by individuals of the military situation—their sense of whether their side seemed to be winning or losing, both at large or in their immediate locality—affected how and where they lived and made their living, and how they evaluated their political and military leaders.

Contemporaries during the Civil War noted the primacy of military events. On that point, individuals as unlike as young Henry Adams and Abraham Lincoln expressed a common sentiment: "The truth is," wrote Henry Adams in 1863, "all depends on the progress of our armies." That opinion was echoed by Abraham Lincoln near the beginning of his Second Inaugural Address in March, 1865, when he spoke of "the progress of our arms, upon which all else chiefly depends." [See *Battle Cry of Freedom* by James M. McPherson (New York, Oxford University Press, 1988), pp. 651, 718.] The writings of the particular Unionists and Confederates included in this volume reflect the varying degrees to which their own individual situations and actions were influenced by wartime conditions and considerations—thus illustrating the Civil War as personal experience.

*   *   *

Lest the reader assume that the editors have not been diligent in proofreading the text of this book, it should be noted that we have reproduced without change the spelling and punctuation used in the various accounts presented. In addition, we have not cluttered the text with the designation "sic" to indicate our awareness of each idiosyncrasy in spelling or punctuation appearing in one or another of the accounts. The only times in which "sic" appears is when it was placed there by the original editor of a particular selection and has been reproduced here, like the rest of the selection, without change.

The editors wish to thank a number of individuals for their assistance in the making of this volume. The students in our classes, for many years, by their enthusiasm for studying the past through the writings of persons who lived in the past, confirmed and strengthened our conviction of the value of that approach to history reflected in *Voices from the House Divided*. Several friends and fellow historians, in particular Dean Brink, Maclyn Burg, and Richard Hume, read the draft of an early portion of the manuscript and offered helpful comments. Three former members of the McGraw-Hill staff gave crucial aid: David C. Follmer expressed the initial support for the book, and Niels Aaboe and Lisa Calberg carried that support to the advanced stages of the completed manuscript. Their help has been continued at McGraw-Hill by Peter Labella, Monica Freedman, and Joseph F. Murphy. The following readers of the manuscript for McGraw-Hill encouraged us by their sympathetic and perceptive reviews; they made useful suggestions, most of which, as they will see, we have accepted and implemented: Hugh Earnhart, Youngstown State University; Phyllis Field, Ohio University; Richard Frucht, Northwest Missouri State University; James McPherson, Princeton University; James Russell, University of Tennessee–Chattanooga; Donald Schaffer, Broward Community College; Terry Seip, University of Southern California–University Park; Wayne Smith, Indiana University of Pennsylvania; Mart Stewart, Western

Washington University; and Harold Wilson, Old Dominion University. Judy Bland with efficiency and speed typed most of the manuscript in its various drafts. Finally, we are grateful for the interest and encouragement of our respective wives, Virginia Linden and Cameron Pressly. It is not possible now for us to thank the one group of persons, without whom the book literally could not exist—the women and men of the 1860s who wrote the selections printed here.

Glenn M. Linden

Thomas J. Pressly

Cast of Characters
(in order of appearance)

Mary Boykin Chesnut
Portrait by Samuel Stillman Osgood c. 1856, on loan to
The National Portrait Gallery, Smithsonian Institution,
in memory of Mrs. Hendrik B. Van Rensselaer. Owned
by her daughter, Mrs. Theodore G. Koven, Lebanon,
New Jersey, and used with her permission.

MARY BOYKIN (MILLER) CHESNUT (1825–1886) was born into the old
and wealthy Boykin family of South Carolina, and in 1840 she married into
the old and wealthy Chesnut family. Her father and her father-in-law each
owned several plantations and hundreds of slaves, thus placing them, in
terms of slave ownership, in the top 1 percent of all whites in the eleven
Confederate states. High political office came to the men in those families
almost as a matter of course, and in 1858 her husband, James Chesnut, Jr.
(1815–1885), was elected United States senator from South Carolina. In
Washington, the Chesnuts became friends of Senator and Mrs. Jefferson
Davis of Mississippi, and that friendship continued after Jefferson Davis
became President of the Confederate States of America early in 1861.
James Chesnut resigned his U.S. Senate seat after the election of Abraham

Lincoln to the Presidency, and then served as aide to Confederate President Davis and as a brigadier general in the Confederate army. The Chesnuts were frequent visitors in the Davis home, and they were acquainted with other top leaders in the Confederacy. Mary Chesnut was an ardent supporter of the Confederacy, although she was often critical of its officials and their actions, and she was frequently fearful of ultimate military defeat. Hostile to various aspects of the institution of slavery, she expressed disgust when she observed the sale of a slave woman ("I felt faint—seasick"), and she indignantly stated her belief that her father-in-law was the father of one or more slave children. She at times linked slavery and the institution of marriage: "You know what the Bible says about slavery—and marriage. Poor women. Poor slaves." During the war years, she asked frequent questions about what the slaves were thinking, and at times she worried about the possibility of slave revolts. She kept a lengthy diary during the war, which she supplemented after the fighting ended, and those writings are the source for the accounts by her in this volume.

David Golightly Harris
Photograph courtesy of the Wofford College Archives.

Emily Jane Liles Harris
Photograph courtesy of the Wofford College Archives.

DAVID GOLIGHTLY HARRIS (1824–1875) and *EMILY LILES HARRIS* (1827–1899) were born and lived in the same state as the Chesnuts, South Carolina, and they owned slaves, but they had few other similarities with the Chesnuts. In contrast to the Chesnut and Boykin families, planters with several plantations and hundreds of slaves, David and Emily Harris were a farm family, owning ten slaves in 1860, four of whom were children, three children under the age of three. David G. Harris at times worked in the fields with his slaves in cultivating approximately a hundred acres of land. Mrs. Chesnut and her husband were part of the South Carolina elite, whether defined in social, political, or economic terms; they had lived in Charleston, Washington, D.C., Montgomery, Alabama, and various other locations. The Harrises were rooted in the upcountry, Piedmont region near the village of Spartanburg, South Carolina (population approximately 1,000 in 1860); David Harris had not been to Charleston until July of 1862, and Emily probably never went to Charleston or to any place that far away from the Harris farm. David and Emily Harris supported the secession of their state, and they supported the Confederate cause, but by 1861 they had eight children, and David Harris was reluctant to leave his family and join the Confederate armed forces. When the conscription age was raised to forty-five, he enlisted in the South Carolina state militia, beginning service in November, 1862, and continuing with interruptions until March, 1865. For much of that time he was stationed in the Charleston area, and he returned home every so often on furloughs; he hired a substitute for six weeks in December, 1863, and January, 1864. Throughout his military service he was an enlisted man; although he suffered hardships and was in areas under enemy fire, he was not often engaged in active combat. He began keeping a journal in 1855 (primarily, but not solely, a record of farm operations), and it was continued, while he was away during the war, by his wife, with a few entries by his daughters. From that journal come the selections printed in this volume.

George Templeton Strong
From a photograph in his diary, dated Washington, October 10, 1863. Reprinted with the permission of Macmillan Publishing Company.

GEORGE TEMPLETON STRONG (1820–1875) was a lawyer in New York City, a member of a prominent family, a graduate and later a trustee of Columbia University, a vestryman of Trinity Episcopal Church, a lover of music and of literature. He was an interested observer of the political scene, beginning in the 1830s and 1840s as an upper-class supporter of the

Whig party in opposition to the Jacksonian Democrats. By the late 1850s, Strong had become an ardent champion of the Union against Southern secessionists. As a patriotic backer of the United States government during the Civil War, Strong became treasurer of the United States Sanitary Commission, an all-purpose organization that performed many of the tasks assigned in later wars to groups such as the Red Cross, the USO, and the medical branches of the various armed services. Strong, through his work in the Sanitary Commission, met and visited President Lincoln on two occasions and was present in the East Room of the White House for Lincoln's funeral in 1865. Strong began to keep a diary in 1835 when he was fifteen years old, and he continued to make regular and often extensive entries there until his death in 1875. It is from that remarkable forty-year diary that the writings by Strong are quoted in the present volume.

Frederick Douglass
Reprinted with the permission of International Publishing Co., Inc.

FREDERICK DOUGLASS (1817?–1895) was born a slave in Maryland and named Frederick Augustus Washington Bailey, but he took the name Douglass after escaping from slavery in 1838. Douglass escaped by traveling by train from Baltimore to New York, using the identification papers of a free black friend. After working as a laborer in Massachusetts, Douglass became an antislavery lecturer and founded and edited a newspaper and a magazine in Rochester, New York. In the 1840s, he published his widely read autobiography, which he updated after the Civil War. By the 1860s he was probably the best-known black in the United States, and perhaps in the English-speaking world, since he had lectured against slavery in Ireland, Scotland, and England. During the Civil War, Douglass supported many of the policies of the Lincoln administration, but he maintained that the administration did not move quickly enough in making the war an attack on the institution of slavery, in enlisting black troops in the Union army, and in paying black soldiers the same wage as white soldiers. Douglass talked with Lincoln on several different occasions while the fighting was in progress, and Lincoln was quoted as saying of Douglass that "considering the condition from which he had arisen and the obsta-

cles that he had overcome, and the position to which he had attained . . .
he regarded him one of the most meritorious men, if not the most meritorious man, in the United States."

A periodical published by Douglass in Rochester, New York, *Douglass's
Monthly*, is the source of most of his writings included in the present volume.

Charles C. Jones, Jr.
"Photograph taken probably in 1859 shows First Lieu-
tenant Jones in the dress uniform of the Chatham
Artillery." From *A Present For Mr. Lincoln* by Alexander
A. Lawrence. Macon, Georgia, The Ardivan Press,
1961. (opposite page 101)

THE JONES FAMILY of Liberty County, Georgia. Letters are included in
the present volume primarily from three members of this striking family:
Rev. *CHARLES COLCOCK JONES* (1804–1863), his wife (and first cousin)
MARY JONES JONES (1808–1863), and their son, *CHARLES COLCOCK
JONES, JR.* (1831–1893).

Rev. Jones and his wife were joint owners of three plantations, containing slightly more than 3,500 acres; their slaves numbered 107 in the 1850
census and 129 in the 1860 census. Rev. Jones had received most of his for-
mal schooling in Northern states, and his diploma and license to preach
came from Princeton University in 1830. Mary Jones had attended various
academies in Georgia, and she married Rev. Jones when he returned to
Georgia after completing his studies at Princeton. During most of his life,
Rev. Jones, with the support of his wife, was a minister to blacks in Liberty
County, arranging for the construction of several churches in which he
preached to blacks and publishing two volumes concerning the religious
education of blacks. He also served as professor at the Presbyterian Theological Seminary in Columbia, South Carolina (1837–1838, 1848–1850), and
he and his family lived in Philadelphia from 1850 to 1853 while he was cor-
responding secretary of the Board of Domestic Missions of the Presbyter-
ial Church.

Charles Colcock Jones, Jr., after private tutoring in Georgia and study at
South Carolina College in Columbia, South Carolina, graduated from
Princeton University in 1852. He then studied law at Dane Law School of
Harvard University and was awarded his law degree in 1855. Beginning
in 1856, he practiced law in Savannah, Georgia, and he served as mayor of

Savannah in 1860 and 1861. When the Civil War broke out, he was an ardent supporter of the Confederacy, and he was an officer in the Confederate army from 1861 to 1865, rising in rank from lieutenant to lieutenant colonel. He had married before the war began, in 1858, but his wife died in 1861, leaving an infant girl who was cared for by Rev. and Mrs. Jones. Charles Jones married for the second time in 1863.

Mary Sharpe Jones, while living with her parents in Philadelphia, attended (1850–1852) a seminary for young ladies. She returned with her parents to Georgia in 1853 and lived there with them until 1857 when she married Robert Q. Mallard, a Presbyterian clergyman. She and her husband and their three children lived in Georgia during the Civil War, and her husband was captured by Union soldiers of Sherman's army in December, 1864. Mary and her children lived with her mother while Sherman's forces occupied the region in which the Jones plantations were located—and Mary's fourth child was born at that time. She and her mother both kept journals describing their life during the occupation, and excerpts from those journals are included in this volume.

The writings of the Jones family reflect their care and consideration for one another, and the harmonious relations between the family members. These writings reflect also the strong support of the Confederacy by the family and their apparently unquestioning acceptance of the institution of slavery.

MARIA LYDIG DALY (1824–1894) was born into an old, wealthy, and distinguished New York City family of Dutch and German merchants. She married Charles Patrick Daly (1816–1899), the son of poor Irish Catholic immigrants, in 1856. Her family objected initially to her marrying Daly, whose background was considered by Maria's parents to be inferior to that of Maria. Her family members did not attend the wedding ceremony, and they provided a dowry that Maria thought inadequate. In fact, Maria's husband, despite the fact that his parents had been poor immigrants and that he was self-educated, was at the time of his marriage a justice of the Court of Common Pleas of the City of New York, the city's highest court. Within two years of his marriage he became chief justice of that court, a position he held for twenty-seven years. By the 1850s he had become a leader in political, intellectual, and social circles in New York. Maria and Judge Daly were in contact with many of the most celebrated figures of the day, including, for example, Secretary of State William M. Seward and Generals Winfield Scott and George B. McClellan.

Maria, like her husband, was a Union (or War) Democrat: She supported the war efforts against the Confederates, but was critical of many Republicans, including President and Mrs. Lincoln. She was also critical of abolitionists and New Englanders, and was unsympathetic to most blacks. Maria kept a diary, beginning in 1861, and the selections in the present volume are taken from that diary.

Marcus Spiegel
Photograph, autumn 1862, in the possession of Jean
Powers Soman, and used with her permission.

MARCUS SPIEGEL (1829–1864) was born in Abenheim, Germany, where
his father, Moses, served as rabbi for the town's Jewish community. Moses
Spiegel, fearing renewed persecution of Jews, emigrated to the United
States in 1846 with his wife and four of their children. Marcus, the oldest
child, remained in Germany and participated in the Liberal Revolution of
1848. When that revolution failed in Germany, Marcus, like other disappointed Forty-Eighters, fled to the United States in 1849. After a brief stay
on New York's Lower East Side, Marcus moved to Chicago in 1850 and
became a peddler of household goods, with Ohio as his assigned territory.
In Ohio, he met a Quaker family, the Hamlins, and in 1853 he married the
daughter of the family, Caroline Hamlin, who converted to Judaism. Marcus became a naturalized citizen in 1857 and took an active role in the
Democratic party in Ohio as a supporter of Stephen A. Douglas. When the
Civil War commenced, Marcus and his wife had three children, and his
restaurant and produce businesses required attention. The regular pay of
an army officer could help his difficult financial situation; he also desired
to preserve the Union for his children, and considered that to be his duty
as an immigrant. He applied for an army commission and became a first
lieutenant in November, 1861.

Spiegel was apparently an effective army officer who was greatly
respected and admired by his soldiers. He fought in the Shenandoah Valley in the spring of 1862, and then later in that year was part of McClellan's
army in the retreat from Richmond after the Seven Days battles. In 1863,
he fought in Grant's army in the assault on Vicksburg; the following year
he participated in the Red River campaign in Louisiana. He rose to the
rank of colonel, one of the few Jewish colonels in the Civil War, and he had
probably been recommended for promotion to brigadier general by the
time of his death in combat in 1864. Throughout his years in the army he
wrote frequently to his wife, to their children, and to his brother. Selections
from those letters are reprinted in this volume. His letters make no mention of hostility to himself because of his religion, but they do express his
own unflattering views of blacks. The letters show a change in Spiegel's
attitudes toward the institution of slavery: In March, 1862, he described
slaves in Virginia as "fat, sleek and hearty looking," adding that "it is not

necessary to fight for the darkies" (that is, the abolition of slavery should not be made a goal of the war). By January, 1864, however, Spiegel, stationed in Louisiana, writes that he has now learned about "the horrors of slavery" and is glad that "the accursed institution" is being closed out—"I am [in] favor of doing away with the institution of slavery," even though that may be opposed to the policies of the Democratic party.

John W. Cotton
"From a picture presumably made during the War."
Used by permission of The University of Alabama Press.

JOHN WEAVER COTTON (1831–1866) and *MARIAH HINDSMAN COTTON* (1833– ?) were both born in Georgia and married there in 1850. In 1853 or 1854, they came to Coosa County, Alabama, and lived there as farmers for the rest of their lives. They farmed some sixty-five acres of improved land, valued at $1,200 in the census of 1860, and were thus "small farmers" or "yeomen farmers." They owned no slaves, although they rented a slave from a neighbor and attempted unsuccessfully to purchase him. As nonslaveowners, the Cottons were among the approximately 70 percent of white families in the Confederate states who owned no slaves. The census of 1860 showed the Cottons as owning two horses, one mule, and four milk cows, plus other cattle, sheep, and pigs. They grew wheat, corn, oats, and potatoes, and there is no mention of their growing cotton. The letters written by the Cottons to each other show little training in spelling or punctuation, and there is no mention of attendance at educational institutions. They were members of the Primitive Baptist Church. John Cotton enlisted in military service in April, 1862, and was paroled at the end of the war in May, 1865; he served as a private in the cavalry throughout his service—first in an Alabama cavalry "legion," which was consolidated into the 10th Confederate Cavalry in December, 1862. The Cottons had seven children at the time of John's enlistment. John Cotton wrote to his wife while he was in the army, and she wrote to him; many of his letters, and a few of hers, have survived, dated from April, 1862, to the beginning of February, 1865. These letters are the primary source of information about the Cottons, and it is from these letters that the selections in this volume are taken.

Charlotte L. Forten Grimké
From page 86 of *Historical Afro-American Biographies* by
Wilhelmena S. Robinson. Cornwells Heights, Pennsylvania, The Publishers Agency, Inc., 1978. Copyrighted
by The Association for the Study of Afro-American
Life and History, and reprinted with its permission.

CHARLOTTE FORTEN GRIMKÉ (1837–1914) was born in Philadelphia to
free black parents, the only child of Robert Bridges Forten and Mary Virginia Woods Forten. Charlotte was of the fourth generation of Fortens who
had been born free in America, and her grandfather, James Forten, Sr., had
become wealthy as the owner of a sailmaking company in Philadelphia.
Her mother was a mulatto member of a prominent Philadelphia abolitionist family, but she died when Charlotte was three years old. Thenceforth, Charlotte's grandmother and aunts became important influences in
her life, as well as her father and grandfather. These and other family
members taught Charlotte the importance of many reform movements,
including the efforts to end slavery and to secure equal rights for blacks.
The homes of those family members were visited by national leaders of
reform such as William Lloyd Garrison, John Greenleaf Whittier, and Harriet Martineau.

When Charlotte was sixteen, she was sent to live with a prominent
black abolitionist family in Salem, Massachusetts, where she could attend
the nonsegregated and excellent schools of that city, rather than the segregated and poorly equipped schools for blacks in Philadelphia. When she
completed her education, she accepted an offer to teach in a grammar
school in Salem, becoming the first black to be offered such a position in
that city. Unfortunately, she had continuing health problems (primarily
respiratory), which had been common in her family, and these problems
made it difficult for her to hold a regular teaching position. Yet, despite
periods of illness and recuperation, she continued, in the late 1850s and
during the first year of the Civil War, whenever she was physically able, to
teach, to remain active in the abolitionist cause, and to write poems and
essays for publication. In 1862, John Greenleaf Whittier suggested that she
could be of great service if she went South and taught escaped slaves who
had fled to Union camps. She accepted this suggestion and sailed at the
end of October, 1862, for Port Royal, South Carolina, teaching in that vicinity for approximately eighteen months.

Charlotte began to keep a journal in 1854, and that journal is the source
of the passages printed in this book.

Samuel Cormany
Photograph probably taken in 1863. Used by permission of the University of Pittsburgh Press.

Rachel and Cora Cormany
Photograph taken in the studio of J. Keagy, Chambersburg, Pennsylvania, 1863. Used by permission of the University of Pittsburgh Press.

SAMUEL CORMANY (1838–1921) and *RACHEL BOWMAN CORMANY* (1836–1899) met while students at Otterbein University, a United Brethren school in Ohio, during the late 1850s. They were both children of farmers: Rachel grew up on a farm in the Province of Ontario in Canada, while Samuel's home was a farm a few miles north of Chambersburg, Pennsylvania. Both Rachel and Samuel were deeply committed to their religion, and it is not surprising that they met at a denominational college. Their religious background was evangelical Protestantism; the United Brethren denomination was formed in late-eighteenth-century revivals among German Reformed and Mennonite congregations in Pennsylvania and Maryland. The United Brethren have been described as "Germanic Methodists," and the denomination did merge ultimately with the present United Methodist Church. The religion of the Cormanys emphasized "intense personal spirituality" and "unwavering commitment to ethical behavior"; they prayed frequently and struggled with their consciences over issues such as the use of alcohol.

The Cormanys were married in November, 1860, and spent most of the next two years in Canada near Rachel's relatives, returning to the United States and settling in Chambersburg in August, 1862. Almost immediately after their return from Canada, Chambersburg was threatened with invasion by Lee's Confederate army, and Samuel, with Rachel's support, enlisted in the Union army. He served until the end of the war in the 16th

Pennsylvania Volunteer Cavalry, participating in most of the major campaigns in the eastern theater of operations after 1862—Chancellorsville, Gettysburg, the siege of Petersburg, Appomattox. Meanwhile, Rachel remained throughout the war in or near Chambersburg with their daughter, Mary Cora (born in May, 1862).

Rachel and Samuel each began to keep a diary in the late 1850s, and they continued to write in their diaries throughout the Civil War. These two diaries, one kept by the wife-mother-housewife in Pennsylvania, the second kept by the husband-father-soldier in various camps, are the source of the accounts printed in this volume. Here we have diaries by two individuals from "middling farm families" who grew up in rural areas and were in many respects "common folk."

JAMES HENRY GOODING (1837–1864), a free mulatto, lived in Troy, New York, and may have been born there. Little or nothing is known about his parents, or about his own life until he came to New Bedford, Massachusetts, in 1856 at the age of nineteen. New Bedford had a thriving community of blacks, some of whom went to sea on whaling or merchant ships. Gooding served as cook or steward on two whaling voyages out of New Bedford, one lasting from 1856 to 1860, and the second from 1860 to 1861. In 1862, he was cook and steward on a voyage of a merchant ship to Argentina that lasted approximately six months. While at sea, he wrote poems, several of which have survived. After the voyage to Argentina, Gooding married a woman from New Bedford on September 28, 1862.

The final Proclamation of Emancipation, January 1, 1863, stated that blacks "will be received into the armed service of the United States," and by the following month the recruitment of a regiment of free blacks was under way in New Bedford. Gooding enlisted in that regiment, the 54th Massachusetts Volunteer Infantry, on February 14, 1863, the eighth person in New Bedford to enlist. After training in Massachusetts, Gooding and his regiment went by boat to Beaufort, South Carolina, and by June were participating in combat operations in the vicinity of Charleston. Gooding took part in the battle of Fort Wagner in July, 1863, and then in early 1864 fought in operations in northern Florida. In one of the Florida engagements, at Olustee in February, 1864, Gooding was captured, and was imprisoned with other Union prisoners of war at Andersonville. There at Andersonville, Gooding died on July 19, 1864.

Almost as soon as he went into the 54th, Gooding began to write letters describing his experiences, for publication in the *New Bedford Mercury*. Selections from those letters are quoted in this volume.

CYRUS GUERNSEY PRINGLE (1838–1911) was born in Vermont of Scottish Presbyterian and English Puritan ancestors. Raised on a Vermont farm, he attended school in a nearby village and then a college preparatory school in Quebec. When his father and an elder brother died, he was obliged to return from Quebec to the farm. He married a Vermont school-teacher in February, 1863, and it may have been due partly to her influence that he joined the Society of Friends and became a conscientious objector. Not long after his marriage, when he was drafted into the Union army, he refused on principle to accept the offer of his uncle to purchase an exemption for him from military service. Once he was in the army, he held that his religious principles did not allow him to perform military service or service in hospitals where soldiers were treated. After approximately six months in the army, he was able through a friend to have his case called to the attention of President Lincoln, and Lincoln ordered his release from military service. He spent the rest of the war as a breeder of plants in Vermont. Pringle kept a diary of his experiences in the army, and the selections in this volume are drawn from that diary.

Esther Hill Hawks
"Esther Hill Hawks as a young woman." Used by permission of the University of South Carolina Press.

ESTHER HILL HAWKS (1833–1906) was born in New Hampshire, where in 1854 she married a physician, Dr. John Milton Hawks, the brother of a friend. Esther Hawks herself became a physician when she graduated in 1857 from the New England Medical College (founded in Boston in 1848). She engaged in medical practice in New Hampshire, although she experienced some prejudice against women as doctors. When the Civil War broke out, she applied for service in the Union armed forces as a physician or as a nurse, but was not accepted. She was accepted, however, as a volunteer teacher of former slaves with the National Freedman's Relief Association, and she was sent by that association to the Sea Islands of South Carolina in October, 1862. There she was reunited with her husband, who was acting assistant surgeon in the Union army, on the staff of General Rufus Saxton, commander of the Union forces in the area.

In January, 1863, Esther Hawks became a teacher with the First South Carolina Volunteer Infantry Regiment, composed of black troops, most of whom had been slaves, and commanded by Colonel Thomas Wentworth Higginson. Later in 1863, she and her husband were both assigned, for a time, to the General Hospital in Beaufort, South Carolina, the first hospital established for black soldiers; her husband was made director of the hospital, and she was in charge when he was absent. After the battle of Fort Wagner in July, 1863, Esther Hawks helped in the care of the wounded troops of the 54th Regiment Massachusetts Volunteer Infantry, and she repeated that assistance after the battle of Olustee, Florida, in February, 1864. She remained in Florida, except for a leave in New England in the autumn of 1864, until she returned to Charleston in March, 1865, following its capture by the Union forces.

She left a diary covering the Civil War years, and that diary is the source of her writings reproduced in this volume.

Thomas Morris Chester
"Chester was appointed brigadier general of the Louisiana State Militia in 1873." Used by permission of Yvonne Martin.

THOMAS MORRIS CHESTER (1834–1892) was born in Harrisburg, Pennsylvania. His mother had been born a slave in Virginia in 1806, but had escaped slavery by fleeing from Baltimore to Pennsylvania in 1825. His father's date of birth was probably 1784, but it is not known whether he was slave or free before he came to Harrisburg in the early 1820s. His father and mother owned and ran a restaurant in Harrisburg that was a social and political center for blacks; it was also a center for abolitionist activity, and William Lloyd Garrison's *Liberator* could be purchased there. Chester's parents supported education for their children, and at the age of sixteen he was enrolled in the recently opened Allegheny Institute (later Avery College) for blacks, across the river from Pittsburgh. Later, from 1854 to 1856, he attended Thetford Academy in Vermont, ten miles from Dartmouth, and enjoyed its rigorous classical curriculum. He was the only black at the school, and most of his expenses were paid by (white) advocates of black colonization. Many graduates of Thetford went on to study at Harvard, Yale, Princeton, Dartmouth, Brown, and other such colleges, but Chester had no funds for that purpose.

From 1853 until 1861, he spent most of the time (with the exception of the two years at Thetford) in Liberia, the colony for blacks established by the American Colonization Society. Back in the United States, Chester in

1863 headed the drive in Harrisburg to recruit blacks to enlist in the 54th and 55th Regiments, which were being formed in Massachusetts. Then later in 1863, when Confederate advance troops reached the outskirts of Harrisburg in June, he helped to raise a company of black troops in the state militia with himself as captain. His company and other black volunteers were not accepted for active service, however, and the military threat to Harrisburg ended with the Union victory at Gettysburg. This and other experiences of hostility to blacks were disillusioning to Chester, and in the autumn of 1863, he went to England, apparently hoping to raise funds so that he could receive legal training there. He gave a series of lectures under the auspices of the British and Foreign Anti-Slavery Society on "The American Crisis and Its Effect on the Negro," but he was not successful in securing funds for his legal education and returned to the United States in the spring of 1864.

The trip to England may have increased his reputation in Pennsylvania, and in August, 1864, he was hired as a war correspondent by John W. Forney's newspaper, the *Philadelphia Press*, to cover the activities of black troops. He has been described as "the first and only black correspondent of a major daily during the war"; attached to the Army of the James, he spent most of his time in the vicinity of Richmond and Petersburg. The first of his dispatches from the front was dated August, 1864, and the last June 12, 1865. He was one of the first reporters to enter Richmond with the victorious Union Forces, led by the black troops of the XXV Army Corps, and he remained in Richmond until mid-June, 1865, reporting on postwar conditions. When he left Richmond it was as one of a committee of ten blacks who visited President Johnson in June, 1865, to protest postwar conditions for blacks in Richmond.

The writings of Chester presented in this volume are from his dispatches to the *Philadelphia Press*.

Voices from the House Divided

The United States Civil War as Personal Experience

INTRODUCTION

"Such Days of Excitement"—The Outbreak of Armed Hostilities at Fort Sumter, April, 1861

"I did not know that one could live such days of excitement."
—MARY B. CHESNUT, April 15, 1861

"At half-past four [in the morning of April 12, 1861], the heavy booming of a cannon" firing against Fort Sumter in the harbor of Charleston, South Carolina, introduced Mary B. Chesnut to the outbreak of armed hostilities in the American Civil War.

"I sprang out of bed," Mrs. Chesnut wrote. "And on my knees—prostrate—I prayed as I never prayed before.

There was a sound of stir all over the house—pattering of feet in the corridor—all seemed hurrying one way. I put on my double gown and a shawl and went, too. It was to the housetop. . . .

I knew my husband was rowing about in a boat somewhere in that dark bay. And that the shells were roofing it over—bursting toward the fort. If Anderson [Robert A. Anderson, commander of the United States forces at Fort Sumter] was obstinate—he [Mary Chesnut's husband] was to order the forts on our side to open fire. Certainly fire had begun. The regular roar of the cannon—there it was. And who could tell what each volley accomplished of death and destruction.

The women were wild, there on the housetop. Prayers from the women and inprecations from the men, and then a shell would light up the scene. . . .

April 13, 1861. . . . the sound of those guns makes regular meals impossible. None of us go to table. . . .

Some of the anxious hearts lie on their beds and moan in solitary mis-

1

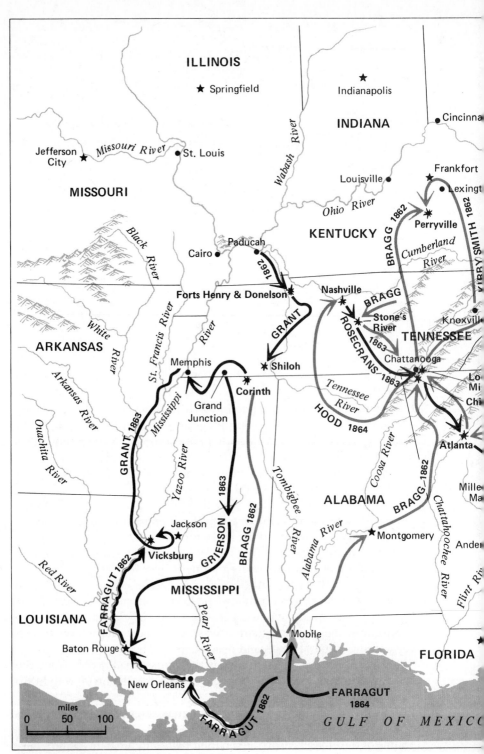

From James M. McPherson, *Ordeal by Fire: The Civil War and Reconstruction*, 2d ed. Copyright © 1992 by McGraw-Hill, Inc. Used by permission of McGraw-Hill, Inc.

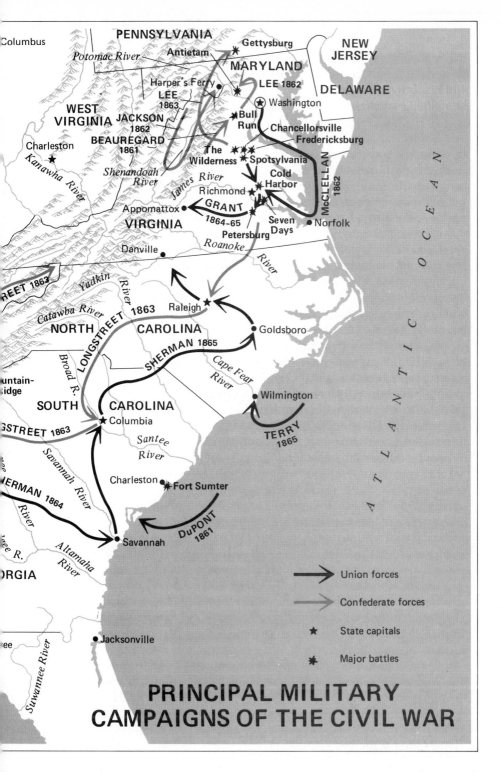

PENNSYLVANIA

Columbus

Potomac River

Antietam

Gettysburg

NEW
JERSEY

MARYLAND

Harper's Ferry

LEE 1862

DELAWARE

WEST
VIRGINIA

LEE
1863

JACKSON
1862

Washington

BEAUREGARD
1861

Bull
Run

Chancellorsville

Charleston

Fredericksburg

Kanawha River

*Shenandoah
River*

The
Wilderness

Spotsylvania

James River

MCCLELLAN
1862

Cold
Harbor

Richmond

Appomattox

GRANT
1864–65

Seven
Days

Norfolk

VIRGINIA

Petersburg

Danville

*Roanoke
River*

REET 1863

*Yadkin
River*

Raleigh

Catawba River

LONGSTREET 1863

NORTH   CAROLINA

Goldsboro

SHERMAN 1865

Broad R.

*Cape Fear
River*

untain-
idge

SOUTH   CAROLINA

Wilmington

GSTREET 1863

Columbia

*Santee
River*

TERRY
1865

Savannah River

Charleston

Fort Sumter

ee R.

*Altamaha
River*

ERMAN 1864

Savannah

DuPONT
1861

RGIA

Jacksonville

Suwannee River

ATLANTIC   OCEAN

→ Union forces

→ Confederate forces

★ State capitals

✳ Major battles

PRINCIPAL MILITARY
CAMPAIGNS OF THE CIVIL WAR

ery. Mrs. Wigfall [wife of former United States senator from Texas Louis T. Wigfall] and I solace ourselves with tea in my room.

These women have all a satisfying faith. 'God is on our side,' they cry. When we are shut in, we (Mrs. Wigfall and I) ask, 'Why?' We are told: 'Of course He hates the Yankees.' . . .

Not by one word or look can we detect any change in the demeanor of these negro servants [i.e., slaves]. Laurence sits at our door, as sleepy and as respectful and as profoundly indifferent. So are they all. They carry it too far. You could not tell that they hear even the awful row that is going on in the bay, though it is dinning in their ears night and day. And people talk before them as if they were chairs and tables. And they make no sign. Are they stolidly stupid or wiser than we are, silent and strong, biding their time? . . .

April 15, 1861. I did not know that one could live such days of excitement.

They called, 'Come out—there is a crowd coming.'

A mob indeed, but it was headed by Colonels Chesnut [Mary Chesnut's husband] and Manning [John Laurence Manning, an aide-de-camp to General P.G.T. Beauregard, as was Colonel Chesnut].

The crowd was shouting and showing these two as messengers of good news. They were escorted to Beauregard's headquarters. Fort Sumter had surrendered. . . .

We have burned our ships—we are obliged to go on now. . . .

April 27, 1861. Montgomery [Alabama, the first capital of the Confederacy]. Here we are. . . .

Everywhere the cars [i.e., train] stopped. The people wanted a speech. There was one stream of fervid oratory. . . .

The [*New York*] *Herald* says, 'Slavery must be extinguished, if in blood. . . .

At Mrs. Toomb's reception [Julia DuBose Toombs, wife of the Confederate secretary of state] Mr. Stephens [Alexander H. Stephens, vice president of the Confederacy] came by me. . . . Today he was not cheerful in his views. I called him halfhearted—accused him of looking back. . . . He was deeply interesting, and he gave me some new ideas as to our dangerous situation. Fears for the future, and not exultation at our successes, pervade his discourse.

Dined at the president's [of the Confederacy, Jefferson Davis]. Never had a pleasanter day. She is as witty as he is wise. He was very agreeable; he took me in to dinner.

The talk was of Washington. Nothing of our present difficulties. . . .

We would have war. And now we seem to be letting our golden opportunity pass. We are not preparing for war.

Talk—talk—in that [Confederate] Congress. Lazy legislators—rash, reckless, headlong, devil-may-care, proud, passionate, unruly raw material for soldiers. . . .

May 13, 1861. Dallas County [Alabama, at the plantation of Mrs. Chesnut's sister and brother-in-law]. . . .

Saw for the first time the demoralization produced by hopes of freedom. My mother's butler (whom I taught to read, sitting on his knife board) continued to keep from speaking to us. He was as efficient as ever in his proper place, but he did not come behind scenes as usual and have a friendly chat. He held himself aloof, so grand and stately we had to send him a 'tip' through his wife Hetty, mother's maid. She showed no signs of disaffection—came to my bedside next morning with everything that was nice for breakfast. She had let me sleep till midday. She embraced me over and over again.

I remarked, 'What a capital cook they have here.'

She curtsied to the ground. 'I cooked every mouthful on that tray. As if I did not know what you like to eat since you was a baby.'

Mrs. Fitzpatrick [Aurelia (Blassingame) Fitzpatrick of Alabama, a friend of the Chesnuts] says Mr. Davis is too gloomy for her. He says we must prepare for a long war and unmerciful reverses at first because they are readier for war and so much stronger numerically. Men and money count so in war. 'As they do everywhere else,' said I, doubting her accurate account of Mr. Davis's spoken words, though she tried to give it faithfully.

We need patience and persistence. There is enough and to spare of pluck and dash among us. The do-and-dare style."

Shortly before the outbreak of armed hostilities at Fort Sumter, Mrs. Chesnut explained the cause of secession and of North versus South conflict through the analogy of divorce from marriage, with ultimate blame for the situation upon the Northerners.

"*March, 1861.* . . . We [Southerners] separated because of incompatibility of temper. We are divorced, North from South, because we hated each other so. If we could only separate—a 'sèparation à l'agréable,' as the French say it, and not a horrid fight for divorce."

After the outbreak of war at Fort Sumter, she continued to use the marriage analogy in discussing the causes of the war:

"*June 10, 1861.* . . . We only want to separate from them [Northerners], and they put such an inordinate value on us, they are willing to risk all—life and limb and all their money—to keep us, they love us so. . . . Anderson fired the train which blew up the Union when he slipped into Fort Sumter that night when we expected to talk it all over. . . .
June 28, 1861. . . . We are an unwilling bride. I think incompatibility of temper began when it was made plain to us that we got all the opprobrium of slavery and they all the money there was in it—with their tariff. . . .

August 18, 1861. . . . The idea that we [Confederates] want to invade or subjugate! We would only be too grateful to be left alone."
[*Mary Chesnut's Civil War.* Edited by C. Vann Woodward. New Haven and London, Yale University Press. Copyright 1981 by C. Vann Woodward, Sally Bland Metts, Barbara G. Carpenter, Sally Bland Johnson, and Katherine W. Herbert, pp. 46, 48–50, 54–57, 59–60, 25, 73, 84, 153. Permission to print these and other passages included in the present volume granted by Yale University Press.]

The emotions and actions which Mary Chesnut reported among the Confederacy's elite in Charleston and Montgomery were matched by the reactions in the rural enclave around Spartanburg, South Carolina, recorded by Piedmont farmer David Golightly Harris. The words in Harris's journal, however, were less elegant and less numerous than those written by Chesnut.

April 12 [1861]. War & Rumors of wars. Great excitement prevails at this time, on account of a report that Fort Sumter is to be bombarded immediately. The volenteers at Spartanburgh has been orderd to repair to Charleston. . . . Laura [wife of David G. Harris] & myself . . . remained in town all night and the next day until the cars came with the all Important News that Fort Sumter was at that time being bombarded. I came home late & found the following note from Camp [Harris's brother-in-law], which at wifes request I poste in my journal.

Golightly Place. April 12th at Sundown.
    Dear Sir Rub up your Rifle the War has begun. The fight Began yesterday Evening a little before Night thar was 9 War Steamers hove in Sight & they Started one in to fort Sumter but it did not get thare. Our batterys opened upon it & then Sumter opened on our batteries. The vessel turned back to Sea and then our Guns were turned on Sumter and they were amusing each other with 10 inch Iron ball at 9 oclock last night which was the last news we have had. All the Compys leave Spartanburg on tomorrow Mornings Train. The highest state of Excitement prevails in Spartanburgh Just Now. . . .
                                        Yours . . . [signed] W C Camp.

April 13. Came home from the village & found that my hands had not done much work in my absence. Rain last night, the land too wet to plow. The negroes sprouting.
April 14. Went to the sunday-school & to church. Great excitement among the people. More soldiers ordered to Charleston. In the evening (Sunday)

heard the cars whistling, and supposeing there something of importance to be heard, I started to the village. While on the road I heard the cannon firing & hurried on to learn what it all meant. When I got to the village I found it alive with people and was told that Fort Sumter was taken. . . . This notorious little battle will have a tendency to bring out the other states, and show the Black Republicans that the South will fight.

April 15. The morning pleasant & the land in working order. . . . The grass is growing finely, & the trees are shoing the effects of the Spring weather. I think that our cattle can now do without any more feeding. . . .

April 16. The land being too wet to plow, I went to the village to hear from the Seat of war. Pres A Lincoln has issued orders for 75,000 men to Keep the peace &c. This begins to look a little squally; but still nobody is afraid. I think this will bring out the Border States. . . . The evening was so cold, windy & a little rain. I declair I had like to froze. . . .

April 19. Beautiful Spring morning. I did intend to kill a turkey-gobler sure, but I was so lazy and sleepy that I could not get up. . . . Quite cold and windy in the evening. Heard the cars whistling as if they had news of importance. Then we heard the cannon fire eight times. From this I infer that another State had forsaken the Abolition rules & has joined the Southern Confederacy.

April 20. White Frost this morning.

In comments that pertained to the causes of secession and war, Harris did not use the analogy of divorce from marriage suggested by Chesnut. But when he wrote of seceding states forsaking "abolition rule," he, like Chesnut, was placing responsibility for the situation upon the North. This was consistent with other comments in which Harris coupled his expressions of support for secession with references to "oppression" of the South by the North, and to war as a lesser evil than subjugation and enslavement by Northerners:

December 6 [1860]. To day the election for delagates to the [Secession] Convention comes off. . . . All the canadates say secede, and, of course it will be done. And I hope it will be done quickly. Then will come the tug of war, but let it come. It can be no worse than the oppression of the North.

The weather is cold to day. A bad time for gathering cotton. . . .

July 24. [1861] The weather is quite cool; but every body is in a fever-heat about the war. We begin to feel that it is a dreadful reality, that we are in the midst of a desperate war, and no one can tell when it will end. It is bad, very bad. But of the two evils, let us choose the least. Better war to the knife, than to be subgagated—than to be slaves to King Abe. Let them come on, Let us fight on to the last man. When they conquor us there will be nothing left for them.

Piedmont Farmer: The Journals of David Golightly Harris, 1855–1870.
Edited by Philip N. Racine. Knoxville, The University of Tennessee Press.
Copyright 1990 by The University of Tennessee Press, pp. 190–191. 165,
203. Permission to print these and other passages included in the present
volume granted by The University of Tennessee Press.]

*While Mary Chesnut and David Golightly Harris were commenting in their
diaries about the momentous events in Charleston and Montgomery in the spring
of 1861, New York attorney George Templeton Strong, many miles to the north of
South Carolina, read in his newspaper about the events at Fort Sumter. But the
reactions Strong expressed and described in his diary were quite unlike those in
South Carolina and Alabama.*

April 12 [1861], *Friday. War* has begun, unless my extra [*New York*] *Herald*
lies, and its Charleston despatch is bogus. . . . The despatch is a column
long, from Charleston, in substance to this effect. The rebel batteries
opened on Sumter at "twenty-seven minutes after four" this morning. . . .
Yet I doubt its genuineness vehemently. I can hardly hope that the rebels
have been so foolish and thoughtless as to take the initiative in civil war
and bring matters to a crisis. . . .
April 13. Here begins a new chapter of my journal, entitled WAR—. . . This
morning's papers confirmed last night's news; viz., that the rebels opened
fire at Sumter yesterday morning. . . . So Civil War is inaugurated at last.
God defend the Right. The Northern backbone is much stiffened already.
Many who stood up for "Southern rights" and complained of wrongs
done the South now say that since the South has fired the first gun, they
are ready to go all lengths in supporting the government. . . . Would I were
in Sumter tonight, even with the chance of being forced to surrender (seventy men against seven thousand) and of being lynched thereafter by the
Chivalry of Charleston. . . .
April 14, Sunday. Fine day. Morning *Herald* announces *Surrender of Fort
Sumter* and great jubilation in Charleston. . . .
April 15. Events multiply. The President is out with a proclamation calling
for 75,000 volunteers and an extra session of Congress July 4. It is said
200,000 more will be called within a few days. Every man of them will be
wanted before this game is lost and won. . . . Expedition to Governor's
Island this morning. . . . Everybody's patriotism is rampant and demon-
strative now. About three hundred recruits on the Island, mostly quite
raw. I discoursed with one of them, an honest-looking, simple-minded
boy from somewhere near Rochester, probably some small farmer's son.
"He had voted for Abe Lincoln, and as there was going to be trouble, he
might as well *fight* for Abe Lincoln," so he enlisted two weeks ago.
"Guessed they were going to get some hard knocks when they went down

South, but then he had always kind o'wanted to see the world—that was one reason why he 'listed'." . . .

April 16. . . . [The *New York Herald*] and other papers say the new war policy will strangle secession in the Border States. But it seems to me that every indication from Virginia, North Carolina, and elsewhere points the other way. No news from Slave-ownia today. . . . Trinity Church Vestry tonight. . . .

Thence to New York Club. Our talk was of war. Subscribed to a fund for equipment of the Twelfth Regiment and put down my name for a projected Rifle Corps, but I fear my near-sightedness is a grave objection to my adopting that arm. . . .

GOD SAVE THE UNION, AND CONFOUND ITS ENEMIES. AMEN. *April 17.* Dull weather, but it has cleared up tonight. . . . I count on the loyalty of no Border State, except Maryland. We are on the eve of a civil war that will be bitter and bloody and probably indecisive. . . .

April 18. Fine day; drizzly evening. . . .

The morning papers give us Jefferson Davis's proclamation of reprisals on Northern commerce. Letters of marque are to be issued to any piratical Spaniard who will accept them. Very well. Then we shall have no scruples about retaliating on Southern property, which is peculiar for possessing a capacity for being invited to go away, and legs to take itself off, and arms wherewith to use such implements as may aid it in so doing, if opposed. . . .

Went to the [City] Hall. The [Sixth] Massachusetts Regiment, which arrived here last night, was marching down on its way to Washington. Immense crowd; immense cheering. My eyes filled with tears, and I was half choked in sympathy with the contagious excitement. God be praised for the unity of feeling here! It is beyond, very far beyond, anything I hoped for. If it only last, we are safe."

When Strong, in the passages from his Diary *quoted above, described "rebels" from "Slave-ownia" who fired the first gun at Fort Sumter and thus began armed hostilities, he clearly implied his view of the causes of the war. A few months earlier, as South Carolina stood on the verge of secession, Strong had spelled out in more detail his view of the background of events producing conflict between North and South that led to war:*

"*December 1.* [1860] . . . What has created our present unquestionable irritation against the South? What has created the Republican party?

Its nucleus was the abolition handful that has been vaporing for thirty years, and which, till about 1850, was among the more insignificant of our *isms.* Our feeling at the North till that time was not hostility to slavery, but indifference to it, and reluctance to discuss it. It was a disagreeable subject

with which we had nothing to do. The battles in Congress about the right of petition . . . made little impression on us. But the clamor of the South about the admission of California ten years ago introduced the question of slavery to the North as one in which it had an interest adverse to the South. That controversy taught us that the two systems could not co-exist in the same territory. It opened our eyes to the fact that there were two hostile elements in the country, and that if we allowed slaves to enter any territorial acquisition, our own free labor must be excluded from it. The question was unfortunate for our peace. But we might have forgotten it had not S. A. Douglas undertaken to get Southern votes by repealing the Missouri Compromise. That was the fatal blow. Then came the atrocious effort to force slavery on Kansas by fraud and violence, with the full support of old Buchanan and his Southern counselors, the brutal beating of the eloquent and erudite Sumner with the cordial approbation and applause of the South, the project to revive the slave trade, and (a little earlier) a sentimental romance, *Uncle Tom's Cabin*, that set all Northern women crying and sobbing over the sorrows of Sambo. The Fugitive Slave Law stimulated sectional feeling by making slavery visible in our own communities, and above all, the intolerable brag and bluster and indecent arrogance of the South has driven us into protest against their pretensions, and into a determination to assert our own rights in spite of their swagger. *December 2, Sunday.* . . . I fear Northerner and Southerner are aliens, not merely in social and political arrangements, but in mental and moral constitution. We differ like Celt and Anglo-Saxon. . . .
[*The Diary of George Templeton Strong.* Edited by Allan Nevins and Milton Halsey Thomas. Copyright 1952 by the Macmillan Publishing Company. Copyright renewed 1980 by Milton Halsey Thomas. Abridged by Thomas J. Pressly. Seattle, University of Washington Press, 1988, pp. 181–188, 169–170. Permission to print these and other passages included in the present volume granted by the Macmillan Publishing Company.]

   Farther upstate than George Templeton Strong in New York, the former slave Frederick Douglass, in Rochester, noted some of the same developments which caught Strong's attention. But Douglass's focus upon what would happen to slavery during the newly commenced hostilities, and upon what blacks would think and do, clearly differentiates his account from that of Strong. Mrs. Chesnut expressed concern over the reactions of slaves to the outbreak of war, although her perspective was obviously light-years away from Douglass's view.
   Frederick Douglass, in April, 1861, was living in Rochester, New York, where he edited and published a periodical, Douglass's Monthly. *He had planned a trip to Haiti, but the firing on Fort Sumter led him to give it up, as he explained in* Douglass's Monthly *(May, 1861):*

"The last ten days have made a tremendous revolution in all things pertaining to the possible future of the colored people of the United States. We shall stay here and watch the current events, and serve the cause of freedom and humanity in any way that shall be open to us during the struggle now going on between the slave power and the government. . . .

The Fall of Sumter. As a friend of freedom, earnestly laboring for the abolition of slavery, we have no tears to shed, no lamentations to make over the fall of Fort Sumter. By that event, one danger which threatened the cause of the American slave has been greatly diminished. Through many long and weary months, the American people have been on the mountain with the wily tempter, and have been liable at any moment of weakness to grant a new lease of life to slavery. The whole power of the Northern pro-slavery press, combined with the commercial manufacturing interests of the country, has been earnestly endeavoring to purchase peace and prosperity for the North by granting the most demoralizing concessions to the insatiate Slave Power. This has been our greatest danger. The attack upon Fort Sumter bids fair to put an end to this cowardly, base and unprincipled truckling. To our thinking, the damage done to Fort Sumter is nothing in comparison with that done to the secession cause. The hail and fire of its terrible batteries has killed its friends and spared its enemies. [Major Robert] Anderson lives, but where are the champions of concession at the North? Their traitor lips are pale and silent. . . .

[The secessionists] have completely shot off the legs of all trimmers and compromisers [in the North], and compelled everybody to elect between patriotic fidelity and pro-slavery treason. . . .

Is it said that we exult in rebellion? We repel the allegation as a slander. Every pulsation of our heart is with the legitimate American Government, in its determination to suppress and put down this slaveholding rebellion. . . .

Sudden Revolution in Northern Sentiment. During the first three weeks after the inauguration of Mr. Lincoln's Administration, there was a general sentiment all over the North looking to a peaceful solution of the revolutionary crisis now upon the country. . . .

But what a change now greets us! The Government is aroused, the dead North is alive, and its divided people united. Never was a change so sudden, so universal, and so portentous. The whole North, East and West is in arms. Drums are beating, men are enlisting, companies forming, regiments marching, banners are flying, and money is pouring into the national treasury to put an end to the slaveholding rebellion. . . .

How to End the War. To our mind, there is but one easy, short and effectual way to suppress and put down the desolating war which the slaveholders and their rebel minions are now waging against the American Government and its loyal citizens. Fire must be met with water, darkness with light, and war for the destruction of liberty must be met with war for the destruction of slavery. *The simple way, then, to put an end to the savage and desolating war now waged by the slaveholders, is to strike down slavery itself,* the primal cause of that war. . . .

Let the slaves and free colored people be called into service, and formed into a liberating army, to march into the South and raise the banner of Emancipation among the slaves. The South having brought revolution and war upon the country, and having elected and consented to play at that fearful game, she has no right to complain if some good as well as calamity shall result from her own act and deed. . . .

We are often asked by persons in the street as well as by letter, what our [black] people will do in the present solemn crisis in the affairs of the country. Our answer is, would to God you would let us do something! We lack nothing but your consent. We are ready and would go, counting ourselves happy in being permitted to serve and suffer for the cause of freedom and free institutions. But you won't let us go. Read the heart-rending account we publish elsewhere of the treatment received by the brave fellows, who broke away from their chains and went through marvelous suffering to defend Fort Pickens against the rebels.—They were instantly seized and put in irons and returned to their guilty masters to be whipped to death! . . . The colored citizens of Boston have offered their services to the Government, and were refused. . . . Until the nation shall . . . make the cause of their country the cause of freedom, until they shall strike down slavery, the source and center of this gigantic rebellion, they don't deserve the support of a single sable arm, nor will it succeed in crushing the cause of our present troubles."

[*The Life and Writings of Frederick Douglass.* Edited by Philip S. Foner. 4 vols., New York, International Publishers, 1950–1952. Vol. 3 Copyright 1952 by International Publishers Co., Inc., pp. 88–89, 91–92, 94–96. Permission to print these and other passages included in the present volume granted by International Publishers Co., Inc.]

As Douglass indicated in the passages quoted above, he identified the institution of slavery as "the primal cause" of the war, "the source and center of this gigantic rebellion." The "insatiate Slave Power" had rebelled against the American government, the South had "brought revolution and war upon the country." Douglass's description of a war caused by slavery and activated by a rebellion of slaveholders was a far cry from Mrs. Chesnut's vision of the South attempting a peaceful divorce from a marriage with a hated and exploitative partner.

CHAPTER I

"We Are Whipping the Yankeys Most Beautifully, but
We Are Loosing Many Good Men"—The Period Marked
by Considerable Confederate Success and Considerable
Union Difficulty, July, 1861–September, 1862

> "We are whipping the yankeys most beautifully,
> but we are loosing many good men."
> —DAVID G. HARRIS, SEPTEMBER 13, 1862

1. THE BATTLE OF BULL RUN (MANASSAS), JULY, 1861, AND ASSOCIATED REPERCUSSIONS

Confederates

The first large-scale military action after the Fort Sumter engagement came near the end of July, 1861, at Bull Run (Manassas) in northern Virginia, not far from Washington, D.C. Mary Chesnut's diary describes how news of that battle was received by individuals close to President Jefferson Davis in Richmond, while the letters between members of the Jones family afford a glimpse of their reactions in Georgia. David Harris made brief reference to the Manassas battle in his journals.

Mary Chesnut:

[Richmond] *July 19, 1861.* Beauregard telegraphed yesterday, they say, to Gen. Joe Johnston, "Come down and help us or we will be crushed by numbers." The president telegraphed General Johnston to move down to Beauregard's aid. . . .

No mistake today. I was too ill to move out of my bed. So they all sat in my room. . . .

July 22, 1861. Mrs. Davis came in so softly that I did not know she was here until she leaned over me <<kissed me>> and said—

"A great battle has been fought—Jeff Davis led the center, Joe Johnston the right wing, Beauregard the left wing of the army. Your husband is all right. Wade Hampton is wounded. Colonel Johnson of the Legion killed—so are Colonel Bee and Colonel Bartow. Kirby Smith is wounded or killed."

I had no heart to speak. She went on in that desperate calm way to which people betake themselves when under greatest excitement. . . .

"The president telegraphs me only that 'it is a great victory.' General Cooper has all the other telegrams." Still I said nothing. I was stunned. Then I was so grateful. Those nearest and dearest to me were safe still. . . .

They got me up. Times were too wild with excitement to stay in bed. We went into Mrs. Preston's room.

She made me lie down on her bed. Men, women, and children streamed in. Every living soul had a story to tell. "Complete victory" you heard everywhere.

We had been such anxious wretches! The revulsion of feeling was almost too much to bear. . . .

A woman from Mrs. Bartow's country was in a fury because they stopped her as she rushed to be the first to tell Mrs. Bartow that her husband was killed. It had been decided that Mrs. Davis was to tell her. Poor thing! She was lying on her bed. Mrs. Davis knocked. "Come in." When she saw it was Mrs. Davis, she sat up, ready to spring to her feet— but then there was something in Mrs. Davis's pale face that took the life out of her. She stared at Mrs. Davis—and then sunk back. She covered her face.

"Is it bad news for me?" Mrs. Davis did not speak. "Is he killed?"

Today she said [that] as soon as she saw Mrs. Davis's face—and then she could not say one word—she knew it all in an instant—she knew it before she wrapped the shawl round her head.

Maria, Mrs. Preston's maid, is furiously patriotic. She came into my room.

"These colored people say it is printed in the papers here that the Virginia people done it all. Now Mars Wade has so many of his men killed—and he wounded—it stands to reason that South Callina was no ways backward. If there was ever anything plain, that's plain." . . .

Today for the first time came a military funeral. As that march came wailing up, they say, Mrs. Bartow fainted. The empty saddle—and the led war horse—we saw and heard it all. And now it seems we are never out of the sound of the Dead March in **Saul.** [George Frederick Handel's oratorio (1739)] It comes and it comes until I feel inclined to close my ears and scream. . . .

<<Mrs. Davis has been so devoted to me since my trouble. . . . Mrs. Johnston told me President Davis said he liked best to have me sit opposite him. He liked my style of chat. . . .>>

July 24, 1861. Here Mr. Chesnut opened my door—and walked in. Of the fullness of the heart the mouth speaketh. I had to ask no questions. He gave me an account of the battle as he saw it (walking up and down my room, occasionally seating himself on a window sill, but too restless to remain still many moments). Told what regiments he was sent to bring up. He took orders to Colonel Jackson—whose regiment stood so stock-still under fire they were called a stone wall. Also, they call Beauregard "Engine" and Johnston "Marlboro" (*s'en va—en guerre*). Mr. C rode with Lay's cavalry after the retreating enemy, in the pursuit, they following them until midnight. There then came such a rain—rain such as is only known in semitropical lands.

In the drawing room Colonel Chesnut was the "belle of the ball"— they crowded him so for news. He was the first arrival that they could get at, from the field of battle—handle, so to speak. . . .

The *[New York] Tribune* said: "In a few days" they would have Richmond, Memphis, New Orleans. "They must be taken and at once." For "a few days" maybe now they will modestly substitute "in a few years."

They brought me a Yankee soldier's portfolio from the battlefield. The letters were franked by Senator Harlan [of Iowa]. One might shed a few tears over some of his letters. Women—wives and mothers—are the same everywhere.

What a comfort the spelling was. We were willing to admit their universal free school education put their rank and file ahead of us *literarily*. Now, these letters do not attest that fact. The spelling is comically bad. . . .

Mrs. Davis drawing room last night was brilliant, and she was in great force. Outside a mob collected and called for the president. He did speak. He is an old war-horse—and scents the battlefields from afar. His enthusiasm was contagious. <<The president took all the credit to himself for the victory—said the wounded roused and shouted for Jeff Davis and the men rallied at the sight of him and rushed on and routed the enemy. The truth is, Jeff Davis was not two miles from the battlefield, but he is greedy for military fame.>> They called for Colonel Chesnut, and he gave them a capital speech, too. . . .

There goes the Dead March for some poor soul. . . .

Everybody said at first: "Pshaw! There will be no war." Those who foresaw evil were called "Ravens"—ill foreboders. Now the same sanguine people all cry "the war is over"—the very same who were packing to leave Richmond a few days ago. Many were ready to move on at a moment's warning, when the good news came.

There are such owls everywhere. But to revert to the other kind—the sage and circumspect, those who say very little, but that little shows they think the war barely begun. Mr. Rives and Mr. Seddon have just called. Arnoldus VanderHorst came to see me at the same time. He said there was no great show of victory on our side until two o'clock, but when we began to win, we did it in double-quick time. I mean, of course, the battle last Saturday. . . .

That was our opportunity. Wigfall can see nothing to stop us. And when they explain why we did not go, I understand it all less than ever.

Yes, here we will dillydally and Congress orate and generals parade, until they get up an army three times as large as McDowell's that we have just defeated.

Trescott says this victory will be our ruin. It lulls us into a fool's paradise of conceit at our superior valor.

And the shameful farce of their flight will wake every inch of their manhood. It was the very fillip they needed.

There was a quieter sort here who know their Yankees well. They say if the thing begins to pay—government contracts and all that—we will never hear the end of it. At least, until they get their pay out of us. They will not lose money by us. Of that we may be sure. Trust Yankee shrewdness and vim for that.

[*Mary Chesnut's Civil War*, pp. 102, 104–111.]

The Jones Family:

Hon. Charles C. Jones, Jr., to Rev. C. C. Jones
Savannah, Wednesday, July 24th, 1861

My dear Father,

Amid the heavy engagements which are upon me I have not had an opportunity until this moment for replying to your kind and valued letter of the 20th inst. I thank God that you are all better at Maybank [one of the Jones's plantations], and that dear little Mary Ruth [infant daughter of Charles C. Jones; her mother had died earlier in the month] improves. . . .

Our city is filled with mingled exultation and sorrow at the news of the recent triumph of our arms at Manassas—a victory without parallel in the history of this western world, an engagement continental in its magnitude, a success whose influence must be felt and acknowledged not only within the limits of our own Confederacy and of the United States but also throughout the civilized world. Surely the God of Battles is with us.

The price of that victory, however, was great. Colonel Bartow and some of our best young men have fallen, and our city is filled with mourning. . . .

What a world of heroism in that act of our worthy President—leaving Richmond and in person leading the center column on that fearful battlefield! . . .

Mr. Colcock writes me that a miniature of my dear wife can be painted by an artist of Charleston, and I am about sending my locket to him for that purpose. . . . You have ever the warmest love of

Your affectionate son,
Charles C. Jones, Jr.

Kiss my dear little daughter for me.

Mrs. Mary Jones to Hon. Charles C. Jones, Jr.

Maybank, *Thursday,* July 25th, 1861

My dear Son,

Mr. McDonald has just brought your last favor, and as he returns immediately, I have only time to send you a few lines to assure you of our tenderest love and constant remembrance and of the continued improvement of our dear little babe. . . . Already she looks up into my face and smiles, and is very bright for her *days*—one month old today! What an age of sorrow that one month has brought to our hearts!

My beloved child, do not let the world draw you away from the one great design of this *deep, deep affliction.* Seek and you shall find your long-neglected Saviour! May the Divine Spirit bring you to Him at once! There is no other rest for the weary and heavy-laden.

Our hearts are filled with gratitude to God for our victory over our enemies, and at the same time we weep at the costly sacrifice. I feel especially for Mrs. Bartow, and shall look most anxiously for further accounts. . . . Enclosed we send you twenty dollars. Please forward it as you know best to some official in Richmond for the use of our suffering and wounded soldiers. I wish it was an hundredfold. . . . In haste, my dear son,

Your ever affectionate mother,
Mary Jones.

Hon. Charles C. Jones, Jr., to Rev. and Mrs. C. C. Jones

Savannah, Saturday, July 27th, 1861

My dear Father and Mother,

I have only a moment in which to thank you for your recent kind letters, and to rejoice in the glad tidings of the good health of dear little Mary Ruth.

You cannot imagine the pressure that has been upon me during the past week. We have been in the midst of the greatest excitement consequent upon this glorious victory at Manassas, and last night we received the body of General Bartow. . . .

It seems to me that I am living in a graveyard. I never have passed through such a period in my life before. . . .

Your affectionate son,
Charles C. Jones, Jr.

David Harris:

August 5 [1861]. Quite clouddy in the morning. Prepairing to go to the village (it being sale-day). All well. Yesterday I found a great many persons at the village. Col. [Oliver E.] Edwards gave us (in public) an interesting history of the Great Battl at Manassas. Many persons volenteered to go to the wars. I came home late, quite tired. . . .

August 27. Sowing turnup seeds. Soon this morning I . . . went to the village. Three companies of soldiers left for the seat of war to day. I hear there was much sign of greaf at parting, among the large crowd that was present to day. No news of importance to day. The impression is that the troops are gradULY closing on Washington. Our arm[s] are very sucssessful so far. Plowing, manuring turnup land.

[*Piedmont Farmer,* pp. 205, 207.]

Unionists

The Confederate victory at the first battle of Bull Run at the end of July, 1861, which so encouraged Mary Chesnut, the members of the Jones family, David Harris, and other Confederates, served to disappoint Frederick Douglass, Maria Daly, and other supporters of the Union. Frederick Douglass, in his despair, even suggested at one point that unless changes were speedily made in the policies and actions of the Union government, Jefferson Davis might as well be invited to replace Abraham Lincoln. Maria Daly in New York City was not as discouraged as Douglass, but she too expressed dismay at the military defeat.

Frederick Douglass:

THE REBELS, THE GOVERNMENT, AND THE DIFFERENCE BETWEEN THEM

Thus far our Government has made very little progress in suppressing the slaveholding rebellion. . . . The defeat of the Government forces at Bull's Run on Sunday, July 21st has inspired the rebels with new confidence, and confirmed their high hopes of ultimate success. . . . The Government has men, money, and munitions of war in abundance, and the complete freedom of the sea. The rebels are poor in men, money, munitions of war, and are suffering all the hardships of a vigorous blockade. Yet with all these, and the disadvantages of an atrociously wicked cause, they are to this hour masters of the field. Who shall explain to us why this is so? Why does wrong so prosper against right? Many answers come to us. One alleges that it is the incompetency of our Generals; another, that it is the strong positions occupied by the rebels; and a third tells us, that it is all owing to the treachery of the late [Buchanan] administration. These, and a thousand other explanations, come to us; but the real difficulty of the case remains untouched.

Our solution of the whole matter is this: The South is *in earnest,* and the North is not. . . . The South hates the North, and the North even yet loves the South, and would rather win her back to loyalty by kind words than by hard blows.

All this is made very manifest in the conduct of both belligerents. Witness the scenes of Bull's Run the other day, when the rebels amused themselves in sticking bayonets in the dead, and setting the wounded up against stumps, and shooting at them as targets.—Witness the deceptions, the cheats, the unscrupulous lying, and the firing upon and killing their prisoners of war, to which they have resorted. . . .

How marked and striking is the contrast between the two peoples, and the two armies. Where the one tortures and sometimes kills its prisoners, the other treats them kindly, and often releases them upon taking the oath of allegiance. Where the one slays only in battle, the other shoots down our unarmed men in cold blood. While the South does not hesitate to employ their slaves against the Government, the Government refuses to accept the services of any colored citizen in suppressing the rebellion, lest they should lead to the freedom of the slaves, and thus inflict too heavy a blow upon the slaveholding rebels. The one is very careful about the rights of property, while the other fills the sea with pirates, and plunders the Government of every thing it can get its hand upon. The slaveholders have no scruples; they wage this war with unrelenting and desperate earnestness, sustained and fed by immeasurable malice, unmixed, and as deadly as the poison from the fang of a rattlesnake. Herein is the secret of their success. It is not their numbers, not their wealth, not the goodness of their cause, not their skill, but the quenchless fire of a deadly hate, which spurns all restraints of law and humanity, and walks to its purpose with a single eye and a determined hand. The battle at Bull's Run has done something to open Northern eyes to the real character of their Southern brethren; but it may require other lessons of the same sort to lead them to strike the South only where it can do so effectually, and that is the abolition of slavery. *Douglass's Monthly,* August, 1861. . . .

THE PROGRESS OF THE WAR . . .
We are writing on the progress of the War; but is not this really a misnomer? Has the Government actually made any progress at all? Are we not now even in a worse condition than at the beginning? The Capital was

in danger in May, and it is in no less danger in August. Our newspapers flamed then with alarming telegrams of the advance of the Confederate forces upon Washington. They so flame now. In fact, we seem to be nearly in the same condition that we were in when Major Anderson was compelled to give up the shattered walls of Fort Sumter. The enemy is now as proud, confident and defiant as at the beginning, and the promised suppression of rebellion seems as far off as ever.

It is not at all surprising that this state of facts should measurably destroy the vast stock of public confidence reposed in the Government at the beginning of the war, and such is really the case whatever show may be made to the contrary by great money loans to the Government. The feeling is becoming general that a new element must be infused into the Government forces, and that unless a new turn is given to the conflict, and that without delay, we might as well remove Mr. Lincoln out of the President's chair and respectfully invite Jefferson Davis or some other slaveholding rebel to take his place. . . .

Douglass's Monthly, September, 1861
[*The Life and Writings of Frederick Douglass.* Vol. 3, pp. 130–132, 145–147.]

Maria Daly:

July 22, 1861. This morning we felt flushed with victory, and I began dictating terms to the rebels. . . .

This afternoon came distressing accounts of the sequel of the capture of the batteries at Bull Run; namely, that a panic had seized our troops, General Johnston had joined General Beauregard and had the Federal Army men in full retreat upon Washington with the loss of all of their artillery and 3,000 killed. . . . God help us if this is so. I trust we may receive better accounts tomorrow. Charles [Maria's husband] has gone to the club to hear the last telegrams.

July 23, 1861. Only 300 or 500 killed, God be thanked. Two batteries saved, but the army is signally defeated. What illumination and rejoicing will there be in the Southern cities! . . . Never in my life did I feel as badly as when I saw this fearful, disgraceful news in the paper yesterday. It will prolong the war another year, if not three, and give European powers cause to consider the matter of recognizing the Confederacy as very probably their best policy.

July 24, 1861. As further intelligence comes in, hope and energy revives. Our loss is not as great as supposed, being perhaps not over 1,000, perhaps little over 500. The rebels, however, have taken a great many prisoners. . . . It has been, as General Scott [stated], no defeat, but only too great odds against us. Great acts of bravery have been done. . . .

The interest which our foreign population have shown, the eagerness with which they have rushed to the rescue of their adopted country, is ir-

repressibly touching. It was all to save this country which they call the
hope of the world. . . .

Down with aristocracy in our free country! Let our people be educated to respect free labor and independence and may God instruct their
hearts and spread so among us the fear and love of Him that dishonesty
and knavery may be banished from among us and we delivered from the
rascally politicians and meddlesome editors and thieving public servants
who dishonor this great republic!

July 28, 1861. The more we hear from those who were in the battle of Bull
Run, the more exasperating does it seem. Had the officers behaved themselves well, had they been fitted to command, the victory would have
been ours. . . .

Brown, the clerk of the Common Pleas, has returned, and he too declared that had they been well-officered, they would have carried the day.
Now the war must be a thing of time. Our prestige is gone and must be re-
conquered. It is a most lamentable and disgraceful thing to acknowledge,
but our people have no moral feeling, no instinct of honor, no principle.
Each man is out for himself; each one seeks how many dollars he can get
out of his friends, his occupation, his place under the government. No one
serves from purely patriotic feeling as in the old republics. Luxury has
done all this, and we women are greatly to blame for our share therein,
and the richer classes are more tainted with the mercenary miserable spirit
than the poorer ones. This uprising of the people will, I trust, put the leaders of fashion, those dead respectables, in the obscurity which they deserve, and give a chance to real aristocracy of nature to invade their ranks
and make them recognize some other title to distinction than money and
dancing masters' manners. . . .

September 2, 1861, West Farms [The Lydig estate in the Bronx]. We have
been here about three weeks and I have not had leisure to sit down and
write the events as they take place. Little has been done, and the papers
only contain a great many extracts from Southern and European papers,
which are very annoying to Northern readers and show what a dreadful
mistake the battle of Bull Run was. We have lost our prestige. The Grand
Army of the United States is not the imposing body it was imagined. . . .

The enlistment goes on slowly. When the enthusiasm of our people
was at its height, the government, with narrow-sighted policy, refused to
take but a certain number, and now it is difficult to fill up the regiments.
Whilst the Confederates have, they say, 300,000 in Virginia alone!

[*Diary of a Union Lady, 1861–1865* (Maria Lydig Daly). Edited by Harold
Earl Hammond. New York, Funk & Wagnalls Company, Inc. Copyright
1962 by Funk & Wagnalls Company, Inc. Copyright renewed, pp. 38–41,
47. Permission to print these and other passages included in the present
volume granted by HarperCollins, Publishers, Inc.]

2. *UNION ADVANCE IN THE WEST—FORTS HENRY AND DONELSON (FEBRUARY, 1862), SHILOH (APRIL, 1862), AND NEW ORLEANS (APRIL, 1862)*

Unionists

Maria Daly's gloom about the Union military prospects was lifted early in 1862, when the Union military forces won a series of victories in Tennessee and Louisiana from February through April:

February 13, 1862. Several victories at last! . . . Fort Henry on the Tennessee River . . . is taken, and our gunboats have run down the river to Florence, Alabama, where the Stars and Stripes were joyously welcomed. This is the best news of all! . . .

February 18, 1862. Fort Donelson taken—fifteen thousand prisoners, including General Albert Johnston, Buckner and Pillow! The rebellion is at last beginning to succumb. Good news from Phil [Maria's brother], who has had active duty. We see by the papers that he was in command of the naval pickets at Roanoke Island.

On Sunday evening last, we paid some visits. Among others, we saw Mr. [William B.] Astor at home. He has as low an opinion of the [Lincoln] Administration as my husband. We freely commented upon the assurance of the wife of a second-rate Illinois lawyer being obliged to choose her company and selecting five hundred élite to entertain at the White House—and then to have the affectation to put on court mourning out of respect to Queen Victoria's recent loss! It is too comical; it is too sad to see such extravagance and folly in the White House with the country bankrupt and a civil war raging.

On Saturday last we dined at Mrs. Stout's with Mr. and Mrs. [George Templeton] Strong, Mr. and Mrs. [George] Bancroft, Miss Thayer, and some other gentlemanly nonentities. . . .

Little Miss Gould provoked me by her abolition. She would hear of no peace that was not a right peace, no compromise with slavery. She ought to have had her ears boxed for intruding her crude eighteen-year-old ideas upon people older and wiser than herself and misleading some poor boy by her influence, probably, for I believe that every woman can do that with one man in her lifetime at least. We do not sufficiently realize how great our influence is.

Agassiz [J. L. R. Agassiz (1807–1873), the great naturalist and biologist] is going to lecture here and we must go and hear him.

February 23, 1862 . . . Nashville is ours and Tennessee once more is in the Union, so there are but the Southern Gulf states left, which will soon give up likewise. Thank God for His protecting providence! . . .

February 26, 1862. Heard Agassiz lecture on Monday. How clear, simple, comprehensive! He evidently spoke from a full mind. His voice is sweet and sympathetic. He speaks a little brokenly and draws what he wishes to represent in outline on the blackboard. . . .

March 11, 1862. The Union flag waves over Manassas; the scandal of Bull's Run is effaced. McClellan is to be superseded. He has not shown sufficient audacity, but has allowed the Confederates to escape. . . . I have great faith that God means the utter overthrow of the Confederates. . . .

April 9, 1862. The news of today is most inspiring: Island No. 10 taken, with 6,000 prisoners, 100 siege guns, etc. etc., three generals, the floating Iron Battery, of which we were so afraid, and all their fleet ammunition, etc. I think the rebels must give up. . . .

May 7, 1862. Yorktown is evacuated, and McClellan in hot pursuit. Corinth likewise, and New Orleans in our possession. . . .

May 11, 1862. What splendid news! Norfolk taken, Portsmouth captured, the Navy Yard secured, the *Merrimac* ours, President Lincoln with the army before Norfolk! All the news seems to come on Sundays. Now there may be truth in what Mrs. McClellan told us yesterday, that the war would be over by the Fourth of July.

I went yesterday with the Judge to see Mrs. General Marcy and Mrs. McClellan. . . . Mrs. McClellan showed Charles a letter of Professor Mahan of West Point in which he highly complimented her husband upon his avoidance of bloodshed in his great successes. He must be a great man. He has such wonderful moderation and has the gift of silence. When *reviled*, he reviles not again. He writes to his wife that in the army he had just whipped were many of his most intimate friends. He ends his telegraph dispatch, "How is the baby?" His favorite project, Mrs. McC. says, is to take her to Europe as soon as the war is over. . . . All feel as though God were aiding us to accomplish some great purpose of His own in the economy of the world. . . .

May 14, 1862. Went this morning with Kate to the Park Barracks to see the wounded and sick soldiers brought on by the *Ocean Queen* from Yorktown. I found a number of ladies there already waiting upon them, some bathing their heads, others giving them their food. The soldiers seemed mostly to suffer from exhaustion. Having taken some cologne and handkerchiefs with me, I went around and distributed it; many of them seemed to find it very grateful. The poor fellows were very patient. Some of them looked grey with pallor and weakness. One young fellow of about eighteen, with a skin like a woman's and bright hazel eyes, looked like a gentleman. He much interested me. I think he was a *deserter*, a Virginian. For he said to me, "How my mother would feel if she knew where I was." I said he was young to go soldiering, and I knew how his mother would feel, for I had a young brother in the army. "Where?" said he. "With Burnside," I answered. I gave him some chicken broth. He ate with relish.

"That is the first thing that I have had that tasted good," said he. "It is better than crackers." He ate it and asked for more cologne, and seemed much refreshed.

Another poor fellow of about 50 was dying of consumption from a kick on the breast by a drunken lieutenant. "Oh," said he, "had I died by a blow from the enemy, I could have borne it better. I was not to blame, and had I my pistol in my hand, I should have shot him. But I remembered I am a Christian, and the lieutenant knew not what he did." Then his mind wandered away to the battlefield. He spoke with tears rolling down his face of the scenes he had witnessed of young fellows dying, moaning for one look at their mothers and sisters or someone still dearer. Kate's beauty seemed to give them great pleasure. Several of the poor fellows would let the older ladies pass, but smiled to attract her attention. Oh, the magic power of youth and beauty!

The rest of the day I have spent on gathering things together for them—shirts, sheets, old linen, towels, clothes of all kinds. . . .

May 30, 1862. . . . The news tonight is that Corinth is evacuated, Beauregard has retreated on the line of railroad towards Mobile, and McClellan is within two miles of the enemy's works. May God grant a speedy end to this war.

The South seems to be desperate, and horrible atrocities are committed. Stragglers from our army are found tied by their feet to the trees with their throats cut, and it seems that what was said of their barbarities at Manassas after the battle of Bull Run was only too true, that they did boil the flesh and carry away the bones of our poor soldiers as trophies, their boasted chivalry rivalling the Indians, exceeding them even in barbarity. [*Diary of a Union Lady,* pp. 103, 106–109, 111, 114–115, 124, 126–130, 139.]

The Union military victories beginning in February, 1862, also encouraged George Templeton Strong. In 1861, Strong had become a national official of the United States Sanitary Commission, and in that capacity he made visits to Lincoln during the winter of 1861–1862. Strong the polished Easterner noted what he considered some crudities of Lincoln, but his overall evaluation of Lincoln was sympathetic.

October 23 [1861]. . . .We had an audience of [President] Lincoln from nine to eleven A.M. . . . He is lank and hard-featured, among the ugliest white men I have seen. Decidedly plebian. Superficially vulgar and a snob. But not essentially. He seems to me clear-headed and sound-hearted, though his laugh is the laugh of a yahoo, with a wrinkling of the nose that suggests affinity with the tapir and other pachyderms; and his grammar is weak. . . .

January 29 [1862]. . . . Bellows [of the Sanitary Commission] and I called on the President yesterday. . . . He is a barbarian, Scythian, yahoo, or gorilla, in respect of outside polish . . . , but a most sensible, straightforward, honest old codger. The best President we have had since old Jackson's time, at least, as I believe. . . . His evident integrity and simplicity of purpose would compensate for worse grammar than his, and for even more intense provincialism and rusticity. . . .

February 4. Fifty years hence John Brown will be recognized as the Hero or Representative Man of this struggle up to 1862. He will be the Wycliffe of the anti-slavery Reformation. A queer, rude song about him seems growing popular:

> John Brown's body lies a-mouldering in the grave
> (repeat)
> But his soul's a-marching on.
> Glory Hally Hallelujah,
> Glory Hally Hallelujah,
> But his soul's a-marching on. . . .

February 8, Saturday. Excellent tidings from Tennessee; Fort Henry, a rebel earthwork on the Tennessee River, bombarded and taken. . . . The war news is decidedly encouraging, but we are very blue indeed. Signs of speedy intervention (probably by France with pharisaical England looking cannily on) increase and multiply.

[*The Diary of George Templeton Strong.* Abridged edition, 1988, pp. 192, 195–197.]

One member of the Union armed forces at the time of their victories early in 1862 was Marcus Spiegel, the German-Jewish immigrant who had become a naturalized citizen in 1857. Spiegel, as a captain and company commander in the Sixty-Seventh Ohio Volunteer Infantry Regiment, participated in military actions in Virginia against Confederate troops led by General "Stonewall" Jackson. In one of those actions, in March, 1862, in the battle of Winchester (Kernstown), the division in which Spiegel served inflicted one of the very few defeats on Stonewall Jackson ever achieved by Union forces.

Spiegel's letters to his wife, his brother Joseph, and his children described his battle experiences. The letters also reflected Spiegel's ardent support of the Union and hostility to secession, his sympathy to the Democratic party, his hostility to blacks, and his view that the war for the Union should not be enlarged to include a war against slavery.

Martinsburg, Va.
March 7, 1862

My Dear and Much Beloved Wife and Children:

"Onward to Richmond" was the celebrated war cry of certain political generals previous to the memorable Bull Run disaster. Onward seems to be, and now is, the word of the gallant defenders of our glorious Union. Onward to victory! Onward to crush rebellion. Onward to bring

this unfortunate and unhappy war, forced upon us by the ambitious leaders of a misguided people, to a successful termination.

In my last I intimated that we might have to march. Even then we
were under marching orders, and fearing you might feel uneasy I determined not to say we were going; but determined rather to wait and say
we have arrived safely at Martinsburg. . . .

On my march yesterday I deviated from my usual practice, and
questioned quite a number of fat, sleek and hearty looking slaves. I asked
them how they were satisfied, and so forth, and whether they would go
North with me. To the first their answer was, pretty well; and to the latter,
"guess not massa." I am the more strongly confirmed in my old faith that
for the Constitution, the Union and the Flag of my country I will fight to
the last; I am ever ready to punish and to shoot traitors; but it is not necessary to fight for the darkies, nor are they worth fighting for. . . . At 12 o'-
clock at night we reached Martinsburg. . . .

Martinsburg, Va
March 9/62

My dear and good wife
My sweet children and beloved brother!

This is Sunday Morning just after Roll Call, . . .

If you and the children and Brother Joseph were here we would
take such a big ride over the City and country and you could see then,
how far men will go when their passions are roused. To see 64
Locomotives of the very best and biggest kind (1 as big as 3 of ours at
home) destroyed, willfully, maliciously and feloniously, the nicest Bridges
of iron and wood destroyed, a magnificent Depot House as nice as I ever
saw in the United States smashed and destroyed, I am satisfied you would
feel Secession is awful and must be subdued. We are here 8 miles from
Bunker Hill, 15 miles from Charlestown and 24 from Harpers Ferry, the
Theater of John Browns fanaticism, 22 miles from Winchester where the
Rebels boast of being strongly fortified and ready to receive us. . . .

Just now the news is spread through town that Winchester was
taken this morning at 5 o'clock by General Banks and his forces. Thus falls
one after the other of the boasted stronghold of Seseshdom; they can not
withstand the fire, earnestness and enthusiasm of those who gather
around the good old flag. I begin to think it will soon be played out. . . .

Your,
Marcus. . . .

Near Winchester, Va.
March 22/62

My dear dear Wife & family!

. . . .We returned last night from a 3-day march to Strousburg
[Strasburg] which was believed and reported to be a strongly fortified

"Rebel Hole", but we were successful in driving them out and chased them 5 miles South towards Woodstock and as I took some notes in the field, you will permit me to give you them just as they are and if they seem a little enthusiastic, you must pass on them and make allowances that they were taken by a Captain proud and elevated by the noble Spirit of the Boys under his command and at the moment of the Excitement of the Battlecry. This is Friday morn. Monday Eve. we received Marching Orders, that is, to cook 3 days rations and be ready to march without Blankets in 3 hours. . . . [Early the next morning] Reveillee beat, the Boys arose, Roll was called and it was then ordered to be ready to march by 10 o'clock. Hurrah for Strasburg was the happy response of everybody, after Stone Wall Jackson, the Bold Rebel General, and a true Soldier Spirit was shown all along the lines of the different Camps as far as the Eye could reach. The Cavelery was trotting briskly, the Artillery was moving, Infantry was passing along the pike in front of our Camp and everybody seemed to be alive for the task before them. We all felt, that if we can catch Jackson, we can whip him and his forces. At last the time came when our gallant Boys were led out commanded by our noble and highspirited Lieutenant Colonel Voris. . . .

We are now South of Middletown and on the battle ground of yesterday between our and the Rebel Cavelery in which my Friend Dr. Ebright was present and captured a Rebel Flag and just now, as we go up quite a little Hill, we hear the Booming of the Cannons some 5 or 6 miles ahead of us and just like an electric Strain it goes through the lines with a Shout of the 12 or 14 Regiments which made the Earth shake and the Heaven tremble. That was enough for the Boys, there was none among them that felt tired. All wanted to go double quick and soon we reached the town of Newtown. . . . We now came to Cedar Creek with smoking ruins of a handsome Bridge which the Rebels had but shortly burned in Order to detain us, but the ingenuity of our Leaders soon threw the ruins down the Creek, put boards on it and so we crossed single file. . . . As we came within 2 miles of Strousburg we were . . . halted and ordered to open Ranks. As we led the advance in the move towards Winchester, we have to take the Rear this time and shall not unless a big battle or a flanking movement [is] contemplated get in very soon. As we open our Ranks a Courier gallops past with all the appearance of something up. Now the Bugles of the Artillery sound the Advance, now the double quick; now they gallop along as fast as the Horses can go, 6 Horses to a cannon. Just imagine 40 Cannons with 80 Ammunition Wagons, 6 Horses to each, galloping past while you hear the Enemies batteries playing at a distant Hill opposite yours, the men hurraing, the Bugles Sounding, the officers commands and then I ask, Who wouldn't be a Soldier? Oh it was truly grant [sic.]; Oh sublime indeed and if ever I live to see the day that I am 80 years old, I think, I can describe that Scene with animation. Now the Cavelery rushes past; now the Ranks are closed and, Battalion forward March, is heard from our Lieutenant Colonel Commanding; forward Company C repeated by me, and my noble Boys start off with as much alacrity and animation as they would do to a 4th of July dance with a pretty Caroline F. Hamlin [Spiegel's wife] with them. Halt is now commanded. The Rebels still throw their Shells which fall as harmless as the leaves of a beautiful Rose after it has been lucritive and sweet. Now Colonel Voris rides up and asks me whether I want to see the Rebels. I started with him on a big Hill where on the top of which, to where I went, stands our Noble General Shields and Staff, our and other Brigade Commanders, Colonels and so forth, through Glasses watching the movements of the Rebels and watching General Shields directing the advance of our men. The Rebels are at a Hill right opposite protecting Strousburg; now a shell bursted in a hallow a great distance below us. Now we see our Artillery advancing and Cavelery following, between us and the Rebels; now the Rebels see them and pull up stakes. Now the Command is given, follow up; now we rush to our respective commands. Forward March, on to Strousburg. We are now in the town, a crooked Streeted old fashion kind of a town; now the Rebel Cannons are still playing. Now through the town, up the Hill, where the Rebels was a little while ago; now off the pike through a long Lane up a Hill, past a large brick House, through a Barnyard, up another Hill, on the level; now our Artillery is being planted on an elevation; now our Brigade is drawn up in line-o-Battle by division [of] 2 Companies; I command the Centre or Color division, my Company and Company H. Oh how big I feel. Now our Artillery commences, boom, boom, boom, more rapid; the Rebels only answer occasionally. Just now General Shields comes galloping apassed our line, commanding our Brigade to double quick down the Side of a Steep Hill of Pinetrees to cut off the retreating Rebels. Now "by the right flank file left, double quick march" down, down as fast as we can get and just as we get on the Pike the 7th Indiana rushes past to get ahead of us. Now Colonel Voris is jumping a high fence with his horse and we follow, double quick through a wheat field, the hardest running I ever done; and how the Balls of the Rebels Cannons are Buzzing over our Heads from Hill top to Hill top, 200 feet over us. Now on the Pike again, over a large Stone Bridge which crosses the north Branch of the Shenandoah River, up a Hill. Here lies 4 dead Horses; 2 Cavelery men are carrying their Saddles passed us, one of them his hand bleeding. Now on top of the Hill; now Halt and rest a little. Now forward march, follow up the fleeing foe, but he is too fast for us, having the Start and knowing the Country. We could not catch them though we chased them for 5 miles; the Infantry never getting a chance to fire at them once. . . . In the morning we dit not know which way to march. Finally at 1/2 past 10 the Order came to march back to Winchester to our Camp; it being I suppose not advisable to follow up farther as the Rebels might attack us in the Rear and cut off our Supply. The March back to Camp was made without one stop; just think, marching 25 miles without stopping once. . . .

At Camp near Winchester, Va.
March 22/62

Master Hamlin M. Spiegel
Miss Lizzie T. Spiegel
Master Moses M. Spiegel
My good sweet children:
    Yesterday I received the second letter from my dear Son Hamlin and since I know that you can not all of you write yet, I thought best to send you all one letter in Partnership which belongs to you all.

    I am very happy indeed that your dear mother always writes me such good news of everyone of you. If she would have to complain of you I would feel very bad, but I always knew that I had just as good Children as there was in the world. I was in a Battle 3 days ago and the Cannon Balls were flying over my head but none hurt me; the good Lord preserved me from any harm and if you will only be right good Children, mind well and pray to the good Lord, I trust soon to see you all well and hearty. Mother writes to me that you all grew nice and learn fast which I hope you will continue to do.

    Good buy, my dear Children; may the Lord keep you in good health is the sincerest wish of your Father who loves you dearly.

M. M. Spiegel

When I come home I will try and bring you just such presents as you want.

. . . .

Strasburg, Va., March 28, 1862

My Dear Beloved Wife and Children,
Brother and Friends:—
    I have a painful yet proud duty to perform in giving you a list of my dead and wounded as well as a history of the battle so fearfully contested, so gallantly fought and so victoriously won. . . .

    All of my boys who were in the battle (except probably two) fought nobly, standing by my Lieutenants and myself, maintaining every position we took, never yielding an inch, gallantly driving the enemy from their position, though mostly exposed to cross fires, and fearlessly and nobly bearing aloft the colors of the Regiment entrusted to our keeping, and their reward is, that their courage and bravery receives encomiums from every one in General Shields's Division. Never was an officer prouder of his command than I am this day of my gallant little band. God bless them. The coolness, courage and skill of my Lieutenants prevented our loss from being much greater than it was. I will now give you a brief account of the battle.

    On Saturday afternoon [March 22], when preparing for dress parade, we heard the firing of the cannon; but paid no attention to it—supposing it to be artillery practice. In less than twenty minutes the long roll beat, and the news spread that Jackson had driven in our pickets. In seven minutes we were moving at double quick towards Strasburg. The 67th was the first Infantry Regiment to report itself on the field, to General Shields. We were therefore deployed as skirmishers on the left to keep the enemy's right at bay until other regiments were brought to our support. While we were deploying the enemy showered shell, grape, canister, and round ball among us.—Three shells passed through my company, one of them very close to L. G. Osborn and the color-bearer. None of them did any damage, since they did not burst very near us, and the boys could dodge them. We advanced rapidly but carefully under the command of our gallant Lieutenant Colonel Voris, and the enemy gave way slowly, until night, when we halted, and at 12 o'clock we were withdrawn, and fell back a mile and a half. We slept until 4 o'clock when Colonel Voris quietly waked us and ordered us to cook some coffee and be ready to fall in. The boys were quickly up and anxious for further orders. We were delayed until 7 o'clock, when we were marched to the support of Daum's celebrated battery, a position of honor assigned us for being first on the field Saturday evening. We remained at this post until 12 o'clock, and all the time shell was showered at us; but fortunately no one was hurt. At noon we were relieved by the 5th Ohio, and ordered further on to our left wing to guard the movements of the rebel Infantry, where we remained for an hour, and then the enemy attempted to outflank our right by their left and we were ordered with a battery of the 1st Ohio to attack their left. At the same time a part of the 2d Brigade under Colonel [Erastus B.] Tyler, were ordered to prevent the enemy from going any further to the left. We retained this position about half an hour when the enemy made an attempt to go further to the left and a volley of musketry was open on them. The second volley had hardly died away when our Regiment was ordered to advance, which we obeyed, at a double quick, in line-of-battle, under a furious fire of shells, grape and canister shot; but the boys having only victory in contemplation, rushed madly, furiously through the open field into a narrow strip of woods, which lay very high with comparatively few trees. As we came into line with the enemy we discovered that we were too much to the right. Yet, to our right, in the woods, was the 29th Ohio and the 110th Pennsylvania, of Tyler's Brigade. They had no orders to advance. When we were drawn into line and with others all along to our left open fire it was perfectly awful. We received an unyielding fire from the company's left and left flank.

   While we were exposed to a galling fire the Colonel of the 29th Ohio, who is strictly military, had no orders to advance, and therefore did not advance; though with orders he might have played on their left flank. Lieutenant Colonel Voris took the responsibility of moving his Regiment to the left, under somewhat of a cover. He took the flag, called for the boys to rally round it, and soon we were in position to play upon the enemy with fearful effect. Such a fire as we let them have. The 8th Ohio, who, from their exposed position had to lay flat on the ground, renderered [sic.] some assistance; and it was not 25 minutes until we made the enemy give, and then the 8th had full play.

Shortly after this we routed them; they leaving the field strewn with their dead and wounded, and our boys pursuing them with all haste. They took another stand in a strip of woods; our boys drove them from this, and pursued them with the most furious yells and shouts of revenge—they occasionally making a stand, but to no effect—until finally they made a stand in a splendid position, high and commanding, in a strip of woods to their left centre, It was necessary for us to charge through an open field of probably a hundred acres to reach them, and most of us, in our eagerness to pursue them, had half crossed the field before we were aware of our position. It was then that Lieutenant Colonel Voris said, "Boys if we don't drive them from these woods, we shall have to go to Richmond or to the d---l. Let them have it." They were then ordered to fall flat upon the ground, laying upon their backs to load and whirling around to take aim at the enemy as they appeared from behind the trees. It then looked most fearful, exposed as we were to a cross fire, very little chance to do them injury, and to advance in a body was madness; but

> When the danger looks most severe,
> Then the help of God is near.

So it proved to us. The gallant 13th Indiana had just come up to our left on a cat-like tread, and were not seen until they were opening a murderous fire on the enemy, to the right, which made them falter, wheel and run. Then our boys spread [sic.] to their feet and run up the field, over the stone fence into another field, through that into the woods, and through that still on, following the panic stricken rebels who threw away guns, bayonets, haversacks, and everything else in order to facilitate their flight. We followed up until dark came on. Our boys were gathered on the field, of which they were complete victors; but how horrible was that field, strewn with dead, and from which came the groans of the wounded and the sighs of the dying. Exhausted and sick at heart we lay down on the field of battle, where we were ordered to remain, and slept without fire or blankets, to awake in the morning stiff and shivering with cold. At daybreak we followed the retreating rebels, without anything to eat. They had left their dead and wounded by the way, and at almost every house our Surgeons were called to minister to the wounded men. That night we had some coffee and slept by fires, though without blankets. We started early the next morning and followed until night. On Monday and Tuesday we fought their rear, taking many prisoners.

Thus ended the careful [fearful?] battle of Winchester. It was fearful. Just think of 10,000 muskets fired continually for hours, the chase and the excitement. All our troops engaged did their best. The rebels fought stubornly and with courage, but the Union boys are bound to win, as one of my Sergeants, J. E. Bruce, told a rebel Major after he had shot him on the third charge. . . .

I am writing this four miles from camp and within three miles of the enemy, where I have been on picket since yesterday; but I expect to be released in an hour.

After we were quartered on Tuesday evening, I went to see General Banks to get permission to look after my dead and wounded. He granted the permission, and shaking my hand said, "I am happy to say, you assisted nobly in gaining a noble victory. . . ." And, in fact, all my boys, except two, should be Colonels, and Sergeant Bruce should be a General.

Good Day.

M. M. SPIEGEL

[*Your True Marcus: The Civil War Letters of a Jewish Colonel.* Edited by Frank L. Byrne and Jean Powers Soman. Kent, Ohio, Kent State University Press. Copyright 1985 by Kent University Press, pp. 59, 62–63, 65–66, 73–74, 77–81, 83–87. Permission to print these and other passages included in the present volume granted by Kent State University Press.]

Confederates

The Union military victories in February, 1862, and the following two months that brought joy to Spiegel, Strong, Daly, and other Unionists were of course defeats that brought dismay to Confederates. But before those events of the late winter and early spring of 1862, Mary Chesnut (back in South Carolina for a time) recorded with horror in her diary in September, 1861, the death of an elderly cousin at the hands of the cousin's slaves.

[Camden, South Carolina] *September 21, 1861.* Last night when the mail came in, I was seated near the lamp. Mr. Chesnut, lying on a sofa at a little distance, called out to me. "Look at my letters and tell me about them."

I began to read one aloud; it was from Mary Witherspoon—and I broke down. Horror and amazement was too much for me. Poor Cousin Betsey Witherspoon was murdered! She did not die peacefully, as we supposed, in her bed. Murdered by her own people. Her negroes.

I remember when Dr. Keitt was murdered by his negroes. Mr. Miles met me and told the dreadful story.

"Very awkward indeed, this sort of thing. There goes Keitt, in the house always declaiming about the 'beneficent institution.' How now?"

Horrible beyond words.

Her household negroes were so insolent, so pampered and insubordinate, that she lived alone and at home. She knew, she said, that none of her children would have the patience she had with these people who had been indulged and spoiled by her until they were like spoiled children. Simply intolerable.

Mr. Chesnut and David Williams have gone over at once. . . .

September 24, 1861. The party to Society Hill [the Witherspoon plantation] have come home again. Nothing very definite so far. William and Cousin Betsey's old maid Rhody in jail. Strong suspicion, no proof of their guilt yet. The neighborhood in a ferment. Evans and Wallaces say these negroes ought to be burnt. Lynching proposed. But it is all idle talk. They will be tried as the law directs, and not otherwise. John Witherspoon will not allow anything wrong or violent to be done. He has a detective here from Charleston. . . .

Hitherto I have never thought of being afraid of negroes. I have never injured any of them. Why should they want to hurt me? Two-thirds of my religion consists in trying to be good to negroes because they are so in my power, and it would be so easy to be the other thing. Somehow today I feel that the ground is cut away from under my feet. Why should they treat me any better than they have done Cousin Betsey Witherspoon?

Kate and I sat up late and talked it all over. Mrs. Witherspoon was a saint on this earth. And this is her reward.

Kate's maid came in—a strong-built mulatto woman. She was dragging in a mattress. "Missis, I have brought my bed to sleep in your room while Mars David is at Society Hill. You ought not to stay in a room by yourself *these times.*" And then she went off for more bed gear.

"For the life of me," said Kate gravely, "I cannot make up my mind. Does she mean to take care of me—or to murder me?" I do not think she heard, but when she came back she said, "Missis, as I have a soul to be saved, I will keep you safe. I will guard you."

We know Betsey well. Has she soul enough to swear by? She is a great stout, jolly, irresponsible, *unreliable,* pleasant-tempered, bad-behaved woman with ever so many good points. Among others, she is so clever she can do anything. And she never loses her temper—but she has no moral sense whatever.

That night Kate came into my room. She could not sleep. Those black hands strangling and smothering Mrs. Witherspoon's gray head under the counterpane haunted her. So we sat up and talked the long night through.

[*Mary Chesnut's Civil War*, pp. 198–199.]

The Confederate defeats in February, March, and April, 1862, caused serious concern to Mary Chesnut, to the members of the Jones family, to David G. Harris, and to John Cotton—although Charles C. Jones, Jr., and David G. Harris at first, on the basis of faulty information, interpreted the battle at Shiloh as a Confederate victory. Intermixed with comments on the military situation was mention of such other topics as Mary Chesnut's continuing observations about blacks, Charles C.

Jones, Jr.'s words about the possibility of foreign intervention in the war, David G. Harris's notations concerning farming and the likelihood of his entering military service, and John Cotton's descriptions of his first weeks in his cavalry unit's camp in Alabama.

Mary Chesnut:

February 11, 1862. Congaree House [A hotel in Columbia, South Carolina] After an illness. . . .

Confederate affairs in a blue way. Roanoke [Island, North Carolina] taken, Fort Henry on the Tennessee River open to them, and we fear the Mississippi River, too. We have evacuated Romney [in western Virginia]—wherever that is. New armies, new fleets, swarming and threatening everywhere. . . .

February 16, 1862. Awful newspapers today. Fort Donelson a drawn battle. You know that means in our mouths that we have lost it.

That is nothing. They are being reinforced everywhere. Where are ours to come from, unless they wait and let us grow some. . . .

February 22, 1862. What a beautiful [day] for our Confederate president to be inaugurated. God speed him. God help him. God save him. . . .

March 13, 1862. . . . Read *Uncle Tom's Cabin* again. . . . These negro women have a chance here women have nowhere else. They can redeem themselves. The "impropers." They can marry decently—and nothing is remembered against them, these colored ladies. It is not a nice topic, but Mrs Stowe revels in it. How delightfully pharisaic a feeling it must be, to rise superior and fancy we are so degraded as to defend and like to live with such degraded creatures around us. Such men as Legare [Legree] and his women.

The best way to take negroes to your heart is to get as far away from them as possible. As far as I can see, Southern women do all that missionaries could to prevent and alleviate the evils. The social evil has not been suppressed in England or New England, London or Boston. And they expect more virtue from a plantation African than they can practice with all their high moral surroundings—light, education, training, and supports. . . .

March 24, 1862. . . . J. C. has been so nice this winter, so reasonable and considerate—that is, for a man. The night I came from Mme Togno's, instead of making a row about the lateness of the hour, he said he was "so wide awake and so hungry." So I put on my dressing gown and scrambled some eggs &c&c there on our own fire. And with our feet on the fender and the small supper table between us, we enjoyed the supper and a glorious gossip. Rather a pleasant state of things, when one's own husband is in a good humor and cleverer than all the men outside. . . .

I did leave with regret Maum Mary. She was such a good, well-informed old thing. My Molly, though perfection otherwise, does not receive the confidential communications of new-made generals at the earliest moment. She is of very limited military information. Maum Mary was the comfort of my life. She saved me from all trouble, as far as she could. Seventy, if she is a day. She is spry and active as a cat, of a curiosity that knows no bounds—black and clean. Also, she knows a joke at first sight. Honest—I fancy they are ashamed to see people as careless as J. C. and myself. . . .

Mr. Chesnut calls Laurence "Adolphe" [the dandified valet who dominates his owner, Augustine St. Clare, in *Uncle Tom's Cabin*.] but says he is simply perfect as a servant for him. Mary Stevens said last winter, "I thought Cousin James was the laziest man alive until I knew his man Laurence!" He will not move an inch or lift a finger for anyone but his master. Mrs. Middleton politely sent him on an errand—and he was very polite about it, too. Hours after, she saw him sitting on the fence of the front yard. "Didn't you go after all?"

"No, ma'am, I am waiting for Mars Jeems."

Mrs. Middleton calls him now "Mr. Take-it-easy." . . .

April 27, 1862. New Orleans gone—and with it the Confederacy. Are we not cut in two? That Mississippi ruins us if lost. The Confederacy done to death by the politicians. What wonder we are lost. Those wretched creatures the Congress and the legislature could never rise to the greatness of the occasion. They seem to think they were in a neighborhood squabble about precedence.

The soldiers have done their duty.

All honor to the army. Statesmen busy as bees about their own places or their personal honor—too busy to see the enemy at a distance. With a microscope they were examining their own interest or their own wrongs, forgetting the interest of the people they represent. They were concocting newspaper paragraphs to injure the government. No matter how vital, nothing—nothing—can be kept from the enemy. They must publish themselves night and day and what they are doing, or the omniscient Buncombe will forget them. . . .

April 29, 1862. Grand smash. News from New Orleans fatal to us.

[*Mary Chesnut's Civil War*, pp. 285–286, 290, 294, 307, 319, 321, 330–331.]

The Jones Family:

Mrs. Mary Jones to Lt. Charles C. Jones, Jr.

Montevideo [Georgia], Friday, February 21st, 1862

My very dear Son,

. . . The hour has arrived when men and women too in the Southern Confederacy must seek to know and to do their duty with fearless hearts and hands. Our recent disasters are appalling. The thought of Nashville, the heart of the country and I may say granary of our Confederacy, falling into the hands of those robbers and murderers casts a terrible gloom over us all. That point in their possession, it really appeared that they might touch every other in North Alabama and Georgia. I trust this day's mail will bring us some encouraging news! . . .

Your affectionate mother,
Mary Jones.

Lt. Charles C. Jones, Jr., to Rev. and Mrs. C. C. Jones
Camp Claghorn, Monday, February 24th, 1862.
My dear Father and Mother,
. . . The recent reverses in the West, most severe as they are, will, I trust, bring our people to a nearer trust in God and to a more faithful and energetic use of those means which are placed in our hands for the preservation of our national honor and for the defense of our soil. Every man capable of bearing arms should be in the field; and the country should be thoroughly alive to the sense of imminent dangers which surround us. . . .

Give many kisses to my precious little daughter. And believe me ever, my dear parents, with warmest love.

Your affectionate son,
Charles C. Jones, Jr.

. . . .

Lt. Charles C. Jones, Jr., to Rev. and Mrs. C. C. Jones
Camp Claghorn, Monday, March 24th, 1862
My dear Father and Mother,
. . . For the present I can see in the future no ray of peaceful sunshine. Clouds and darkness are about us. That we shall, if we but prove true to our God and to ourselves, be eventually successful I entertain not the shadow of a doubt; but this consummation will, as matters now stand, be reached only after months and probably years of severe struggle, heroic endurance, and patient patriotism. Foreign intervention is entirely out of the question. I wish our people had thought it so long ago; we would have gone more earnestly about our work. I am glad it is out of the question, and that no foreign power shall attempt to intervene for the supposed settlement of our present difficulties. No compromise can by any possibility be made. We must make ours a self-sustaining government, developing at home resources of every description and remanding ourselves to the day of Roman virtue and Spartan simplicity. Mr. Yancey, I see in a recent speech, suggests that our ministers, now knocking for admission into the cold reception rooms of European palaces, be recalled. I think his idea more than half correct. The time is, I trust, not far distant when the world will feel our power, and in turn itself honored by our friendship and benefited by our commercial alliances. . . .

Your affectionate son,
Charles C. Jones, Jr.

. . . .

Lt. Charles C. Jones, Jr., to Rev. and Mrs. C. C. Jones
                        Camp Claghorn, Monday, April 7th, 1862
My dear Father and Mother,
    . . . The morning papers have just been received, and we are
thanking God for our grand victory near Corinth [i.e., Shiloh], the
Solferino of the war. I trust the accounts as reported are correct. I do not
feel entirely confident as yet. . . .

                                            Your affectionate son,
                                            Charles C. Jones, Jr.

                        . . . .

Lt. Charles C. Jones, Jr., to Mrs. Mary Jones
                        Camp Claghorn, Monday, April 21st, 1862
My dear Mother,
    We have nothing of special interest in our vicinity today. The
enemy appears to be operating quietly down the river, but the exact character and extent of their labors are not, I believe, definitely ascertained.
Most of the ships have returned northward, either with a view to returning with reinforcements at some early day, or for the purpose of swelling
the immense force which now threatens our army on the [Virginia]
Peninsula.
    The approaching conflict there will doubtless be terrific. The
shock of that battle will be felt in the remotest bounds of our Confederacy,
and its results will exert a most material effect upon the duration of this
war. If driven from our positions there and discomfited, God alone knows
when the war will end; while on the other hand, if He in mercy crowns the
valor of our arms with success, the annihilation of that boasted Grand
Army of the Potomac under the leadership of McClellan will, at least for
the present, in that direction work a practical cessation of hostilities, and
may conduce in no small degree to an early and final restoration of peace.
    One after another our fortifications and strong places have fallen
before the superior forces and untiring industry of our unrelenting enemy.
So far our foe is without a permanent check to his general advance, except
upon the memorable hills of Shiloh. But I think if we can hold our own
until August, we will see more light and somewhat of joy and immediate
hope. The present exertions of the Lincoln government are wonderful,
and their resources marvelous. . . .
    I have no fears of our ultimate success; but as matters now stand,
and at the rate at which we have been for some time retrograding, the
amount of blood, loss, and deprivation to be incurred before that consummation devoutly to be wished for is reached will be enormous. . . .
    The existing difficulties about the continuance of the late state
forces in service, and the disagreements which recently arose between
those in authority, are peculiarly unfortunate just at this time. . . .

Give much love to dear Father. Many kisses for my precious little daughter. And believe me ever

Your affectionate son,
Charles C. Jones, Jr.

. . . .

Lt. Charles C. Jones, Jr., to Rev. C. C. Jones
Savannah, Monday, May 12th, 1862

My dear Father,
        . . . The telegraphic communications of today cast additional gloom over our prospects: Norfolk evacuated, the navy yard burnt, our vessels, dry dock, and all destroyed, the *Virginia* blown up, the city in the occupancy of the enemy, Commodore Tattnall resigned, and our army in Virginia falling back generally. Add to this that General Beauregard is said to be suffering severely in the Army of the Mississippi for want of provisions; the report that Atlanta is suffering from the supposed Lincoln incendiaries; and the further rumor that both Charleston and Savannah are to be evacuated at no distant day—and we have a chapter of evil tidings which it is almost impossible to consider with composure.

There is no disguising the fact that our country's fortunes are in a most desperate plight, and thus far I see nothing ahead but gathering gloom. . . .

The passage of this [Confederate] conscript law—a law good in itself—just at this time exerts a most disorganizing and deleterious effect upon our armies. The elections thus far evidence the fact that almost all of the good officers have been thrown overboard in the reorganization of companies, battalions, and regiments, and that in their steads men of inferior qualifications . . . have been entrusted with the command. All the worst phases of low, petty electioneering have been brought to light, and military discipline and becoming subordination are in frequent instances quite neglected. . . . The election in the Chatham Artillery occurs on Friday or Saturday next. What the result will be I have not inquired. Of one thing you may rest assured: I will compromise neither name nor honor to compass a reelection. . . .

Your affectionate son,
Charles C. Jones, Jr.

[*The Children of Pride*, pp. 852–853, 867–871, 880–881, 893–894.]

David G. Harris:

February 20 [1862]. The sun is shining to day. It is a sight that we have not been blessed with lately. . . . We had bad news from the war on day before yesterday. Fort Donelson has been taken and thirteen thousand Confederate prisners. This is bad, very bad. But yet it might be much worse. These are distressing times, & we can not tell how long they will continue or how they will terminate. The weather is warm again. There has scarcely been any winter weather yet. I do not think I have seen any ice for a month. In fact there has been but little this winter. My clearing is nearly complete except the rails and fencing. But as soon as I can plow, I shall quit the clearing & go to sowing oats.

March 9, Sunday. A beautiful morning. Though ther was a heavey frost. . . . We have done but th[r]ee days plowing yet, but the weather has been so cold that the plows has not done much.

The war is assumeing a rather ugly appearance. The people are becoming alarmed. I think that war is not the game of fun that they did at the commencement. But now is the time for patriots to show their vaunted patriotism. When it is most needed, I fear it will be the hardest to find. Now that we have put our hands to the plow, and our necks are in the haulter. We must not look back, nor dispond, but strain ever more to accomplish our independence. Times are hard, because every thing is so high priced. So much money is needed and is hard to get. Our taxes are heavey, and they must be paid. For they like Time and Tide waits for no man. But the government must have money, and it [is] our duty to support it and it is not right for us to complain. [We must] conquer or be conquered, & subjugated. . . .

March 19. Having received orders to enroll myself at the White Plains, to day I started at 9 o'clock and by driving hard arived there at 12 o'clock. I did nothing ther but returned by 4 o'clock. At 12 it began raining and continued until night. Wet cold evening. . . .

March 20. Quite sore after my long ride yesterday. But if I have saved my fine, it will to some extent compensate me.

March 21. . . . My hands have been hauling leaves, and firewood & working about the new-ground. Hard times is here & worse is coming. Wife, (and me too) are in a peck of trouble about the probability of my being drafted for the war. I confess I did not think that I would be liable to go so soon, but now I think my chance is as good as any ones. If I was to go; I had much rather have gone as a volenteer. Then I could choose my company and arms &c but now, I fear that privaledge is denyed me. But if I go, I will try to go as reconciled as well as I can. Hoping that all will go well with me while in the army and at home with my family. Somthing has to be done, and I should do my part. The milatary life will be a new life for me, as I have never been in ranks in my life, and scarsely know a word of command. If I go, I hope my wife will be reconciled to it. Parting with my family will be worse then meeting the yankeys. . . .

April 8. Clouddy, damp, and rather cold. Yesterday I engaged Mr Rogers to make me an every day pair shose [shoes]. He charges me $4.00. This is terable. But I suppose it is the ligiamate [legitimate] effects of the war. . . . My black bull died this evening. My boar, ram goats, ram sheep & now my bull is dead.

Great Victory at Corinthe [Corinth] [Shiloh]. Rainy day. I have just heard of the battle & victory at Corinth. The report is that the yankeys are badly whipped. I wish they was all whipped out of there skins. The evening is quite wet, and the day has been rather cold. I expected to do lots [of] plowing this week, but shall be disappointed again. *The first mess of lettuce. . . .*

April 27. Sunday. The land very wet, and the morning rather cool. But we have had *NO FROST* in a long time. . . . Bad news from the war. The yankeys are giving it to us on every hand.

April 29. Went to the village to get Mr Lanford to shear my sheep. While ther, heard still more bad news from the war. Our [forces] are not in ascendency at this time. But the darkest time is just before day. Matters may alter soon, and we may hear a better account from our forces. Broke up and planted the hill side in the lower Bottom.

Broke up the turnup-pach and replowed the garden. The land is still wet and prospect of more rain. . . .

May 3. . . . Some of our lands gets too hard before the wet weather springs cease runing. There has been a great amount of wet this winter & Spring. But still I fear to see it turn dry, for then the land will be so hard we can not work it. Not much news to day from the war. But the yankey's are still in the ascendency. Taking our rivers, sea course, and citties as fast as they can. But still I am not discouraged. We can give them all they can get with these gun boats, and then whip them, until they come to their senses. War is not the thing for sport. I do not fear the yankey's, but I fear the scarcity of provisions may induce some of the Southerns to cry out enough. But for myself, I am willing to live on bread & parched corn for a long time before I will yeald to their rule. If the South will remain firm and united there is no danger.

May 4. Sunday morning. Raining again.

[*Piedmont Farmer,* pp. 230, 235–236, 238, 241, 244, 245.]

John Cotton:

Alabama Montgomery Aprile the 24, 1862

Mariah Cotton dear wife for the first time in life take my pen in hand to write you a few lines to let you no that we are all well William lessley [a neighbor] has been sorta puny but he is better he is down in town garding the yankes there is 744 yankeys here in a old ware house and we have to help gard them we have been examined and received and they say our horses will be praised today and our legion will also be organized today I would bee very glad to see you and the children I am very well satisfyed concidering the way I left home If I could see you and the children when I wanted to see you I could make out very well we are camped two miled south east of montgomery we received our bounty money [a bounty of fifty dollars was granted to all privates who enlisted for three years or the duration of the war] yesterday it is uncertain how long we will stay here

I dont recken I will come home til wheat gets ripe unless we git orders to leave if we get orders to march I wil come home sooner I would bee glad to bee there and see how things are going on and look around a little rite to me and tell me how my wheat is doing and how things are going on nothing more at present but remain your affectionate husband til death

John W Cotton to Mariah Cotton

Montgomery Camp Mary Alabama May 1 1862
Mariah Cotton Dear Wife I take my pen in hand to drop you a few lines to let you no that I am tolerable well I have had a very bad cola but I am bet-ter I am not atall sick but feel sorta bad I hope these lines will find you all well and I hope you have got more reconciled about my leaving you and the children I think if you could see these yankeys that we have to gard down here you would yap, whip them or dye on the battle field I have hope to gard them for days and nights there is over eight hundred of them in all some of them wants to get home very bad and other dont seem to care mutch about it I would bee very well satisfyed if I could see you and the children when I wanted to I want to see you all very bad and I would bee glad to here from you all for I have not herd nary word from you all since I left home. . . . now we here that the yankeys have taken neworleans some of the people here are very badly scared and are moveing out there families and they are halling oft the cotton. . . . we are doing very well now we got plenty to eat and nothing to do but to gard the yankeys our com-pany has been received and our horses praised and we have got our bounty money but we have not got our saddles yet nor I dont no when we will get them we cant drill any until we get our saddles for a heap of our men have not got no saddles. . . . nothing more at present but remain your affectionate husband til death

John W. Cotton

Alabama Montgomery County May the 5 1862
Mariah Cotton Dear wife I again take the opportunity to rite you a few lines to let you no that I am well and doing well we get a plenty to eat but it is badly Cooked we had nothing fit to Cook with but we have bought some things but not enough yet we draw meal flour pickled pork pickled beef and some times fresh beef rice sugar molasses and soap I am very sorry to here that the wheat has got the rust so bad I am glad to here that manuel [a slave hired from a neighbor] is trying to do comething and get-ting along so well. . . . If I could see you and talk with you I could tell you of a great many things that has passed since I left you I think if nothing happens I will bee at home about the 20 of this month the most of our men is gone home now but the captain says they shant go no more I could have come two but I thought as I could not come but once that I would wait a while I recived a letter from you this morning dated the 29 of Aprile. . . . I

recken you herd that the yankeys had taken neworleans we are still garding what yankeys we have got here yet one of our men killed one of them
the other day for disobeying orders one of our sodiers belonging to our legion shot another the same day and the day before one of our men got
drounder in the river. . . . our colonel says that we may have our first battle here at this place I expect we will stay here a good while and we may
never leave here while the war lasts we have not drilled any yet but the
captain says we will have to go at it the 10 of this month he thinks that we
will draw our saddles the ninth my horse is very bad off with the distem-
per he has eat nothing hardly for about a week. . . . I would bee glad to see
little ginny [the Cottons' baby child] and give her a kiss and see the rest of
the children frolic around and play on my lap and see babe suck his thum
if it had not have bee the love I have for them and my country I would
have been ther now nothing more but remain your affectionate husband
til death J W Cotton to Mariah Cotton there is about fore thousand soldiers
stationed here now and there is more comeing in direct your letters to
John W. Cotton Montgomery Alabama in care of Capt M G Slaughter
May the 6 1862. . . . I have just now received a letter from you and I was
glad to here from you and to here that you all was well and that all was
going on well and that the wheat was doing better I want to see you and
the children as bad as any body can
[*Yours Till Death: Civil War Letters of John W. Cotton.* Edited by Lucille
Griffith. University, Alabama, University of Alabama Press. Copyright
1951 by University of Alabama Press, pp. 1–5. Permission to print these
and other passages included in the present volume granted by University
of Alabama Press.]

3. CONFEDERATE DEFENSE OF RICHMOND AND ADVANCE INTO MARYLAND AND KENTUCKY, MAY–SEPTEMBER, 1862

Confederates

*The Confederate defeats in the western theater of war from February through
April of 1862 were soon overshadowed in the public mind when Confederate
armies in Virginia, led by Generals Robert E. Lee and Thomas J. ("Stonewall")
Jackson, among others, won a series of spectacular victories, beginning in May of
1862. In one of those victories, Richmond was successfully defended from the
Union forces under the command of General George B. McClellan in the Seven
Days battles at the end of June and the beginning of July, 1862.*

*The Confederate defense of Richmond can be seen through the eyes of both
soldier and civilian in Mrs. Chesnut's diary since she includes in her diary letters
from the fighting front by her husband. She also includes some observations about
her view of the unfairness of men to women.*

Mary Chesnut:

[Columbia, South Carolina] *June 12, 1862*. . . . Here came in Mary Cantey's strident voice: "I may not have any logic, any sense—I give it up. My woman's instinct tells me, all the same, slavery's turn has come. If we don't do it, they will." . . .

After all this—tried to read *Uncle Tom*. Could not. Too sickening. A man sends his little son to beat a human being tied to a tree? . . . Flesh and blood revolts. You must skip that—it is too bad—or the pulling out of eye-balls in *Lear*. . . .

June 29, 1862. Victory! Victory heads every telegram now, one reads on the bulletin board. . . .

June 30, 1862. . . . At church every face was anxious. It is a great deliverance, but the list of killed and wounded is to come. . . .

Richmond
June 29th, 1862

My dear Mary,

For the last three days I have been witness of the most stirring events of modern times. On my arrival here I found the government so absolutely absorbed in the great pending battle that I found it useless to talk of the special business that brought me to this place. As soon as it is over, which will probably be tomorrow, I think I can easily accomplish all that I was sent for. I have no doubt that we can procure another general and more forces, &c&c.

The president and General Lee are inclined to listen to me and to do all they can for us. General Lee is vindicating the high opinion I have ever expressed of him, and his plans and execution of the last great fight will place him high in the role of really great commanders.

The fight on Friday was the largest and fiercest of the whole war—some 60,000 or 70, with great preponderance on the side of the enemy. Ground, numbers, armament, &c all in favor of the enemy. But our men and generals were superior. The higher officers and men behaved with a resolution and dashing heroism that has never been surpassed in any country or in any age.

Our line, by superior numbers and superior artillery impregnably posted, was three times repulsed when Lee, assembling all the generals to the front, told them that victory depended on carrying the batteries and defeating the army before them, ere night should fall. If night came without victory, all was lost, and that the work must be done by the bayonet. Our men then made a rapid and irresistible charge, without powder, and carried everything. The enemy melted before them and ran with the utmost speed, though of the regulars of the federal government. The fight between the artillery of the opposing forces was terrific and sublime. The field became one dense cloud of smoke, so that nothing could be seen but the incessant flashes of fire through the clouds.

They were within sixteen hundred yards of each other, and it rained storms of grape and cannister.

We took 23 pieces of their artillery, many small arms, and some ammunition. They burnt most of their stores, wagons, &c&c.

The victory of the second day was full and complete. Yesterday there was little or no fighting, but some splendid maneuvering which has placed us completely around them.

I think the end must be decisive in our favor. We have lost many men and many officers. I hear Alex Haskell and young McMahon among them, as well as a son of Dr. Trezevant. Very sad indeed. We are fighting again today, will let you know the result as soon as possible. Will be at home sometime next week. No letter from you yet.

With devotion, yours,

James Chesnut, Jr. . . .

Telegram from my husband:

Richmond
June 29th

Was on the field—saw it all. Things satisfactory so far. Can hear nothing of John Chesnut—he is in Stuart's command. Saw Jack Preston—safe so far. No reason why we should not bag McClellan's army or cut it to pieces. From four to six thousand prisoners already.

J.C.

Dr. Gibbes rushed in like a whirlwind to say we were driving McClellan into the river. . . .

July 1, 1862. No more news. It has settled down into this—the great battle, the decisive battle, has to be fought yet. . . .

July 3, 1862. . . . "Why do we wait and whimper so in our soft Southern speech—we poor women?"

"Because," said Mrs. Singleton, in quick and emphatic way, "you are always excusing yourselves. Men here are masters, and they find fault and bully you. You are afraid of them and take a meek, timid, defensive style."

Mary C dramatically explains: "Dogmatic man rarely speaks at home but to find fault or ask the reason why. Why did you go? or: why, for God's sake, did you come? I told you never to do that. Or: I did think you might have done the other. My buttons are off again—and be d————d to them. Coffee cold! Steak as tough as the devil! Ham every day now for a week! What a blessed humbug domestic felicity is—eh? At every word the infatuated fool of a woman recoils as if she had received a slap in the face. And for dear life, she begins to excuse herself for what is no fault of hers.

And explains the causes of failure, which he knows beforehand as well as she does. She seems to be expected to put right every wrong in the world. Mrs. S. fought, she did not apologize; hence her freedom from slavish whining, etc., etc." . . .

July 10, 1862. J.C. [Mary Chesnut's husband] has come. He believes from what he heard in Richmond that we are to be recognized as a nation by the crowned heads across the waters at last.

Mr. Davis was very kind. He asked J.C. to stay at his house, which he did and went every day with General Lee and Mr. Davis to the battlefield, as a sort of amateur aide of the president. Likewise they admitted him to the informal cabinet meetings at the president's house, etc., etc.

He is so hopeful now that it is pleasant to hear him. . . .

After all, suppose we do all we hoped. Suppose we start up grand and free—a proud young republic. Think of all these young lives sacrificed! If three for one be killed, what comfort is that? . . . The best and bravest of one generation swept away!

[*Mary Chesnut's Civil War*, pp. 381, 400, 402–403, 405–408, 410, 412.]

The Confederate military victories in the summer of 1862 did not end with the successful defense of Richmond. When it became clear that McClellan was withdrawing his army from its unsuccessful siege, the Confederate troops of Lee and Jackson began to move northward, defeating the Union forces under General Pope at the second battle of Bull Run, at the end of August, 1862. Continuing their northward advance, the Confederate army crossed into Maryland in September, passing to the west of Washington, D.C., and posing a potential threat to Harrisburg, Philadelphia, and other communities in Pennsylvania.

The optimism and hope inspired by these Confederate military victories were reflected in both the journal of David G. Harris and the letters between members of the Jones family.

David G. Harris:

May 10 [1862]. Saturday. The negroes have holaday to day, & I went to muster at Bagwell'[s] old-feild, and did milatary duty for the first time in my life. I was not much pleased with our performance. It looked so much like childrens work. . . .

May 12. . . . The news from the war is more favourable and is particularly pleasant after repeated reverses. We will whip the yankeys yet, inspite of all their Gun-Boats. Commenced breaking up the Lower Bottom. It is late to be doing such work but it is the best that I could do, oweing to the wet. . . .

May 16. WHEAT. I have just been over my wheat crop and am satisfied that I will not make more than one fourth (1/4) of a crop. This is bad to think about at this time, now that the war is upon us, and provision so scarce and so high. A failur at this time would conquor us much sooner than the Yankey could do it. FRUIT. There has been no frost for a long time. Indeed there has been but little this winter & none this Spring, consequently all our fruit trees is loaded with fruit, every peach-tree on hill[s] and in the hollows are very full of peaches. There is so much fruit that I think we can live on it for a while and fight the Yankey's without wheat or bacon. . . .

May 31. Laura [his daughter] & I went to the village to day. The day was rather warm for comfort. Laura wanted her tooth drawn, thinking it would add to her beauty. But I was not willing to have it taken out. Not much news from the war though two big battles are expected soon. All well. . . .

June 6. Another rain this morning, and the day is cool. Finish plowing the new-ground. All well. Expected much news to day, so soon after the battle of Richmond. . . . I went to Mr. Zimmermans to read his papers, but did not learn much of importance. This is an important time with us. Many important battles depending; and all are so anxious to heare, and still afraid to here. . . .

July 1. Yesterday I went to the village. I called at the school house to see if they had a paper for me. Spent a few minutes in pleasant chat with the children, then hurried on to the post office and heard the *Glorious news* that our army had attacked and routed McClens' [Gen. George B. McClellan's] Army. Taking many priseners, Destroying many Stores, But at a great loss to human life. Takening [taking] the day all togather, the day has been an important & pleasant one. I hope we will have many such.

To day the Conscripts are enrolling themselves. This is a bitter pill to the most of them, for they are the crew that does not want to fight for their country. I would hate to wate to be forced out in defence of my needy country. . . .

July 2. . . . This rain has made us many a bushel of corn. And the Lord knows we will need it, judging from all that I can hear & see. I fear that starvation may conquor us sooner then the Yankeys. We have no one to depend upon but ourselves. . . .

July 10. To day I have been riding over the neighborhood and have heard of the death of many of our soldiers, and many more are wounded. The battle around Richmond has been a fatal one, and a dear bought victory. But I hope it will return value Recieved. . . .

July 21. . . . .

Sunday the 20 wife & I went to the village to see the conscripts take their leave. They bid farewell to their friends and left with as good grace as possibl. They are gone, and we (who are over thirty-five) are ordered to enroll ourselves, and be in readiness to take our places in the rank[s]. . . .

July 23. Went to the village, but did not make much by the trip. . . . We (the men over the age of thirty five & under fifty) are ordered on parade Monday next to organize ourselves, and then go into camp for instructions. This will be hard on us *old men*. But we must do our share as well as the younger. Warm and clouddy to day; but no rain. I do wish it would rain. . . .

July 27. Wife, children and I went to church at Ceder Springs to day. Mr. Bonner preched. The weather is rather cool. Tomorrow the men of the age between 35 & 50 meet at the White Plains to organize ourselves in companies for the defence of our country. The younger men are all gone, now we have to follow. It would be hard on us to take the feild at this season. But we must divide the labour with the others, all must do their share, be it ever so hard. . . .

August 2. Put my poor tired horse to the buggy this morning and went to the village. I was somewhat disappointed in the pleasure that I inticepated. I heard but little news from the war but saw several wounded soldiers. They have become quite common of late. Showing the effects of the late well contested battles. . . .

August 11. . . . More good news from the seat of war.

August 12. *Stonewall Jackson* has won another victory over the infirnal yankeys. Our arms are victorious in almost every engagement. . . .

September 13. . . . Times are hard and seems promising to be worse. What we are to do for food and clothing, I can not tell. I have bought some rye and barly, which I want to sow soon for pastureage for my stock. I hear good news from the war. We are whipping the yankeys more beautifully, but we are loosing many good men. . . .

September 17. Went to the village through the heat and dust. Did not hear much news, only our noble army was doing well in Maryland.

[*Piedmont Farmer*, pp. 246, 248–249, 251–254, 256, 259.]

In the Jones family letters, optimism and hope over the Confederate military victories were tempered by discussions of the escape, and the threatened escape, of Georgia slaves to the Union forces along the coastline of the state.

Lt. Charles C. Jones, Jr., to Rev. and Mrs. C. C. Jones

Savannah, Friday, July 4th, 1862

My dear Father and Mother,

I had hoped that this, the anniversary of our former national independence, would have been rendered memorable in the history of our young Confederacy by the unconditional surrender of McClellan and his boasted army of invasion. It may be that such will be the case before this newly risen sun shall have performed his daily journey. . . .

The effect of this defeat of their arms before Richmond must exert a most depressing influence upon the Federals. It must teach them the utter impracticability of any theory which looks towards a subjugation. It will strengthen the hands of the peace party in their midst. It will bring desolation to their hearts and sorrow to their eyes. . . .

The result in Europe must prove most favorable to us, and we will look with interest for reports from that quarter.

On our part this great victory—while it will cost many a pang to the state who has lost so many brave defenders, while many a sorrowing home will attest the magnitude of the sacrifice . . . will nevertheless give to us, one and all, assurance of the favor of God, of the greatness of our cause, of the value of the liberties for which we are contending, and of our absolute invincibility by the proudest force which our enemy may send against us. The tide has indeed turned. I trust that we have been sufficiently punished for our transgressions, and that the avenging rod will be now lifted. . . . I trust we shall soon hail the return of white-winged peace. . . .

Your affectionate son,
Charles C. Jones, Jr.

. . . .

Lt. Charles C. Jones, Jr., to Rev. and Mrs. C. C. Jones
Camp Stonewall Jackson, Wednesday, July 9th, 1862
My dear Father and Mother, . . .

The recent successes of our arms, by the blessing of God, have been even more remarkable and encouraging than were our former reverses depressing and unexpected. A degree of rather painful uncertainty still lingers about our final operations in the vicinity of our capital, and the reported reinforcements of McClellan may cost us yet many a brave life. . . .

Your affectionate son,
Charles C. Jones, Jr.

Rev. C. C. Jones to Lt. Charles C. Jones, Jr.
Walthourville, Thursday, July 10th, 1862
My dear Son, . . .

The series of brilliant victories which have been achieved by the Army of Eastern Virginia (as our President terms it in his admirable congratulatory address) has infused new life and energy into our citizens and soldiers; . . . We long to see the *finale* of McClellan's army. It will be difficult to force his position, and it will require great skill and resolution on the part of our commander in chief and his army. So far it has been a tremendous blow. May it please our Heavenly Father to continue his smiles upon us! . . .

A public meeting of the citizens was called on the 8th at Hinesville to adopt some measures for suppressing if possible the escape of our Negroes to the enemy on the coast. *Fifty-one* have already gone from this county. Your Uncle John has lost five. *Three* are said to have left from your Aunt Susan's and Cousin Laura's; one was captured, two not; and one of these was *Joefinny!* Such is the report. The temptation of *cheap goods, freedom, and paid labor* cannot be withstood. None may be absolutely depended on. The only preservation is *to remove them beyond the temptation,* or *seal* by the most rigid police all ingress and egress; and this is most difficult. We have petitioned General Mercer to quarter Captain Thomson's company in our country. We need the corps, and trust he may be able to accede to our request. Our people [i.e., the slaves of the Jones family] *as yet* are all at home, and *hope* they may continue faithful. . . .

Mother has just come in. Your aunt's and cousin's Negroes were Joefinny, his brother Dick, and their nephew *Cato.* Cato is taken; the other two, with others, are said to be on the Island. Little Andrew, who married into the family, knew all about it and has told. I go to Dorchester this afternoon to see Brother Buttolph and family and to consult. My determination is to turn them over to the proper authorities and let them be tried and dealt with as the public welfare may require. Some example must be made of this matter. They are traitors who may pilot an enemy into your *bedchamber!* They know every road and swamp and creek and plantation in the county, and are the worst of spies. If the absconding is not stopped, the Negro property of the county will be of little value. Should you see General Mercer before our petition reaches him, tell him that we have petitioned for Captain Thomson's company. Do let me know your opinion on the proper disposition to be made of these absconding Negroes. What would you do with *white men?* . . .

Your affectionate father,
C. C. Jones.

. . . .

Lt. Charles C. Jones, Jr., to Rev. C. C. Jones
Camp Stonewall Jackson, Saturday, July 19th, 1862
My very dear Father, . . .

I reached camp on Friday morning at two o'clock A.M. with twenty-one conscripts, all able-bodied, active, honest men from Middle Georgia, a valuable acquisition to the strength of our battery. On Monday night next, D.V., I leave again for the camp of instruction at Calhoun to secure some twenty more, which will entirely fill the vacancies in our battery—vacancies to be caused by the discharge from our ranks, by virtue of the operation of the Conscript Act, of all men over thirty-five and under eighteen years of age some ninety days hence. . . .

You have observed our recent success in Tennessee. This, I am led to believe, is but an earnest of a forward movement on the part of our troops, who are heavily massed at and near Chattanooga, which will swell the triumph which now rests upon our arms. . . .

It is a most mortifying reflection that intemperance exerted its baneful influences even in the very midst of our brilliant victories in the vicinity of Richmond; and that we were prevented from reaping the full reward of our achievements, and from compassing the full success of our plans, by the drunkenness of some of our officers high in command. . . .

I deeply regret to learn that the Negroes still continue to desert to the enemy. Joefinny's conduct surprises me. You ask my opinion as to the proper disposition to be of absconding Negroes, and also inquire what would be done with white men detected in the act of giving over to the enemy. If a white man be apprehended under such circumstances, he would doubtless be hung, and in many instances, if the proof be clear, by an indignant and patriotic community without the intervention of either judge or jury. In the case of a Negro, it is hard to mete out a similar punishment under similar circumstances. Ignorance, credulity, pliability, desire for change, the absence of the political ties of allegiance, the peculiar status of the race—all are to be considered, and must exert their influences in behalf of the slave. If, however, a Negro be found digesting a matured plan of escape and enticing others to do the same; or if, after having once effected his escape to the enemy, he returns with a view to induce others to accompany him, thus in fact becoming an emissary of the enemy; or if he be found under circumstances which indicate that he is a spy, it is my opinion that he should undoubtedly suffer death, both as a punishment for his grave offense and as an example to evildoers. In the case, however, of a Negro endeavoring to effect escape to the enemy detected in the effort, my opinion is that he should not be put to death, but that he be taken to the county seat of the county in which the offense was committed and there *publicly* and *severely punished*. . . .

Your affectionate son,
Charles C. Jones, Jr.

. . . .

Lt. Charles C. Jones, Jr., to Mrs. Mary Jones
Savannah, Monday, September 8th, 1862

My dear Mother, . . .

The news from Virginia comes in slowly. We have gained a signal but not altogether a decisive victory. . . . My own impression is that the main body of the army will avoid Alexandria and Arlington heights and, crossing the Potomac higher up, invade Maryland, and, passing in the rear of Washington, subject that city to either a partial or total isolation. An excellent strategic point for occupation would be Harrisburg, Pennsylvania. This in our possession, Pennsylvania would furnish abundant supplies for our army, while Philadelphia, Baltimore, and Washington would be cut off to a very great extent from the rich tributes from the West which have ever furnished them with every necessary. . . .

We have cheering news from Tennessee, and we look from that quarter for results even more decisive than in Virginia. Tennessee and Kentucky will soon be entirely relieved from the Lincoln yoke. . . .

I am sorry to learn that the Negroes of the county still continue to desert to the enemy. I am doing all that I can to ascertain some place of retreat for us. . . .

Your affectionate son,
Charles C. Jones, Jr.

. . . .

Lt. Charles C. Jones, Jr., to Rev. C. C. Jones
                              Savannah, Wednesday, September 10, 1862
My dear Father, . . .

It is a most difficult matter to secure a place to which the Negroes can be removed. I have corresponded with gentlemen in various portions of the state, and have made every inquiry from the factors here, but without success. . . .

My own impression is that the principal danger to which we will be subjected will be the voluntary desertion of the Negroes. I very much doubt if the enemy will attempt to penetrate the interior except at strategic points. And the truth is, if God still favors our cause and inspires our armies and leaders as He has done in such a marked manner for some time past, the enemy will be forced to keep his troops for home defense.

The fall campaign opens on our part with a brilliancy and success absolutely wonderful. Contrasted with the position the Confederate States occupied three months since, our present is almost incredible. Already is the promise of our worthy chief magistrate redeemed, and the war is being carried "beyond the outer confines of our Confederacy"—Smith thundering at the gates of Cincinnati; Lee, Jackson, and Longstreet surrounding the beleaguered capital of Lincolndom and pressing to the rescue of Maryland. Ohio and Pennsylvania will both soon feel the presence of actual, present warfare; while a hasty retreat will be all that is left for the scattered armies of our invaders. . . .

Every act in this drama but reveals more and more closely the wisdom of our rulers, vindicates the energy and the ability of the administration, and afford ever-increasing assurance of the favor of the Ever-Living God, to whom all thanksgivings are due, and are humbly and fervently paid by many a pious heart. Never in the annals of the world has a nation in such short period achieved such a history. . . . Whatever else the nations of the earth may think or say or do, we have already wrested from them unbounded respect and admiration.

Have you noticed one very interesting fact in the history of this war—that the *pious leaders* have been specially blessed in all of their enterprises? . . . Stonewall Jackson, Lee, Stuart: pious men all—another illustration of the fact that the truly pious man is the best man for every walk and every emergency in life, and for the simple reason that he carries with him the favor of Him from whom alone all success and all strength can come. . . .

                              Your affectionate son,
                              Charles C. Jones, Jr.

[*The Children of Pride,* pp. 923–924, 927–930, 933–935, 959–964.]

The Jones family letters note that the Confederate armies by September, 1962, had not only invaded Maryland but were also advancing in the western theater into Kentucky and "thundering at the gates of Cincinnati."

By that date in 1862, the cavalry unit in which John Cotton served was part of the western Confederate army pushing into Kentucky. But also by that date John Cotton was separated from his unit and in a hospital in Atlanta stricken with typhoid fever. In addition to John's letters to his wife, Mariah, two letters from her to him at this time have survived and are included here. Mariah and John wrote primarily about matters other than the overall progress of the war, but John did say that he had heard that General Kirby Smith's Confederate forces were in Kentucky, within thirty miles of Louisville. It was John's understanding that when he rejoined his company he would be in Kentucky as part of Smith's army, and he suggested that his wife address her letters to Lexington, Kentucky.

Atlanta Georgia July 13th 1862
Mariah dear wife I again take my pen in hand to drop you a few lines to let you no where I am and that I am well and I hope these few lines may find you all enjoying the same blessing I want to here from you very bad worse than I ever did in my life. . . . I want you to rite to me as soon as you get these direct your letter to Chatanuga tennessee in care of Captain M.G. Slaughter hilliards legion I reckon that we will stay there til we get equiped and armed they are expecting to have a fight there before long they have just now come here with the drays after our baggage to carry it to the cars to be ready to start in the morning I dont want you to uneasy yourself about me for I am doing very well. . . .

your affectionate husband til death
John W Cotton. . . .

Chattanooga Tennessee July the 16 1862
Dear wife I now once more take my pen in hand to rite you a few more lines to let you no where I am and how I am I am as well as I ever was in my life and I hope these few lines may reach you all the same. . . . they say the yankeys are in about fifteen miles of here but the main armey is about thirty miles of here on the tennessee river it is clost to us about a half mild we have got nearly all of our company to gether now. . . . there is about forty thousand of our troops here and about forty thousand yankeys but our men dont appear to fer them no more than if they wernt here. . . . when we came up the people cheered us al the way men women and children they were collected on the road in great quantities and there was a continuel hollow nearly all the way we passed some of the higest bridgs that ever I saw and we passed the tunnel under the stone mountain but it was night and we couldnot see mutch. . . .

John W. Cotton. . . .

Chattanooga Tennessee August 1th 1862
Great god what a thunder bolt struck my ear yesterday when Asa come up here to the horsepitle and gave me a letter from you and told me that

Cricket [The Cotton's daughter, Nancy Hanner, born February 3, 1858. She had died July 12.] was dead I no not how to address you on the subjectt I hop she is better off but it almost brakes my hart to think I could not bee at home and see the last of her I want you to grieve as little as possible I hope the time is near at hand when I can come home and stay with you and the rest of the children. . . . you need not bee uneasy about me if I get killed just say I dyed in a good cause ould abe lincon and his cabinet could not daunt me now I could fall his hole army rite now I don't feel like riting now but I will try to rite you another letter in a few days forgive me for not riting no more if I could see you I could talk to you a weak but I cant rite what I could tell you if I could see you. . . .

John W. Cotton

Chattanooga Tennessee August the 3 1862
My dar wife and children I now with mutch sorrow attempt to rite you a few more lines to let you no that I am not very well I have got a bad cold but not very bad off I left the horsepitol yesterday eavning. . . . I never want to go to a horsepital again men are dying there constant there was about a dozen men dyed while I was there three of our own men and we have two more that I think well dye and lots more sick but I dont no how many. . . . I dont want you to grieve two mutch about the death of our lettle daughter we must only hope that she is better off then we are but oh how I will miss her when I come home she will not be there to fondle on my nees with the rest of the children I hope the rest may do well til I come home and want you to take care of yourself and not expose your self two mutch. . . . I hant mutch to rite to console you for I am in two mutch trouble myself I shall bee uneasy til I here that all of the children has had the measles and well of them I never new what pleasure home afforded to a man before If it wer not for the love of my country and family and the patriotism that bury in my bosom for them I would bee glad to come home and stay there but I no I have as much to fite for as any body else but if I were there I no I could not stay so I have to take it as easy as possible. . . .
John W. Cotton to his wife at home.

Alexandres Hospital Atlanta Ga August 15/62
Mrs. Cotton Dear Madam [This letter of course was not written by John W. Cotton but there is no further knowledge as to who the scribe is. As is revealed in the next letter Cotton had typhoid fever and his low spirits evidenced in earlier letters may be in part explained by this illness.]
I take pleasure in writing you few lines for Mr. Cotton or rather his request to inform you that he is not improving very much yet Dr. giving him quinine very heavey today which makes his head in an awfull fire his fever has never broke yet the Dr has never given hem any strong medisin until today since he has been here he came here last Thursday

evening which was the 14th of the month I think he looks better today than he did yesterday I think he will be up in a few days he said for you to write to him soon as you get this let him know how you all are getting on how your crops is Mrs Cotton I will keep you posted how Mr Cotton get on as long as I stay here but I may have to leave for my company this week we both belong to the same company we are not in the same Hospital though I can go and see him every day write to him Atlanta Ga Alexander Hospital as for the health of our company I cant tell anything about for I have not been with the Company 3 weeks or more I learn that they are at or above Knoxville tenne Nothing more at present will write again in a few days to you believe me to be your friend & yours trula
To Mrs Cotton

W. G. Johnston
John W. Cotton

Atlanta August 17, 1862
Mariah dear wife I now attemp to let you no that am in the All-Scrandrer horsepitle I am god deale better than I was when I come heare the Dr Says I have got the typhoid fevor but he says he will have me up in afew days I come hear the 14th of this month I cant write much as I am Sick and Nurvess I had to git the nurs to do my writeing I hope I will be able to giv you afull histor of all things i afew days I want you to write to me as soon as you git this letter direct your letter to Allesander atlanta ga Hospitle at-lanta ga I clos my letter by Singing my Name

John W. Cotton. . . .

Alabama Coosa Count August the 21 1862
        my dear husband I now seat my self to rite you a few to let you hear from me and the children the children is all at well at time and as for my self I am not atall sick but I trouble all most to death about you and our little cricket death it all most breaks my hart to think that you are gone so farr off from me and the children but I can ony hope that the time is com-ing when you will get home to us all again I hope thes few lines many find you well evreything is doing very well you stock is all doing vary well so far I hant much of importen to rite to you for I cant hear of eny thing hear but war all the time they say tha are fixing for a big battle at richmond again I want you to rite to me weth you gon fether of than you wer before or not and rite to me all about how you far wether you get annuf to eat or not I hear of som not getting anuf to eat I so uneasy about you not geting anuf to eat so I want to no. . . . I dont no what will become of us all crop is sarrow and worms is eaten up the grass and ther is some on the fodder I dont no whether tha will hurt the fodder or not you brouther William and the rest of the conscript men started from around hear the 19 of this thear is a tauke of thear taken of than hier than thirty five but I hope that wont

take no more I wont than that is thear to com home wever do you want me to sell any of you weet for seed or not you rite to me about what to do about it you must rite me all the good advice you can for I need advice you no I received a letter from you a Monday it is now thursday it was date the third of this I was glad to fom you. . . . I so uneasy about you I dont what to do I wood this hold world if you was at home with me so I cood no when you sick or well you sed that you wood bee uneasy till you heard that the children was all well of the measels tha are all well of them now sweet and Jinny has no had than yet I dont think tha will have them now so you must not uneasy you self about the measells. . . . you dont no how bad I felt to hear of you beeing in a horsepitol sick Oh that I ony cood bee ther to wate on you I will bee so uneasy till hear from you I cant rest but I hope you are better by this time and I hope by the time you get this letter you will bee well. . . . I nevery was as uneasy in my life nuth mor at present but remain you affecttion wife until death.

Mariah Cotton. . . .

August the 25 1862
my dear husband I wonce more with sorrow and trouble I take my pen in hand to rite you a few lines to let you hear from me and the children the children is all well at this time. . . .I have gest now receive a letter from you it give me relief for I did not no wher you was I never was as glad to hear fom any boddy in my life as I was to hear from you I am so sarrow to hear of you beein sick I dont no how to address you on it I dont want you to bee uneasy about home I wont you to take good cear of you self and try to get well again I want to come and see you if you are willing and are a gouing to stay ther long anuft for me to come and if you are rite me about it whether I must try to come or nor. . . . you must excuse my bad spelling and riten for it is hard task for me to rite to you now I wish I cood hear from you every our rite to me if you dont want some clouse while you are ther and if you do rite what it is and I will try to send it or fetch it I wood bee son glad if you cood come home and stay till you got well. . . . rite soon. . . .

Mariah Cotton to her loving husband John W. Cotton. . . .

October the 2 1862
Atlanta Ga Medical college horsepittol Dear wife it is with pleasure that I take my pen in hand to rite you a few line to let you no that I am well and will leave here this eavning for my company there is several of the legion going with me but none of my company we will start half past 7 oclock this eavning. . . . I am a fraid that when I leave here that I never will here from you all again nor see you until the war ends if I never come back again I want you to do the best you can for your self and the children lern them to love you and obey you and try to lern them to bee good children

and if I never return I want you to keep you land and such things as you need and raise your children the best you can I don't want you to bee uneasy because I have rote this but bee of good cheer. . . . I herd from general smith—[General Kirby Smith.] he is three hundred miles from chattanooga in kentucky at a little place in thirty miles of louisville I rote to you before that my company left knoxville on the 18 of september I dont expect they have got to smith yet I expect that I shall bee bothered to get to them I hant herd from them since they left knoxville. . . . I wish I was there it will not bee worth while for you to rite to me any more until you here from me again I am so bothered that I dont no what else to rite to you dont bee uneasy about me if you dont here from me you may no I am doing the best I can for my self tho in distant land I rome I will think the more about home if on yankey soil I bee dont think eyle ever forget the. . . .

John W Cotton to Mariah Cotton and children at home

Tennessee Camp Convalescence near Noxville Oct the 8 1862
Mariah Cotton dear wife. . . . I am at the convalescent camp at Knoxville waiting for company to go with me to my company there is one of my company here and I expect we will start to the company soon about day after tomorrow. I will rite again when I leave here I don't no whether we can get to our company or not but we will go as far as we can I understand that the army is still moveing on north. . . . if you want to rite to me direct your letter to lexington kentucky our company may bee there yet I am to go from here there I will bee very glad to here from you if I should ever get there but I have a dangerous road to travoil for about two hundred miles I only have to hope that I will go threw safe I want you to pray for me that I may go threw safe to my company and threw the war til we have moved the yankeys back from our soil and peace is maid and that I may return safe home to you all again nothing more but remain your best friend.

John W. Cotton. . . .

Knoxville Tennessee October the 18 1862
Mariah dear wife it is again that I take my pencil in hand to let you no that we are about to leave knoxville the order is to leave this eavning for kentucky. . . .I want you to rite to me as soon as you get this letter if you call it one and direct you letter to lexinton kentucky in care of captain M G Slaughter Hilliands legion cavalry battalion I cant tell you how bad I want to see you all so I must close nothing more at present only remain you most affectionate husband til death.

John W Cotton to Mariah Cotton
[*Yours Till Death,* pp. 9–10, 13–19, 24–26, 28–29.]

Unionists

When the successful Confederate defense of Richmond in June and July, 1862, forced the retreat of McClellan's army, one of the Union regiments sent to join McClellan's forces included Marcus Spiegel. Spiegel received a furlough in May, 1862, and early in July, his regiment was sent by boat to join McClellan's retreating army of the Potomac. Spiegel participated in a few military engagements near City Point, Virginia, but by the end of August much of McClellan's army was being withdrawn to northern Virginia. Spiegel's regiment was part of the forces left behind at Suffolk, Virginia (near Norfolk), and from there he commented in his letters on the defeats suffered by the Union forces near Washington and in Kentucky in the late summer of 1862.

> Camp in the Field near
> City Point Va.
> July 6/62

My dear good Wife, my beloved Children and Brother!

This Sunday a.m., a beautiful but very hot morning, and . . . I am compelled to lay on my front in consequence of two monster big "Boils" in the rear. . . .

Since I have written the above I received an order to report to the Field at once, as a Battle was impending. Sick and weary as I was, with 2 Boils about my Stern, the weather to a perfect fever heat, I started and came just in time to see our Pickets driven in by the Rebel Cavelery, where upon we immediately started out, in line of Battle and they skedatled. . . .

> Camp in the Field near
> Harrison Landing
> July 10/62

My dear dear Wife and Children
and Brother if he is there yet.

God bless you! I am well, hearty, cheerful and in better spirit than I have been since I left home. We are still near the Landing but not in front of all the troops. Neither are we in a low miserable swamp, but on a high Bank of the James River. . . . I think we have a position now which is impregnable and we are strengthening it daily, so that I came to the conclusion there will be no fight here, neither will we advance until after we get plenty of reinforcement. I never thought it possible that one man could be so beloved by so many thousands of men, as is General McClellan, [whom] the Army of the Potomac fairly Idolizes. . . .

The Balloons are up every clear day and from them McClellan gets information as to the position of the Enemy. I think McClellan is a splendid General, all the Croakers may say to the contrary notwithstanding. . . .

Harrison Landing, Va.
July 11/62

My dear, dear good Wife! . . .

    If I only knew you were all well and hearty, I could feel perfectly easy but think of it, my good sweet wife, I left you my love, my joy, my all, the mother of my four beloved children, one only two weeks old, our sweet Babe, you scarcely able to stand up, careworn and sad at the departure of your true husband, troubled as I know you was and subject to those dangerous reverses likely to fall on a woman in child bed, and then think of me away from home in War for three long weeks and over, and not a word from you. May God grant that all is right. . . .

Your ever true
Marcus

Camp in the Field near
Harrisons Landing Va.
July 18/62

My dear dear good wife and children, good mother,
my good Brother,

    You never in all my life was as dear to me as you are this morning for I just received your loving, good, dear letter of the 13th which assures me that you all are O.K. My God what a weight that takes from my mind. I feel young, well, cheerful and in excellent spirits. . . .

    The late withdrawal or rather repulse of McClellan from before Richmond I look upon as a great disaster to the national cause, though at the same time it can not be denied that the giant Retreat has been conducted by General McClellan in a manner which stamp[s] him at once the greatest as well as gallant, magnificient as well as Scientific General in the World. He is truly a General; the Rebels were worsted at every engagement and their loss is immense, . . . yet they have the moral triumph of forcing our Army to retreat. . . .

Suffolk Va. Sept. 3/62

My dear Good Wife and Children! . . .

    We are now in Camp near Suffolk. . . . I have not as yet had an opportunity of seeing as to getting a house here for us and thought best to wait until I hear from you and also from the effects of the Battles near Washington.

    Things do not look very bright in that quarter. We begin to feel

here as though every effort the loyal men in the north can make will have
to be made ere this Rebellion can be crushed. . . .

Your ever true and loving
Marcus

Camp near Suffolk Va.
Sept. 7/62

My dear good Wife! . . .

I will come some time this Fall or Winter. I somehow took it in my
head that the War would not last over winter. Our last defeats will call out
spontaneously such a powerful Army and all our resources will at once be
opened and used for a quick and successful termination of the struggle
and if we should or God forbid should not be successful, the War will have
to end this Winter.

The people of Ohio must be awfully excited at the daring onward
course of the Rebels in Kentucky but in my opinion they need not be
alarmed. The Rebels will never cross the Ohio River. [No closing signature
for this letter]
[*Your True Marcus*, pp. 121–122, 125–127, 129, 131, 163–167.]

*Spiegel's letters in September, 1862, expressed confidence that the Union
military forces would rebound from their defeats and be successful. Those defeats,
however, occurring in both the eastern and western theaters of operation, had led
to widespread dismay and frustration among many Unionists, and to severe criticism of the Union leaders, including Abraham Lincoln. Among the Unionists
who expressed those sentiments were George Templeton Strong, Maria Daly, and
Frederick Douglass.*

*Strong, Daly, and Douglass all criticized Lincoln—Strong with reluctance,
Daly with scorn and contempt, and Douglass with disillusionment. Of the three,
it was only Douglass who found much ground for hope, maintaining that the desperate military and diplomatic situation would force the Lincoln government to
make war upon the institution of slavery, and thus save the nation.*

Strong:

August 31 [1862], *Sunday.* Eleven-thirty A.M. Waiting for news. The suspense is trying. Anticipations not brilliant. No further particulars that are
at all reliable in morning papers—an ominous stillness. Mcdowell
telegraphs that it's "decidedly" a victory. The adverb produces a negative
impression on my mind. . . . Ten P.M. This citizen does not despair of the
republic. Most of his friends do. But though things look bad, and there is
reason enough for anxiety and apprehension, people are making up their
minds to the worst much too fast. I can find no tangible evidence of serious disaster, yet. . . .

we went after dinner to the upper end of Central Park and walked down. . . . The long lines of carriages and the crowds of gents and giggling girls suggested peace and prosperity. There was nothing from which one would have guessed that we are in a most critical period of a great Civil War, in the very focus and vortex of a momentous crisis and in imminent peril of grave national disaster. . . . received George Anthon at about eight o'clock in the evening. He was a messenger of evil. Pope has fallen back on Centreville, if the reports that prevail be reliable. That does not look like decided victory! But the situation is utterly obscure and we can form no opinion about it.

September 3. It has been a day of depressing malignant dyspepsia, not only private and physical, but public and moral. . . . The morning papers and an extra at mid-day turned us livid and blue. Fighting Monday afternoon at Chantilly, . . . and Pope retreating on Alexander and Washington to our venerable field-worn fortresses of a year ago. Stonewall Jackson (our national bugaboo) about to invade Maryland, 40,000 strong. General advance of the rebel line threatening our hold on Missouri and Kentucky. Cincinnati in danger. A rebel army within forty miles of the Queen City of the West. Martial law proclaimed in her pork shops. . . . Everybody talks down McClellan and McDowell. . . .

September 4. It is certain now that the army has fallen back to its old burrows around Washington. It will probably hibernate there. So, after all this waste of life and money and material, we are at best where we were a year ago. McClellan is chief under Halleck. Many grumble at this, but whom can we find that is proved his superior? He is certainly as respectable as any of the mediocrities that make up our long muster roll of generals. . . .

September 7, Sunday. . . . Rebellion is on its legs again, East and West, rampant and aggressive at every point. Our lines are either receding or turned, from the Atlantic to the Mississippi. The great event now prominently before us is that the South has crossed the Potomac in force above Washington and invaded Maryland and occupied Frederick, proclaimed a provisional governor, and seems advancing on the Pennsylvania line. . . . A very strong [Union] force, doubtless, has rushed up the Potomac to cut off the rebel communications. If it succeed, the rebellion will be ruined, but if it suffer a disorganizing defeat, the North will be at Jefferson Davis's mercy. I dare not let my mind dwell on the tremendous contingencies of the present hour. . . .

The nation is rapidly sinking just now, as it has been sinking rapidly for two months and more. . . .

September 13, Saturday. . . . I fear our Army is in no condition to cope with Lee's barefooted, ragged, lousy, disciplined, desperate ruffians. They may get to Philadelphia or New York or Boston, for fortune is apt to smile on audacity and resolution. What would happen then? A new and most alarming kind of talk is coming up, emitted by old Breckinridge

Democrats (like W.L. Cutting) mostly, and in substance to this effect: "Stonewall, Lee, and Joe Johnston were all anti-secessionists till the war broke out. No doubt, they still want to see the Union restored. They are personally friends, allies, and political congeners of Halleck, McClellan, F.-J. Porter, and others. Perhaps they will all come together and agree on some compromise or adjustment, turn out Lincoln and his 'Black Republicans' and use their respective armies to enforce their decision North and South and reëstablish the Union and the Constitution." A charming conclusion that would be of our uprising to maintain the law of the land and uphold republican institutions! But we have among us plenty of rotten old Democrats . . . , capitalists . . . , traders and money dealers . . . , and political schemers . . . , who would sing a *Te Deum* over any pacification, however infamous, and would rejoice to see Jefferson Davis our next President. Perhaps he may be. If he is magnanimous and forgiving he may be prevailed on to come and reign over us. I would rather see the North subjugated than a separation. Disgust with our present government is certainly universal. Even Lincoln himself has gone down at last, like all our popular idols of the last eighteen months. This honest old codger was the last to fall, but he has fallen. Nobody believes in him any more. I do not, though I still maintain him. I cannot bear to admit the country has no man to believe in, and that honest Abe Lincoln is not the style of goods we want just now. But it is impossible to resist the conviction that he is unequal to his place. His only special gift is fertility of smutty stories. . . . If McClellan gain no signal, decisive victory within ten days, I shall collapse; and we have no reason to expect anything of that sort from him.

Rebel ravages in southern Pennsylvania may stir up a general arming and enrolment, but even that would give us only an undisciplined mob for months to come. O Abraham, *O mon Roi!*
[*The Diary of George Templeton Strong*. Abridged edition, 1988, pp. 199–201, 203–204.]

Daly:

September 11, 1862

Since I have been in the city, we have been deeply humiliated, Stonewall Jackson having forced our splendid army and our over-prudent civilian generals across the Potomac, threatening Washington and invading Pennsylvania whilst the pothouse administration in Washington seems as sanguine as ever. McClellan has been deposed and Halleck has been reinstated as commander in chief. A lady went to ask Halleck, whom she knew very well, a favor to aid in getting a ward of her husband appointed. His answer was that he had always been and was still opposed to the Administration and the Secretary of War and would never ask any favor of them. I feel ashamed of being an American now. To think that we should be conquered by the bare feet and rags of the South, fed from our wagons, supplied from our caissons! Stonewall Jackson told a prisoner (a Major Lee now in our hands) that with three brigades in the position of Pope and McDowell's troops he could have captured the whole of Longstreet's advance. A dying soldier writes to his brother in Michigan, "I die fearlessly. I have fought bravely, but I fall a victim to Pope's imbecility and McDowell's treachery." . . .

Baron Gerolt tells us that fifteen hundred men were lying for five days, still alive, on the battlefield, and that thousands died from mere starvation, no one going to their succour. The wretched heads of departments know nothing of their duties, and the *honest* fool at their head is content playing President. God forgive the authors of all these horrors and enlighten the mind of the poor creature who dared to take upon himself the high office of President in such a time with no ability to fill the office! Better a dishonest but clever man! Honesty, unfortunately, is often an attribute of imbecility—I suppose to fill the law of compensation which seems to pervade all things in this world. I am sure I would not willingly sit at the table of Lincoln or his wife, much less receive them at mine. In the *World* of this morning there was a very bold article against the Administration. I hope it is a sign of public opinion. I wish the army would take Washington and defend it for the nation and drive Lincoln and his host of locusts, like those which infested Egypt of old, into the sea. Phil writes that everyone now wonders that anyone is desirous of entering the army.

September 12, 1862 . . .

There seems to be a panic at the North at Jackson's success. As far as I am concerned, I would as willingly be ruled by Jefferson Davis as by poor Lincoln, and I suppose many feel the same. Treason, however, should not prosper. Had the Southerners waited four years, this bloodshed would have been spared and they would again have been in the ascendant with the whole Democratic party. But they certainly have the military talent. . . .

Generals Shields and Blenker the President leaves unemployed. He so fears the abolitionists to whom they are opposed, and yet they are two brave, able men. Jefferson Davis would be wiser. His danger makes him so. Lincoln and his crew are likewise in danger. They may be displaced sooner than they imagine by an outraged, indignant people whom they have sold out to contractors. McClellan, after all, has most greatness of mind of all. To the thousands of attacks made upon him he returns no answer, but keeps a dignified silence. This is either the result of great intrepidity and calmness or of weakness. His wife told an uncle of mine that he had telegraphed to Stanton after his retreat from before Richmond: "In attempting to ruin men, you have nearly ruined your country." . . .

What is truth? As Pilate once asked so must we do now among the many contradictory assertions we everywhere hear. In truth, Northern

men are educated to act individually and are unwilling to submit to discipline of any kind. This begins in the family, thence to the private soldier, who dissents from his captain, the captain from his colonel, the colonel from his general, the general from the commander in chief, and the generals are all rivals—whilst at the South, Jefferson Davis is the head; Lee's and Jackson's orders are obeyed.
[*Diary of a Union Lady*, pp. 167–168, 170–172.]

Douglass:

THE PRESIDENT AND HIS SPEECHES

The President of the United States seems to possess an ever increasing passion for making himself appear silly and ridiculous, if nothing worse. Since the publication of our last number he has been unusually garrulous, characteristically foggy, remarkably illogical and untimely in his utterances. . . . Notwithstanding his repeated declarations that he considers slavery an evil, every step of his Presidential career relating to slavery proves him active, decided, and brave for its support, and passive, cowardly, and treacherous to the very cause of liberty to which he owes his election. . . .
Douglass's Monthly, September, 1862

ANTI-SLAVERY PROGRESS

Notwithstanding the apparent determination of the Government and of Generals commanding in the field, to preserve slavery and save the Union at the same time, notwithstanding the exaltation of proslavery over antislavery commanders, and the steady purpose of the Government to check and arrest all anti-slavery measures and tendencies in the army and country, it is evident that the idea that this horrible slaveholding rebellion can only be speedily and successfully put down by suppressing its cause, in the entire abolition of slavery, has gained decided ground during the last few weeks among the loyal people.—The defeats and disasters on the field which have visibly thinned the ranks of the loyal army, and the call for six hundred thousand more men, and the prospect of heavily increased national debt, and grinding taxation, are doing their legitimate work among the people, however little they may seem to affect the Government at Washington. . . . A few weeks more of sufferings, disasters, defeats, and ruin of the slaughter of our country's first born, a few weeks more of successful rebellion and threatened intervention from abroad, a few weeks more of gloomy prostration of business and of earnest protest on the part of the suffering people will, we trust, arouse the Government to a just and wise sense of the demands of the age and of the hour. We are to be saved as by fire. . . .

By some, it is even now thought too late. We have. . . bowed so low to the dark and bloody spirit of slavery, that it is doubted whether we have the requisite moral stamina to save our country from destruction, whether we shall not at last give up the contest, patch up a deceitful peace and restore the slave power to more than its former power and influence in the republic. . . .

Nevertheless we have yet strong grounds of hope. The rebels are firm, determined, enthusiastic and wonderfully successful. They have beaten off McClellan, hold Richmond securely, and are menacing Washington, and all the Border States. With slavery undisturbed they can prolong the war indefinitely. . . . Considerations of this character will make the South slow to listen to any compromise, and will, we still hope, compel the Federal Government to take at last *the* step, which it ought to have taken at the first, i.e. destroy this slaveholding contagion, by destroying the filthy cause which produced it. Than this there is no other way, slavery must die if the nation lives, and the nation must die if slavery lives.
Douglass's Monthly, September, 1862
[*The Life and Writings of Frederick Douglass,* Vol. 3, pp. 266, 268, 270–272.]

The writings by Douglass, by Daly, by Strong, and by Spiegel all expressed explicitly their authors' reactions to the military situation at the times they wrote. In striking contrast was the journal kept in the summer of 1862 by Charlotte Forten, the free black woman in her twenties who was away from her Philadelphia home to teach school in Massachusetts. Charlotte Forten's journal, instead of chronicling the military victories or losses, was filled with descriptions of her friends, her reading, her fascination with the world of nature (the ocean, the sunsets, the flowers, the singing of birds, the green hills). Even her description of a white man who refused to eat at the same boardinghouse table with her because she was black was not related to the war, although the white man in question happened to be a naval officer.

Thus, a reader of her journal might almost be unaware that the country in 1862 was in the midst of a gigantic war—almost unaware, but not entirely so. For Charlotte Forten mentioned in her journal that she had heard speeches by abolitionist leaders, William Lloyd Garrison, Susan B. Anthony, and Wendell Phillips, among others. She heard Phillips speak, for example, in the Music Hall in Boston in July, 1862, and she obviously agreed with Phillips' criticism of Lincoln ("the poor miserable President") and admired Phillips' lifelong labors to free the slaves. Above all, Forten's journal described her efforts to secure permission and sponsorship to go to Port Royal, South Carolina, now in 1862 in Union hands, to assist the former slaves there who had escaped to the Union military forces.

Salem. June 22, 1862. More penitent than ever I come to thee again, old Journal, long neglected friend. More than two years have elapsed since I last talked to thee. . . .

It is a lovely June Sunday,—the air sweet and cool, the birds singing, the sun shining, and soon the church bells will ring. . . .

Sunday, June 29. Little worth recording has occurred during the past week. Have taught school, as usual, wrote letters, played chess, and listened to "Chronicles of Carlingford," which Miss S.[hepard] has been reading. . . . Have had a grand walk on the turnpike this morning. How fresh and invigorating the breezes were. How peaceful the green hills, and gray old rocks looked,—sleeping in the June sunlight. . . . Mr. Manning of the "Old South," preached here this morning; and greatly as I admire this fearless young apostle of freedom, I could not prevail upon myself to go to church. I felt such a strong drawing toward my dear old hills. T'was irresistible.

Sunday, July 6. Let me see? How did I spend last week! In teaching as usual, until Friday, on which, being the "glorious Fourth," we had no school, and I went to Framingham to the Grove Meeting. . . . Greatly to my disappointment Mr. [Wendell] Phillips was not there. . . . Mr. [William Lloyd] G.[arrison] and all his children were there looking as well and happy as possible. He and Mr. [Ezra] Heywood and Miss [Susan B.] Anthony made the best speeches. . . . After the meeting, spent a day or two in Boston. Had a lovely walk on the Common, Saturday morning. How fresh and beautiful the grass and trees looked. . . .—In the afternoon S. [arah] P. [itman?] and I spent a little time at the [Boston] Atheneum. . . . To-day—Sunday—had the great happiness of hearing Mr. [Wendell] Phillips. . . . It was a grand, glorious speech, much as he alone can make. I wish the poor miserable President whom he so justly criticised c'ld have heard it. It grieved me to see him looking so pale and weary. And his throat troubles him much. I cannot bear to think of his health failing. . . . let us pray to the good All-Father to spare this noble soul to see the result of his life-long labors—the freedom of the slaves. . . . I must not forget to tell. . . . [you] about a little adventure I met with to-day. I was boarding with Mrs. R.[,] a very good anti-slavery woman, and kind and pleasant as can be. Well, when I appeared at the dinner-table to-day, it seems that a *gentleman* took umbrage at sitting at the same table with one whose skin chanced to be "not colored like his own," and rose and left the table. Poor man! he feared contamination. But the charming part of the affair is that I with eyes intent upon my dinner, and mind entirely engrossed by Mr. Phillips' glorious words, which were still sounding in my soul, did not notice this person's presence nor disappearance. So his proceedings were quite lost upon me, and I sh'd have been in a state of blissful ignorance as to his very existence had not the hostess afterward spoken to me about it, expressing the wish, good woman—that my "feelings were not hurt." I told her the truth, and begged her to set her mind at ease, for even had I have noticed the simpleton's behavior it w'ld not have troubled me. I felt too thorough a contempt for such people to allow myself to be wounded by them. This wise gentleman was an *officer in the navy,* I understand. An honor to his country's service isn't he? but he is not alone, I know full well. The name of his kindred is Legion,—but I defy and despise them all. I hope as I grow older I get a little more philosophy. Such things do not wound me as deeply as of yore. But they create a bitterness of feeling, which is far from desirable. "When, when will these outrages cease?" often my soul cries out—"How long, oh Lord, how long?" . . .

Saturday, August 2. Have spent the last few weeks as usual in teaching, alternating with walking, reading or listening to Mary read. . . . School closed to-day. . . .

Monday, August 4. L.[izzie], S.[allie] and I went to Marblehead Beach. Had a delightful time on the rocks. S.[allie] and I waded and frolicked like a couple of children. . . .

Wednesday, August 6. Spent the day at Nahant. . . . Soon after I reached home dear M.[ary Shepard] came, bringing me the kindest note from [John Greenleaf] Whittier in answer to one I had written asking what day we sh'ld come. (His sister had urgently invited us to come before I left N.[ew] E.[ngland].) We are to go on Saturday. . . .

Saturday, August 9. Another "day to be marked with a white stone." Mary and I started early at the station. . . . We changed cars at L.[ynn] then proceeded to Amesbury. Did not see Whittier at the station. Drove to the house; met with a warm welcome from his sister. She looks very frail. Just as we entered the door of the house a lady came in behind us, whom we found afterward to be Lucy Larcom—a pleasant mothering, unassuming kind of person, really quite lovable. W.[hittier] was in one of his most delightful genial moods. His sister as lovely, childlike—I had almost said as angelic as ever. . . . The conversation turned on many topics, and was most enjoyable throughout. . . . We left the poet's home with regret. . . . W.[hittier] advised me to apply to the Port-Royal Com.[mission] in Boston. He is very desirous that I sh'ld go. I shall certainly take his advice. . . .

Boston. Monday, August 11. Left S.[alem] with Sallie [Cassey Smith Watson] this morn. Farewell, farewell again old town! . . .

Wednesday, August 13. Had gone to see some members of the P.[ort] R.[oyal] Com.[mission] and finding them all out of town, felt somewhat discouraged, when I rec'd the kindest letter from Whittier, advising me again to apply to the Com.[mission] and giving me the names of several friends of his [to] whom to apply, also his permission to use his name as a reference. How very kind he is. I shall go see those whom he mentions at once. . . .

Sunday, August 17. My twenty-fifth birthday. . . . The accomplishments, the society, the delights of travel which I have dreamed of and longed for all my life, I am now convinced can never be mine. If I can go to Port Royal, I will try to forget all these desires. I will pray that God in his goodness will make me noble enough to find my highest happiness in doing my duty. Since Mrs. J. has given me such sad accounts of the sufferings of the poor freed people my desire of helping them has increased. . . .

Wednesday, September 3. . . . Last week I heard from home that there was now no doubt of my being able to go from the Phil.[adelphia] Com.[mittee]. Mr. [J. Miller] McK.[im] had spoken to them about it. So if I cannot go from Boston I am sure of going from P.[hiladelphia] but I w'ld rather go under Boston auspices. . . .

Phila[delphia]. Sunday, September 14. Back again in old abominable P.[hiladelphia]. H.[enry] and I went from W.[orcester] to B.[oston] on Tuesday afternoon. I got little satisfaction from the B.[oston] Com.[mission]. "They were not sending women at present" etc. Dr. R.[ogers] promised to do all he c'ld for me, but I am resolved to apply to the Com.[mittee] here. . . .

Monday, September 15. Through Mr. [J. Miller] McK.[im]'s kindness have seen the Com.[mittee]. They are perfectly willing for me to go. The only difficulty is that it may not be quite safe. They will write to Port Royal at once, and inquire about my going. I shall wait anxiously for a reply.

[*The Journals of Charlotte Forten Grimké.* Edited by Brenda Stevenson. New York, Oxford University Press. Copyright 1988 by Oxford University Press, pp. 362, 366–376, 380–381. Permission to print these and other passages included in the present volume granted by Moorland-Spingarn Research Center, Howard University.]

Charlotte Forten was a firm supporter of the Union, but her anxiety over the fate of her application to go to Port Royal to help the freed slaves was not the same as the anxiety expressed by many other supporters of the Union by September, 1862. By that date, what many Unionists were anxious about was the fate of the Union itself, in view of the desperate military situation. That widespread anxiety was expressed particularly by Maria Daly and George Templeton Strong. "There seems to be a panic at the North" over the military situation, wrote Daly in her diary on September 12. A few days earlier, on September 7, Strong had written that if the Union forces opposing the Confederate invasion of Maryland were defeated, "The North will be at Jefferson Davis's mercy. . . . The nation is rapidly sinking just now."

CHAPTER II

"Our Army Is Still Folling Back and the Yankeys Are Advancing Slowly"—The Period in Which the Tide of Battle Turned, September, 1862–December, 1863

> "Our army is still folling back and the yankeys are advancing slowly."
> —JOHN W. COTTON, DECEMBER 14, 1863

By mid-September, 1862, the perceptions of impressive Confederate successes and of the possibly imminent failure of the Federal attempt to preserve the Union were not confined to such anxious Unionists as George Templeton Strong or to such hopeful Confederates as Charles C. Jones, Jr. Those perceptions were also expressed by the two highest-ranking officials of the British government:

"The detailed accounts . . . of the battles of August 29 and 30 between the Confederates and the Federals," wrote Prime Minister Palmerston to his Foreign Minister, Lord John Russell, on September 14th, 1862, "show that the latter got a very complete smashing; and it seems not altogether unlikely that still greater disasters await them, and that even Washington or Baltimore may fall into the hands of the Confederates.

"If this should happen, would it not be time for us to consider whether in such a state of things England and France might not address the contending parties and recommend an arrangement upon the basis of separation?"

Foreign Minister Russell's reply to his Prime Minister expressed agreement with the Prime Minister's proposal. "Whether the Federal army is destroyed or not," wrote the Foreign Minister on September 17th, "it is clear that it is driven back to Washington, and has made no progress in subduing the insurgent States. . . . I agree with you that the time is come for offering mediation to the United States Government, with a view to the recognition of the independence of the Confederates. I agree further that, in case of failure, we ought ourselves to recognise the Southern States as an independent State. . . ."

"We ought then, if we agree on such a step, to propose it first to France, and then, on the part of England and France, to Russia and other powers, as a measure decided upon by us."
[Spencer Walpole, *The Life of Lord John Russell,* 2 vols. London, Longmans, Green, and Co., 1891. Vol. 2, pp. 360-362.]

George Templeton Strong, Lieutenant Charles C. Jones, Jr., and other Unionists and Confederates had no way of knowing what the British prime minister and foreign minister were writing to each other. Even without that knowledge, however, it was not difficult to see in the autumn of 1862 that much was riding on the outcome of the Confederate advances into Maryland and Kentucky.

4. THE OUTCOME OF THE CONFEDERATE MILITARY ADVANCES INTO MARYLAND AND KENTUCKY, AND THE ISSUING OF THE EMANCIPATION PROCLAMATION

Unionists

The Confederate advance into Maryland figured prominently in the diary of Samuel Cormany and that of Rachel Cormany, his wife. The Cormanys, supporters of the Union, lived in Chambersburg, Pennsylvania, a town threatened with invasion by the advancing Confederate army in September, 1862. From Chambersburg, the Cormanys heard the sounds of battle when the Confederates commanded by General Robert E. Lee engaged the Union army led by General George B. McClellan at Antietam Creek (Sharpsburg), Maryland, on September 17, 1862.

In that battle, there were 25,000 casualties, with at least 5,000 dead or mortally wounded, and it may have been the bloodiest single day in United States military history. ["By way of comparison: on D-Day in World War II, American forces suffered 6,000 casualties—about one-fourth the number of casualties at Antietam. More than twice as many Americans were killed or mortally wounded in a single day at Antietam as in the War of 1812, the Mexican War, and the Spanish-American War combined." James M. McPherson, Ordeal by Fire. New York, Alfred A. Knopf, 1982, p. 285n.]

George Templeton Strong was in and around Washington, D.C., from September 15 to September 24, involved in the activities of the United States Sanitary Commission. Included in those activities was an inspection of the battlefield facilities of the commission in the vicinity of Antietam, and he described the battle area in a long entry in his diary when he returned to New York on September 24.

From a military standpoint, the battle of Antietam was something of a draw. But it did stop the northward push of the Confederate army, which withdrew to the south, crossed the Potomac River, and went into winter quarters in Virginia. Lincoln hoped for vigorous attacks on the retreating Confederates and the destruction of that army, but those attacks did not come from McClellan's forces. Lincoln did, however, use the checking of the Confederate invasion as the occasion for issuing the Preliminary Proclamation of Emancipation (September 22, 1862), declaring free all the slaves in the states that were still in rebellion against the United States government on January 1, 1863.

The Cormanys did not mention the Proclamation, although they probably favored it. Strong indicated his support of the Proclamation, and stated that it was "generally approved" except for a "few old Democrats." Two of the Democrats who criticized the Proclamation were Maria Daly and her husband. At the opposite pole of opinion from the Dalys was Frederick Douglass, who enthusiastically supported this enlargement of the war's goals to include emancipation as well as preservation of the Union.

Samuel Cormany:

[Near Chambersburg, Pennsylvania] *September 7, 1862* Sunday. We all went to [religious] Camp Meeting—War excitement great—A Battery went down the road en route for Baltimore. Rebels reported near Hagerstown [Maryland] and coming this way—

Meetings were not in good form—Too much War excitement—. . . .
September 9, 1862 Tuesday. Brother brought us to Chambersburg. I went to see about enlisting. There is great excitement about Drafting men into The Army—The air is full of calls for men who are patriotic to enlist—I really inwardly feel that I want to go and do my part—as a Man—as a Volunteer—leaving others to wait and be drafted—and Darling [Samuel's wife, Rachel] is likeminded—That is, she is loyal and true—and wants to see the South subdued—and however hard it would be to be alone here amongst strangers—and to have me exposed—and away. She calmly consents—That if I desire to go and make the sacrifice for our Country—our Homes, our firesides, she calmly says, though hard it is to say it—"Yes I am willing." "There will be a way" and thus we wrestled with the problem. Spending a great deal of time on our knees, before our God—and agreed that as a loyal, patriotic Man I should Enlist—

The fear of being drafted, if I did not volunteer—had possibly some weight in inducing decission—
September 10, 1862 Wednesday. NEWS! The Rebels are surely advancing on Hagerstown—Today—P.M. I enlisted in Capt. W. H. Sollenbergers Cavalry Company. . . . I was offered drink—I refused—Capt. approved my stand. Tho he drank himself—Brother John was in town today. Said to me Sam, weight it well, I did so, and considered it a duty to serve my Country in her time of need.

September 11,1862 Thursday. . . . This evening Martial Law was proclaimed—Many families are leaving Chamb'g. . . .
September 13, 1862 Saturday. . . . Had a long talk with Mother seeking to
get her reconciled to my going into the Army—She became pretty well
convinced that I could even be saved [i.e., his soul could be saved] if killed
in battle defending my Mother and Home and Country—I promised
Mother and Pet [his wife, Rachel] that I would keep evidence bright as to
being right and at peace with God. . . .
September 16, 1862 Tuesday A.M. . . . The Enemy has been halted and battle
is on beyond Hagerstown. So the tension is slightly relieved about
Chambersburg—If our men win, the enemy will surely need to fall back—
south—if not gobbled up. . . .
September 17, 1862 Wednesday. The noise of battle is in the air—occasionally—["Reverberations of field artillery at the Battle of Antietam could be
heard in Chambersburg, some twenty-five miles north of the Union gun
emplacements."] . . .
September 18, 1862 Thursday. Our Boys won out at Anteitam—and we'll
hear later what next!

Rachel Cormany:

September 21, 1862 . . . now we [Samuel and herself] are separated he has
gone to defend the rights of his country in Sulenbergers Cavalry company.
It went hard to see him go. for he is more than life to me. When he told me
that he had enlisted, I felt an undescribable heaviness in my heart. We
prayed earnestly over it. I became calm & felt more resigned, at times still
I am overcome, tears relieve me very much, my heart always seems lighter
after weeping freely. In daytime I get along very well but the nights seem
very long. I pray for him quite often & trust he will be spared to me—
[*The Cormany Diaries: A Northern Family in the Civil War.* Edited by James
C. Mohr. Pittsburgh, University of Pittsburgh Press. Copyright 1982, by
University of Pittsburgh Press, pp. 228–232, 253. Permission to print these
and other passages included in the present volume granted by University
of Pittsburgh Press.]

George Templeton Strong:

September 24, Wednesday. . . . From all accounts, Abe Lincoln is far
from easy in his mind. Judge Skinner, who knows him intimately, says he
wanders about wringing his hands and wondering whom he can trust
and what he'd better do. What's very bad, he has been heard to utter the
words "war for boundaries," to speak which words should be death.
Heaven help our rulers. Never was so great a cause in the keeping of
much smaller men. But I still have faith in Abe Lincoln. . . .

[Harrisburg, Pennsylvania was] swarming with Pennsylvania militia and all the paraphernalia of war. Men were drilling in all the streets. The great battle of Wednesday [Antietam] and the withdrawal of the rebels from Maryland were not yet fully understood, and people looked grave enough. . . .

[In Hagerstown, Maryland] Mrs. Dorsey told me much of the rebel forces that occupied the town some four days; how dirty and wretched they were, how they scampered at midnight on the news of McClellan's approach, and what a smell they left behind them. Stuart, a chaplain from Alexandria, told her they meant to take Philadelphia—"Philadelphia or death."

Next morning . . . we soon entered an atmosphere pervaded by the scent of the battlefield—the bloody and memorable field of Antietam ("Antee´tum") Creek. Long lines of trenches marked the burial places; scores of dead horses, swollen, with their limbs protruding stiffly at strange angles, and the ground at their noses blackened with hemorrhage, lay all around. Sharpsburg, a commonplace little village, was scarified with shot. In one little brick house I counted more than a dozen shot-holes, cleanly made, probably by rifle projectiles. Here and there was seen the more extensive ravage made by an exploding shell. . . .

At Sharpsburg, we found the little church used as a hospital for the 118th Pennsylvania; some fifty wounded lay there on straw. The regiment had suffered badly. . . . We went to McClellan's headquarters and to Fitz-John Porter's. McClellan has twenty regimental standards and more, and guns, substantial trophies. But for the miserable misconduct that lost us Harper's Ferry . . . the rebel retreat would have been a rout. . . . [At French's division Hospital, there was a horrible] congregation of wounded men . . . and at Porter's—our men and rebel prisoners both—on straw, in their bloody stiffened clothes mostly, some in barns and cow-houses, some in the open air. It was fearful to see; Gustave Doré's pictures embodied in shivering, agonizing, suppurating flesh and blood.

Walked with Hartshorne over another section of the battlefield, strewn with fragments of shell and conical bullets; here and there a round shot or a live shell, dangerous to handle. We traced the position in which a rebel brigade had stood or bivouacked in line of battle for half a mile by the thickly strewn belt of green corn husks and cobs, and also, *sit venia loquendi,* by a ribbon of dysentric stools just behind. . . .

September 27, Saturday. President's Emancipation Manifesto much discussed and generally approved, though a few old Democrats (who ought to be dead and buried but persist in manifesting themselves like vampires) scold and grumble. It will do us good abroad, but will have no other effect.

[*The Diary of George Templeton Strong.* Abridged edition, 1988, pp. 207–210.]

Maria Daly:

September 19, 1862 The wheel of Fortune has turned around once more and the rebels seem to be caught in their own trap. The Potomac has risen and cut off their retreat, being no longer fordable, and McClellan has been gaining victory after victory. . . . One dare scarcely believe it, so often has the sequel been just the contrary of what first we heard. I must sincerely trust that McClellan will prove himself all that was first hoped. . . .

September 24, 1862 Mr. Barney, the Collector of the Port, was here on Sunday last. He seems much discouraged and wished the Judge to go on to Washington. "You," said he, "have the ear of the President, and he needs advice." He spoke about raising Negro brigades, which the Judge disapproved. Charles said that if that was done he would wash his hands of the whole matter; that recruiting was difficult enough now because of the everlasting Negro question; that President Lincoln was sufficiently unpopular. The Judge said he had done what he could to support the government, not because he thought well of it or its measures, but because he feared the consequences if it should be overthrown.

The new levies came in very slowly. Fifty thousand were as yet last week in the field, and the government had neither arms nor clothing for another 50,000 encamped in Illinois. We are heartily sick of the whole business, and in the face of all this, yesterday the President issued a proclamation freeing all slaves in those states which shall be in rebellion on the first of January next. Better wait until we have the power to perform than utter these weak threats. . . .

Sunday, September 28, 1862 Yesterday was our wedding day. Six happy years of marriage. Few can say this in this world of change. . . . Judge Pierrepont tells us that the President told him that the Emancipation Act was his own doing. The Cabinet were not consulted. He told them it was there for them to criticize verbally, not to argue upon. What supreme impertinence in the railsplitter of Illinois! "It is my last trump card, Judge," said he. "If that don't do, we must give up." Father O' Reilly says we are under a worse despotism than they have in France or Russia. There is no law but the despotic will of poor Abe Lincoln, who is worse than a Knave because he is a *cover* for every knave and fanatic who has the address to use him. Therefore we have not one devil, but many to contend with. Yet he only stands between us and internal revolution. It is terrible. God help our unhappy country!
[*Diary of a Union Lady,* pp. 174, 176–177, 179.]

Frederick Douglass:

EMANCIPATION PROCLAIMED
Common sense, the necessities of the war, to say nothing of the dictation of justice and humanity have at last prevailed. We shout for joy that we

live to record this righteous decree. *Abraham Lincoln*, President of the United States, Commander-in-Chief of the army and navy, in his own peculiar cautious, forbearing and hesitating way, slow, but we hope sure, has, while the loyal heart was near breaking with despair, proclaimed and declared: *"That on the First of January, in the Year of Our Lord One Thousand, Eight Hundred and Sixty-three, All Persons Held as Slaves Within Any State or Any Designated Part of a State, The People Whereof Shall Then be in Rebellion Against the United States, Shall be Thenceforward and Forever Free."* "Free forever" oh! long enslaved millions, whose cries have so vexed the air and sky, suffer on a few more days in sorrow, the hour of your deliverance draws nigh! Oh! Ye millions of free and loyal men who have earnestly sought to free your bleeding country from the dreadful ravages of revolution and anarchy, lift up now your voices with joy and thanksgiving for with freedom to the slave will come peace and safety to your country. President Lincoln has embraced in this proclamation the law of Congress passed more than six months ago, prohibiting the employment of any part of the army and naval forces of the United States, to return fugitive slaves to their masters, commanded all officers of the army and navy to respect and obey its provisions. He has still further declared his intention to urge upon the Legislature of all the slave States not in rebellion the immediate or gradual abolishment of slavery. But read the proclamation for it is the most important of any to which the President of the United States has ever signed his name.

Opinions will widely differ as to the practical effect of this measure upon the war. All that class at the North who have not lost their affection for slavery will regard the measure as the very worst that could be devised, and as likely to lead to endless mischief. All their plans for the future have been projected with a view to a reconstruction of the American Government upon the basis of compromise between slaveholding and non-slaveholding States. The thought of a country unified in sentiments, objects and ideas, has not entered into their political calculations, and hence this newly declared policy of the Government, which contemplates one glorious homogeneous people, doing away at a blow with the whole class of compromisers and corrupters, will meet their stern opposition. Will that opposition prevail? Will it lead the President to reconsider and retract? Not a word of it. Abraham Lincoln may be slow, Abraham Lincoln may desire peace even at the price of leaving our terrible national sore untouched, to fester on for generations, but Abraham Lincoln is not the man to reconsider, retract and contradict words and purposes solemnly proclaimed over his official signature.

The careful, and we think, the slothful deliberation which he has observed in reaching this obvious policy, is a guarantee against retraction. But even if the temper and spirit of the President himself were other than what they are, events greater than the President, events which have slowly wrung this proclamation from him may be relied on to carry him forward in the same direction. . . . The whole situation having been carefully scanned, before Mr. Lincoln could be made to budge an inch, he will now stand his ground. . . .

The effect of this paper upon the disposition of Europe will be great and increasing. It changes the character of the war in European eyes and gives it an important principle as an object, instead of national pride and interest. It recognizes and declares the real nature of the contest, and places the North on the side of justice and civilization, and the rebels on the side of robbery and barbarism. It will disarm all purpose on the part of European Government to intervene in favor of the rebels and thus cast off at a blow one source of rebel power.

Douglass's Monthly, October 1862.

[*The Life and Writings of Frederick Douglass*, vol. 3, pp. 273–275.]

Confederates

While the outcome of the Battle of Antietam (Sharpsburg) was pleasing to the Cormanys, to George Templeton Strong, and to Maria Daly, the massive clash between Confederate and Union armies on September 17, 1862, was to the members of the Jones family and to Mary Chesnut "a terrible battle," "a dreadful battle," which brought death to individuals they had known. In a similar fashion, the counterpart to the elation of Frederick Douglass over the issuance of the Emancipation Proclamation was the dismay, anger, and indignation that marked the reaction to the Proclamation by the members of the Jones family. Rev. and Mrs. Jones moved further inland to avoid attacks launched from Union gunboats. Rev. Jones described one such attack in a neighboring county that took off "every Negro" (i.e., slave) from one plantation, and Charles C. Jones, Jr., wrote that the move of his parents further inland "must be viewed very much in the light of an insurance upon Negroes."

The Jones Family:

Lt. Charles C. Jones, Jr., to Rev. C. C. Jones

Savannah, *Saturday*, September 27th, 1862

My dear Father, . . .

Yesterday we have the sad intelligence of the death of Spalding McIntosh (who married Sis Morris), an aide to General McLaws with the rank of major, and of the fact that both Randolph and Charlie Whitehead are wounded. This at the terrible battle of Sharpsburg. It is said by General Lee that the shock of this battle was more terrific than any which has as yet occurred in the present war. We held the honors of the field, but the long list of killed and wounded which has already reached us attests the severity of the struggle and the heavy price at which the victory was purchased. The present status of our army in Virginia and along the line of the Potomac seems involved in a degree of uncertainty which causes painful anxiety.

It occurs to me that our government ought, upon the termination of a general engagement of such magnitude and unquestioned importance, to furnish at the earliest practicable moment to the country at large at least an announcement of the general result. . . . I still indulge the hope that the report of McIntosh's death may not be correct. I obtained for him his appointment in the army. . . . Maria Morris, his wife, was tenderly attached to him, and I feel deeply for her.

The news from the West is cheering. Bragg reported near Louisville; has demanded the surrender of the city. . . .

You notice in the morning papers the announcement that Lincoln has issued his proclamation liberating the slaves of all rebels on the 1st January next—the crowning act of the series of black and diabolical transactions which have marked the entire course of his administration. I look upon it as a direct bid for insurrection, as a most infamous attempt to incite flight, murder, and rapine on the part of our slave population. With a fiendish purpose he has designedly postponed the operation of this for a future day in order that intermediately the mind of the slave population may if possible be prepared to realize and look forward to the consummation of the act proposed and thus prepare for the same. Practically, under present circumstances, I do not think the proclamation will have any effect. But this does not in the least detract from the character of the act, or lessen one iota the enormity of its crime. . . .

The question occurs, what are we now to do with future prisoners captured from such an enemy? Are they within the pale of civilization? Are they entitled to consideration as prisoners of war? By the law of England an outlaw could be pursued and captured with hue and cry wherever found in the King's realm and killed at the first crossroad. Shall a less punishment be meted out to these robbers, murderers, plunderers, violators of virtue and outlaws of humanity? By the statute law of the state any one who attempts to incite insurrection among our slaves shall if convicted suffer death. Is it right, is it just to treat with milder considerations the lawless bands of armed marauders who will infest our borders to carry into practical operation the proclamation of the infamous Lincoln, subvert our entire social system, desolate our homes, and convert the quiet, ignorant, dependent black son of toil into a savage incendiary and brutal murderer?

Surely we are passing through harsh times, and are beset with perils which humanity in its worst phases has not encountered for centuries. The Age of Gold has yielded to the Age of Iron; and the North furnishes an example of refined barbarity, moral degeneracy, religious impiety, soulless honor, and absolute degradation almost beyond belief. . . .

Your affectionate son,
Charles C. Jones, Jr.

Rev. C. C. Jones to Lt. Charles C. Jones, Jr.

Walthourville, *Tuesday,* September 30th, 1862

My dear Son,

Your interesting letter of the 27th came yesterday. . . . from present appearances it will not be surprising if the enemy begins his campaign on our coasts early in the season. It will be a great relief when our people [i.e., slaves] are *removed.*

It is not without full advisement that Lincoln has issued his Emancipation Proclamation. . . . There is no other policy in all the old United States but the war policy. The old Northern Democratic party is nothing. Peace party there is none. Military dictatorship is a fancy; and the abolition and anti-South party waxes stronger and stronger. We have nothing but war before us. The enemy considers our subjugation but a question of time only. They can beat us and give us three or four in the game, for they say that they can call out three or four soldiers to our one and their resources are as many times greater than ours, and consider us well-nigh exhausted now. Wonderful is it how they leave out in their calculations right and justice and God, who rules over the nations—even Him who can save by few as by many; and moreover, that the invader works at a disadvantage of three or four to one. Up to this hour we can say the Lord has been on our side; to Him let us constantly commit our cause.

Am happy to see that this execrable proclamation has been called up to notice in our Congress. I fully agree with you in your views of it. The war has become one for the perpetration of every brutal crime—for robbery, arson, and insurrection; and our government would be justifiable in putting every prisoner taken to instantaneous death, unless the war be wholly altered in its character and the proclamation be withdrawn. The Northern people will uphold the proclamation. England will uphold it, and so will France and every nation in Europe practically. There will be no remonstrances, no protests, unless great changes occur speedily. What Seward threatened them with if they interfered—the abolition of slavery and their loss of cotton, rice, and tobacco—is coming upon them without their interference. We must hope for the best from General Lee's army. A dreadful battle, that of Sharpsburg! . . .

Your ever affectionate father,
C. C. Jones. . . .

Rev. C. C. Jones to Lt. Charles C. Jones, Jr.
Walthourville, *Thursday,* October 2nd, 1862

My dear Son, . . .

What a judgment is falling upon our country! When we view it in its extent, its ramifications, its intensity, its miseries, and its destruction and mourning and woe, it is enough to sober the most inconsiderate and soften the most obdurate and bring our whole people to humiliation before God, who is thus dealing with us. And while He has most signally and mercifully aided us thus far, yet His hand is still stretched out over us; for the war continues, and the enemy is laying his plans more resolutely and extensively to swallow us up. As we have survived his first great effort, trusting in the Lord may we not hope for a second deliverance? I have faith to believe we may.

The invasion of Maryland and the return of our army to Virginia I look upon *as a special providence in our behalf.* Success began to intoxicate, and incline many to cry out for invasion of the enemy's territory. General Lee was induced to make the experiment in the most favorable moment and upon the most favorable soil—at least one upon which the people were, to a good degree, at least, so friendly as not to rise upon us. He could advance but a little way. The people did not come to his standard. The enemy gathered with energy and promptness an army far outnumbering his and gave him the bloodiest battle (on their own ground, as they deemed it) ever fought on this continent; and nothing saved his army from defeat and ruin but the blessing of God upon his skillful disposition of his forces, and the indomitable courage of his men—men to be annihilated but never defeated! I hope this taste of invasion will be satisfactory—at least for the present. If the enemy with superior numbers and equipments cannot invade our thinly populated territories with large armies without being starved back if not driven back, how can we fare better invading a more densely populated country? The Maryland pear certainly is not ripe yet. When it will be, no one can tell. If we can free the other border states, it will be well. A desperate stand is to be made by the enemy to save both Tennessee and Kentucky. The fighting has not fairly begun there yet. . . .

Your ever affectionate father,
C. C. Jones. . . .

Lt. Charles C. Jones, Jr., to Mrs. Mary Jones
Savannah, *Tuesday,* October 7th, 1862

My dear Mother,

I trust that all at home are well.

You probably noticed in the papers of yesterday morning an announcement of the fact that West had been killed during the recent desperate engagement at Sharpsburg. He was a private in Captain Read's light battery, and has shared the fate of many a brave fellow whose bones lie unmarked, commingled with those of the many slain upon the bloody battlefield. Poor West! . . .

Your son,
Charles C. Jones, Jr.

Lt. Charles C. Jones, Jr., to Rev. C. C. Jones
Savannah, *Wednesday,* October 8th, 1862

My dear Father, . . .

The advices from the West are not encouraging. . . . A battle is regarded as imminent between Bragg and Buell near Louisville, and we are told that Generals Lee and McClellan will soon meet again in deadly conflict. I see no cessation to present hostilities—unless some unlooked-for pressure is brought directly and forcibly to bear—except in absolute exhaustion. The mask is fairly lifted—and by their own hands—from the face of Northern duplicity and Yankee tyranny; and we can now expect from the Lincoln government nothing but renewed attempts and redoubled efforts to effect our annihilation. . . . I have, under God, no fear for the final issue; but when our triumph will come, as matters now stand, can be known only to Him in whose hands are the issues of all things. . . .

By the train of tomorrow, Father, I send you a cask of pale Scotch ale—the only one in the city. I have tried to procure a cask of porter for you in Charleston, Columbia, and elsewhere, but without success. . . .

Your affectionate son,
Charles C. Jones, Jr. . . .

Lt. Charles C. Jones, Jr., to Rev. C. C. Jones
Savannah, *Thursday,* October 16th, 1862

My dear Father,

I have just returned from Middle Georgia, and have purchased Mr. Henry J. Schley's Buckhead plantation containing fourteen hundred and twelve acres at ten dollars per acre, and also his present corn crop (say, four thousand bushels) at seventy-five cents per bushel.

The place is situated about one hundred miles, in round numbers, from this city, and is without exception the best place I have seen. . . .

I think the purchase a valuable one, and that by the blessing of God we may find it a safe, comfortable, and remunerative retreat for our people.

As to the question of possession, Mr. Schley tells me if at any time danger threatens, to send the Negroes up at once, and that they shall be quartered as best they can be with present accommodations. . . .

I propose, Father, to assume the entire responsibility of the purchase of the plantation: $14,120—one-third cash, balance in one and two years. I am unwilling that you should at your time of life, and in your present health, be troubled with any additional moneyed arrangements or new cares. . . . If I may believe the opinions of others, I have secured a planta- tion far above the average. . . . I have asked the blessing of God on the ad- venture, and trust with His blessing that we may find the investment safe and remunerative. For the present it must be viewed very much in the light of an insurance upon Negroes. . . .

Do give warmest love to dear Mother, Sister, Robert, and the little ones. Kiss my precious daughter for me. And believe me ever, my dear fa- ther,

Your affectionate son,
Charles C. Jones, Jr. . . .

Rev. C. C. Jones to Lt. Charles C. Jones, Jr.
Walthourville, *Saturday,* October 18, 1862
My dear Son,

Yours of the 16th Mother handed me last evening on my return from Montevideo. . . .

Your account of Mr. Schley's place is very satisfactory, and have no doubt that your purchase is a judicious one and as good as could well be made in any part of the cotton districts of our state. And the payment in three installments is more liberal than I had anticipated. And although you so generously offer to assume the whole payment for the place on your own account, yet I shall feel bound to render you every aid in my power to meet the payments as they come to maturity. . . .

Your affectionate father,
C. C. Jones

[*The Children of Pride,* pp. 966–977, 979–980.]

Mary Chesnut:

[During a Union military raid near Richmond early in May, 1863, Mary Chesnut destroyed her diary from August 1, 1862. Under date of September 23, 1863, she "tried to fill up the gap from memory."]

"Then came fatal Sharpsburg. My friend Colonel Means—killed on the battlefield, his only son wounded and a prisoner. His wife had not recov- ered from the death of her other child, Emma, who had died of consump- tion early in the war. She was lying on a bed when they told her of her hus- band's death—and then they tried to keep Stark's [the only son] condition from her. They think now that she misunderstood and believed him dead, too. She threw something over her face. She did not utter one word. She remained quiet so long, someone removed the light shawl which she had drawn over her head. She was dead. Miss Mary Stark said afterward: "No

wonder! how was she to face life without her husband and children. That was all she had ever lived for."
[*Mary Chesnut's Civil War*, p. 426.]

In the midst of the sad reports concerning the Battle of Antietam (Sharpsburg), Lt. Charles C. Jones, Jr., had found the news from Kentucky "cheering"—General Bragg's Confederate army was said to be near Louisville, Kentucky. In response, Jones's father had predicted that the Union forces would make "a desperate stand" to save Kentucky and Tennessee, and that prediction was proved accurate. The Confederate thrust into Kentucky was repulsed in the autumn of 1862, the principal battle being the Union victory at Perryville, Kentucky, on October 8.

John Cotton's battalion was part of the Confederate forces in Kentucky, and he had optimistically told his wife to send letters to him at Lexington, Kentucky. But John had not been able to join his comrades in Kentucky, as he explained to his wife near the end of October, 1862, and by that time, almost three weeks after the Confederate defeat at Perryville, "the whole army," in Cotton's words, "[had] left Kentucky." The Confederate forces had retreated southward into Tennessee, and by December, Cotton wrote of desertions by Confederate soldiers there: "Our army is in a heap of Confusion and mitely out of hart."

Knoxville Tennessee Ocotber 26, 1862 Dear wife I again take my pen in hand to rite you a few more lines to let you no I am well and am at knoxville and battalion is coming back here. . . . we were ordered to kentucky and we went about a mild and stopped to stay all nite and go on next morning next we had orders to start and before we got off we had orders not to go and we moved back clost to where we were before and nere here October the 27 Mariah I will rite you a few more lines. . . . the whole army has left kentucky but I recien you have herd that there is more soldiers about here than I ever saw I hant got any news from you since I left Atlanta but I have looked for a letter from you for some time but I hant got nary one yet I want you to rite to me again as soon as you get these few lines direct your letter to knoxville to J. W. Cotton knoxville tennessee . . . . I hant got much to rite to you it is not worth while to try to tell you how bad I want to see you all or here from you if I could here from you all and here that little ginney has go well and all of the rest of you I woul bee very glad to come home and see you all and see how things is going on and make arrangements for another year but there is no chance nw you must do the best yu can for your self and the children only remain your affectionate husband til death

John W. Cotton to Mariah Cotton. . . .

Winchester Tennessee December the 1 1862
Mariah Cotton dear wife it is again that I take my pen in hand to rite you a few lines to let you no that I am still well and enjoying good health but I am not satisfyed in mind I hand got nary letter from you in some time

the last I got was rote the 30 of october I would like very much to here from you all and to no that you were still doing well I want to come home very bad but but it is a bad chance now and the chance dont get any better I dont no whether I will get to come home atall or not but that dont keep from wanting to come. . . . I was in hopes a while back that the war would end this christmas or some time this winter but I dont see any chance now for it to end soon but we must live in hopes if we dy in dispare. I dont dread the fighting that I will have to do all I hate is having to stay from home and being exposed to the weather I dont want you to bee uneasy about me for I am fatter than ever was in my life I way 179 pounds I have out fattened any body you every saw since you left me I hope these few lines may find you all enjoying as good health as I am I want you to cary on your business as if you never expected to see me any more do the best you can and you will please me if I dont come home you must make your arrangements for another year and the best you can. . . . nothing more at present but remain your loving husband til death

John W Cotton to Mariah Cotton

Tennessee Camped to stay all nite December 9th 1862
My dear beloved wife it is again I take my pen in hand to answer a letter that I recieved last nite it was dated the 15 of november I was glad to here from you but I was sorry to here that the children was sick. . . . you said you did not no what you would do for salt I am afraid you will have to do without it salt is very scarce up here. . . . there is some of our men running away and going hom there is fore that went home without leave has come back they were court marshaled and put under gard for ten days and live on bread and water and deduct there wages for one month. . . . our army is in a heep of confusion and mitely out of hart a man told me today in manchester that there had been as many as 50 of there briggade deserted in one nite I could rite a heap but when I go to rite I cant think of half I want to rite if I could see you all I could tell you all a heap. . . . I want to come home the worst perhaps I want to come home to see the children before they forget me nothing more at present I remain your affectionate husband till death

John W. Cotton

[Cotton, *Yours Till Death*, pp. 29-30, 34-36.]

5. THE "TIME OF TROUBLES" FOR THE LINCOLN ADMINISTRATION IN THE WINTER OF 1862–1863

The defeat of the Confederate military advances into Maryland and Kentucky was noteworthy. In particular, the checking of Lee's army at the battle of Antietam, which in turn provided the opportunity for the issuance of the Preliminary Proclamation of Emancipation, was prominent among the factors

that insured that England and France would not intervene in the Civil War in the autumn of 1862. The battle of Antietam was thus, considering its effects upon both the military situation and the developments in foreign relations, one of the most important single battles of the entire war.

But many Union supporters at the time were aware that the Confederate armies had not been destroyed, and perhaps were not even severely crippled, and they were also aware that the casualties in the Union armed forces had been numerous and that many new recruits would be needed as replacements. In addition, the war brought changes in society and in personal lives that many individuals in the Union states found inconvenient, troubling, and threatening to patterns of ideas and of behavior common before 1861. One of those changes, for example, was the enlarging of the purpose of the war to add the ending of slavery to the original purpose of preserving the Union. Against this background, war weariness and opposition to the policies of the Lincoln administration became prominent by the winter of 1862–1863 in the Union states.

By that winter, similar developments had taken place in the Confederate states, with comparable attitudes toward the Davis administration. There was no Emancipation Proclamation in the Confederacy to enlarge the original goals of the war, but there was growing debate over how slaves should be employed in the war effort and over whether the military strategy and tactics of the Confederacy should be offensive, with invasions into the Union states, or purely defensive, with Confederate troops confined to Confederate soil.

While war weariness and criticism of the policies of the government were present in both Union and Confederacy, there was one major difference in the two societies: Congressional and state elections were to be held in the Union states by early November, 1862, but not in the Confederacy until the autumn of 1863. Those elections in the Union states served as a focus for discontent and a channel through which the discontent could be expressed.

Frederick Douglass, George Templeton Strong, and Maria Daly all commented on the 1862 elections. Douglass and Strong championed the Republicans—Unionists—and equated the Democrats with supporters of the Confederacy. Daly sympathized with the Democrats, although she wanted Democrats to support the war effort. All three commentators focused their remarks on their home state, New York, but their attitudes had implication for all the Union states.

The Elections of 1862

Frederick Douglass:

THE SLAVE DEMOCRACY AGAIN IN THE FIELD

The next two months must be regarded as more critical and dangerous than any similar period during the slaveholders' rebellion. Our grounds of apprehension are far more political than military. . . .

The re-animation of the Democratic party at this juncture and its entrance upon a vigorous campaign for place and power, with elements of strength given to it by the mistakes and imperfections of the present administration, constitute our chief danger during the next two months. . . . It is clear that he who at this crisis votes for Horatio Seymour [The Democratic candidate for governor of New York], votes against the loyal administration, and in effect for Jefferson Davis and his rebel Government. If the Democratic party had received direct orders from the rebel Government at Richmond, its programme and the manner of executing it could not have been more satisfactory to the rebels. . . .

One other cause of alarm is the fact that the anti-slavery men of the country, the men whose votes are needed at home to keep the Government of this State in harmony with the Government of the United States, have naturally flocked to the war against the rebels, while the devotees of slavery have stayed at home, to work against the Government and for the rebels, as openly and as actively as they dare. Their leaders have long had an eye to this advantage, and have taken no real interest in promoting enlistments. . . .

The party of Union represented by General Wadsworth is the party of the Union, and that of Seymour, is the Northern wing of slavery and disunion. Anti-slavery men need not be told how to vote in such a contest. *Douglass's Monthly,* November 1862
[*The Life and Writings of Frederick Douglass,* vol. 3, pp. 293–296.]

George Templeton Strong:

October 8 [1862], Wednesday. . . . Canvass for fall elections fairly begun. Wadsworth and Seymour candidates for governor. I hope Wadsworth and the so-called radicals may sweep the state and kick our wretched sympathizers with Southern treason back into the holes that have sheltered them for the past year and from which they are beginning to peep out timidly and tentatively to see whether they can venture to resume their dirty work. . . . Seymour's election would be an encouragement to Jefferson Davis worth 100,000 men. . . .

October 15, Wednesday. . . . McClellan's army [is as] immovable as the Pyramids. That general has sent for his wife, his mother-in-law, and his baby, and is going to go into housekeeping, it seems, somewhere near Sharpsburg. He may move next first of May, but I fear he is settled until then. Heaven Help us! . . .

October 17. . . . Election news from Pennsylvania and the West were cold, but I hope the opposition men elected are "War Democrats." . . .

October 23. . . . Our war on rebellion languishes. We make no onward movements and gain no victories. . . . One thing is clear: that unless we gain decisive [military] success before the November election, this state will range itself against the Administration. If it does, a dishonorable peace and permanent disunion are not unlikely. . . .

October 25.   Philharmonic rehearsal this afternoon; Beethoven's

Symphony in B flat (No. 2), one of the two that I know but little if at all
. . . . Expected little, but it turns out to be a very noble symphony, and for
one hour I forgot all about the war and the Sanitary Commission, and was
conscious of nothing but the marvelous web of melodic harmony and
pungent orchestral color that was slowly unfolding. . . .

October 29. At Niblo's last night with Ellie and George Anthon; first
part of *King Henry IV.* Hackett's Falstaff seems to me beyond criticism, incapable of improvement in a single detail of look, gesture, or intonation—
the only perfect impersonation I have ever seen of any character. . . .

October 30, Thursday. Private advices from the War Department are
that the Virginia rebels are greatly reinforced and that McClellan is to wait
a little longer. Alas for next Tuesday's election! There is danger—great and
pressing danger—of a disaster more telling than all our Bull Run battles
and Peninsular strategy: the resurrection to political life and power of the
Woods, Barlows, LaRocques, and Belmonts, who have been dead and
buried and working only underground, if at all, for eighteen months, and
every one of whom well deserves hanging as an ally of the rebellion. It
would be a fearful national calamity. If it come, it will be due not so much
to the Emancipation Manifesto as to the irregular arrests the government
has been making. They have been used against the Administration with
most damaging effect, and no wonder. They have been utterly arbitrary,
and could be excused only because demanded by the pressure of an un-
precedented national crisis; because necessary in a case of national life or
death that justified any measure, however extreme. But not one of the
many hundreds illegally arrested and locked up for months has been publicly charged with any crime or brought to the notice of a Grand Jury. They
have all been capriciously arrested, so far as we can see, and some have
been capriciously discharged; locked up for months without legal authority and let out without legal acquittal. All this is very bad—imbecile, dangerous, unjustifiable. It gives traitors and Sey-Mourites an apology for opposing the government and helping South Carolina that it is hard to answer. I know it is claimed that these arrests are legal, and perhaps they are,
but their legality is a subtle question that government should not have
raised as to a point about which people are so justly sensitive. . . .

November 3, Monday. . . . Tomorrow's prospects bad. The
Seymourites are sanguine. Vote will certainly be close. A row in the city is
predicted by those who desire one, but it is unlikely, though people are
certainly far more personally bitter and savage than at any election for
many years past. A Northern vote against the Administration may be
treated by Honest Old Abe as a vote of want of confidence. He may dis-
miss his Cabinet and say to the Democrats, "Gentlemen, you think you
can do this job better and quicker than Seward and Chase. Bring up your
men, and I'll set them to work." It would be like him. . . .

Have we the people, or have we not, resolution and steadiness enough to fight on through five years of taxation, corruption, and discouragement? All depends on the answer to that question.

November 4, Tuesday. A beautiful bright day, but destined to be memorable, I fear, for a national calamity. Voted this morning, and did not much beside. . . .

November 5. As anticipated, total rout in this state. Seymour is governor. Elsewhere defeat, or nominal success by a greatly reduced vote [i.e., margin]. It looks like a great, sweeping revolution of public sentiment, like general abandonment of the loyal, generous spirit of patriotism that broke out so nobly and unexpectedly in April, 1861. Was that after all nothing but a temporary hysteric spasm? I think not. We the people are impatient, dissatisfied, disgusted, disappointed. We are in a state of dyspepsia and general, indefinite malaise, suffering from the necessary evils of war and from irritation at our slow progress. We take advantage of the first opportunity of change, for its own sake, just as a feverish patient shifts his position in bed, though he knows he'll be none the easier for it. Neither the blind masses, the swinish multitude, that rule us under our accursed system of universal suffrage, nor the case of typhoid, can be expected to exercise self-control and remember that tossing and turning weakens and does harm. Probably two-thirds of those who voted for Seymour meant to say by their votes, "Messrs. Lincoln, Seward, Stanton & Co., you have done your work badly, so far. You are humbugs. My business is stopped, I have got taxes to pay, my wife's third cousin was killed on the Chickahominy, and the war is no nearer an end than it was a year ago. I am disgusted with you and your party and shall vote for the governor or the congressman you disapprove, just to spite you."

If I am mistaken, and if this vote does endorse the policy of Fernando Wood and John Van Buren, it is a vote of national suicide. All is up. We are a lost people. . . . But I will not *yet* believe that this people is capable of so shameful and despicable an act of self-destruction as to disembowel itself in the face of the civilized world for fear Jefferson Davis should hurt it.

[*The Diary of George Templeton Strong*. Abridged edition, 1988, pp. 211–220.]

Maria Daly:

October 4, 1862. . . .

Judge Pierrepont told us that the French are watching our November elections with the greatest earnestness, and hope that the government will be so embarrassed if Seymour is elected that they may interfere with advantage. . . .

I have just received a most interesting letter from Adam Badeau from New Orleans which contains statements as to the disaffection and dissensions in the South, some of which may be useful to the government if they are known. I shall copy the letter and beg the Judge to send it to Seward or Lincoln himself. . . .

October 23, 1862. . . . The whole North seems to be going for the Democrats. What a revolution of public opinion since Lincoln's election. I almost feel sorry for the Republicans, struggling 20 years for power and losing it after one year's possession. . . .

October 31, 1862. . . . People are very much afraid of the draft. The authorities here seem to declare that they are not to be governed by any of the rules laid down in August last. Tuesday next is election day.

November 6, 1862. The election is over and Seymour is the Democratic Governor; 36 congressmen and senators probably elected. There has never been so great a revolution of public feeling. Everything two years ago was carried by the Republicans, but now radicals have ruined themselves and abolitionism. As a popular Democratic song describes it: "It has died before it was weaned, weaned, weaned; it has died before it was weaned." Seymour, however, is not the man that the Democrats should have nominated. Their nominee should have been Dix, or someone who exerted himself for the war. . . . I seem to feel that there is now some hope of a return to good feeling in the South.

I sometimes wish that Charles were more ambitious. He would shine in public life and be an ornament to the country. Had we a settled competency, I sometimes think he would allow himself to run for a seat in Congress, or as senator. Perhaps, however, we might not be so happy together were he a greater man in public estimation. . . . The Republican press seem more exasperated than the Democratic with the Administration, and attributes their defeat to its incompetency and want of energy. . . .

November 9, 1862. Those whom the gods wish to destroy, they first must make mad. President Lincoln has removed McClellan and appointed Secretary [Caleb B.] Smith of the Interior, a poor country lawyer, Judge of the Supreme Court. Burnside succeeds McClellan. I trust that he will not allow himself to be goaded on by the public clamor to do anything rash with the new levies.

[*Diary of a Union Lady*, pp. 182, 191, 194–196.]

The victory of Democrats in the 1862 elections in New York was matched by similar victories in other Union states. The number of Democrats in the United States House of Representatives greatly increased, although the Republicans retained control by a narrow margin. The editor of the New York Times, *a supporter of Lincoln, called the election "a vote of want of confidence in the President."*

The Republican losses in the elections ushered in what turned out to be a "time of troubles" for the Lincoln administration, and those troubles were continued and increased by Union military defeats in Virginia at the battles of Fredericksburg (December 13, 1862) and Chancellorsville (May 1–4, 1863). The comments on those two battles by George Templeton Strong and by Maria Daly reflected the gloom of Union supporters. Not gloom but relief was expressed in the comments of staunch Confederate Charles C. Jones, Jr., concerning the battle of Fredericksburg ("nobly won"), but he noted also the loss of the "valuable lives" of Confederates in that battle. (Jones, by the time of the battle of Fredericksburg, had been promoted to the rank of colonel.)

The Battles of Fredericksburg (December 13, 1862) and Chancellorsville (May 1–4, 1863)

George Templeton Strong:

December 11 [1862], Thursday. The crisis seems to have come at last. Burnside commenced throwing his pontoons across the Rappahannock at daylight, and being met by a fusillade from the houses of Fredericksburg, opened on that unhappy town with 143 guns from our side of the river . . . . God help us. I have little faith in the men to whom our destinies seem confided. . . .

December 13. Burnside, having established himself on the right bank of Rappahannock, seems to have engaged the rebels at nine this morning . . . . We know nothing of the progress of the fight. I anticipate only disaster, and an addition to the catalogue of Bull Runs, Big Bethels, and so on already so large. Defeat at this point, with a broad river in our rear, is destruction. But Burnside may be only feeling the enemy. . . .

Want of discipline in the army is our great danger, and that is due to want of virility in those who should enforce it—the ultimate cause being the weakness of the President himself. At all our battles, nearly one man out of three has shirked and straggled, and not one man has been shot down by his commanding officer.

Olmsted tells me he called on the President the other evening to introduce some ladies (members of his recent "Honorable Convention" from relief societies all over the country), and Abe Lincoln expatiated on this terrible evil. "Order the army to march to any place!" said Abe Lincoln. "Why it's jes' like *shovellin' fleas.* Hee-yah, ya-hah!" Whereupon one of the ladies timidly asked, "Why don't you order stragglers to be *shot,* sir?" and the query not being immediately answered, was repeated. Olmsted says the presidential guffaw died away and the President collapsed and wilted down into an embodiment of everything weak, irresolute, perplexed, and annoyed, and he said, "Oh, I ca-an't do *that,* you know." It's an army of lions we have, with a sheep for commander-in-chief. O for a day of the late Andrew Jackson! . . .

December 14, Sunday. I think the fate of the nation will be decided before night. The morning papers report a general engagement that lasted all yesterday, with no result but a little advance by part of our line, and heavy loss apparently on both sides. Taken together, the little scraps of fact and incident and humor that have come over the wires look unpromising but they might be much worse.

December 15. Sultry weather. Nothing definite from the Rappahannock. There was only skirmishing yesterday. . . . Peace Democrats and McClellanites call it a repulse and say that our main body was engaged . . . .

Poor Bayard [Brigadier-General George D. Bayard], killed last Saturday [at Fredericksburg], was to have been married next Wednesday to a pretty girl of seventeen, daughter of the commandant at West Point. Her trousseau was all ready, and Miss Bessy Fish was to have gone up the river on special service as bridesmaid. Such details help one to appreciate the depth of meaning embodied in the words battle, war, rebellion. . . .

December 17. Burnside recrossed the Rappahannock, unmolested, Monday night. . . . Burnside pleads guilty to failure and repulse. This news, arriving yesterday afternoon, has produced serious depression and discouragement. The battle of Fredericksburg was a defeat with heavy loss, damaging to the national cause.

[*The Diary of George Templeton Strong.* Abridged edition, 1988, pp. 224–228.]

Maria Daly:

December 14, 1862. . . . Today the papers say a battle is raging at Fredericksburg. It began yesterday and at night neither side had the advantage. It was to begin at daylight again this morning. God help us and protect my brother! . . .

December 20, 1862. I have had no heart to write. Since I opened my diary last, the battle of Fredericksburg has occurred and our repulse with the loss of 14,000 killed, wounded, and missing. Burnside hoped to surprise the enemy, but our dilatory government officials kept his bridges and supplies so long behind-hand they had two weeks to fortify themselves. Poor Burnside will therefore have to suffer.

It is surprising how people spend despite the present distress. The artists say they have never been so busy. Bierstadt is even offered more than he has asked for his pictures, and every place of amusement is crowded. . . . there was a ringing of the bell, and who should come in but Phil, Captain Phil, just arrived from Fredericksburg. How glad we were to see him! . . . We shall have him for Christmas. . . .

January 4, 1863. . . . Day before yesterday, Phil dined with us. . . . Phil is very modest and talks but little of his experiences. The Judge mentioned that he had met a colonel at Judge Pierrepont's on New Year's Day who said that had it not been for the want of heart in the brigadier generals, they could have carried the entrenchments [at Fredericksburg]. . . .

McClellan has injured himself by too much tampering with the ultra-Democrats. Seeing how the rebels act, it would seem that we might as well accept the issue as they offer it. They have inaugurated the war, declared slavery incompatible with our free institutions, invited the aid of foreign nations against us, and we have therefore little cause to consider them. Slavery may as well be abolished if it is possible. The only question with the Judge was, is it practicable? . . .

May 10, 1863. Caught a dreadful cold at the lecture on Monday last which has confined me to the house and to my bed. [General] Hooker has crossed the Rappahannock, but been obliged to retreat with the loss of ten thousand men [at the battle of Chancellorsville] which, after his boastful proclamations and arrogant criticisms of other generals, must be to him a great mortification. He was so sure of victory that he declared that Lee's army was now the legitimate property of the Army of the Potomac, but on going to take possession, he found that the nine points of law, namely, possession were all in their favor and the legitimacy of his claim was entirely overlooked. . . . I care not who conquers so that this dreadful waste of blood and treasure be but stopped.

[*Diary of a Union Lady*, pp. 206–209, 211–212, 237–238.]

Charles C. Jones, Jr.:

Col. Charles C. Jones, Jr., to Rev. C. C. Jones

Savannah, *Monday*, December 15th, 1862

My dear Father,

The telegraphic intelligence from Virginia and elsewhere, although of a cheering character, does not as yet give assurance of any decided victory.

We are not, in all human probability, just on the verge of that tempest which has for some time been gathering. In view of the paucity of our troops when compared with the immense hosts opposed to us, fortified with all the most approved appliances of modern warfare; in view of the further fact that we are almost entirely unable to procure better arms and more soldiers, it does seem that we can alone in God look for deliverance. It is a time for universal prayer. The recent battle near Fredericksburg, although nobly won, has cost us the loss of valuable lives—Cobb, Gregg, and (more than all) *Hood,* one of the bravest of the brave. Priceless is that liberty purchased at such a cost. Twenty-five hundred of our troops from this military district left the city last night—destination probably North Carolina or wherever else the storm cloud may hang most darkly. We are anxiously expecting tonight more intelligence from Virginia. Our capital is grievously beset. But I have an abiding confidence in the valor and ability of our generals, the almost miraculous courage of our soldiers, and above all in the justice of our cause and the favoring protection of Heaven, and will expect a timely deliverance from all our troubles. . . .

Your affectionate son,
Charles C. Jones, Jr.

[*The Children of Pride*, pp. 1000–1001.]

6. GETTYSBURG AND VICKSBURG, JULY, 1863

The months-long "time of troubles" for the Lincoln administration finally came to an end early in July, 1863, with two major military victories by the Union armed forces at Gettysburg, Pennsylvania, and Vicksburg, Mississippi.

Gettysburg was the meeting place between two huge armies during the first three days in July. The Confederate forces under the command of Lee moved northward across the Potomac, just as in the autumn of 1862—only this time they crossed Maryland without significant opposition and advanced into Pennsylvania. The Union army, led by General George Meade, entrenched itself on a range of hills near the town of Gettysburg.

Among the Union forces were Samuel Cormany and his fellow soldiers of the 16th Pennsylvania Volunteer Cavalry. They had engaged in more or less continuous skirmishing with the Confederate cavalry commanded by General J. E. B. Stuart for the last two weeks in June, as the cavalry units followed their respective armies northward. During the battle of Gettysburg itself, Cormany's unit was located on the right wing of Meade's army, at time engaging in combat and at other times serving as part of the reserve. A few miles from Gettysburg, Rachel Cormany and the couple's daughter, in Chambersburg, Pennsylvania, witnessed both Union and Confederate forces march through their town and occupy it for brief periods. Ultimately, when the big battle ended, the Cormanys were reunited in Chambersburg for a few days. The Cormany diaries describe these events in graphic detail.

Samuel Cormany:

June 15, 1863 Monday. . . . Took line of march at noon via Manassas, Great Fortifications. 9 P.M. we put up in old rebel camp near Bull Run—News comes "Rebels in Chambersburg." Men incensed—Here we are burning old Rebel Camps while they are destroying our public property at home, and distressing our wives and babies—. . . .

June 17, 1863 Wednesday. Took up line of march at 5 A.M. Crossed Bull Run at R. R. Bridge—Went several miles wrong—had to retrace and make up lost time. Very hot! Got a mess of good cherries—About 4 P.M. got to Aldie at Bull Run Mountains. Had a hard fight—Rebs fall back—we capture 2 Majors, 3 Captains—4 or 5 Lieutenants—75 Men. A canon ball fell very close to me, but I was not hurt—Tho bullets whizzed all about me—not one quite touched me. Thank God. Went into camp at a splendid spring near Hotel and Picketed—

June 18, 1863 Thursday. Hot—Took fine Bath—At 10 AM took up the march via Dover Mills—to Middleburg—a fine little village—Reb skirmishers met us close to town, and we pressed them hard for several hours with hard firing—and little dashes—Then lined up and at it again—I fired 45 to 50 rounds of cartridges. I was struck in my hat once—The fence was struck many times very close to me—and slivers flew about me and my horse, but I stood my ground till enemy began to yield some. Then was foremost charging into town—captured a few—saw some dead on the streets—The wounded escaped, either with their comrades—or were taken in and concealed—We lost none—Had a few wounded—Held the place—Scouted out after the retreaters—Came back—established a Picket line and Reserve. Then fell back 1-1/2 miles and put up for the night—The Brigade camping near us—I was never so completely exhausted—being on the firing line about all day—either dismounted or mounted—mostly mounted—Turned cool, cloudy, rained some—not much sleep. . . .

June 26, 1863 Friday. Rainy—Recd 2 such good letters from Darling . . .—Pet gives details of the Rebs trip to and through Chambersburg—10A.M. we took up line of march. A very zigzag course—very hilly—fine farms—rainy day—very little show for foraging! About 9 P.M. we struck Grove Creek on Leesburg Pike—Lay on arms—but later encamped—Rumor—Rebels at Carlisle—and our destination Gettysburg Pa. . . .

June 28, 1863 Sunday. Fed and rested til noon. Then took up the march via Fyatesville to Frederick City—we can see a clear difference between the people here [Maryland] and over in Virginia—Everyone greets us with welcome looks and words—Ladies waive their h'd'k'fs &c &c and all seem to look to us for protection against invasion—Pretty fair nights rest for men and horses— . . .

July 1, 1863 Wednesday. I had a fine chicken breakfast—and a feast of other good things. Took up march for Hanover. Very fine rich country—and such fine water—Settlers are Old Style People. Many Dunkerds. We were given any amount to eat all along the way—The Rebs who had passed this way acted very meanly—All around—demanding setters to pay money to exempt horses from being taken and barns and houses from being burned—One old man said he paid $100 to exempt 2 horses—another paid $23 to save his horse—Still another—$100 to save his barn. We found this hideous thing to be quite common—

We struck Hanover at dark. Found N.C. R. R. badly torn up—During the day we heard heavy canonading—and later musketry firing—in the direction of Gettysburg. Rumor was, "Theres a Battle on at Gettysburg" and was not hard to believe—Some of our Cavalry had fought desperately here today, early—Charging into the enemy's rear and flanks—

Killed some 30 rebs and hustled large forces on their way. So they had to abandon their dead and some of their wounded—

We lay on arms in a field for the night—we were well fed, but awfully tired and sleepy—A shower of rain failed to awaken me—I was lying in a furrow, an old furrow. I partially awakened in the night feeling coolish on my lower side—but didn't fully awake. In the morning I discovered that water had run down the furrow—and I had "dam'd" it somewhat and so was pretty wet from below, while my poncho had kept me dry from the top—

July 2, 1863 Thursday. More or less Picket firing all night—We were aroused early, and inspection showed a lot of our horses too lame and used up for good action—So first, our good mounts were formed for moving out, and were soon off—with the Brigade and took Reb. Genl. Steward [Stuart] by surprise on the Deardorf Farm—on right and rear of the army line—where Steward was expected to at least annoy the rear of Genl Mead—But our boys charged him—and after severe fighting dealt him an inglorious defeat and later in the day came in and lay on arms in the rear of Meads right—While our mounted men were paying attention to Genl Steward, we fellows had our horses cared for and were marched down to the right of the main line—to occupy a gap and do Sharpshooting—at long range, with our Carbines—we soon attracted attention, and later an occasional shell fell conspicuously close—but far enough to the rear of us so we suffered no serious harm. Towards noon firing became more general and in almost all directions—and we were ordered to our horses—and joined our returned heroes, and lay in readiness for any emergency—The general battle increaced in energy—and occasional fierceness—and by 2 P.M. the canonading was most terrific and continued til 5 P.M. and was interspersed with musketry—and Charge-yells and everything that goes to making up the indescribable battle of the best men on Earth, seemingly in the Fight to the Finish——At dark, our Cav Brig—2nd Brig 2" Div—was moved to the left—many wounded came in—Taken as a whole from all one can see from one point—it seems as tho our men—The Union Army—is rather overpowered and worsted—

Lay on arms to rest—Little chance to feed and eat.

July 3, 1863 Friday, canonading commenced early—and battle was on again in full intensity——at 10 ock we were ordered to the Front and Center, but immediately removed to the right of the Center—had some skirmishing. Pretty lively—Our squadron almost ran into a Rebel Battery with a Brigade of Cavalry maneuvering in the woods. They didn't want to see us, but moved left-ward and we held the woods all P.M.—All seemed rather quiet for several hours—From 1-1/2 til 4 P.M. there was the heaviest canonading I ever have heard—One constant roar with rising and falling inflections—

Our Boys opened 54 guns at the same time on the Rebel lines and works from a little conical hill, Cemetary Ridge. We were picketing in the rear and on the right of it—Many shells came our way—some really quite near—But it is wonderful how few really made our acquaintance.

July 4, 1863 Saturday. . . . Rained furiously during the night—We had fed, eaten, and were standing "to horse" when about 6 ock NEWS CAME—"The Rebs are falling back!" and "Our Forces are following them" and our Regt went out towards Hunterstown reconnoitering. We found some confederates who had straggled, or were foraging, not knowing yet what had

happened and was taking place—Of course, our Boys took them in—
Making a little detour I captured two. Sergt. Major J. T. Richardson and
Private Cox 9th Va Cav—disarming them and bringing them in—I
guarded them—while the Regt gathered in some others—P.M. Captain
Hughes came along and paroled them—and we were ordered to camp
near Hanover—where we first lay on arriving near Gettysburg—

Evening awfully muddy and disagreeable—I saw much of the de-
structiveness of the Johnies today—

July 5, 1863 Sunday. Rained awfully during the night. I got very wet—

Early we took up the march for Chambersburg—Crossing the battlefield—Cemitary Hill—The Great Wheat Field Farm, Seminary ridge—
and other places where dead men, horses, smashed artillery, were strewn
in utter confusion, the Blue and The Grey Mixed—Their bodies so
bloated—distorted—discolored on account of decomposition having set
in—that they were utterly unrecognizable, save by clothing, or things in
their pockets—The scene simply beggars description—Reaching the west
side of the Field of Carnage—we virtually charged most of the way for 10
miles—to Cashtown—Frequently in sight of the Rebel rear guard—taking
in prisoners—in bunches—We captured some 1,500 wounded men, and
300 stragglers—we went as far as Goodyears Springs, where we rested (?)
for the night. (I had to guard a Reb all night.)

July 6, 1863 Monday. Had a good breakfast. Turned my prisoner over to
others—We took up the march—via Fayeteville for Quincy—I told Corp.
Metz I intended going on—To Chambersburg—To see wife and Baby—
and would report in the morning again. He understood and I slipped
away—and was soon making time for home— . . .—on approaching
Chambersburg I was assured there were still squads of rebs about town—
Near town I was met by town folk inquiring about the battle. I was the
first "blue coat" they had seen—and the first to bring direct news of the
Enemy's defeat—as communications had been cut. As I struck the edge of
town, I was told "The Rebel rear-guard had just left the Diamond." So I
ventured out 2nd Street and ventured to strike Main near where Darling
and Pussy lodged—and behold They were at the door—had been watching the Reb Rear leaving town—and Oh! The surprise and delight thus to
meet after the awful battle they had been listening to for passing days—
My horse was very soon stabled. My Cavalry outfit covered with hay—
and myself in my citazens clothes—So should any final "rear" come
along, I would not be discovered—

To attempt to describe my joy and feelings at meeting and greeting
my dear little family must prove a failure—We spent the P.M. and evening
very sweetly and pleasantly, but only we had a few too many inquiring
callers.

[*The Cormany Diaries*, pp. 317–319, 321–327.]

Rachel Cormany:

June 14, 1863 Read . . . & wrote letters this A.M.—P.M. went to S. School, took Cora along—she did pretty well—was in Bro. Hokes Bible class. How much better I feel to get out to religious gathering. Intend to go more. Mrs. Dulany was there with her little one too. I got such a good book to read. Some excitement about the rebels come. Evening the excitement pretty high.

June 15, 1863 Monday. This morning pretty early Gen Milroys wagon train (so we were told) came. Contrabands [black refugees] on ahead coming as fast as they could on all & any kind of horses, their eyes fairly protruding with fear—teams coming at the same rate—some with the covers half off—some lost—men without hats or coats—some lost their coats as they were flying, one darky woman astride of a horse going what she could. There really was a real panic. All reported that the rebels were just on their heels. Soon things became more quiet—& all day government wagons & horses were passing through. For awhile before dark the excitement abated a little—but it was only like the calm before a great storm. At dusk or a little before the news came that the rebels were in Greencastle & that said town was on fire. Soon after some of our guard came in reporting that they had a skirmish with them. Soon followed 100-200 cavalry men—the guard. Such a skedadling as their was among the women & children to get into the houses. All thought the Rebels had really come. The report now is that they will be here in an hour. If I could only hear of My Samuels safety—Many have packed nearly all of their packable goods—I have packed nothing. I do not think that we will be disturbed even should they come. I will trust in God even in the midst of flying shells—but of course shall seek the safest place possible in that case—which I hope will not come to us. I have just put my baby to sleep & will now sit at the front door awhile yet—then retire, knowing all will be well.

June 16, 1863 Retired at 11 oclock. . . . At 11-½ I heard the clattering of horses hoofs. I hopped out of bed & ran to the front window & sure enough there the Greybacks were going by as fast as their horses could take them down to the Diamond. Next I heard the report of a gun then they came back faster if possible than they came in. But a short time after the whole body came. the front ones with their hands on the gun triggers ready to fire & calling out as they passed along that they would lay the town in ashes if fired on again. . . .—At 2 oclock A.M. all was quiet again save an occasional reb. riding past. We went to bed again & slept soundly until 5 the morning. All seemed quiet yet. . . . Soon however they became more active. Were hunting up the contrabands & driving them off by droves. O! How it grated on our hearts to have to sit quietly & look at such brutal deeds—I saw no men among the contrabands—all women & children. Some of the colored people who were raised here were taken along—I sat on the front step as they were driven by just like we would drive cattle. Some laughed and seemed not to care—but nearly all hung their heads. One woman was pleading wonderfully with her driver for her children—but all the sympathy she received from him was a rough "March along"—at which she would quicken her pace again. It is a query what they want with those little babies—whole families were taken. Of course when the mother was taken she would take her children. I suppose the men left thinking the women & children would not be disturbed. . . .

June 20, 1863 Went to bed early & slept well all night. This morning there is great excitement again. . . . If we could only have regular mails. a mail came last night—but was not opened until this morning—Got a letter from My Samuel. it is but short. He is still safe—but were under marching orders again. it has been over a week on the way—I almost feel like getting out of this to some place where the mail is uninterrupted, but then I fear, My Samuel might chance to come here & I would not see him so I shall stay—Will write to him now. . . .

June 23, 1863 . . . Evening—The Reb's have been cutting up high. Sawed down telegraph poles, destroyed the scotland bridge again, took possession of the warehouses & were dealing out flour by the barrel & mollasses by the bucket ful—They made people take them breat—meat—&c to eat—Some dumb fools carried them jellies & the like—Not a thing went from this place. . . . Well whatever betides us the good Lord is able to protect us. And He will protect us. . . .

June 24, 1863 Another eventful day has passed—All morning there was considerable riding done up & down street. At 10 A.M. the infantry commenced to come & for 3 hours they just marched on as fast as they could. it is supposed that about 15,000 have already passed through, & there are still more coming. Ewel's brigade has pas. I do not know what others. Longstreet & Hill are expected this way too. It is thought by many that a desperate battle will be fought at Harisburg. This P.M. the Rebs are plundering the stores. some of our merchants will be almost if not entirely ruined. . . .

June 26, 1863 12-½ oclock Cannon-waggons & men have been passing since between 9 & 10 this morning—42 Cannon & as many amunition waggons have passed—so now there are 62 pieces of artillery between us & Harrisburg & between 30,000 & 40,000 men. O it seems dreadful to be thus thrown into the hands of the rebbels & to be thus excluded from all the rest of the world—I feel so very anxious about Mr. Cormany—& who knows when we will hear from any of our friends again. It is no use to try to get away from here now—we must just take our chance with the rest—trusting in God as our Savior then come life come death if reconciled with God all is well. . . .

June 27, 1863 Got up early & wakened Annie. . . . Before we got started the rebels poured in already. they just marched through. Such a hard looking set I never saw. All day since 7 oclock they have been going through.

Between 30 & 40 pieces of canno[n]—& an almost endless trail of wag-gons. While I am writing thousands are passing—such a rough dirty ragged rowdyish set one does not often see—Gen's Lee & Longstreet passed through today. A body would think the whole south had broke loose & are coming into Pa. It makes me feel too badly to see so many men & cannon going through knowing that they have come to kill our men—Many have chickens as they pass—There a number are going with honey—robed some man of it no doubt—they are even carrying it in buckets. The report has reached us that Hooker & Sickel & Stoneman are after them. & at Harisburg the north has congregated en masse to oppose the invaders. Many think this the best thing in the wor[l]d to bring the war to a close—I hope our men will be strong enough to completely whip them—Now it is on our side—While down there our army was in the en-emys country & citizens kept the rebels posted in our army movements—now *they* are in the enemys country. Scarcely any are willing to give them anything—in fact none give unless the have to except perhaps the Copperheads. . . . I hope that all the rebels have passed that intended to pass through—After they quit coming once then I shall look for our men . . . .

June 29, 1863 Got up early & washed. . . . After I was dressed I put the baby to sleep then went to Ditmans & got a Gallon molasses for 50 cts—Also to Hok[e]s & got 3 qts. syrup for 45 cts—Hoke told me that the Rebs's had taken about 500 $ worth of sugar & molasses—they went into the private cellar & took Mrs Hokes canned fruit & bread—Mr. H looks down this morning. The news reached us this A.M. that Stoneman & Stuart had a fight last week in which Stuart was whipped & ten pieces of artillery were taken from him. Also that our men hold Hagerstown again. Also that the rebel mail carryer could not get through the lines. If our men hold Hagerstown it will not be long before they will be here. . . .

June 30, 1863 Nothing special transpired today. The Rebs are still about doing all the mischief they can. They have everything ready to set fire to the warehouses & machine shops—Tore up the railroad track & burned the crossties—They have cleared out nearly every store so they cannot rob much more—Evening—Quite a number of the young folks were in the parlor this evening singing all the patriotic & popular war songs. Quite a squad of rebels gathered outside to listen & seemed much pleased with the music—"When this cruel war is over" nearly brought tears from some. they sent in a petition to have it sung again which was done. they then thanked the girls very much & left—they acted real nicely. . . .

July 2, 1863 At 3 A.M. I was wakened by the yells & howls of this dirty ragged lousy trash—they made as ugly as they could—all day they have been passing—part of the time on the double quick. At one time the report came that our men had come on them & that they were fighting—the ex-citement was high in town—but it was soon found out to be untrue—but the shock was so great that I got quite weak & immagined that I could already see My Samuel falling—I feel very uneasy about him—I cannot hear at all—They had quite a battle with Stuart—I almost fear to hear the result in who was killed & who wounded—still I want to know.

July 3, 1863 Started out with Cora & a little basket on the hunt for something to eat out of the garden. I am tired of bread & molasses. . . . when I got back Daddy Byers was standing at the gate. he came to see how I was getting along & told me how the rebels acted—they robbed him of a good deal—they wanted the horse but he plead so hard for him that they agreed to leave him & while one wrote a paper of securety others plundered the house. I guess Samuels silk hat & all that was in the box is gone. took Ellies best shoes—took towels sheets & c &c—After they were gone others came & took the horse too yet—they did not care for his security. . . . There are no rebels in town today except the sick—& two or three squads passed through, in all not much over a hundred if that many. . . . Canonading was heard all day.

July 4, 1863 At daybreak the bells were rung—Then all was quiet until about 8 oclock when a flag was hoisted at the diamond. Soon after the band made its appearance & marched from square & played national airs—two rebels came riding along quite leisurely thinking I suppose to find their friends instead of that they were taken prisoners by the citizen—some 13 more footmen came and were taken prisoners. those were willing prisoners they had thrown their guns away before they reached this. The report has reached us that 6000 prisoners had been taken yesterday in Adams Co. near College Hill. . . . Wild rumors of a dreadful fight are numerous.

July 5, 1863 I was roused out of sleep by Mr Early coming into Wampler & telling him something about wounded & prisoners. so I got up took a bath dressed & went for a pitcher of water when I was told the 10, 4 or 6 horse waggons filled with wounded from the late battle were captured by citizens & brought to town—the wounded were put into the hospitals & the waggons & drivers were taken on toward Harisburg. . . . P.M. A report has reached us that the whole rebel army is on the retreat—later that they are driven this way & are expected on soon—Have church S. School here today—seems like Sunday again Evening. At or after 4 P.M. I dressed myself & little girl and went to Mrs. Sulenbargers & while there we heard a fuss outside & when we got out lo our (Union of course) soldiers were coming in—she came along upstreet then to see them. They are of Milroys men—Just at dusk they went out the Greencastle road enroute to capture the waggon train which is trying to get over the river again. It is frightful how those poor wounded rebels are left to suffer. they are taken in large 4 horse waggons—wounds undressed—nothing to eat. Some are only about 4 miles from town & those that are here are as dirty and lousy as they well can be. The condition of those poor rebels all along from

Getysburg to as far as they have come yet is reported dreadful. I am told they just beg the people along the road to help them—many have died by the way.

July 6, 1863 I was sitting reading, Pussy playing by my side when little Willie Wampler came running as fast as he could to tell me a soldier had come to see me & sure enough when I got to the door Mr Cormany just rode up. I was so very glad to see him that I scarcely knew how to act. He was very dirty & sweaty so he took a bath & changed clothes before he got himself dressed A. Holler & Barny Hampshire called—next Rev. Dixon & Dr Croft & others. Eve we went down into the parlor to hear some of the girls play—Mr. C. was very much pleased with the music.

[*The Cormany Diaries*, pp. 328–334, 336–341.]

> At the same time that the Cormanys were witnessing the end of the battle at Gettysburg in early July, 1863, fighting also ended at Vicksburg on the Mississippi River. On July 4, 1863, the Confederate defenders of Vicksburg surrendered to the besieging Union troops of General U.S. Grant. Vicksburg's surrender came only after a long military campaign and encirclement of the city, which together occupied several months.
>
> It is difficult to overestimate the importance of the capture of Vicksburg by the Union forces. This victory solidified the Union control over the entire Mississippi River, thereby cutting off Arkansas, Texas, and a portion of Louisiana from easy and effective contact with the rest of the Confederacy.
>
> Marcus Spiegel, now promoted in rank to colonel, was part of Grant's army. His letters to his wife provided both a vivid picture of the extended military effort to capture Vicksburg and an indication of Spiegel's opposition to the views of the "peace" faction of the Democratic party.

In the field before Vicksburg
May 23/63

My dear dear good wife

After five days of the hardest kind of fighting in the front we were about a half an hour ago relieved to fall back here about a mile to the Rear and rest. The fighting so far has been terrific and as yet we have not taken Vicksburg; we have taken two forts and were driven out of them again.

My Regiment made two charges, the first one perfectly terrific awful; I never saw shot, shell, crape [grape] and Bullets fly thicker in my life and yet I had but four men wounded and my men stood and kept their line as on dress parade while on the charge and during the hottest Brigadier General Lee (who had taken charge of our Brigade in the morning) came up to me and said, "Spiegel by God you are a man after my own heart; you are doing bully and your men are the bravest I ever saw." The Regiment was at least 20 yards in front of any of the 10 charging Regiments.

The loss so far has been in my Regiment miraculously light, only 8 wounded and I am struck by a piece of shell on my left knee which knocked the skin off, bruised it some and makes it a little painful. I did not suffer it to be published for fear you would see it and be uneasy.

General Lee was wounded by the same shell badly; he had to leave the field. I am sorry; he is a brave and gallant Officer and a Gentleman.

We have Vicksburg already surrounded and it must fall. From our position we can see the Church steeples but they have a heavy line of fortifications clear around.

The greatest consolation I have during the last two weeks of continual fighting, marching and hardship, is that lovely picture of you and the dear children. I sent one of my men 34 miles to the Rear for it where I had left it in my trunk. I am looking at it about 5 times an hour and I fear that some times I am talking to it. . . .

I think Vicksburg will fall within a week and let us pray to God that I may get out as safe as I have so far and then I will come home and tell you more news than you *ever heard*. . . .

I must close as the man who agrees to carry this to Helena, Arkansas, is leaving. God bless you and the children and all friends.

> Your
> Marcus

> In the field near R.R. Bridge Big Black River Mis.
> May 25/63

My dear good and kind Wife!

You will see by the above that the whereabouts and plans of a soldier are frequently as uncertain as his life is insecure. When last (two days ago) I wrote to you a few hasty penciled lines from the front in the Battlefield of Vicksburg, I surely thought that my next one would more apt to be written in Vicksburg, than 15 miles back here to the rear. But such is war. Now for the facts.

After fighting for five days and nights with but two days rations before Vicksburg . . . we received an Order to get ready to march in an hour.

How is that? Well, Osterhaus who is known as a careful, brave and discreed General who is always sent with his fighting Division to the most difficult places, was Ordered out here in consequence of news being received that the Rebel General Joe Johnston was advancing on our Rear with a force of fifteen thousand. Well, here we are eleven miles from the Battle field and in fact I feel relieved; I was almost tired of hearing the incessant roar of the hundreds of Cannons and Mortars, the rattling of musketry, which latter never ceased for a minute the five days and the former never stopped any for the last five days or nights. You are perhaps anxious to know how it stands with Vicksburg. Well we have it perfectly surrounded; we are close up to their works on every side, but their works are almost impregnable besides being so situated that you can not approach one of their numerous forts without going over ravines, abattis, fallen timber and every hindrance possible. . . .

We are so situated that Vicksburg *must fall* shortly with all the force therein contained, providing our Government will keep its forces elsewhere engaging the Enemy in such shape that he can not take away one of his Armies from the front of Rosencranz, Hooker, Hunter or otherwise. Vicksburg and its powerful Army captured and Secessia in the South West is gone up. General Grant has shown in this campayne more true, gay, dashing, bold and strategic military skill than has been displayed by all the Generals combined since the Rebellion broke out. He deceived the Enemy all the time; they as well as many of the Generals in his Army knew not what he was agoing to do until he whipped the Enemy at five different points and had his whole Army surrounding Vicksburg and, if no unforeseen event [occurs], Vicksburg will soon be ours. . . .

If Johnston advances as he has for two days past, he will be on us by to morrow noon. My Regiment has been extremely fortunate thank God. Since we landed on the Mississippi Shore and in all the fights, I have only lost 33 in killed and wounded and perhaps 10 as prisoners. . . .

As for myself I feel in good spirits. I have already wrote to you that I was struck by a piece of shell on my kneecap. It knocked the skin and bruised the flesh and bone a little but I never left the field and have not been off duty on [its] account. In a few days I will be all right, scarcely feel it in walking now. . . .

My boys will follow me anywheres. I have it so now that I can go in as cool as on Battalion Drill; everything must be learned and I really think I had a good School. It is no Science in my estimation to *send* a lot of men in a hot place where they will get mixed up and frequently slaughtered and then have a big list of killed and wounded and make a *big fuss* while the Commander is admiring the bravery of his men at a distance, but it is a pretty and difficult study to *lead* your men carefully into dangerous places and do the most damage to the Enemy and least to yourself; the latter I am endeavoring to study and I believe that at least I am favored with a little consolation in knowing that in this Army I have the reputation of being somewhat of an apt Scholar.

My Sergeant Major, a very nice young man by the name of McCay, had his shoulder badly shaddered by a shell; Sergeant Waters of Company D, a splendid young man, had the socket of his shoulder knocked and afterwards taken out by the Surgeon. . . .

As for resigning dear Caroline, I do not feel that I can as long as my Country needs my services for the suppression of this unholy and wicked rebellion. I am not in favor of settling this until the miserable cusses that would ruin our beloved Country are thoroughly convinced of their error and completely whipped. It makes but little difference to me whether the Holmes County Republican or democratic party give me credit for anything; you can feel perfectly easy on that score, for I do also. One thing is certain, that my fighting in this War will leave an inheritance to my beloved children of more value then all the Gold in India. I hope to live to see the day when my boys will point with pride to their father's history during his country's trouble. If this War should come to a close soon and the Rebs whipped, God knows I would love it, for I long for home with all its blessings and I think I ought to be at home and assist in raising my children. . . .

> In the field Big Black Bridge Mis.
> May 31, 63

My dear dear Wife!

. . . We are still in the same place as when I last wrote to you, a very quiet place where we hear the cannonading of our folks at Vicksburg Day and night. . . .

I would very much wish, if you would write me a little more incoraging as to my military career, but I know you write as you feel at the time you write and although you say in every letter resign and so forth, I am nevertheless satisfied that you feel as proud in my achievements and as I do and I am satisfied that in your heart you do not now want me to resign, when you know that resignation is "disgrace" unless a man is sick, which thank God I am not.

Cary my love, my heart and soul are in the cause, though I make no blow, though I write no letters for popularity, though I say it but to you, yet I am satisfied as I am that "God liveth" that our cause is just and that as an honorable man I must stay in the service as long as my Country needs me and while I can serve my dear family more by an honest and honorable name then by leaving a stain on my name in forsaking my Country and her flag, just then when she needs me and when by my experience and influence I can do her some service.

. . . As soon as Vicksburg falls, I expect to start for home and expect to stay with you quite awhile, go to Uniontown, Lima and so forth with you . . . .

I love you my dear my sweet Wife and have a chance to show it some time I hope.

> Ever yours
> Marcus. . . .

> In the field near Big Black Mis. June 3/63

My dear good wife!

. . . We are just near enough to hear the terrific cannonading of our folks at Vicksburg day and night without being in any danger from that source. Yet we do not know how soon we may expect some fun here of our own inasmuch as General Johnston is this afternoon positively reported to come this way. If we can only prevent reinforcements from reaching the Rebels at Vicksburg, we can take the town with all its Garrison. This Army has had the most brilliant chain of Successes of any Army since the beginning of the War, yet the crowning Victory would only then be won if Vicksburg is taken. . . .

Adjeu. . . .

Big Black Miss, June 29/63

My dear dear Wife!

Your very good letter of the 9th instant I received three days hence and the pleasure of hearing of your and the dear Childrens health and of receiving sweet little Hattie's picture is indescribable. . . . The reason why I have not written for several days was simply owing to the fact that I had expected "Vicksburg to fall" and go home, but yesterday I was to the front and looked at all the positions and I must confess that the place looks no nearer taken than it dit when we left 5 weeks ago. Although our folks are nearer, the only advantage I see is that we are fixed to hold them easy and can use most of our force against Johnston, should he attack us. Everything here looks at least satisfactorily for the Government; not so I fear with the Eastern Army and the people at home.

Looking to Virginia, where we have dates to the 23rd, I fear Lee is too much for Hooker; all our Generals, Officers and men feel so. McClellan should have that Army. Major General Sherman, an Army Officer and perhaps the most accomplished General in this Army, told me a week ago, "McClellan is the only man that can successfully cope with Lee" he knows them both from West Point and understands their Calibre.

Not only that it looks bad in that Army, but judging from the Reports of Holmes County in the Papers (and also other places), there seems to be a spirit to resist the Government and bring on a Collision, resulting in Civil War at home; I tremble when I think of it. Though I fear nothing from "Camp Napoleon" as it is called, yet the signs are bad and I wish you were out of the County. If you can sell the house for $1200, do so and I will agree to clear off all Mortgages and when I come home you can move away. They may have difficulty in Millersburg and I could not bear the Idea of you living in a town where you would be in danger of suffering the trials of War. You need not say anything about me saying that, yet still I do not care. It is a shame. I can scarcely think of anything else. I think it wrong to arrest Citizens in the loyal States for Civil offences and try them by Court Martials but it is ten times as bad to resist the laws of the Government.

Since I wrote to you last, we moved again; we are again near Big Black Bridge, close to the Rifle Pits. We are daily looking for Johnston to attack and if he does he will get a warm reception. I consider Grant's situation perfectly safe as against all the forces the Confederates can bring in this Section of Country against him. . . .

We are at present more excited about Hookers Army and the Raids into Maryland and Pennsylvania than we are about Vicksburg, because the latter is sure to fall, while Hooker seems in a precarious position. Let us trust to God for the best. . . .

The paymaster is here and will pay us two months pay in a few days and then I will send you about three hundred Dollars again; if he pays us 4 months I will send you seven hundred.

If God only spares my health I think I begin to see bottom. I do hope my love that we may soon see the time that we can live as people like us should and raise our beloved Children, becoming to them and us who love them as we do. . . .

Big Black Miss. July 1/63

My dear dear Wife:

. . . Our situation is as it was when last I wrote; we are fortifying and expecting the Rebels to attack us, which may happen in a few days; the latest reports say that Johnstons Advance is within five miles of us. His Army is reported fifty thousand strong, yet I feel confident if he attacks us we can whip him. Vicksburg is not yet taken, very little firing to day. If we whip Johnston, Vicksburg will surrender; the only hope Pemberton has, is to be relieved by Johnston. We have St. Louis and Chicago Papers of the 26th and I must confess everything looks gloomy in Pennsylvania; it seems Lee is bound to go to Philadelphia, My God, what is our Potomac Army doing. Would to God, President Lincoln would recall McClellan; he would make Lee pay dearly for his impudence. McClellan is the only man in America that can do it, so says Grant, Sherman and nearly every General here and I, though a much, much lesser light, would bet my life upon it.

I am still saying if Vicksburg falls I shall come home, and am still in great hopes that it will soon fall. . . .

How do you live? I hope good. Don't live stinchy. Don't be hankering for any thing and too "geitzig" [stingy] to buy it. I want you and the dear ones to live as well as anybody, for if I come home and find out you have lived stinching along, I shall not be pleased. . . . Oh that this accursed Rebellion might be crushed, peace restored to our unhappy Country so that the many good and true men and noble woman, husbands and wifes, Parents and Children might be united again and live in peace. I do not believe that ever a greater sin was perpetrated in the Eyes of the Lord, than was by those who brought about this State of Affairs. . . .

Ever ever your true,
Marcus

Big Black Miss July 4/63

My dear dear Wife!

This is a glorious day for our noble boys here; all of us feel wild with enthusiasm; our forces entered Vicksburg this A.M. We took 27,000 prisoners and 227 pieces of Artillery. The grandest Victory of modern history. We raised a Liberty Pole in my Regiment, made Speeches and hurrah and so forth.

My God, such a happy set of boys; this splits the Confederacy. I am only sorry we have to go further right off; it seems Jackson is our next place, Grant is determined to follow up his Victory. He is the greatest Chieftain of the Age; the boys worship him. I will have to postpone my going home until we get to some place where we stop awhile.

Such a fourth of July I never saw, without anything to drink and yet everybody wild.

God bless you
Your loving
Marcus

Hd. qrs. Division Hospital
in the rear of Jackson Miss.
Sunday 12th 63

My dear dear Wife,

This morning I was very severely but not in the least dangerously wounded in my left leg, by a shell, a large flesh wound, in the groin, Dont be scared by reports; I am doing as well as I could. I sent for Brother Josey and will start home as soon as he comes and I am satisfied that under your kind care I will be able for duty in two months.

The enemy charged on me yesterday but I drove them splendidly and fearfully. Day before yesterday I opened the Ball. My wound is doing well, but from our own shell. I lost so far here 4 officers wounded and 14 men.

Good bye my love; I will see you soon, God willing. God bless you and the children.

Ever yours
Marcus

Hd qrs Division Hospital
before Jackson Miss.
May [July] 15/63

My dear dear Wife!

This is the fourth day of my wound and thank God I am doing exceedingly well. I expect to be able to be moved in an ambulance to the River in the course of two weeks and when at the River I can easy get home. You must feel easy my good wife, dont be discouraged; if I only were at home and had you attend to me I am satisfied I would be well shortly.

With Gods help I mean to be home soon and will have much, much to tell you. I think I had better have a bed in the big Room below, dont you? . . .

Ever your true

Marcus

[*Your True Marcus*, pp. 281–286, 288–291, 293–297, 299–302.]

The Confederate defeats at Vicksburg and Gettysburg brought gloom and foreboding to such Confederate supporters as David G. Harris and the members of the Jones family. Harris was preparing to enter the Confederate army (since conscription had now been extended to include persons up to the age of forty-five), and he feared that many of his compatriots were losing hope of ultimate victory. Charles C. Jones, Jr., and his mother urged each other, in the face of the unfavorable military news, to put their trust in God (Charles C. Jones, Sr., had died on March 16, 1863).

David G. Harris:

July 13. Cutting oats at the Camp Place. Yesterday & to day the boys are cuting oats. My oat-crop is fine, but I am looseing much in my corn-crop while cutting oats. Vixburg [Vicksburg] has fallen and to day I hear that the yankeys have made or are making another attack on Charleston. May they get what they deserve. . . .

July 15. *Finished cutting oats.* Went to the village to get six bushels of salt that I had engaged while I was stationed on Mount Pleasant. I pay eight dollars per bushel (of 50 lb). Salt is now selling at 30 cents per lb. The weather is still clouddy. Every one is uneasy about the war. Bou[gh]t three gallons of whiskey for $12 per gal. . . .

July 17. More rain last night. Rain forever. I hauled in part of my oats to day, and many of them rotted. My oat crop is badly damage[d] already, & the weather too damp to dry them. . . .

July 19. As usual not much doing to day. Hoeing the goobers, tobacco &c. Land too wet to plow. MORE RAIN last night. . . . Yesterday I heard that the conscription was extended up to 45 years. That will take me in for the war. It had as well be me as any one. . . .

July 25. The morning was (as usual) dark and clouddy, with as little rain. Emily & I went to Allens. I left E there to go to church, while I went to the village to learn the news. All that I can learn is dark and gloomy. This is certainly the dark hour of the night. Our arms are not in the ascendency at this time. Our people are discouraged and I fear will soon be disposed to give up the contest. I hope this confined to the few, not the majority. The conscription has been extended to age of 45. This embraces me. I was drafted (into six month service). Now I come under the conscription act. Our drafted company is to remain in force for the time they was drafted for (six month) in the servise of the State. The conscription takes us in the Confederate service.

This is the time that is calculated to try men's souls. No time during this war has the prospect seemed so gloomy & forbiding as at the present time but still I am not frightend at all. If our own men will be true to there country their will be no doubt of the contest whatever. Yet I am uneasy about the dissatisfaction that is showing itself. I am making all arrangements to go into servise. This time it will be something serious for we, probably, we will have to remain during the war. Yet I am confident that it will all go right. No orders have as yet come for us to start to the feild, but they are expected constantly. I carried our flat fly broom and several fans to the village with me. I sold the broom readily for seven dollars and one of the fans for $2 & few days since had the First *Mess of Roasting* ears. July 26. Sunday. This morning I road to Col Balengers to learn what we had to do concerning going to the war, but I did not hear as much as I knew before. Father paid us a hasty visit to day. The first for a long time. He is wearing away & comes to see us but seldom. Clouddy and thundering in the evening. Emily reading a novel & the boys in the fish-pon & c. Our Garden is very fine. An abundance of all vegetables, beans, cabbage & c. Our cabbage are heading fast & are large and fine. My corn is silking rappidly, though it is mighty grasy. My oats are not yet all housed.

How tired some of us are getting of the war. I am tired of asking for, & hearing the news. At this time everything wears a gloomy aspect. Our army that was in Pensyvania [Pennsylvania], have recrossed the Potomac. Having accomplished but little, but lost thousands of men. Vicksburg have fallen, and our armys in the West are retreating. The Mississippi is in the control of the Yankeys. Charleston is beseiged and will probable fall. Then we will certainly see, feel, & taste what we have so far escaped, but if it must be it will be. So we must make the best we can of it. As for me, I am far from saying that we are conquored, or will be conquored so long as our men are united. I can see nothing so desperate but that it could be much worse. And nothing so bad, but that it may be redeemed. So we must put our trust in providence & fight on. I expect soon to be called away, to take my place in the ranks that has been too sadly thined. Our [courage] must be kept up or we must submit to the yankey rule. I only wish that all who are as able as I am, was only as willing.

July 27. Having some 1300 Confederate money on hand, & having paid almost all my debts & beleiving cotton would be a good investment, I started to hunt cotton this morning. After riding some time, I could only buy two bags. One for 35 cents and the other for 30. I once thought that I would be a happy man if I only could sell cotton at such figures, but now I am glad to buy at those figures. Confederate money is very plenty, and people do not fancy it much & I fear that it will still be more valueless. For that reason, I am anxious to get rid of it. So does every other person. This is the reason of such high prices. Bought three bushels of wheat at $3 per bushel. Employed a lady to spin wool for 50 cents per lb and weave jeans at 33 1/3 cents per yd. *Another hard rain, rain always. . . .*

July 29. Went to the factory for my rools, and to carry some wheat to have ground. Another *Hard rain.* Too wet to plow & always is. Ther surely has never has been such a summer as this, always raining. There has been no time since harvest that we could sun wheat with safty. Ther is much complaint of injured wheat. Some sick-wheat that is said to vomit those that eat it immediately. There is war, & rumors of war. A dark and gloomy time indeed. Some have already given up in despair & I fear many others will.

July 31. Went to our musterground to elect feild officers, and making other little arrangement for going to servise. We have until the 20 of August to choose our Companys to Volenteer into. After that time the men are to be conscripted and put where they pleas to put them. Still too wet to plow. My hands are hoeing at home. *Making cider* & c. Just weighed the flour that was sent me from Bivingsville = 27 1/3 lbs to the bushel. Not much to brag on at that, this wheat I bought. I hope mine will do better than that. [*Journals of David . . . Harris*, pp. 300–303.]

The Jones Family:

Savannah, *Thursday*, July 2nd, 1863

My very dear Mother,

. . . General Lee appears to be pressing onward, and with marked success, into Pennsylvania. The enemy will now have a taste of actual warfare. . . .

Your affectionate son,
Charles C. Jones, Jr. . . .

Walthourville, *Tuesday*, July 7th, 1863

My dear Son,

. . . Our hearts are anxiously looking for tidings from our army, which seems in peril at so many points. . . .

Ever your affectionate mother,
Mary Jones. . . .

Walthourville, *Tuesday*, July 14th, 1863

My dear Son,

. . . How long will this awful conflict last? And to what depths of misery are we to be reduced ere the Soverign Judge of all the earth will give us deliverance? It does appear that we are to be brought very low. . . . I do bless God for the spirit of true patriotism and undaunted courage with which He is arming us for this struggle. Noble Vicksburg! From her heroic example we gather strength to hold on and hold out to the last moment. I can look extinction for me and mine in the face, but *submission* never! It would be degradation of the lowest order. . . .

Your mother
Mary Jones. . . .

Savannah, *Wednesday,* July 15, 1863

My very dear Mother,

    . . . The heavens above us are indeed dark; but although for the present the clouds give no reviving showers, let us look and pray earnestly for His favor who can bring order out of chaos, victory out of apparent defeat, and light out of shadow. All these reverses should teach us our absolute dependence upon a Higher Power, and lead to sincere personal and national repentance. . . .

Your affectionate son,
Charles C. Jones, Jr.

[*The Children of Pride*, pp. 1071–1074, 1076–1077.]

While Charles C. Jones, Jr., his mother, and David G. Harris were dismayed at the outcome of the battles at Gettysburg and Vicksburg, those battles elicited responses that were the opposite of dismay, as would be expected, from George Templeton Strong and Maria Daly. Strong and Daly both rejoiced at the tidings from those two big battles, and both reported similar feelings of jubilation among their friends and associates. "This [the victory at Gettysburg] ends the Rebellion," Strong was told. Strong disagreed, holding that many more battles would be needed to crush the Rebellion, but both he and Daly called Gettysburg one of the most decisive battles of all time. Easterners Strong and Daly wrote much more about Gettysburg than Vicksburg, although Daly's brother, Phil, was in the Union forces at Vicksburg.

George Templeton Strong:

July 3. Half-past nine of a muggy morning. We can scarcely fail to have most weighty news before night.

There was a battle at or near Gettysburg on the first, resulting apparently in our favor. . . .

Evening. No definite news at all. We were told by the bulletin boards at noon that Vicksburg had surrendered, and I believed the story till about one in the afternoon, when it turned out not entirely authentic. Never mind. Do not the *Times, Tribune, Post* and *Commercial* daily certify that the "fall" of Vicksburg is "only a question of time," as distinguished from one of eternity?

July 4, Saturday. A cloudy, muggy, sultry Fourth. . . .

At half-past five appeared Walter Cutting with news from the army up to eight last night. There was fighting on the afternoon of the second, renewed yesterday, when the rebels attacked Meade's left centre in great force and were twice repulsed with severe loss. Our cavalry was operating on their flank. Both armies seem to have held their original position . . . .

July 5. A memorable day, even should its glorious news prove but half true. Tidings from Gettysburg have been arriving in fragmentary instalments, but with a steady crescendo toward complete, overwhelming victory. If we can believe what we hear, Lee is smitten hip and thigh, and his invincible "Army of Northern Virginia" shattered and destroyed. But I am skeptical, especially as to news of victory, and expect to find large deductions from our alleged success in tomorrow morning's newspapers. There has been a great battle in which we are, on the whole, victorious. The woman-floggers are badly repulsed and retreating, with more or less loss of prisoners, guns, and matériel. So much seems certain, and that is enough to thank God for most devoutly, far better than we dared hope a week ago. This may have been one of the great decisive battles of history. . . .

July 6. Mugginess continues. Morning papers give us little additional light, if any. Evening papers do. I regret to see no official statement of guns captured. But an extra *Herald* despatch dated at noon today gives us a splendidly colored picture of Lee's retreat and tells how teamsters and artillery men are cutting their traces and riding off for life on their draft-mules. . . .

The results of this victory are priceless. Philadelphia, Baltimore, and Washington are safe. Defeat would have seriously injured all three. The rebels are hunted out of the North, their best army is routed, and the charm of Robert Lee's invincibility broken. The Army of the Potomac has at last found a general that can handle it, and it has stood nobly up to its terrible work in spite of its long disheartening list of hard-fought failures, and in spite of the McClellan influence on its officers.

Government is strengthened four-fold at home and abroad. Gold one hundred and thirty-eight today, and government securities rising. Copperheads are palsied and dumb for the moment at least. . . .

People downtown very jolly today. "This ends the Rebellion." So I was told a dozen times. My cheerful and agreeable but deluded friends, there must be battles by the score before that outbreak from the depths of original sin is "ended." . . .

July 15. . . . News from the South is consolatory. Port Hudson surrendered. Sherman said to have beaten Joseph Johnston somewhere near Vicksburg. Operations commencing against Charleston. Bragg seems to be abandoning Chattanooga and retiring to Atlanta. *Per contra,* Lee has got safely off. I thought he would. . . .

[*The Diary of George Templeton Strong.* Abridged edition, 1988, pp. 230–233, 241.]

Maria Daly:

June 17, 1863

. . . Today there is news from Pennsylvania that Harrisburg is in danger from Lee's army, which (just as they did last year) has crossed the Potomac and is laying waste the Cumberland Valley. It is dispiriting in the extreme. . . .

Phil is at Vicksburg with the Ninth Army Corps. It is not taken yet, though the flags were hung out in honor of its capture six weeks ago. . . .

June 18, 1863

Another rebel raid into Pennsylvania by Lee has been more successful than the last. Our wretched Administration have allowed all the three-years' men to return without making any provision whatever to replace them. Truly God has a controversy with this people. He raises for us no deliverer. There is not one honest, clever man left; at least such are not permitted to have influence. One would not admit the men who rule us in Washington, with the exception of Chase and Seward, even into the drawing room. The Republicans who place them where they are are equally disgusted. It saps all patriotism! Vicksburg is not yet taken. . . .

June 29, 1863

How virulent Republicans are against McClellan. . . . It is wonderful to see the apathy which prevails. Whatever troops can be raised will be but state, not United States troops. None will consent to put themselves at the disposition of the Federal government. It is extraordinary to hear the violence that the Republicans indulge in against the Democrats. They hate them worse than the secessionists.

. . . . .

July 12, 1863

Much has occurred since I opened this book last. Hooker has been displaced, and General Meade has led the Army of the Potomac to victory, driving Lee back to the Potomac where they are now probably fighting the decisive battle of this war. Vicksburg was at last surrendered on the fourth, on which day Meade likewise defeated Lee, so that there has never been a Fourth of July kept before so grandly by the nation. God seems to have at last sent us a leader. General Meade is a native of Spain, but his parents were Americans. Now if Lincoln had but the sense to publish a general amnesty and annul his emancipation act, we might once more be a united nation, for we have great reason to be proud of the courage and talent exhibited on both sides. This last battle has never been surpassed by any in history. The North and South will now have learned to respect each other. . . .

July 14, 1863

. . . The news from the army is most encouraging. It is thought that Lee will not be able to escape. It would seem as though this war might now be brought to an end. . . .

[*Diary of a Union Lady*, pp. 240–241, 244–245, 248.]

7. A NOTABLE MONTH: JULY, 1863

The Union military victories at Gettysburg and Vicksburg would have made the month of July, 1863, memorable, even if nothing else had happened during that thirty-one-day period. It turned out, however, that several other events in that month were also noteworthy, two of which were the draft riots in New York City, July 13 to 16, and the assault on Fort Wagner (located in the approach to the Charleston, South Carolina, harbor) by the black troops of the 54th Massachusetts Volunteer Infantry on July 18.

Draft Riots, New York City

The joy with which George Templeton Strong, Maria Daly, and other residents of New York City greeted the victories at Gettysburg and Vicksburg was not shared by all the inhabitants of that city. In particular, the joy was not shared by a number of poor laborers of Irish and other ethnic and immigrant backgrounds who were scheduled to be drafted into the Union army in July. The Union government had passed a national conscription law in March, 1863; the names of men in New York City who were selected for the draft under that law were published on Sunday, July 12, and on the following day rioting against the draft began and lasted for the next four days. At least 105 persons were killed in those days. There were riots against the draft in various communities, but the mid-July disturbances in New York City were by far the most extensive and attracted the most attention. One of the most criticized provisions of the 1863 conscription act was the possibility of avoiding the draft by paying $300 or providing a substitute to go in one's place (George Templeton Strong provided a substitute for himself). The rioters in New York attacked the draft headquarters and other places associated with the national government; they also attacked blacks, seen as, among other things, economic competitors who would take the jobs of persons who were drafted.

Both Strong and Daly witnessed portions of the riots and described them graphically. Their identifications of the rioters differed, but they both were horrified by what they observed.

George Templeton Strong:

July 12 [1863]

. . . Draft has begun here and was in progress in Boston last week. *Demos* takes it good-naturedly thus far, but we shall have trouble before we are through. The critical time will be when defaulting conscripts are haled out of their houses, as many will be. . . .

July 13, Monday. . . . [I heard] of rioting in the upper part of the city. . . . Reached the seat of war at last, Forty-sixth Street and Third Avenue. Three houses on the Avenue and two or three on the street were burned down: engines playing on the ruins—more energetically, I'm told, than they did when their efforts would have been useful.

The crowd seemed just what one commonly sees at any fire, but its nucleus of riot was concealed by an outside layer of ordinary peaceable lookers-on. Was told they had beat off a squad of police and another of "regulars" (probably the Twelfth Militia). At last, it opened and out streamed a posse of perhaps five hundred, certainly less than one thousand, of the lowest Irish day laborers. The rabble was perfectly homogeneous. Every brute in the drove was pure Celtic—hod-carrier or loafer. They were unarmed. A few carried pieces of fence-paling and the like. They turned off west into Forty-fifth Street and gradually collected in front of two three-story dwelling houses on Lexington Avenue, just below that street, that stand alone together on a nearly vacant block. Nobody could tell why these houses were singled out. Some said a drafting officer lived in one of them, others that a damaged policeman had taken refuge there. The mob was in no hurry; they had no need to be; there was no one to molest them or make them afraid. The beastly ruffians were masters of the situation and of the city. After a while sporadic paving-stones began to fly at the windows, ladies and children emerged from the rear and had a rather hard scramble over a high board fence, and then scudded off across the open, Heaven knows whither. Then men and small boys appeared at rear windows and began smashing the sashes and the blinds and shied out light articles, such as books and crockery, and dropped chairs and mirrors into the back yard; the rear fence was demolished and loafers were seen marching off with portable articles of furniture. And at last a light smoke began to float out of the windows and I came away. I could endure the disgraceful, sickening sight no longer, and what could I *do?*

The fury of the low Irish women in that region was noteworthy. Stalwart young vixens and withered old hags were swarming everywhere, all cursing the "bloody draft" and egging on their men to mischief.

Omnibussed down to No. 823, where is news that the Colored Half Orphan Asylum on Fifth Avenue, just above the reservoir, is burned. "*Tribune* office to be burned tonight." Railroad rails torn up, telegraph wires cut, and so on. If a quarter one hears be true, this is an organized insurrection in the interest of the rebellion and Jefferson Davis rules New York today. . . . then to St Nicholas Hotel to see the mayor and General Wool. . . . We begged that martial law might be declared. Opdyke said that was Wool's business, and Wool said it was Opdyke's, and neither would act. . . .

We telegraphed, two or three of us, from General Wool's rooms, to the President, begging that troops be sent on and stringent measures taken. The great misfortune is that nearly all our militia regiments have been despatched to Pennsylvania. . . .

These wretched rioters have been plundering freely, I hear. Their outbreak will either destroy the city or damage the Copperhead cause fatally.
Could we but catch the scoundrels who have stirred them up, what a
blessing it would be! God knows what tonight or tomorrow may bring
forth. We may be thankful that it is now (quarter past twelve) raining
briskly. Mobs have no taste for the effusion of cold water. . . .

July 14. Eleven P.M. Fire bells clanking, as they have clanked at inter-
vals through the evening. Plenty of rumors throughout the day and
evening, but nothing very precise or authentic. There have been sundry
collisions between the rabble and the authorities, civil and military. . . .
Many details come in of yesterday's brutal, cowardly ruffianism and
plunder. Shops were cleaned out and a black man hanged in Carmine
Street, for no offence but that of Nigritude. . . . Sally forth, and find the
Eighteenth Ward station house, Twenty-second Street, near First Avenue,
in full blaze. A splendid blaze it made, but I did not venture below Second
Avenue, finding myself in a crowd of Celtic spectators disgorged by the
circumjacent tenement houses. They were exulting over the damage to
"them bloody police," and so on. I thought discretion the better part of curiosity. . . .

July 15. Wednesday begins with heavy showers, and now (ten A.M.)
cloudy, hot, and steaming. Morning papers report nothing specially grave
as occurring since midnight. But there will be much trouble today.
Rabbledom is not yet dethroned any more than its ally and instigator,
Rebeldom. . . .

July 19, Sunday. . . . Not half the history of this memorable week has
been written. I could put down pages of incidents that the newspapers
have omitted, any one of which would in ordinary times be the town's
talk. Men and ladies attacked and plundered by daylight in the streets;
private houses suddenly invaded by gangs of a dozen ruffians and
sacked, while the women and children run off for their lives. Then there is
the unspeakable infamy of the nigger persecution. They are the most
peaceable, sober, and inoffensive of our poor, and the outrages they have
suffered during this last week are less excusable—are founded on worse
pretext and less provocation—than St. Bartholomew's or the Jew-hunting
of the Middle Ages. This is a nice town to call itself a centre of civilization!
Life and personal property less safe than in Tipperary, and the "people"
(as the *Herald* calls them) burning orphan asylums and conducting a mas-
sacre. How this infernal slavery system has corrupted our blood, North as
well as South! . . .

I am sorry to find that England is right about the lower class of Irish.
They are brutal, base, cruel, cowards, and as insolent as base. Choate (at
the Union League Club) tells me he heard this proposition put forth by
one of their political philosophers in conversation with a knot of his
brethren last Monday: "Sure and if them dam Dutch would jine us we'd

drive the dam Yankees out of New York entirely!" These caitiffs have a trick, I hear, of posting themselves at the window of a tenement house with a musket, while a woman with a baby in her arms squats at their feet. Paddy fires on the police and instantly squats to reload, while Mrs. Paddy rises and looks out. Of course, one can't fire at a window where there is a woman with a child!! But how is one to deal with women who assemble around the lamp-post to which a Negro had been hanged and cut off certain parts of his body to keep as souvenirs? Have they any womanly privilege, immunity, or sanctity?

No wonder St. Patrick drove all the venomous vermin out of Ireland! Its biped mammalia supply that island its full average share of creatures that crawl and eat dirt and poison every community they infest. Vipers were superfluous. But my own theory is that St. Patrick's campaign against the snakes is a Popish delusion. They perished of biting the Irish people.

July 20. . . . I see a frequent placard bearing these two words, "Sam, Organize!" It plainly means that there is a movement to revive the old Native American party with its Know-Nothing Clubs; a very natural consequence of the atrocities just perpetrated by our Irish *canaille*. Talking with Americans of the middle and laboring class, even of the lowest social grade, I find they fully appreciate and bitterly resent these Celtic outrages. But the obstacle in the way of a revived Know-Nothingism is that it would be obliged to discriminate between Celts and Teutons. The Germans have behaved well and kept quiet. Where they acted at all, they volunteered against the rabble, as they did, most effectively, in the Seventh Ward. A mere anti-Hibernian party would have no foundation on principle, would seem merely vindictive and proscriptive, and would lead to no lasting result, I fear. For myself, personally, I would like to see war made on Irish scum as in 1688.

[*The Diary of George Templeton Strong.* Abridged edition, 1988, pp. 236–241, 244–245.]

Maria Daly:

July 14, 1863

The draft began on Saturday, the twelfth [the 11th], very foolishly ordered by the government, who supposed that these Union victories would make the people willing to submit. By giving them Sunday to think it over, by Monday morning there were large crowds assembled to resist the draft. All day yesterday there were dreadful scenes enacted in the city. The police were successfully opposed; many were killed, many houses were gutted and burned: the colored asylum was burned and all the furniture was carried off by *women:* Negroes were hung in the streets! All last night the fire-bells rang, but at last, in God's good mercy, the rain came down in torrents and scattered the crowds, giving the city authorities time

to organize. Today bodies of police and military patrolled the city to prevent any assembly of rioters. A Virginian, last evening, harangued the
crowd. Fearful that they might attack a Negro tenement house some
blocks below us, as they had attacked others, I ordered the doors to be
shut and no gas to be lighted in front of the house. . . . this news of the riots
here will give the rebels encouragement. The principal cause of discontent
was the provision that by paying three hundred dollars any man could
avoid serving if drafted, thus obliging all who could not beg, borrow, or
steal this sum to go to the war. This is exceedingly unjust. The laboring
classes say that they are sold for three hundred dollars, whilst they pay
one thousand dollars for Negroes.

Things seem quiet this morning. People are returning to their homes,
though the tops of the stages are crowded with workingmen and boys.

Mr. Leslie at Long Branch told me that he was in disgrace with Mrs.
Lincoln for having published in his paper a likeness of her taken at
Springfield by a skillful photographist sent there for the purpose just after
Lincoln's election. At the time she was entirely satisfied with the likeness,
but after she had been dressed by city mantua-makers and milliners, she
considered it a libel. It was certainly the likeness of a very common looking country body, whilst now she looks like a vulgar, shoddy, contractor's
wife who does not know what to do with her money. . . .

July 23, 1863

At last the riot is quelled, but we had four days of great anxiety.
Fighting went on constantly in the streets between the military and police
and the mob, which was partially armed. The greatest atrocities have been
perpetrated. Colonel O'Brian was murdered by the mob in such a brutal
manner that nothing in the French Revolution exceeded it. Three or four
Negroes were hung and burned; the women assisted and acted like furies
by stimulating the men to greater ferocity. . . . This mob seems to have a
curious sense of justice. They attacked and destroyed many disreputable
houses and did not always spare secessionists. . . . Mrs. Hilton said she
never saw such creatures, such gaunt-looking savage men and women
and even little children armed with brickbats, stones, pokers, shovels and
tongs, coal-scuttles, and even tin pans and bits of iron. They passed her
house about four o-clock on Monday morning and continued on in a constant stream until nine o'clock. They looked to her, she said, like Germans,
and her first thought was that it was some German festival. . . .

Among those killed or wounded have been found men with delicate
hands and feet, and under their outward laborers' clothes were fine cam-
bric shirts and costly underclothing. A dressmaker says she saw from her
window a gentlemen whom she knows and has seen with young ladies,
but whose name she could not remember, disguised in this way in the
mob on Sixth Avenue. . . .

I saw Susanna Brady, who talked in the most violent manner against the Irish and in favor of the blacks. I feel quite differently, although very sorry and much outraged at the cruelties inflicted. I hope it will give the Negroes a lesson, for since the war commenced, they have been so insolent as to be unbearable. I cannot endure free blacks. They are immoral, with all their piety.

The principal actors in this mob were boys, and I think they were Americans. Catherine, my seamstress, tells me that the plundering was done by the people in the neighborhood who were looking on and who, as the mob broke the houses open, went in to steal. The police this morning found beds, bedding, and furniture in the house of a Scotch Presbyterian who was well off and owned two cows and two horses. The Catholic priests have done their duty as Christians ministers in denouncing these riotous proceedings. One of them remonstrated with a woman in the crowd who wanted to cut off the ears of a Negro [who] was hung. The priest told her that Negroes had souls. "Sure, your reverence," said she, "I thought they only had gizzards."
[*Diary of a Union Lady*, pp. 246, 248–251.]

The Assault on Fort Wagner, and the 54th Massachusetts Volunteer Infantry

At almost the same time when blacks in New York City were being hunted down by mobs, other blacks dressed in the uniforms of Union soldiers were risking their lives in battle near Charleston, South Carolina. On July 18, an attack on Fort Wagner, near the entrance to the Charleston harbor, was led by the black Union soldiers of the 54th Massachusetts Volunteer Infantry. The 54th was one of the first black regiments raised in the North, regiments which had been foretold when Lincoln's final Proclamation of Emancipation (January 1, 1863) declared that blacks "will be received into the armed service of the United States." The 54th had been recruited in New Bedford, Massachusetts, beginning in February, 1863. Its officers were white (as was the case with all other regiments of blacks during the war), and its commander was Colonel Robert Gould Shaw, a Harvard graduate whose parents were prominent abolitionists. Shaw, although he was only twenty-six years old in 1863, already had combat experience in the almost two years he had served with white regiments.

The 54th trained at a camp near Boston until near the end of May and was then transported by boat to Beaufort, South Carolina. It saw its first combat early in June, engaging in a series of actions that led up to its assault on Fort Wagner on July 18. In the 54th's frontal attack on Fort Wagner it faced murderous fire and suffered casualties of almost 50 percent; some of the regiment reached the parapet of the fort, including the color bearer and Colonel Shaw, both of whom were killed there. The attack was repulsed and Fort Wagner was not captured, but the bravery, skill, and heroism of the 54th's men did much to convince many whites that blacks could and would fight as effectively as whites. (It was the 54th Massachusetts that was pictured in the movie Glory.)

James Henry Gooding, private and later corporal in the 54th, described his experiences in the regiment in a series of letters published in the New Bedford *[Massachusetts]* Mercury *at the time. Gooding, like a number of other soldiers in the 54th, was a free black from New Bedford; in September, 1863, he wrote to President Lincoln, requesting that black soldiers be paid the same salary as white soldiers, and that letter is among those reprinted here.*

[*Mercury*, June 19, 1863]
Port Royal, June 3
Messrs. Editors:—After a long passage of seven days, we have arrived at Port Royal. We are still on board the vessel, and I write my first letter on the top of my knapsack. . . . There is nothing interesting to write as yet, for the very good reason that we have none of us been ashore. I write this letter to let the friends of the men know that we are all safe, except one, who jumped overboard the first night out from Boston. I think he must have been cracked or drunk, more likely the latter. The men are all in good health and spirits, not one man in the whole regiment being now on the sick list. After we are quartered on shore, and have an opportunity to look around, you may expect better letters.

J.H.G.

Beaufort, S.C., June 8th
Messrs. Editors:—We arrived at this town on the evening of the 4th, not debarking at Hilton Head. On the morning of the 5th, we left the steamer and marched to our camp ground about a quarter of a mile out of the town, near the 55th Pennsylvania and 8th Maine regiments. Our reception was almost as enthusiastic here in Beaufort, as our departure from Boston was. You know probably how universal the enthusiasm was in Boston. The 54th has already won the reputation here of being a first class regiment, both in drill, discipline and physical condition. When the 54th marched through the streets of this town, the citizens and soldiers lined the walks, to get a look at the first black regiment from the North. The contrabands did not believe we were coming; one of them said, "I nebber bleeve black Yankee comee here help culer men." They think now the kingdom is coming sure enough. The yarns the copperhead press have so studiously spun, that the slaves were better satisfied in their old condition than under the present order of things, is all bosh. So far as I have seen, they appear to understand the *causes* of the war better than a great many Northern editors. . . .

The slaves, hereabouts, are working for the government mostly, although they can make a pretty snug little sum, peddling among the soldiers, selling fruit, &c.

The 2d South Carolina volunteers [composed primarily of freed slaves] have made a successful expedition. . . . We leave tonight for, the Lord knows where, but we shall try to uphold the honor of the Old Bay State wherever we go.

The wagons are being packed, so I must close.

J.H.G.

. . . .

[*Mercury*, August 1, 1863]
Morris Island, July 20, 1863
Messrs. Editors:—At last we have something stirring to record. The 54th, the past week, has proved itself twice in battle. The first was on James Island on the morning of the 16th. There were four companies of the 54th on picket duty at the time; our picket lines extending to the right of the rebel battery, which commands the approach to Charleston through the Edisto river. About 3 o'clock in the morning, the rebels began harassing our pickets on the right, intending, no doubt, to drive them in, so that by daylight the coast would be clear to rush their main force down on us, and take us by surprise. They did not suppose we had any considerable force to the rear of our pickets on the right, as Gen. Stevenson's brigade was plain in sight on the left; and their plan, I suppose, was to rush down and cut Gen. Stevenson off. They made a mistake—instead of returning fire, the officer in charge of the pickets directed the men to lie down under cover of a hedge, rightly expecting the rebels to advance by degrees toward our lines. As he expected, at daylight they were within 600 yards of the picket line, when our men rose and poured a volley into them. That was something the rebels didn't expect—their line of skirmishers was completely broken; our men then began to fall back gradually on our line of battle, as the rebels were advancing their main force on to them. On they came, with six pieces of artillery and four thousand infantry, leaving a heavy force to drive Gen. Stevenson on the left. As their force advanced on our right, the boys held them in check like veterans; but of course they were falling back all the time, and fighting too. After the officers saw there was no chance for their men, they ordered them to move on to a creek under cover of the gunboats. When the rebels got within 900 yards of our line of battle, the right wing of Gen. Terry's brigade gave them three volleys, which checked their advance. They then made a stand with their artillery and began shelling us, but it had no effect on our forces, as the rebels fired too high. The 6th Connecticut battery then opened fire on them from the right, the John Adams and May Flower from the creek between James and Cole Islands, and the Pawnee and a mortar schooner from the Edisto [i.e., Stono], when the rebels began a hasty retreat. It was a warmer reception than they had expected. Our loss in the skirmishing before the battle, so far as we can ascertain, was nine killed, 13 wounded,

and 17 missing, either killed or taken prisoners; but more probably they were driven into the creek and drowned. Sergeant Wilson, of Co. H, was called upon to surrender, but would not; he shot four men before he was taken. After he was taken they ordered him to give up his pistol which he refused to do, when he was shot through the head.

The men of the 54th behaved gallantly on the occasion—so the Generals say. It is not for us to blow our horn; but when a regiment of white men gave us three cheers as we were passing them, it shows that we did our duty as men should.

I shall pass over the incidents of that day, as regard individuals, to speak of a greater and more terrible ordeal the 54th regiment has passed through. I shall say nothing now of how we came from James to Morris Island; suffice it to say, on Saturday afternoon we were marched up past our batteries, amid the cheers of the officers and soldiers. We wondered what they were all cheering for, but we soon found out. Gen. Strong rode up, and we halted. Well, you had better believe there was some guessing what we were to do. Gen. Strong asked if we would follow him into Fort Wagner. Every man said, yes—we were ready to follow wherever we were led. You may all know Fort Wagner is the Sebastopol of the rebels; but we went at it, over the ditch and on to the parapet through a deadly fire; but we could not get into the fort. We met the foe on the parapet of Wagner with the bayonet—we were exposed to a murderous fire from the batteries of the fort, from our Monitors and our land batteries, as they did not cease firing soon enough. Mortal men could not stand such a fire, and the assault on Wagner was a failure. The 9th Me., 10th Conn., 63d Ohio, 48th and 100th N.Y. were to support us in the assault; but after we made the first charge, everything was in such confusion that we could hardly tell where the reserve was. At the first charge the 54th rushed to within twenty yards of the ditches, and, as might be expected of raw recruits, wavered— but at the second advance they gained the parapet. The color bearer of the State colors was killed on the parapet. Col. Shaw seized the staff when the standard bearer fell, and in less than a minute after, the colonel fell himself. When the men saw their gallant leader fall, they made a desperate effort to get him out, but they were either shot down, or reeled in the ditch below. One man succeeded in getting hold of the State color staff, but the color was completely torn to pieces.

I have no more paper here at present, as all our baggage is at St. Helena yet; so I cannot further particularize in this letter. Lieut. Grace was knocked down by a piece of shell, but he is not injured. He showed himself a great deal braver and cooler than any line officer.

J.H.G.

Our correspondent gives a list of killed, wounded and missing. It is the same that we have already published.
[*Mercury* Editor]

"They mowed us down like grass" one survivor wrote to his mother; and Lieutenant Grace gave the following account to Brigadier General Pierce:

Knowing your deep interst in the officers and men of the Regiment, I thought I would let you know how we are after our Skirmish and retreat from James Island and Fight at Morris Island. We were on the move three days and nights before the Fight on this Island. When we arrived here, we were very much exhausted, tired and hungry, not having any thing to eat for twenty four hours. I simply speak of this to let you know what condition we were in before the Fight. We arrived on the Island about 3 o'clock, rested a short time, and then moved forward to the upper end of the Island (the Island is about four miles long). When we arrived within one thousand yards of Fort Wagner, we laid down waiting for our support to come up. We laid there about thirty minutes when we were ordered to rise up and charge on the works, which we did at double quick time with a tremendous scream. When we arrived within a short distance of the works, the Rebels opened on us with grape and canister accompanied with a thousand muskets, mowing our men down by the hundreds. This caused us to fall back a little, but we soon made another rush to the works, when we received another tremendous discharge of musketry, and also grape and canister. Such a tremendous fire right in our faces caused us to fall back, which we did in very good order. Our men are highly spoken of by military men as showing great bravery. They did fight when they were in front of the works [and a] good many of our men went on to the works and fought hand to hand with the Enemy.

[*Mercury*, August 4, 1863]
Morris Island, July 24
Messrs. Editors:—Since my letter of the 20th last, our forces have been busily engaged, preparing for the grand sortie on Wagner and Sumter. When everything is complete, you may expect to hear of decisive results. It is very probable that Fort Wagner would have been in our possession now, had the rebels not sent a flag-of-truce boat out on the 22d inst. to exchange prisoners. The monitors, gunboats and batteries were blazing away on her (Wagner) that forenoon, and from the look of things, it seemed as though they were in a pretty tight place. I do not think, with the vast preparations now being made, that Wagner can hold out 48 hours if our side push matters a little when they do begin. Ere this meets the eyes of the readers of the Mercury, the Union troops may garrison both forts, Wagner and Sumter; but the people at home must not expect Charleston to be taken in two minutes, for even if Forts Wagner and Sumter are soon reduced, there is still a few miles between Sumter and the city, backed by

heavy batteries on each shore. Winning victories by theory, in easy chairs at home, and *fighting* to win them on the field, are different things.

We have since learned by the flag-of-truce boat that Colonel Shaw is dead—he was buried in a trench with 45 of his men! not even the commonest respect paid to his rank. Such conduct is in striking contrast to the respect paid a rebel Major, who was killed on James Island. The Commander of the 54th regiment had the deceased rebel officer buried with all the honors of war granted by the regulations; and they have returned the compliment by tossing him into a ditch.

We hope the London Times will make note of that fact. They did not say how many of our men they had buried, beyond the 45 with the Colonel, nor how many of them they have as prisoners; they merely said they would not exchange them then, but should hold them for future consideration. So we can give no definite news of those who are killed or prisoners. We have never been allowed to approach near enough to hold any parley with them since the night of the assault. It seems though, from the proceedings since the truce, that there might have been some "kid glove handling" of the negro volunteer question, as the two boats were side by side nearly three hours; though I may be wrong in my surmises. But since that day our regiment has not been out on picket duty, either as outposts or reserves; and this may be prompted by a desire of those in charge not to place a regiment of black men in an exposed position under such peculiar circumstances, until they know definitely what is to be the fate of those in the hands of the rebels. If such be the case I think it is for the best. The regiment is hardly fit for service in the field at present for want of officers. Capts. Russell and Simpkins have never been heard of since the memorable night of the 18th. All the other company commanders are so severely wounded that it is feared some of them will never be able to resume the field again, and it is to be hoped that the steps for reorganizing the regiment will be speedily taken. It is due to what few officers we have left with us, to reward them with a step higher up the ladder. Col. Littlefield, of the 3d S.C. Regiment, has temporary charge of the 54th.

I did intend to give you an account of our evacuation of James Island; but as we may have occasion to "play it over again," for strategic reasons, I'll keep dark on it.

In my last letter I put down Abram P. Torrance as killed. I have subsequently learned that he is wounded, and is in the hospital at Beaufort. The rest of the list is, I think, correct. The total number of men now killed, wounded and missing, is 357. It is estimated that about 70 of the wounded will be again fit for service.

J.H.G.

P.S.—Two more monitors arrived this afternoon, ready to take a part in the combat. The men of the regiment are raising a sum to send the body of the

Colonel home, as soon as Fort Wagner is reduced. They all declare that they will dig for his body till they find it. They are determined this disgrace shall be counteracted by something noble.
[*Mercury,* August 5, 1863]

Our correspondent, "J.H.G." is a member of Co. C., of the 54th Massachusetts regiment. He is a colored man, belonging to this city, and his letters are printed by us, *verbatim et literatim,* as we receive them. He is a truthful and intelligent correspondent, and a good soldier.
[*Mercury* Editor] . . .

Camp of the 54th Mass. Colored Regt. Morris Island
Dept of the South. Sept. 28th, 1863
Your Excellency, Abraham Lincoln:

Your Excellency will pardon the presumption of an humble individual like myself, in addressing you, but the earnest Solicitation of my Comrades in Arms beside the genuine interest felt by myself in the matter is my excuse, for placing before the Executive head of the Nation our Common Grievance.

On the 6th of the last Month, the Paymaster of the department informed us, that if we would decide to receive the sum of $10 (ten dollars) per month, he would come and pay us that sum, but that, on the sitting of Congress, the Regt. would, in his opinion, be *allowed* the other 3 (three). He did not give us any guarantee that this would be, as he hoped; certainly he had no authority for making any such guarantee, and we cannot suppose him acting in any way interested.

Now the main question is Are we *Soldiers,* or are we *Labourers?* We are fully armed, and equipped, have done all the various Duties pertaining to a Soldier's life, have conducted ourselves to the complete satisfaction of General Officers, who were, if any[thing], prejudiced *against* us, but who now accord us all the encouragement and honour due us; have shared the perils and Labour of Reducing the first stronghold that flaunted a Traitor Flag; and more, Mr. President. Today the Anglo-Saxon Mother, Wife, or Sister are not alone in tears for departed Sons, Husbands and Brothers. The patient, trusting Descendants of Afric's Clime have dyed the ground with blood, in defense of the Union, and Democracy. Men, too, your Excellency, who know in a measure the cruelties of the Iron heel of oppression, which in years gone by, the very Power their blood is now being spilled to maintain, ever ground them to the dust.

But When the war trumpet sounded o'er the land, when men knew not the Friend from the Traitor, the Black man laid his life at the Altar of the Nation,—and he was refused. When the arms of the Union were beaten, in the first year of the War, and the Executive called [for] more food for its ravaging [ravenous?] maw, again the black man begged the privilege of aiding his Country in her need, to be again refused.

And now he is in the War, and how has he conducted himself? Let their dusky forms rise up, out [of] the mires of James Island, and give the answer. Let the rich mould around Wagner's parapets be upturned, and there will be found an Eloquent answer. Obedient and patient and Solid as a wall are they. All we lack is a paler hue and a better acquaintance with the Alphabet.

Now your Excellency, we have done a Soldier's Duty. Why Can't we have a Soldier's pay? You caution the Rebel Chieftain, that the United States knows no distinction in her Soldiers. She insists on having all her Soldiers of whatever creed or Color, to be treated according to the usages of War. Now if the United States exacts uniformity of treatment of her Soldiers from the Insurgents, would it not be well and consistent to set the example herself by paying all her *Soldiers* alike?

We of this Regt. were not enlisted under any "contraband" act. But we do not wish to be understood as rating our Service of more Value to the Government than the service of the ex-slave. Their Service *is* undoubtedly worth much to the Nation, but Congress made express provision touching their case, as slaves freed by military necessity, and assuming the Government to be their temporary Guardian. Not so with us. Freemen by birth and consequently having the advantage of *thinking* and acting for ourselves so far as the Laws would allow us, we do not consider ourselves fit subject for the Contraband act.

We appeal to you, Sir, as the Executive of the Nation, to have us justly Dealt with. The Regt. do pray that they be assured their service will be fairly appreciated by paying them as American *Soldiers,* not as menial hirelings. Black men, you may well know are poor; three dollars per month for a year will supply their needy Wives and little ones with fuel. If you, as Chief Magistrate of the Nation, will assure us of our whole pay, we are content. Our Patriotism, our enthusiasm will have a new impetus, to exert our energy more and more to aid our Country. Not that our hearts ever flagged in Devotion, spite the evident apathy displayed in our behalf, but We feel as though our Country spurned us, now that we are sworn to serve her. Please give this a moment's attention.

[signed] James Henry Gooding.

[*On the Altar of Freedom: A Black Soldier's Civil War Letters From the Front— Corporal James Henry Gooding.* Edited by Virginia Matzke Adams. Amherst, University of Massachusetts Press. Copyright 1991 by University of Massachusetts Press, pp. 25–27, 29, 36–43, 118–120. Permission to print these and other passages included in the present volume granted by University of Massachusetts Press.]

Charlotte Forten had arrived in the South Carolina Sea Islands near the end of October, 1862. She visited the camp of the 54th Regiment not long after it arrived in South Carolina in June, 1863. She had known one of the regiment's offi-

cers before the war and met Colonel Shaw and other officers there in South Carolina. The news that the regiment had left on a combat mission made her apprehensive; she was shocked when she learned of the death of Colonel Shaw and the death or wounding of other members of the regiment at the battle of Fort Wagner. When the wounded returned after the battle, she served as a nurse in the local army hospital. Then, at the end of July, 1863, she returned to the North on a furlough because of her health.

Charlotte Forten:

Tuesday, June 30. [1863] . . .

This eve. Mrs. H.[unn], L.[izzie] and I rode with Col. [Quincy] G.[illmore] down to see the 54th Mass.[achusetts] which is encamped at Land's End. . . . It was very pleasant to see my old friend J.[ames] W.[alton]. He is a Lieut. in the 54th. But surely he is not strong enough to be a soldier. . . .

Thursday, July 2. Col. [Robert] Shaw and Major H.[allowell] came to take tea with us, and afterwards stayed to the shout. Lieut. W.[alton] was ill, and c'ld not come. I am perfectly charmed with Col. S.[haw]. He seems to me in every way one of the most delightful persons I have ever met. There is something girlish about him, and yet I never saw anyone more manly. To me he seems a thoroughly lovable person. And there is something so exquisite about him. The perfect breeding, how evident it is. Surely he must be a worthy son of such noble parents. I have seen him but once, yet I cannot help feeling a really affectionate admiration for him. We had a very pleasant talk on the moonlit piazza, and then to the Praise House to see the shout. I was delighted to find that it was one of the very best and most spirited that we had had. The Col. looked and listened with the deepest interest. And after it was over, expressed himself much gratified. He said, he w'ld like to have some of the hymns to send home. I shall be only too glad to copy them for him. . . .

Monday, July 6. . . . After school, though very tired, did not neglect my invitation to tea with the officers of the 54th. Drove down to Land's End with J.[ack], Mrs. H.[itchcock] and L.[izzie]. Met Col. [Quincy] G.[illmore] who went with us. Were just in time to see the Dress Parade. Tis a splendid looking regt. An honor to the race. Then we went with Col. Shaw to tea. Afterward sat outside the tent and listened to some very fine singing from some of the privates. Their voices blended beautifully. "Jubilo" is one of the best things I've heard lately. I am more than ever charmed with the noble little Col. [Shaw]. What purity[,] what nobleness of soul, what exquisite gentleness in that beautiful face! As I look at it I think "The bravest are the tenderest." I can imagine what he must be to his mother. May his life be spared to her! Yesterday at the celebration he stood, leaning against our carriage and speaking of mother, so lovingly, so tenderly. He said he wished she c'ld be there. If the regt. were going to be stationed there for some time he sh'ld send for her. "'But you know," he said "we might be suddenly ordered away, and then she w'ld have nobody to take care of her." I do think he is a wonderfully lovable person. Tonight, he helped me on my horse, and after carefully arranging the folds of my riding skirt, said, so kindly, "Good-bye. If I don't see you again down here I hope to see you at our house." But I hope I shall have the pleasure of seeing him many times even down here. He and his men are eager to be called into active service. . . .

Wednesday, July 8. . . . The regt. has gone. Left this morning. My heart-felt prayers go with them—for the men and for their noble, noble young Colonel [Shaw]. God bless him! God keep him in His care, and grant that his men may do nobly and prove themselves worthy of him!

Monday, July 20. For nearly two weeks we have waited, oh how anxiously for news of our regt. which went, we know[,] to Morris Is.[land] to take part in the attack on Charleston. To-night comes news oh, so sad, so heart sickening. It is too terrible, too terrible to write. We can only hope it may not all be true. That our noble, beautiful young Colonel [Shaw] is killed, and the regt. cut to pieces! I cannot, cannot believe it. And yet I know it may be so. But oh, I am stunned, sick at heart. I can scarcely write. There was an attack on Fort Wagner. The 54th put in advance; fought bravely, desperately, but was finally overpowered and driven back after getting into the Fort. Thank Heaven! they fought bravely! And oh, I still must hope that our colonel, *ours* especially he seems to me, is not killed, But I can write no more to-night.

Beaufort, July 21. Come to town to-day hearing that nurses were sadly needed. Went to Mrs. L.[ander]'s. Found Col. H.[igginson] and Dr. R.[ogers] there. Mrs. L.[ander] was sure I sh'ld not be able to endure the fatigues of hospital life even for a few days, but I thought differently, and the Col. and Dr. were both on my side. So at last Mrs. L[ander] consented and made arrangements for my entering one of the hospitals to-morrow. . . .

Wednesday, July 22. My hospital life began to-day. Went early this morning with Mrs. L.[ander] and Mrs. G[,] the surgeon's wife, saw that the Dr. had not finished dressing the wounds, and while I waited below Mrs. S[axton] gave me some sewing to do—mending the pantaloons and jackets of the poor fellows. (They are all of the 54th.) It was with a full heart that I sewed up bullet holes and bayonet cuts. Sometimes I found a jacket that told a sad tale—so torn to pieces that it was far past mending. After awhile I went through the wards. As I passed along I thought "Many and low are the pallets, but each is the face of a friend." And I was surprised to see such cheerful faces looking up from the beds. Talked a little with some of the patients and assisted Mrs. G. in distributing medicines. Mrs. L.[ander] kindly sent her carriage for me and I returned home, weary, but far more pleasantly impressed than I had thought possible, with hospital life.

Thursday, July 23. . . . Took a more thorough survey of the hospital to-day. It is a large new brick building—quite close to the water,—two-storied, many windowed, and very airy—in every way well adapted for a hospital. Yesterday I was employed part of the time in writing letters for the men. It was pleasant to see the brave, cheerful, uncomplaining spirit which they all breathed. Some of the poor fellows had come from the far west—even so far as Michigan. Talked with them much to-day. Told them that we had heard that their noble Colonel was not dead, but had been taken prisoner by the rebels. How joyfully their wan faces lighted up! They almost started from their couches as the hope entered their souls. Their attachment to their gallant young colonel is beautiful to see. How warmly, how enthusiastically they speak of him. "He was one of the best little men in the world," they said. "No one c'ld be kinder to a set of men than he was to us." Brave grateful hearts! I hope they will ever prove worthy of such a leader. And God grant that he may indeed be living. But I fear, I greatly fear it may be but a false report. One poor fellow here interests me greatly. He is very young, only nineteen, comes from Michigan. He is very badly wounded—in both legs, and there is a ball—in the stomach—it is thought that cannot be extracted. This poor fellow suffers terribly. His groans are pitiful to hear. But he utters no complaint, and it is touching to see his gratitude for the least kindness that one does him. Mrs. G. asked him if he w'ld like her to write to his home. But he said no. He was an only son, and had come away against his mother's will. He w'ld not have her written to until he was better. Poor fellow! that will never be in this world.

Another, a Sergeant, suffers great pain, being badly wounded in the leg. But he too lies perfectly patient and uncomplaining. He has such a good, honest face. It is pleasant to look at it—although it is black. He is said to be one of the best and bravest men in the regiment.

When I went in this morning and found my patients so cheerful some of them even quite merry, I tho't it c'ld not be possible that they were badly wounded. Many, indeed have only flesh wounds. But there are others— and they among the most uncomplaining—who are severely wounded;— some dangerously so. Brave fellows! I feel it a happiness, an honor, to do the slightest service for them. True they were unsuccessful in the attack of Fort Wagner. But that was no fault of theirs. It is the testimony of all that they fought bravely as men can fight, and that it was only when completely overwhelmed by superior numbers that they were driven back.

Friday, July 24. To-day the news of Col. Shaw's death is confirmed. There can no longer be any doubt. It makes me sad, sad at heart. They say he sprang from the parapet of the fort and cried "Onward, my brave boys, onward"; then fell, pierced with wounds. I know it was a glorious death. But oh, it is hard, very hard for the young wife, so late a bride, for the invalid mother, whose only and most dearly loved son he was,—that heroic mother who rejoiced in the position which he occupied as colonel of a colored regiment. My heart bleeds for her. His death is a very sad loss to us. I recall him as a much loved friend. Yet I saw him but a few times. Oh what must it be to the wife and the mother. Oh it is terrible. It seems very, very hard that the best and the noblest must be the earliest called away. Especially has it been so throughout this dreadful war.

Mr. P.[ierce] who has been unremitting in his attention to the wounded—called at our building to-day, and took me to the Officers Hospital, which is but a very short distance from here. It is in one of the finest residences in Beaufort, and is surrounded by beautiful grounds. Saw Major Hallowell, who, though badly wounded—in three places—is hoped to be slowly improving. A little more than a week ago I parted with him, after an exciting horseback ride, how strong, how well, how vigorous he was then! And now thoroughly prostrated! But he with all the other officers of the 54th, like the privates, are brave, patient—cheerful. With deep sadness he spoke of Col. Shaw and then told me something that greatly surprised me;—that the Col. before that fatal attack had told him that in case he fell he wished me to have one of his horses—He had three very fine spirited ones that he had brought from the North. (I afterward found this to be a mistake. He only wished me to take charge of the horses until [they] c'ld be sent North to his wife.—) How very, very kind it was! And to me, almost a perfect stranger. I shall treasure this gift most sacredly, all my life long. . . .

Sunday, July 26. Had a pleasant morning under the trees, near the water, while Dr. R[ogers] read Emerson to us. Then had a long talk with him, after which came to the very sudden determination to go North in the next steamer. It is necessary for my health, therefore, it is wiser to go. My strength has failed rapidly of late. Have become so weak that I fear I sh'ld be an easy prey to the fever which prevails here, a little later in this season. . . . I take my good Dr.'s advice, therefore, and shall go North on a furlough—to stay until the unhealthiest season is over.
[*Journal of Charlotte Forten*, pp. 490–499.]

The 54th Massachusetts Volunteer Infantry was the unit in which two of the three sons of Frederick Douglass enlisted in 1863. One of the two sons in the 54th, Lewis H. Douglass, took part in, and survived, the assault on Fort Wagner in July, 1863, just as did James Henry Gooding. Frederick Douglass himself visited Lincoln in the White House in August, 1863, and according to Douglass's account of his visit, Lincoln mentioned Fort Wagner in response to a comment by Douglass concerning protection of Union "colored soldiers and prisoners" in combat equal to that accorded to white soldiers and prisoners. Lincoln's remarks on the "equal protection" of black soldiers, as well as on the other topics discussed with Douglass, were described by Douglass in a sympathetic vein—unlike some of Douglass's earlier criticism of the President.

Our Work Is Not Done

Speech Delivered at the Annual Meeting of the American Anti-Slavery Society Held at Philadelphia, December 3–4, 1863

Ladies and Gentlemen: . . .

I have been down there to see the President; and as you were not there, perhaps you may like to know how the President of the United States received a black man at the White House. I will tell you how he received me—just as you have seen one gentlemen receive another [great applause]; with a hand and a voice well-balanced between a kind cordiality and a respectful reserve. I tell you I felt big there! [Laughter.] Let me tell you how I got to him; because everybody can't get to him. He has to be a little guarded in admitting spectators. The manner of getting to him gave me an idea that the cause was rolling on. The stairway was crowded with applicants. Some of them looked eager; and I have no doubt some of them had a purpose in being there, and wanted to see the President for the good of the country! They were white; and as I was the only dark spot among them, I expected to have to wait at least half a day; I had heard of men waiting a week; but in two minutes after I sent in my card, the messenger came out, and respectfully invited "Mr. Douglass" in. I could hear, in the eager multitude outside, as they saw me pressing and elbowing my way through, the remark, "Yes, damn it, I knew they would let the n—r through," in a kind of despairing voice—a Peace Democrat, I suppose. [Laughter.] When I went in, the President was sitting in his usual position, I was told, with his feet in different parts of the room, taking it easy. [Laughter.] Don't put this down, Mr. Reporter, I pray you; for I am going down there again to-morrow! [Laughter.] As I came in and approached him, the President began to rise, [laughter,] and he continued rising until he stood over me [laughter]; and, reaching out his hand, he said, "Mr. Douglass, I know you; I have read about you, and Mr. Seward has told me about you"; putting me quite at ease at once.

Now you will want to know how I was impressed by him. I will tell you that, too. He impressed me as being just what every one of you have been in the habit of calling him—an honest man. [Applause.] I never met with a man, who, on the first blush, impressed me more entirely with his sincerity, with his devotion to his country, and with his determination to save it at all hazards. [Applause.] He told me (I think he did me more honor than I deserve) that I had made a little speech, somewhere in New York, and it had got into the papers, and among the things I had said was this: That if I were called upon to state what I regarded as the most sad and most disheartening feature in our present political and military situation, it would not be the various disasters experienced by our armies and our navies, on flood and field, but it would be the tardy, hesitating, vacillating policy of the President of the United States; and the President said to me, "Mr. Douglass, I have been charged with being tardy, and the like"; and he went on, and partly admitted that he might seem slow; but he said, "I am charged with vacillating; but, Mr. Douglass, I do not think that charge can be sustained; I think it cannot be shown that when I have once taken a position, I have ever retreated from it." [Applause.] That I regarded as the most significant point in what he said during our interview. I told him that he had been somewhat slow in proclaiming equal protection to our colored soldiers and prisoners; and he said that the country needed talking up to that point. He hesitated in regard to it, when he felt that the country was not ready for it. He knew that the colored man throughout this country was a despised man, a hated man, and that if he at first came out with such a proclamation, all the hatred which is poured on the head of the Negro race would be visited on his administration. He said that there was preparatory work needed, and that the preparatory work had now been done. And he said, "Remember this, Mr. Douglass; remember that Milliken's Bend, Port Hudson and Fort Wagner are recent events; and that these were necessary to prepare the way for this very proclamation of mine." I thought it was reasonable, but came to the conclusion that while Abraham Lincoln will not go down to posterity as Abraham the Great, or as Abraham the Wise, or as Abraham the Eloquent, although he is all three, wise, great and eloquent, he will go down to posterity, if the country is saved, as Honest Abraham [applause]; and going down thus, his name may be written anywhere in this wide world of ours side by side with that of Washington, without disparaging the latter. [Renewed applause.]

Proceedings of the American Anti-Slavery Society at Its Third Decade, Held in the City of Philadelphia, December 3, 4, 1863, New York, 1864, pp. 110–118. [*Life and Writings of Frederick Douglass.* Vol. 3, pp. 378, 383–386.]

8. CONSCIENTIOUS OBJECTION TO THE WAR

In both the Union and the Confederacy, there were individuals who objected on grounds of conscience to the warmaking efforts of their respective governments. A number of these conscientious objectors were adherents to the Quaker faith, and one of the Quaker conscientious objectors from Vermont left a diary of his experiences, beginning when he was drafted into the Union army in July, 1863. That diary by Cyrus Pringle is the source of the following selection.

At Burlington, Vermont, on the 13th of the seventh month, 1863, I was drafted. . . .

I was to report on the 27th. Then loyal to our country, Wm. Lindley Dean and I appeared before the Provost Marshal with a statement of our cases. We were ordered for a hearing on the 29th. On the afternoon of that day W.L.D. was rejected upon examination of the Surgeon, but my case not coming up, he remained with me, much to my strength and comfort. . . . By his encouragement much was my mind strengthened; my desires for a pure life, and my resolutions for good. In him and those of whom he spoke I saw the abstract beauty of Quakerism. On the next morning came Joshua M. Dean to support me and plead my case before the Board of Enrollment. On the day after, the 31st, I came before the Board. Respectfully those men listened to the exposition of our principles; and, on our representing that we looked for some relief from the President, the marshal released me for twenty days. Meanwhile appeared Lindley M. Macomber and was likewise, by the kindness of the marshal, though they had received instructions from the Provost Marshal General to show such claims no partiality, released to appear on the 20th day of the eighth month.

All these days we were urged by our acquaintances to pay our commutation money; by some through well-meant kindness and sympathy; by others through interest in the war; and by others still through a belief they entertained it was our duty. But we confess a higher duty than that to country; and, asking no military protection of our Government and grateful for none, deny any obligation to support so unlawful a system, as we hold a war to be even when waged in opposition to an evil and oppressive power and ostensibly in defense of liberty, virtue, and free institutions. . . . Appearing finally before the marshal on the 24th, suits and uniforms were selected for us, and we were called upon to give receipts for them. L.M.M. was on his guard, and being first called upon, declared he could not do so, as that would imply acceptance. Failing to come to any agreement, the matter was postponed till next morning, when we certified to the fact that the articles were "with us." Here I must make record of the kindness of the marshal, Rolla Gleason, who treated us with respect and kindness. He had spoken with respect of our Society, had given me furloughs to the amount of twenty-four days, when the marshal at Rutland considered himself restricted by his oath and duty to six days, and here appeared in person to prevent any harsh treatment of us by his sergeants, and though much against his inclinations, assisted in putting on the uniform with his own hands. We bade him farewell with grateful feelings and expressions of fear that we should not fall into as tender hands again; and amid the rain in the early morning, as the town clock tolled the hour of seven, we were driven amongst the flock that was going forth to the slaughter, down the street and into the cars for Brattleboro. . . .

Herded into a car by ourselves, we conscripts, substitutes, and the rest, through the greater part of the day, swept over the fertile meadows along the banks of the White River and the Connecticut, through pleasant scenes that had little of delight for us. At Woodstock we were joined by the conscripts from the 1st District—altogether an inferior company from those before with us, who were honest yeomen from the northern and mountainous towns, while these were many of them substitutes from the cities.

At Brattleboro we were marched up to the camp. . . .

Brattleboro, 26th 8th Month, 1863—. . . .

L.M.M. and I addressed the following letter to Governor Holbrook and hired a corporal to forward it to him.

Brattleboro, Vt, 26th, 8th month, 1863

Frederick Holbrook,

Governor of Vermont:—

We, the undersigned members of the Society of Friends, beg leave to represent to thee, that we were lately drafted in the 3rd Dist. of Vermont, have been forced into the army and reached the camp near this town yesterday.

That in the language of the elders of our New York Yearly Meeting, "We love our country and acknowledge with gratitude to our Heavenly Father the many blessings we have been favoured with under the government; and can feel no sympathy with any who seek its overthrow."

But that, true to well-known principles of our Society, we cannot violate our religious convictions either by complying with military requisitions or by the equivalents of this compliance—the furnishing of a substitute or payment of commutation money. That, therefore, we are brought into suffering and exposed to insult and contempt from those who have us in charge, as well as to the penalties of insubordination, though liberty of conscience is granted us by the Constitution of Vermont as well as that of the United States.

Therefore, we beg of thee as Governor of our State any assistance thou may be able to render, should it be no more than the influence of thy position interceding in our behalf.

Truly Thy Friend,

Cyrus G. Pringle.

P.S.—We are informed we are to be sent to the vicinity of Boston tomorrow.

27th—On board train to Boston. The long afternoon of yesterday passed slowly away. This morning passed by, the time of our stay in Brattleboro, and we neither saw nor heard anything of our Governor. We suppose he could not or would not help us. . . .

Camp Vermont: Long Island, Boston Harbor. 28th—In the early morning damp and cool we marched down off the heights of Brattleboro to take train for this place. Once in the car the dashing young cavalry officer, who had us in charge, gave notice he had placed men through the cars, with loaded revolvers, who had orders to shoot any person attempting to escape, or jump from the window, and that any one would be shot if he even put his head out of the window. . . . we came into the City of Boston, "the Hub of the Universe." Out through street after street we were marched double guarded to the wharves, where we took a small steamer for the island some six miles out in the harbor. . . .

Here on this dry and pleasant island in the midst of the beautiful Massachusetts Bay, we have the liberty of the camp, the privilege of air and sunshine, and hay beds to sleep upon. So we went to bed last night with somewhat of gladness elevating our depressed spirits. . . .

This is one gratification: the men with us give us their sympathy. They seem to look upon us tenderly and pitifully, and their expressions of kind wishes are warm. Although we are relieved from duty and from drill, and may lie in our tents during rain and at night, we have heard of no complaint. . . . Yesterday L.M.M. and I appeared before the Captain commanding this camp with a statement of our cases. He listened to us respectfully and promised to refer us to the General commanding here, General Devens; and in the meantime released us from duty. . . .

In Guard House. 31st—Yesterday morning L.M.M. and I were called upon to do fatigue duty. The day before we were asked to do some cleaning about camp and to bring water. We wished to be obliging, to appear willing to bear a hand toward that which would promote our own and our fellows' health and convenience; but as we worked we did not feel easy. Suspecting we had been assigned to such work, the more we discussed in our minds the subject, the more clearly the right way seemed open to us; and we separately came to the judgment that we must not conform to this requirement. So when the sergeant bade us "Police the streets," we asked him if he had received instructions with regard to us, and he replied we had been assigned to "Fatigue Duty." L.M.M. answered him that we could not obey. He left us immediately for the Major (Jarvis of Weathersfield, Vt.). He came back and ordered us to the Major's tent. The latter met us outside and inquired concerning the complaint he had heard of us. Upon our statement of our position, he apparently undertook to argue our whimsies, as he probably looked upon our principles, out of our heads. We replied to his points as we had ability; but he soon turned to bullying us rather than arguing with us, and would hardly let us proceed with a whole sentence. "I make some pretension to religion myself," he said; and quoted the Old Testament freely in support of war. Our terms were, submission or the guardhouse. We replied we could not obey. . . .

The subjects of all misdemeanors, grave and small, are here [in the guardhouse] confined. Those who have deserted or attempted it; those who have insulted officers and those guilty of theft, fighting, drunkenness, etc. In *most*, as in the camps, there are traces yet of manhood and of the Divine Spark, but some are abandoned, dissolute. There are many here among the substitutes who were actors in the late New York riots. They show unmistakably the characteristics and sentiments of those rioters, and especially, hatred to the blacks drafted and about camp, and exhibit this in foul and profane jeers heaped upon these unoffending men at every opportunity. In justice to the blacks I must say they are superior to the whites in all their behavior. . . .

3rd—A Massachusetts major, the officer of the day, in his inspection of the guard-house came into our room to-day. We were lying on the floor engaged in reading and writing. He was apparently surprised at this and inquired the name of our books; and finding the Bible and Thomas á Kempis's *Imitation of Christ*, observed that they were good books. I cannot say if he knew we were Friends, but he asked us why we were in here.

Like all officers he proceeded to reason with us, and to advise us to serve, presenting no comfort if we still persisted in our course. . . .

At the Hospital. *7th*—Yesterday morning came to us Major Gould again, informing us that he had come to take us out of that dirty place, as he could not see such respectable men lying there, and was going to take us up to the hospital. We assured him we could not serve there, and asked him if he would not bring us back when we had there declared our purpose. He would not reply directly, but brought us here and left us. When the surgeon knew our determination, he was for haling us back at once; what he wanted, he said, was willing men. We sat on the sward without the hospital tents till nearly noon for some one to take us back; when we were ordered to move into the tents and quarters assigned us in the mess-room. The Major must have interposed, demonstrating his kindness by his resolution that we should occupy and enjoy the pleasanter quarters of the hospital, certainly if serving, but none the less so if we declined. Later in the day L.M.M. and P.D. were sitting without, when he passed them and, laughing heartily, declared they were the strangest prisoners of war he ever saw. He stopped some time to talk with them and when they came in they declared him a kind and honest man. . . .

13th—Last night we received a letter from Henry Dickinson, stating that the President, though sympathizing with those in our situation, felt bound by the Conscription Act, and felt liberty in view of his oath to execute the laws, to do no more than detail us from active service to hospital duty, or to the charge of the colored refugees. For more than a week have we lain here, refusing to engage in hospital service; shall we retrace the steps of the past week? Or shall we go South as overseers of the blacks on the confiscated estates of the rebels, to act under military commanders and to report to such? What would become of our testimony and our determination to preserve ourselves clear of the guilt of this war?
P.S. We have written back to Henry Dickinson that we cannot purchase life at cost of peace of soul. . . .

16th—Yesterday a son-in-law of N.B. of Lynn came to see us. He was going to get passes for one or two of the Lynn Friends, that they might come over to see us today. He informed us that the sentiment of the

Friends hereabouts was that we might enter the hospital without compromising our principles; and he produced a letter from W.W. to S.B. to the same effect. W.W. expressed his opinion that we might do so without doing it in lieu of other service. How can we evade a fact? Does not the government both demand and accept it as in lieu of other service? Oh, the cruelest blow of all comes from our friends.

17th—Although this trial was brought upon us by our friends, their intentions were well meant. Their regard for our personal welfare and safety too much absorbs the zeal they should possess for the maintenance of the principles of the peaceableness of our Master's kingdom. . . .

Regimental Hospital, 4th Vermont [Near Culpeper, Virginia]. *29th*—On the evening of the 26th the Colonel came to us apologizing for the roughness with which he treated us at first, which was, as he insisted, through ignorance of our real character and position. He told us if we persisted in our course, death would probably follow; though at another time he confessed to P.D. that this would only be the extreme sentence of court-martial.

He urged us to go into the hospital, stating that this course was advised by Friends about New York. We were too well aware of such a fact to make any denial, though it was a subject of surprise to us that he should be informed of it. He pleaded with us long and earnestly, urging us with many promises of indulgence and favor and attentions we found afterwards to be untrue. He gave us till the next morning to consider the question and report our decision. In our discussion of the subject among ourselves, we were very much perplexed. If all his statements concerning the ground taken by our Society were true, we seemed to be liable, if we persisted in the course which alone seemed to us to be in accordance with Truth, to be exposed to the charge of over-zeal and fanaticism even among our own brethren. Regarding the work to be done in hospital as one of mercy and benevolence, we asked if we had any right to refuse its performance; and questioned whether we could do more good by endeavoring to bear to the end a clear testimony against war, than by laboring by word and deed among the needy in the hospitals and camps. We saw around us a rich field for usefulness in which there were scarce any laborers, and toward whose work our hands had often started involuntarily and unbidden. At last we consented to a trial, at least till we could make inquiries concerning the Colonel's allegations, and ask the counsel of our friends, reserving the privilege of returning to our former position.

At first a great load seemed rolled away from us; we rejoiced in the prospect of life again. But soon there prevailed a feeling of condemnation, as though we had sold our Master. And that first day was one of the bitterest I ever experienced. It was a time of stern conflict of soul. . . . L.M.M. wishing to make a fair, honest trial, we were brought here—P.D. being already here unwell. We feel we are erring; but scarce anything is required of us and we wait to hear from Friends.

Of these days of going down into sin, I wish to make little mention. I would that my record of such degradation be brief. . . .

It is with pleasure I record we have just waited upon the Colonel with an explanation of our distress of mind, requesting him to proceed with court-martial. We were kindly and tenderly received. "If you want a trial I can give it to you," he answered. . . .

When lately I have seen dear L.M.M. in the thoroughness and patience of his trial to perform service in hospital, his uneasiness and the intensity of his struggle. . . and seen him fail and declare to us, "I cannot stay here," I have received a new proof, and to me a strong one, because it is from the experimental knowledge of an honest man, that no Friend, who is really such, desiring to keep himself clear of complicity with this system of war and to bear a perfect testimony against it, can lawfully perform service in the hospitals of the Army in lieu of bearing arms. . . .

At Washington. 6th [10th month]—At first, after being informed of our declining to serve in his hospital, Colonel Foster did not appear altered in his kind regard for us. But his spleen soon became evident. At the time we asked for a trial by court-martial, and it was his duty to place us under arrest and proceed with the preferring of his charges against us. For a while he seemed to hesitate and consult his inferior officers, and among them his Chaplain. The result of the conference was our being ordered into our companies, that, separated, and with the force of the officers of a company bearing upon us, we might the more likely be subdued. Yet the Colonel assured L.M.M., interceding in my behalf, when the lieutenant commanding my company threatened force upon me, that he should not allow any personal injury. When we marched next day I was compelled to bear a gun and equipments. My associates were more fortunate, for, being asked if they would carry their guns, declined and saw no more trouble from them. The captain of the company in which P.D. was placed told him he did not believe he was ugly about it, and that he could only put him under arrest and prefer charges against him. He accordingly was taken under guard, where he lay till we left for here.

The next morning the men were busy in burnishing their arms. When I looked toward the one I had borne, yellow with rust, I trembled in the weakness of the flesh at the trial I felt impending over me. Before the Colonel was up I knocked at his tent, but was told he was asleep, though, through the opening, I saw him lying gazing at me. Although I felt I should gain no relief from him, I applied again soon after. He admitted me and, lying on his bed, inquired with cold heartlessness what I wanted. I stated to him, that I could never consent to serve, and, being under the war-power, was resigned to suffer instead all the just penalties of the law. I begged of him release from the attempts by violence to compel my obedience and service, and a trial, though likely to be made by those having no sympathy with me, yet probably in a manner conformable to law.

He replied that he had shown us all the favor he should; that he had, now, turned us over to the military power and was going to let that take its course; that is, henceforth we were to be at the mercy of the inferior officers, without appeal to law, justice, or mercy. He said he had placed us in a pleasant position, against which we could have no reasonable objection, and that we had failed to perform our agreement. He wished to deny that our consent was only temporary and conditional. He declared, furthermore, his belief, that a man who would not fight for his country did not deserve to live. I was glad to withdraw from his presence as soon as I could.

I went back to my tent and lay down for a season of retirement endeavoring to gain resignation to any event. I dreaded torture and desired strength of flesh and spirit. My trial soon came. The lieutenant called me out, and pointing to the gun that lay near by, asked if I was going to clean it. I replied to him, that I could not comply with military requisitions, and felt resigned to the consequences. "I do not ask about your feelings; I want to know if you are going to clean that gun?" "I cannot do it," was my answer. He went away, saying, "Very well," and I crawled into the tent again. Two sergeants soon called for me, and taking me a little aside, bid me lie down on my back, and stretching my limbs apart tied cords to my wrists and ankles and these to four stakes driven in the ground somewhat in the form of an X.

I was very quiet in my mind as I lay there on the ground [soaked] with the rain of the previous day, exposed to the heat of the sun and suffering keenly from the cords binding my wrists and straining my muscles. And, if I dared the presumption, I should say that I caught a glimpse of heavenly pity. I wept, not so much from my own suffering as from sorrow that such things should be in our own country, where Justice and Freedom and Liberty of Conscience have been the annual boast of Fourth-of-July orators so many years. It seemed that our fore-fathers in the faith had wrought and suffered in vain, when the privileges they so dearly bought were so soon set aside. And I was sad, that one endeavoring to follow our dear Master should be so generally regarded as a despicable and stubborn culprit.

After something like an hour had passed, the lieutenant came with his orderly to ask me if I was ready to clean the gun. I replied to the orderly asking the question, that it could but give me pain to be asked or required to do anything I believed wrong. He repeated it to the lieutenant just behind him, who advanced and addressed me. I was favored to improve the opportunity to say to him a few things I wished. He said little; and, when I had finished, he withdrew from the others who had gathered around. About the end of another hour his orderly came and released me.

I arose and sat on the ground. I did not rise to go away. I had not where to go, nothing to do. As I sat there my heart swelled from joy from above. The consolation and sweet fruit of tribulation patiently endured.

But I also grieved, that the world was so far gone astray, so cruel and blind. It seemed as if the gospel of Christ had never been preached upon earth, and the beautiful example of his life had been utterly lost sight of.

Some of the men came about me, advising me to yield, and among them one of those who had tied me down, telling me what I had already suffered was nothing to what I must yet suffer unless I yielded; that human flesh could not endure what would be put upon me. I wondered if it could be that they could force me to obedience by torture, and examined myself closely to see if they had advanced as yet one step toward the accomplishment of their purposes. Though weaker in body, I believed I found myself, through divine strength, as firm in my resolution to maintain my allegiance to my Master.

The relaxation of my nerves and muscles after having been so tensely strained left me that afternoon so weak that I could hardly walk or perform any mental exertion.

I had not yet eaten the mean and scanty breakfast I had prepared, when I was ordered to pack up my things and report myself at the lieutenant's tent. I was accustomed to such orders and complied, little moved.

The lieutenant received me politely with, "Good morning, Mr. Pringle," and desiring me to be seated, proceeded with the writing with which he was engaged. I sat down in some wonderment and sought to be quiet and prepared for any event.

"You are ordered to report to Washington," said he; "I do not know what it is for." I assured him that neither did I know. We were gathered before the Major's tent for preparation for departure. The regimental officers were there manifesting surprise and chagrin; for they could not but show both, as they looked upon us, whom the day before they were threatening to crush into submission, and attempting also to execute their threats that morning, standing out of their power and under orders from one superior to their Major Commanding E.M. As the bird uncaged, so were our hearts that morning. Short and uncertain at first were the flights of Hope. As the slave many times before us, leaving his yoke behind him, turned from the plantations of Virginia and set his face toward the far North, so we from out a grasp as close and as abundant in suffering and severity, and from without the line of bayonets that had so many weeks surrounded us, turned our backs upon the camp of the 4th Vermont and took our way over the turnpike that ran through the tented fields of Culpeper.

At the War Office we were soon admitted to an audience with the Adjutant General, Colonel Townsend, whom we found to be a very fine man, mild and kind. He referred our cases to the Secretary of War, Stanton, by whom we were ordered to report for service to Surgeon General Hammond. Here we met Isaac Newton, Commissioner of Agriculture, waiting for our arrival, and James Austin of Nantucket, expecting his son, Charles L. Austin, and Edward W. Holway of Sandwich, Mass., conscripted Friends like ourselves, and ordered here from the 22nd Massachusetts.

We understand it is through the influence of Isaac Newton that Friends have been able to approach the heads of Government in our behalf and to prevail with them to so great an extent. He explained to us the circumstance in which we are placed. That the Secretary of War and President sympathized with Friends in their present suffering, and would grant them full release, but that they felt themselves bound by their oaths that they would execute the laws, to carry out to its full extent the Conscription Act. That there appeared but one door of relief open—that was to parole us and allow us to go home, but subject to their call again ostensibly, though this they neither wished nor proposed to do. That the fact of Friends in the Army and refusing service had attracted public attention so that it was not expedient to parole us at present. That, therefore, we were to be sent to one of the hospitals for a short time, where it was hoped and expressly requested that we would consent to remain quiet and acquiesce, if possible in whatever might be required of us. That our work there would be quite free from objection, being for the direct relief of the sick; and that there we would release none for active service in the field, as the nurses were hired civilians.

These requirements being so much less objectionable than we had feared, we felt relief, and consented to them. I.N. went with us himself to the Surgeon General's office, where he procured peculiar favours for us; that we should be sent to a hospital in the city, where he could see us often; and that orders should be given that nothing should interfere with our comfort, or our enjoyment of our consciences.

Thence we were sent to Medical Purveyor Abbott, who assigned us to the best hospital in the city, the Douglas Hospital.

The next day after our coming here I.N. and James Austin came to add to our number E.W.H. and C.L.A., so now there are five of us instead of three. We are pleasantly situated in a room by ourselves in the upper or fourth story, and are enjoying our advantages of good quarters and tolerable food as no one can except he has been deprived of them.

8th—Today we have a pass to go out to see the city.

9th—We all went, thinking to do the whole city in a day, but before the time of our passes expired, we were glad to drag ourselves back to the rest and quiet of D.H. During the day we called upon our friend I.N. in the Patent Office. When he came to see us on the 7th, he stated he had called upon the President that afternoon to request him to release us and let us go home to our friends. The President promised to consider it over-night. Accordingly yesterday morning, as I.N. told us, he waited upon him again. He found there a woman in the greatest distress. Her son, only a boy of fifteen years and four months, having been enticed into the Army, had deserted and been sentenced to be shot the next day. As the clerks were telling her, the President was in the War Office and could not be seen, nor did they think he could attend to her case that day. I.N. found her almost wild with grief. "Do not despair, my good woman," said he, "I guess the President can be seen after a bit." He soon presented her case to the President, who exclaimed at once, "That must not be, I must look into that case, before they shoot that boy"; and telegraphed at once to have the order suspended.

I.N. judged it was not a fit time to urge our case. We feel we can afford to wait, that a life may be saved. But we long for release. We do not feel easy to remain here. . . .

13th—L.M.M. had quite an adventure yesterday. He being fireman with another was in the furnace room among three or four others, when the officer of the day, one of the surgeons, passed around on inspection. "Stand up," he ordered them, wishing to be saluted. The others arose; but by no means L. The order was repeated for his benefit, but he sat with his cap on, telling the surgeon he had supposed he was excused from such things as he was one of the Friends. Thereat the officer flew at him, exclaiming, he would take the Quaker out of him. He snatched off his cap and seizing him by the collar tried to raise him to his feet; but finding his strength insufficient and that L. was not to be frightened, he changed his purpose in his wrath and calling for the corporal of the guard had him taken to the guard-house. This was about eleven A.M. and he lay there till about six P.M., when the surgeon in charge, arriving home and hearing of it, ordered the officer of the day to go and take him out, telling him never to put another man into the guard-house while he was in charge here without consulting him. The manner of his release was very satisfactory to us, and we waited for this rather than effect it by our own efforts. We are all getting uneasy about remaining here, and if our release do not come soon, we feel we must intercede with the authorities, even if the alternative be imprisonment.

The privations I have endured since leaving home, the great tax upon my nervous strength, and my mind as well, since I have had charge of our extensive correspondence, are beginning to tell upon my health and I long for rest.

20th—We begin to feel we shall have to decline service as heretofore, unless our position is changed. I shall not say but we submit too much in not declining at once, but it has seemed most prudent at least to make suit with Government rather than provoke the hostility of their subalterns. We were ordered here with little understanding of the true state of things as they really exist here; and were advised by Friends to come and make no objections, being assured it was but for a very brief time and only a matter of form. It might not have been wrong; but as we find we do too much fill the places of soldiers (L.M.M.'s fellow fireman has just left for the field, and I am to take his place, for instance), and are clearly doing military service, we are continually oppressed by a sense of guilt, that makes our struggles earnest.

21st—I.N. has not called yet; our situation is becoming intolerable. I query if patience is justified under the circumstances. My distress of mind may be enhanced by my feeble condition of health, for today I am confined to my bed, almost too weak to get downstairs. This is owing to exposure after being heated over the furnaces.

26th—Though a week has gone by, and my cold has left me, I find I am no better, and that I am reduced very low in strength and flesh by the sickness and pain I am experiencing. Yet I still persist in going below once a day. The food I am able to get is not such as is proper.

5th, 11th month—I spend most of my time on my bed, much of it alone. And very precious to me is the nearness I am favored to attain unto the Master. Notwithstanding my situation and state, I am happy in the enjoyment of His consolations. Lately my confidence has been strong, and I think I begin to feel that our patience is soon to be rewarded with relief; insomuch that a little while ago, when dear P.D. was almost overcome with sorrow, I felt bold to comfort him with the assurance of my belief, that it would not be long so. My mind is too weak to allow of my reading much; and, though I enjoy the company of my companions a part of the time, especially in the evening, I am much alone; which affords me abundant time for meditation and waiting upon God. The fruits of this are sweet, and a recompense for affliction.

6th—Last evening E.W.H. saw I.N. particularly on my behalf, I suppose. He left at once for the President. This morning he called to inform us of his interview at the White House. The President was moved to sympathy in my behalf, when I.N. gave him a letter from one of our Friends in New York. After its perusal he exclaimed to our friend, "I want you to go and tell Stanton that it is my wish all those young men be sent home at once." He was on his way to the Secretary this morning as he called.

Later—I.N. has just called again informing us in joy that we are free. At the War Office he was urging the Secretary to consent to our paroles, when the President entered. "It is my urgent wish," said he. The Secretary yielded; the order was given, and we were released. What we had waited for so many weeks was accomplished in a few moments by a Providential ordering of circumstances.

7th—I.N. came again last evening bringing our paroles. The preliminary arrangements are being made, and we are to start this afternoon for New York.

Note. Rising from my sick-bed to undertake this journey, which lasted through the night, its fatigues overcame me, and upon my arrival in New York I was seized with delirium from which I only recovered after many weeks, through the mercy and favor of Him, who in all this trial had been our guide and strength and comfort.

[*The Civil War Diary of Cyrus Pringle*, Pendle Hill Pamphlet 122, Wallingford, Pennsylvania, 1962, pp. 7–16, 18, 20–22, 27–39.]

9. UNION MILITARY VICTORY IN EAST TENNESSEE, NOVEMBER, 1863

One of the major military developments during the autumn of 1863 was the Union success in driving the Confederate forces from eastern Tennessee back into Georgia. Just as the capture of Vicksburg (July 4, 1863) signaled the isolation of the western third of the Confederacy, so the Union victory at Missionary Ridge, Chattanooga (November 23 to 25, 1863) and the subsequent retreat of General Bragg's Confederate army south into Georgia meant that the Confederate forces in the west were now restricted to the area south of the state of Tennessee.

John Cotton's cavalry unit was part of General Bragg's army, and the correspondence between John and Mariah Cotton reflected the defeat and retreat of that army. Mariah wrote John in mid-July, 1863, of her hope that the war would "com to a close." John's reply from Tennessee in August expressed his fear of defeat unless the military situation changed. By November, John wrote from Georgia, noting that "Braggs armey is falling back from chattanooga" into Georgia. When John wrote in December, he told his wife that most of the Confederate soldiers thought that the Confederate army would retreat to Atlanta. "I am worse out of hart about whipping the yankeys" he added, "than I have every been."

Mariah Cotton:

Alabama Coosa County July the 16 1863

Dear beloved husband it is again I seat my selft to try to rite you a few lines to let you no the children is all well at this time and I hope thes few lins may find you well and doing well I hant much of inportent to rite to you but I thought I wood rite for I expect it will bee som sadfaction to you to here from home if it was only to here we was well I wish I cood here from you every day I wish I node wher you was to day and node you was well but I dont no wher you you are nor what you are a doing you may in a battle now while I am ritin you this letter if I node wher you was in a battle I dont thing I cood set still to rite nor do any thing else but I hope the lorde willbee on your side and gide you saft threw all you trouble and enable you to reach home saft won time mor I hope that happy day will soon com when you can com to see me and you little children I hope the war will con com to a close and you can com home to me to stay it wood bee a day of joy to see you a com home saft again I think if peace was made it wood be the joyfullest times that ever has ben in wood bee to me if you was to come saft. . . . I re main you true loving wife till death Mariah Cotton to her dear beloved husband in the war good by my dear husband.

John Cotton:

Tennessee Camps near Concord August 7th 1863

Dear beloved wife it is again that I take my pen in hand to let you no that I got back to camps again I got here yesterday I got here without any trouble. . . . some of our men went to kentucky and some of them has got back and some hant they got into a battle and got cut all to pieces and some killed and some wounded and some taken prisoners but it is not noun how many they are coming in yet it is thought that 4 or 5 of our company is killed but there cant bee no correct account given about it yet I found our boys very much dishardened and whiped there is a heap of them ready to give it up I am awfully afraid if a change dont take place soon for the better that we will be whipped I cant rite much now for my mind is bothered and the ink I have got to rite with ant no account at all when I get somethin I can rite with I will rite more. . . . I remain your true devoted husband

John W. Cotton. . . .

Georgia Camps near dalton November the 29. 1863

Dear beloved wife I again take my pen in hand to rite you a few lines to try to rite you a few lines to try to let you no that I am well and hope these few lines may find you all enjoying the same blessing I hant rote to you in more than a weak we have been riding almost day and nite for 8 days we have been riding up and down tennessee river the most of the time trying to keep the yankeys from crossing but they crossed anyhow we went to east tennessee and they crossed at the mouth of chicamauga and we was ordered back and we found them at cleavlen day before yesterday morning and we had a fite with them that lasted about two hours. . . . I would rite more but I hant got the time now Braggs armey is falling back from chatta nooga again they are at dalton the most of them I dont no where he will make another stand nothing more I will rite again soon

John W Cotton. . . .

Georgia Camps 7 miles above dalton December 14th 1863

Dear beloved wife I again take my pen in hand to try to rite you a few lines to try to let you no that I am well and hope these few lines may find you all well and doing well I hant got but very little to rite to you we are here and have been 3 days but I dont think we will stay here long our army is still folling back and the yankeys are advancing slowly I dont no where we will make a stand at the most of our men thinks we will fall back to atlanta georgia I think our cavalry is only staying here to til the infantry gets out of the way Mariah I am sorry to say to you that I am worse out of hart about whipping the yankeys than I have every been there is lots of our men says there is no use to fite them any more they say that bowth congresses has met and I hope they will make peace on some sort of terms of peace so we can come home and live as we have done before it ant worth while to try to tell how bad I want to come home I am afraid from what you rote in your last letter that you and little geney is borth sick I would love to here that you were all well one time more I want you to take good care your self and the children and I will come home as soon as I can. . . . I remain your true devoted husband till death

John W Cotton

[*Yours Till Death*, pp. 76–78, 96–98.]

After the defeat of the Confederate forces commanded by General Bragg in east Tennessee late in November, 1863, Mary Chesnut had begun to expect bad news about the war effort. Most Confederates had not given up hope of victory, but Mary Chesnut's comment, like the words of John Cotton, symbolizes the change in expectations as the tide of battle had turned by the end of the year 1863.

November 28, 1863. Richmond. . . . Bragg defeated and separated from Longstreet. It is a long street that knows no turning. And [Union General] Rosecrans not taken, after all!

One begins the day with "What bad news next, I wonder?"
[*Mary Chesnut's Civil War*, p. 494.]

CHAPTER III

"This Wild Adventurous Work of Crushing the Southern Cause"—The Period Marked by Union Victories and Confederate Defeats, January, 1864–April, 1865

> *"This wild adventurous work of crushing the Southern Cause"*
> —SAMUEL CORMANY, APRIL 6, 1865

10. UNION MILITARY OFFENSIVES, FEBRUARY–AUGUST, 1864

In Florida: February, 1864

The changed military complexion of the war by January, 1864, led to expectations in the Union states that their armed forces would take the offensive in all theaters of military operations. James Gooding of the 54th Massachusetts Volunteer Regiment and Marcus Spiegel of the 120th Ohio Regiment were both participants in the Union military offensives of early 1864, with tragic consequences in each case.

President Lincoln in January, 1864, directed that steps be taken "to reconstruct a loyal State government in Florida." To carry out that directive, some 7,000 troops were sent by boat in February, 1864, from the Sea Islands to Jacksonville, Florida. Among those troops was the 54th Massachusetts Regiment, including James Gooding, now a corporal in rank. Letters from Gooding to the New Bedford Mercury *described the landing of the 54th in Jacksonville under small arms fire.*

[*Mercury,* February 22, 1864]

Jacksonville, Fla., Feb. 8, 1864

Messrs. Editors: . . . Yesterday afternoon the "Lincoln Gunboats" brought up before Jacksonville, so as to feel the way, before transports

149

ventured up. At last the gunboats signalized that the way was clear, and the imposing fleet of steamers and vessels of all classes and sizes moved majestically up the St. John's river. As we neared the town, say within three or four miles, the people along either bank of the river saluted the fleet by the waving of hats and handkerchiefs and other demonstrations of evident satisfaction. But as the long file of steamers swept by the town, preparing to near the docks, the women and children flocked to the wharves, or looked out of the windows, with a seemingly sullen silence— no waving of handkerchiefs greeted the old flag as it proudly floated from the peak of each vessel. It may be fairly presumed that the people of Jacksonville remember the heartless burning of their homes on a previous occupation by the Union forces. But Gen. Seymour is not the commander to tolerate the repetition of any such savagery.

To resume; the flag steamer Mapleleaf had touched the dock, and some of the crew landed to make her fast, while the steamer "Gen. Hunter" about the same time touched another dock, when a volley of musketry was poured into the latter, wounding one of her mates, and one soldier, a member of the 54th Massachusetts regiment. The excitement on board the Hunter was at once intense—every man began to load without orders and rushed for the gangways to get on shore—and almost before those in command could give the necessary orders, the men were rushing pell-mell up through the streets, to catch, if possible, the cowardly crew who had fired on an unarmed transport. Major Appleton soon got off, with two companies, A and D, Capt. Grace in command of A, and Lieut. Durand, of D, who moved at double-quick through the town till they came to the woods, when they deployed as skirmishers. The rebels retreated however, faster than our men could pursue, as the roads were obstructed by felled trees making a successful pursuit impossible. The detachment from the 54th captured 13 prisoners, and those from the 1st Mass. cavalry 5, with a horse, cart and a little booty, about three miles from the town. Seven companies of the former regiment were posted as advanced pickets, supported by a detachment of mounted rifles from the 40th Mass.

We are now encamped half a mile from the town, with the 47th and 48th New York, and the 8th U.S., waiting for the artillery to debark before proceeding on the march into the interior.

The faces of the ladies in Jacksonville indicated a sort of Parisian disgust as the well-appointed Union army, composed in part of Lincoln's "niggers," filed through the streets. I am happy to say, that the 54th behaved in the most exemplary manner—not a low jest was indulged as they passed through the streets, in most cases lined with women. A respectful silence was maintained by the men, some of whom have experienced the misfortune of being black by the treatment they have received from those now in rebellion. To-day those, who at first greeted us with frowns, are treating us with respect and courtesy; in fact more than we should expect to receive in some parts of the free North. And that respect is not due to the presence of an overwhelming army—lasting only so long as cannon are ranged on their homes—but respect paid to men who by their deportment show that they are christianized, if not very refined.

10th—Our forces were in motion at 12 M., of the 8th, following the railway, and at 7 P.M., captured a rebel battery of five pieces, the rebels skedaddling, and the 4[0]th Mass. in hot pursuit. The vanguard rushed into a rebel camp last night and captured a whole company under command of a lieutenant. The prisoners were brought down to Jacksonville this afternoon in two cars drawn by mules, as the engines on the road have been purposely damaged to prevent our using them. At last accounts, the right of our column was beyond Pilatka, having met with no strenuous opposition as yet.

[The letter above was the last from James Gooding to the *Mercury*. The next letter came from an officer in the 54th.]

[*Mercury*, March 9, 1864]
Jacksonville, Fla., Feb. 25, 1864
Messrs. Editors:—I am pained to inform you that Corporal James H. Gooding was killed in battle on the 20th inst. at Olustee Station. He was one of the Color Corporals and was with the colors at the time. So great was the rout of our troops that we left nearly all our dead and wounded on the field. The fight lasted four hours. We were badly beaten that night, and the next day we kept falling back, until we reached Jacksonville. The fifty-fourth did honor to themselves and our city. All concede that no regiment fought like it. . . .

The regiment is pleased to learn that the bill to pay them $13 per month passed.

The total loss of the regiment, I am unable to give you at this time. All we want now is more troops; with them we would go forward again and drive the rebels from the State.

Your friend/James W. Grace/Captain Fifty-Fourth Regiment

EPILOGUE
[This epilogue is an extract from a letter from Beaufort, dated Feb. 26, from "a gentleman who accompanied General Seymour" (*The Liberator*, March 18, 1864, p. 47).]

A word about the terrible defeat in Florida. . . . The rebels allowed us to penetrate, and then, with ten to our one, cut us off, meaning to 'bag' us. *And had it not been for the glorious Fifty-fourth Massachusetts, the whole brigade would have been captured or annihilated.* This was the only regiment that rallied, broke the rebel ranks, and saved us. *The 8th United States Colored lost their flag twice, and the Fifty-fourth recaptured it each time.* They have lost in killed and missing about 350. They would not retreat when ordered, but charged on them with the most fearful desperation. . . . If this regiment has not won glory enough to have shoulder straps, where is there one that ever did.

[*On the Altar of Freedom: A Black Soldier's Civil War Letters From the Front,* pp. 112–115.]

The report that James Gooding was killed in the Battle of Olustee was premature; he was not killed, but was severely wounded, and was taken prisoner by the Confederates. He was sent as prisoner of war to the notorious Confederate prison at Andersonville, Georgia, and there he died in July, 1864.

A few days after James Gooding and the 54th Regiment had moved to Jacksonville, Florida, in February, 1864, they were followed by the 3d United States Colored Troops Regiment. Attached to the 3d Regiment at the time was Dr. Esther Hill Hawks, of New Hampshire, who had been sent to the Sea Islands in October, 1862, by the National Freedman's Relief Association. Dr. Hawkes served in the Sea Islands both as physician and as teacher in schools for former slaves. She assisted in caring for the wounded from the 54th Regiment after the battle of Fort Wagner in July, 1863, and was to serve again as doctor and nurse to survivors of the 54th and other regiments after their defeat at the battle of Olustee, in which Gooding was captured. In her diary, she described, among other things, cooperation between black soldiers and white soldiers, her opinions of freed slaves and of various Union officers and soldiers she met, her disappointment at not having a child, and "outrages" committed on white women by black men and on black women by white men.

Our Regt has recieved orders to be ready to move at an hours' notice. This was on Friday, the 11th of Feb./64. Simultaneously with the order the teams came into camp to move such things as are to be taken. I begged the Col. to take me, and he consented. In spite of all the precautions taken many of the men succeeded in getting out of Camp, so as to avoid going on the expedition—so that the Regt. that was marched on board the *Charles Houghton* was a small one, and I was counted *one of* it.

We made the trip without incident, in about twenty hours. . . . It was 4 P.M. when we reached the wharf—but the sun had set before I went ashore. Dr. [Dr. J. M. Hawks, husband of Esther] . . . came in with the joyful intilligence that he had found a chance . . . for us to spend the night. It was in the Fla. House. The Surg. of the 2 S.C. had taken possession of it for Hd. Qrs. and we might have *half*. My spirits arose immediately. . . .

Our Stay in Jack.-ville was short the Regt being ordered out to Camp Finnegan [Finegan], about 14 miles from the city. . . . —We find Camp Finnigan has only been vacated by its rebel occupants a few days before we take possession—and their is every evidence that they left in a hurry. The next day being Sunday was spent in writing letters for the men—to their wives and sweet-hearts left behind. One of the officers, Capt. Poppy

[Poppe], enjoyed the fun with me and such vigarous love-letters as we wrote, must have quite astonished the young ladies of color to whom they were sent. Here are the views of one of our soldiers on love, "Arter you lub, you lub, you know boss! You cant broke lub, Lub. stan—'e' aint gwine broke! Man hab. to be berry strong and smart for broke lub. Lub is a ting dat stan jes like tar, arter he stick, he stick he aint gwine move: he cant move less dan you burn him. Hab. to kill all two arter he lub, fo' you broke lub!"—You can imagine the warmth of the letters dictated by such sentements. . . .

The guard house is just in the rear of our cabin, and some unusual excitement has kept up a constant talking through the night. This morning, seeing the Provo-Marshal, Capt. Willoughby, standing near the guard-house, I enquired if there was any trouble, and he pointed to three boyish looking prisoners belonging to the *55th* Mass., who were under guard. — They had been arrested about mid-night, taken directly before acting Brig. Gen Littlefield, tried and condemned, to suffer death by hanging on the afternoon of the same day. —They had committed an outrage on a white woman. At the time appointed 3 p.m. our Regt and the 2. S.C. were drawn up in line and the poor fellows, launched into eternity. They showed no sign of emotion of any kind, but our soldiers sobbed aloud and were all greatly affected. Gen Seymore [Seymour], who had come from J.ville to witness the execution, after it was over turned to the men, and said, loud enough for them all to hear "Served them right, now let any other man try it if he dares." The bearing of the Gen. and his manner of speaking left an impression on our officers of his utter heartlessness. If the same measure had been meted out to white officers and men who have been guilty of the same offense towards black women, Gen. S. [Seymour] might have grown hoarse in repeating his remarks. This dreadful affair has spread a feeling of gloom over our camp. . . .

20th This morning there are rumors of an engagement of our forces under Gen Seymore, at the front, near Lake City [Olustee] and that our soldiers are driven back. . . . At 5 p m an order came for the Col. Commanding the Post for the Regt. to be ready to march forward at a moments notice. Hamiltons Battery is entirely destroyed, the guns falling into the hands of the enemy, and that we have lost a thousand killed and wounded and as many taken prisoners: Our Regt was under arms waiting for the order to march when an order came for the men to be provided with 3 days rations—this throws us into a state of anxious expectation. The men in hospital are cooking rations, as we have no "hard tack" flour has been served. This they mix with water and fry in bacon fat—in masses about 10 in. across and 1 1/2 in. thick. 6 of these will be furnished each man of the hospital staff. If they could be worn as armor, it would make the men invulnerable! how it will affect them as rations remains to be proved! Our horses stand saddled, all night at the door. I shivered with terror at every sound, expecting the order to march, but the long hours dragged slowly on and morning came with no change. At noon the 2nd S.C. were ordered back to Ja-ville, and our Regt was left alone in charge of Camp Finnegan [Finegan]. The air was heavy with forebodings of evil. Our officers go about with anxious faces. Stragglers from the front tell terrible stories of our defeat and losses. The rebel forces are under the command of Gen Hardee, and we have been most disasterously out-generaled—our soldiers are retreating as rapidly as possible. . . . The retreating army was only ten miles ahead—so all our baggage and Regimental stores, had to be left, in Camp under charge of a small guard—with slight prospect of our ever seeing any of them again!—It was 7 p.m. when we got started. I rode at the head of the column with the Col.—The surgeon being obliged to ride in the rear to see that no [one] falls by the way. . . . We reached J. [Jacksonville] at about 11 o'clock. —The men camped on the ground and we found a welcome at Col. Montgomerys Hd. Qtrs. 500 wounded had arrived—and the Surgeon went directly to the hospital to assist in their care. —After a few hours rest, I went to a church near, where I found 50 wounded men who had come in during the night and had entered the church for shelter they had not been attended to so getting some men to bring water: and sending another to the Sanitary Com. [Commission] for rags and bandages, we commenced work on such as most needed immediate care.

The S. Com. also sent me some coffee and a fire in the yard soon gave us plenty of warm water for bathing and a drink of hot coffee all round for the half famished boys: Soon Dr. H. [J. M. Hawks] and an assistant came in and the work of repairs went bravely on—and by 1 p.m. the wounds are all dressed. The men fed and supplied with clean shirts and clean straw to lie in. Most of the wounds are comparatively light—but many of them may prove severe from the fatigue and exhaustion of their long march. Many touching instances of friendliness occurred, among our patients, who were a mixed company of black and white, in very close quarters the black Regts. had borne the fiercest onslaught of the enemy, and the white soldiers were loud in their praise and when I saw white soldiers sharing their tobacco with the black ones, I concluded that the end of the war was near for the millennium had begun!

As I was carefully removing the pieces of clothing carried by a spent ball through the fleshy part of the arm of a colored soldier, I saw that he took unusual interest in my work—his admiring eyes followed every movement, and as I finished, he said "Is you Mrs Hawks," there is'nt only one woman in dis world who could do that, s. I know you is. My brudder told what you did for the *54th* soldiers in the hospital. —On enquiry I learned that this was the brother who had stayed at home of one of those who were wounded at Ft. Wagner—and he had come out with the *55th*.

Our force is entirely routed, we had but 5000 men, while the enemy brought 20,000 against us, but the officers say even this might not have been so disastrous if only there had been a Gen. in command—but with our superior offices 80 miles away the disaster was inevitable! —and why the rebels do not follow up their victory and bag the whole of us is very strange *and* gratifying. Our loss is estimated, at 1400. The Col. of the 3.U.S. Ct. was killed—and many other officers but we cannot know the whole extent of our loss yet. The men especially the colored troops fought like demons—the white soldiers say this of them. A great many troops have come in today and our army surrounds the city, they are drawn up in line of battle and expect an attack at sunset but no attack was made and in a few days many of the troops were withdrawn and sent to Morris Is.

Sunday Eve. Apr. 24th
     Alone! The day has been very long! The morning warm and rainy. — couldn't sleep—the noise of the men and teams, who, not-withstanding the rains, were busy in removing the boards timbers and other things of any value, left by the 24th Mass. in their camp—when they broke up housekeeping last night, and went on board the *Dictator* 'en rout for Fortress Monroe! Strange how much I miss them—especially when I re-member that I had hardly a speaking acquaintance with a single officer or man in the Regt. but they were so quiet and gentlemanly that I felt a sort of protection in their nearness which I now miss! . . .
     29th The day has been cool and windy: an agreeable change from the oppressive heat of the just past days. . . . 'Ben' one of our Regt. left here in hospital came to see me—told me of three other of my boys who are sick here so I went over to see them—the first time I have been in a hospital since the wounded from Olustee were sent away. The boys were very glad to see me, and begged me to come again. Went from there to P.O. found letter from Dr. [J. M. Hawks]—and by his description of Morris Is. I think a further residence in this place more desirable. . . .

Jacksonville Fla Sunday May 1st 1864
     What can be sadder than to pass through life with nothing to love. To live though the long, weary months and years with an ever increasing yearning in the heart for some object dearer than all the world besides, on which to lavish the strong pure heart love. The *mother love*—dearer than all other!
     I have longed for this, prayed for it with all the passionate entreaty of a desolate nature. Why am I denied. Why can no softening purifying in-fluences be sent to lead me through life's tangled pathway. Am I less wor-thy, less capable of such high trust—than the many I meet who do not even realize their blessedness? I *do* need something to love. I grow selfish and hard externally until I am sometimes tempted to think there is no *love* in my heart, but I will not believe it. I *have* the power to love earnestly—

passionately. O God! give me something to break through the bonds which chain it! Give me something to love.

[*A Woman Doctor's Civil War: Esther Hill Hawks' Diary*. Edited by Gerald Schwartz. Columbia, South Carolina, University of South Carolina Press. Copyright 1984 by University of South Carolina Press, pp. 59–64, 66, 68. Permission to print these and other passages included in the present volume granted by University of South Carolina Press.]

It seemed for a time that David G. Harris would be one of the Confederate soldiers in Florida opposing that Union offensive. Harris had served in the South Carolina state armed forces in 1863, but by February, 1864, he was faced with the choice either of being drafted into the Confederate army or of volunteering in that army so that he could choose the unit in which he would serve. The entries in his journal by himself and by his wife explain what happened.

David G. Harris:

February 19 [1864]. I have heard that I had to choose my company for the war by the 20 or be conscripted and sent to some company without regard to my choice. So I must choose tomorrow or take my chances. . . .

February 20. . . . I went to the village to volenteer & to choose my company. I have made choice of an infantry company in the Holcomb Legion. Comn C., Capt [Joseph M.] Boss's Company.

February 21. . . . This week I have been in a peck of trouble about choosing my place in the army. I do not know but that the Cavelry would suit me the best, for I am hardly able to do much marching on foot, but all places are hard at this time. All well to day.

February 22. The weather is more like Spring, but is still cold. I had an idea of trying to get in the Cavelry servise and went today to see Mr. Williams Bobo on the subject, hearing that he had joined them, but we have concluded to remain in the infantry. . . .

February 28. Been busy this week trying to get readdy for my departure for the wars. . . . Every man should do his duty, & I must do mine. I have to day learned that the Holcome Legion had gone on to Florida. That is more than I had bargained for, but what is the differance, war is everywhere & there is no easy place. I am willing to go, & I am glad that I am willing.

February 29. Wife, I, and the two baby-boys have been to the village to day to make the final arangement for my departure for my company which is now is Florida. . . . I expect to have fine fun in Florida part of the time, and part of the time, I do not expect it will be so funny. . . . Late in the evening and my wife is busy fixing me off for the war. Boo, hoo, hoo.

Emily L. Harris:

March 1. About 3'oclock this morning Mr. Harris again left his home for the "soldier's tent." He has gone into Confederate service and there is no telling when I shall see him again. After he had started and I had cried until I could cry no longer I slept a little nap, waked with the heaviest heart I ever had and spent a sad and lonely day with no company but little D.G. Pour little fellow, he was happy as a bird little knowing the dangers to which his best friend is exposed.

March 2. A little rain last night. Sold a [turkey] gobler for $10.00. . . .

David G. Harris:

March 6. Last evening I came home from Columbia. After I went to Columbia I concluded to get into the Cavelry servise if I could, not feeling able to do much hard marching, & not feeling disposed to remain in Florida during the summer season, I suceeded in making the desired arangement & have joined the I. S. C. Cavelry, Col. [John L.] Black's Regiment, Capt. [Thomas W.] Whatley. I was given a furlough for 25 days & I have came home to make the necessary arangement. I will now have to purchase a horse, or deprive my family of my celebrated Gray which I hate very much to do. I am aware that cavelry is expensive, but I had rather make a horse of Gray, than to make one of myself. . . .

[*Piedmont Farmer*, pp. 321–323.]

Harris's service in the 1st South Carolina Cavalry took him, not to Florida, but to the Charleston area, where he became part of the Confederate defense of that city.

In Louisiana: April–May, 1864

Not quite three months after the attempted Union offensive in Florida, Marcus Spiegel, now a colonel, led his regiment in another attempted Union military offensive, this one up the Red River in Louisiana.

Spiegel, as we have seen, received wounds in July, 1863, in skirmishes which followed the battle of Vicksburg, and he spent several months at home in Ohio while his wounds healed. By December, he had resumed command of his regiment, which was in Louisiana. Spiegel's letters to his wife in the early months of 1864 reveal that he was now strongly in favor of ending the institution of slavery—even though he realized that his stand might be in opposition to that of the Ohio Democratic party, and even though he still described blacks as "naturally lazy and indolent." His regiment began offensive operations up the Red River at the end of April, 1864, and that move proved to be disastrous for Spiegel and his family.

Plaquemine La Jan 22/64

My dear Wife, my sweet Cary!

. . . You must not expect any news inasmuch as this [is] as monotonous a place as ever Millersburg can be. We are living here right on the

Mississippi River and with exception of three or four Steamboats landing here every day which are called Coast Packets and travel from Baton Rouge to New Orleans and back, we have no news. . . . we are building a very large and formidable Fort here. . . .

There was a report yesterday that there were a lot of Rebels twelve miles form here, so I started out with a Company of Cavelery. . . . but we found "nary Reb" after a hard ride. . . .

I have at present 12 Sergeants in Ohio on the recruiting Service; I do not know how well or whether at all, they succeed. It takes so long somehow to hear from Ohio and the North generally that we do not know what is going on. In New Orleans they have news once a week at least but here it is very irregular. . . .

Since I am here I have learned and seen more of what the horrors of Slavery was than I ever knew before and I am glad indeed that the signs of the times show, towards closing out the accursed institution. You know it takes me long to say anything that sounds antidemocratic [That is, opposed to the policies of the Democratic party.] and it goes hard, but whether I stay in the Army or come home, I am [in] favor of doing away with the institution of Slavery. I am willing for the Planters to hire them and in favor of making the negro work at all events, inasmuch as he is naturally lazy and indolent, but never hereafter will I either speak or vote in favor of Slavery; this is no hasty conclusion but a deep conviction. Yet I never mean hereafter to be a politician, but quietly as a good citizen doing duty to my God, my family, my Country and myself. . . .

One of my men who deserted in Covington and was brought up by the Provost Marshal was tried by a Court Marshal and sentenced to forfeit all his pay and condemned for six months hard labor on Fort Espararox [Esperanza], Texas, with a Ball and Chain on his right leg, a very very hard sentence indeed; I would rather they would have shot him, for death is not so hard as degradation. . . .

My leg still hurts me most all the time and I come to the conclusion it always will, yet not enough to hurt me in the common avocation of life. . . .

Plaquemine La Feby 12/64

My dear good and kind Cary!
Yesterday I received your very good and loving letter of the 22nd ultimo and I have been joyous ever since. . . .I will first try and answer your every question you ask in yours and then give you the news which is very slim. Of course the time will come when we will have a fine Horse, Carriage and sleigh and drive ourselves and enjoy it and let me assure you my love that time is not very far distant.

As for moving and leaving Millersburg, I am perfectly willing. If you can sell the House you may; it ought to bring $1400.00 or at least $1300 with the new stable. . . .

As for our "Affair" you may rest perfectly easy; I will be home if God spares my health whenever it comes off and long enough before hand so as to be sure of not missing it, though really in your last you do not seem very certain whether is agoing to be an "Affair" at all or whether it is all "*wind*". I suppose though ere long the matter will be positively decided and you must not omit to inform me as I think I have a very large share of interest in the matter. Your "Kindbett" [childbed] present shall not be very slovenly you may bet; it must be O.K. . . .

I have been to see several large Planters and find them very hospitable; they live like princes, are proud and aristocratic, but exceedingly pleasant and agreeable to the Federal Officers. Slavery has been abolished in Louisiana and they are just as keen to get the negro to work for pay as they used to while slaves, and I am satisfied in twenty five years from now, the negro will be an educated, well to do laborer and the white man none the worse. This you know I see from my own experience; I am now a strong abolitionist, but I want laws and regulations by which the negro must be made to work and educated and the present Master be compelled to do it. Slavery is gone up whether the War ends to day or in a year and there is no use crying over it; it has been an awful institution. I will send you the "black code" of Louisiana some of these days and I am satisfied it will make you shudder.

Now understand me when I say I am a strong abolitionist, I mean that I am not so for party purposes but for humanity sake only, out of my own conviction, for the best Interest of the white man in the south and the black man anywheres. I find some few large slaveholders concur in my opinion; of course the major part of them would prefer the old System. The poor white man, the mechanic and laborer in this country however, find that a new era is dawning for them in this Country (South); herethefore they were almost worse [off] then the negro slave here. . . .

As to my plan I can not tell you; we will I am satisfied agree upon some plan when I come home. As long as the war looks so important and call after call for men, it seems as though a soldier and patriot could have no rest except in the Army. I have an excellent Regiment, my men almost worship me, and if I were to resign to day, one half of my officers would also and perhaps demoralize the Regiment which could be doing the Government more harm then my humble efforts perhaps ever done it good; but never mind, I do not believe you really want me to resign. I think you are really proud of your Soldier man, only you do not like to let on.

Good bye. God bless you, my love to the children and all friends.

Ever your true
Marcus. . .

Baton Rouge La. April 10/64

My dear dear Wife and good Children,

. . . You will see by the above that my Regiment moved from Plaquemine to this City Baton Rouge, the Capital of the State of Louisiana.

Here I arrived safe day before yesterday after a long monotonous and tedious trip. . . . I landed here and found my [regiment] pleasantly situated here at the West End of the City by the penitentiary, a powerful and commodious Building. My Boys were happy indeed and I received a cordial and warm reception such as King could feel proud of. . . .

This certainly was a beautiful and thriving City before this Cruel War. The State House, a magnificent as well as Gigantic structure, is situated on as lovely and romantic a spot as you could wish to see, on an eminent slope on the Banks of the Mississippi. . . .

Baton Rouge La. April 20/64

My dear dear Wife

. . . Since my arrival here I have been busier than I had previously been for a year; am working very hard with my Regiment and I am happy to say the fruits show worthy of the labor—For a week past we had to rise at the early *"peep of dawn"* about half past 3 o'clock A.M. and are ordered to remain under arms until after "Sunrise" owing to a big "scare" they get up in this town about twice a month, lasting from the morning of the 1st to the Evening of the 15th and the 2nd scare from the morn of the 15th to the Eve of the last of the month. . . .

A very pleasant little affair took place night before last. As I was quietly laying on my couch, preparing my lesson for the next day School, my door was opened and in came Captains Jones, Frowenfelder and Miller; Jones commencing to make a speech presenting me with a beautiful "Meershamm pipe" worth about $50, a beautiful Present indeed. I was taken by surprise truly, yet I rallied and made (they say) a very good reply. It is just what I always wanted. I shall send it home to have it taken care of, and let us hope that when in after years I sit by my own fireside surrounded by my true and loving wife, my good children, smoking my "meersham", I may be able to enjoy with you, my love, the comforts of life due to us and tell you many a little tale of my military campayne, and may the days be many and happy ones for all of us. . . .

We suffered a very severe defeat at Red River [Sabine Crossroads, La., April 8th], lost 22 Guns, 250 Wagons and 3500 men. I should not be surprised if our Brigade would be moved. I send this letter by a young man going to Ohio. Good bye my love. God Bless you.

Your true and loving
Marcus

Baton Rouge La. April 23/64

My dear dear Cary!

I got your very good and kind letter. . . . Shall be very glad to get my new Clothes, as mine are beginning to look very shabby; yet inasmuch as we have marching Orders for Red River I am not so very particular as I would have been if we stayed here. . . . for reasons of the health of my recruits I should have preferred staying here, but the Eastern troops got whipped up Red River and we Western boys will be relieved here from Garrison duty by them and go and perhaps retrieve the defeat they sustained.

We may not however start for a week or so. I understand McClernand is to take Command of the Expedition; if so I look to the result as a Success, as almost foregone conclusions.

Here we expected an attack; were up early, two hours before day every morning and under Arms, but I never felt there was any use for it, but our old General "Philip St. George Cooke, Brigadier General, United States Army", is an Alarmist and a regular old Granny but a very clever Gentleman.

When we leave here we go to Alexandria and should not be surprised, if we were successful, but I might someday or other write you a letter from Texas, that is Galveston. . . .

I received a very kind and encouraging letter from Simon Wolf giving me positive assurance that I will be "Starred" [i.e., be promoted to rank of General] though it takes time, perseverance, money and pluck, but he says it shall be done. I will send you the letter as soon as I answered it. Petitions will flow into Washington on my behalf, I think, and all will be right; then you will be "Generalin" [a General's wife]. . . .

This is Shabbath and I am invited to a regular Shabbath Dinner at Mrs. Baer, a Jewish Widow here; a place that would seen very pleasant to go to if it were not for 6 as mean children as I ever saw. . . . this Lady is [as] thoroughly educated in French, German as [in] English, but for all the world like Yette. She has a Store, is making money. It is a place of resort for Dinner and so forth for the Union Officers and of course she is smart enough to get permits and so forth for them to send Goods out. . . .

Baton Rouge La April 27/64

My dear good Caroline!

Your very good kind sweet and long letter came together with yours of the 2nd packed up in the Clothing and I must say it made me feel full of love and admiration. . . .

General McClernand & Staff passed here the other day to go up Red River and if possible retrieve the great disaster we sustained up there, by the utter & gross inefficiency of Genl. Banks, perhaps since the first Bull Run fight we have not sustained so disgraceful a defeat as we dit up Red

River, Our Army is demoralized and disheartened up there & if Banks is not removed I know not what will follow. . . .

We are ordered up Red River and are awaiting transportation, I hope by the time we get up there we may have Genl. Jno. A. McClernand command the Dept. I have no doubt the next letter you get from me will be written on board of the Transport on our way up the River. . . .

The weather here is very hot, as hot as it is in Ohio in July, everything is in full growth & we get beans new Potatoes & any kind of Vegetables our living is very good but not near as good as it was some time

[The letter stops in mid-page]

What happened to Spiegel after his letter of April 27 was interrupted in mid-page has been described by the editors of his letters:

On April 30, 1864, at Baton Rouge, Spiegel and almost four hundred men of his regiment boarded the steamboat *City Belle*. Their destination was Alexandria, Louisiana, where Banks's defeated army was delaying its retreat until the Union fleet could pass the rapids of the Red River. Stopping en route at Port Hudson, the *City Belle* picked up a hundred more troops belonging to other units before beginning to ascend the Red River on May 2. . . . on May 3 the *City Belle* passed Fort De Russy.

Realizing that this captured fort near Marksville was the last Union strong point before Alexandria, Spiegel took precautions against attack. He placed some two hundred of his men on guard with loaded weapons and instructed his officers to be alert. He was ready for a guerrilla attack but was not ready—on his unarmored transport he could not have been ready—for the large force which the Confederates were able to insert below Alexandria because of the chaotic situation produced by Banks's retreat. At Davide's Ferry near Snaggy Point, a position about thirty river miles from Fort De Russy, some thousand dismounted cavalry with four or five cannons waited behind the levee. Two days earlier they had captured a Union steamboat and the unconvoyed *City Belle* was their next target. About 4 P.M. on May 3, after Spiegel's transport had unwittingly passed one concealed battery, the Confederate guns opened fire from above and below the hapless *City Belle,* with volleys from rebel cavalrymen's muskets completing the ambush. According to one of Spiegel's captains, "such a torrent of shot and shell as was poured into the boat I never saw before and never want to witness again."

Spiegel was in or near the cabin, which the first shell traversed, doing great damage. Uninjured, he rallied his men and encouraged them to maintain a steady counterfire—to no avail. The second shell hit the pilothouse and killed the pilot. Almost immediately thereafter, a shell cut the steam pipe and entered the boiler. While the boat drifted helplessly, about a hundred panicky soldiers jumped overboard. In his hopeless plight, according to some of the confused accounts, Spiegel may have exposed himself on the hurricane deck to wave a white flag. In any event, he was on the upper deck when a rifle ball struck him in the abdomen. He was carried below to the shattered, bloodstained cabin. Lt. Col. Williard Slocum then sent a man with a line to the bank opposite the Confederates and, having fastened the boat, escaped with about 150 men. The remaining 250 members of the 120th were lost; most, like Spiegel, becoming prisoners. The whole engagement had lasted only thirty to forty minutes.

Spiegel, who had survived major battles, knew as soon as he was hit that in this obscure clash his luck had finally run out. A gunshot wound to the intestines was almost invariably mortal because of infection. Still, he had no wish to die in agony and expressed great concern when the Confederates prepared to set fire to the *City Belle*. Several of his "boys" waded through four feet of water to carry him ashore. In a nearby house he was cared for by his regimental surgeons. His beloved brother Joseph, who had received a flesh wound in the arm, was also at his side and was of great comfort to him. To them, Spiegel spoke mainly of those at home. "This is the last of the husband and father, what will become of my poor family?" he cried out to Surgeon Stanton. . . . During the night, Spiegel suffered intense pain but next morning he felt better and dared to hope that he might recover. Conscious almost to the end, he sank into death about 4 P.M. on May 4. The following morning, the odyssey that had begun thirty-four years earlier on the Rhine ended in a muddy grave on the bank of the Red River.

[*Your True Marcus: The Civil War Letters of a Jewish Colonel*, pp. 314–322, 324, 326–331, 334–337.]

In Virginia: May–August, 1864

The unsuccessful attempted offensives of Union forces in Louisiana and Florida early in 1864, in which Marcus Spiegel and James Gooding lost their lives, were preludes to the major forward movement of Union troops which General Grant would lead in Virginia against the Confederate armies of General Lee, beginning early in May, 1864. General Grant had moved in March, 1864, from the western theater of operations to Washington, D.C., to accept the post of general-in-chief of all Union armies, with the rank of lieutenant general. On May 4, the Union forces crossed the Rapidan River in Virginia, moving south toward Richmond. For the next several months, the army led by Grant was locked in a titanic struggle with the army led by Lee, starting with the battle of the Wilderness, some fifty-five miles north of Richmond, and continuing on through battles at Spottsylvania, Cold Harbor, and Petersburg, fifteen miles south of Richmond. Grant, in preparation for the battles with Lee, had reorganized the Union cavalry in the eastern theater, placing General Philip Sheridan in overall command. Sheridan's troops included the 16th Pennsylvania Cavalry Regiment, with Sergeant (soon to be commissioned 2d Lieutenant) Samuel Cormany. Cormany and the 16th Regiment were to take an active part in the fighting from the Wilderness to Petersburg, advancing at one point to the outskirts of Richmond, as Cormany recorded in his diary:

May 4, 1864 Wednesday. Aroused at 2 A.M. Marched at 4—Got to Ealies Fort at daybreak—Our whole 2nd Division and 3 Divisions (30,000) of 2nd Army Corps advanced—Captured some half dozen Johnie Pickets. . . .

May 5, 1864 Thursday. Early called in from line—Took up march at 8 A.M. to Chancellorville 4 mls to R.R. train for Forage—Great columns of infantry and heavy artilleryists from Washington D.C. acting as infantry—are moving front and in various directions. Their faces express business—Their step is elastic—firm—and one is inspired with courage to be a part of such a body of Men.

P.M. Skirmishing and canonaiding hearable in almost every direction—save in the rear— . . .

May 6, 1864 Friday. We were in column by dawn. My platoon is in good shape—At sunrise heavy musketry and canonading set in—The heaviest musketry I ever heard—and continued 4 to 5 hours—about 10 A.M. Custers Cavalry [Brig. Gen. George Armstrong Custer, who died in 1876 at the Little Big Horn, was a rising young cavalry officer.] became engaged and soon our 2nd Division took some part—Our brigade supporting and lightly engaged came in for some shelling—tho not severe. . . . The tension was so high all day—and all energies so aroused and wound up that all our sleep was more than half awake.

May 7, 1864 Saturday. Early the famous "Clean them out" order was read to the men. The order congratulated the men on their fine work yesterday and before—and proposed that we "clean them out today"—The cheers and roars all along the lines and everywhere were simply indiscribable . . . . I had some pine logs before me and was sharp shooting—picking, now and then during the lull, some Johny who showed himself busy as I was—we were not supposed to advance at all, simply hold the line and await orders—A Johny got my range—I saw where his shot—ball—struck the ground in front of me—some distance—"buddy" called my attention, saying "some Johny is getting range of you" I replied "you find and peck him" a little later a ball struck a smoothe cut pine knot close in front of me—glanced, flatened some and struck me flatly above my right eye—Knocked me senseless. As I dropped on my face, I heard "Cormany's shot" uttered by some one—Later, Capt Brooks rolled me over on my back, dashed some water from a canteen into my face, and the shock brought me to consciousness—I was in bad shape. My head became kind of benumbed, but I would not be taken from the line—but lounged around close to my post on the line— . . .

May 8, 1864 Sunday. Thus far only 4 or 5 of H. Co. wounded, none killed yet—I have a fearful bump over my eye, but with a bandage over it—

which I keep wet, I greatly prefer remaining on the line with the Boys. . . .
10 P.M. we lie on arms and sleep some. The roar of battle having quieted
down—up at 3 A.M. Orders! Be very quiet—Strike no light—To move out
at once—Keep sabers from dangling, so as to make no noise—avoid all
possible noise—First 1/2 hour we move rather slowly, but gradually increase to rapid movement—We realiz that we are striking for the rear of
Lees Army. That we are on a hazardous trip—and that it demands haste—
and quiet for a time—

We find no resistance—So we know we've succeeded in slipping
away unobserved. Sometime Monday night 9th we neared the North Ann
River and bivouaced.

May 10, 1864 Tuesday. Wide awake! Just at daybreak the enemy opened
on us with shell, and but for the dense fog hiding our maneuver we would
have been awfully endangered—

At sunrise we cross the North Ann River and pass on to Beaver Dam
Station where where our 1st Brigade—last evening—with wonderful
tact—captured 3 engines with 3 trains of cars in which were 400,000.
Rations for Lees Army—and 300 prisoners recently taken about
Chancellorsville and Todds Tavern &c, and kept on the cars for safety—

Our (2nd) Brigade was supporting the 1st—which cautiously came in
on the Telegraph Operator—and by persuasion of several revolvers, compelled the Operator to be mum, but order the trains—which were lying
near Richmond awaiting orders—to come to the front with all speed--and
the trains came—and the 1st helped themselves and started the destruction of the surplus, and this morning our Brigade came on the scene—and
replenished their light haversacks well and then Joined in the hasty destruction of about everything excepting the train crews, and the 300 prisoners and the Confeds who were guarding them—

Well! We had the Confeds to turn over their arms—and the late prisoners had the pleasure of guarding them as our prisoners now— . . .

And now our Cavalry Corpse moves rapidly toward Richmond. . . .

May 11, 1864 Wednesday. Last night—for the first time since we crossed
the River at Ealies Ford on the 4th—we got nearly a full nights sleep——
At daybreak our squadron went out on Picket 1 mile west of Squirrel
Court House—At 10 OCK firing commenced and we were ordered back
to the Regiment. In the meantime our division had moved and the enemy
had driven our men out of the position they were holding on the Cross
roads, and 2nd Brigade artilery were in position and ready to open on
them when they would make a charge. They charged and the 10th N.Y.
broke and fled, and somehow got into the range so the artilery could not
be used to good advantage. Just at this juncture our squadron—coming
off Picket with orders to join the Regiment (which had left) came marching out of the roads, and in full view of the Rebel Charge—and the 10th
N.Y. skedaddle—We, although ordered off duty, and to report to our reg-

iment—at once formed for a charge—and as the Rebs made for a second charge—and were almost sure to capture the 2 Pieces and a lot of prisoners We charged them to fine effect, saving all—and empting a number of their saddles, and causing the Johnies to skedaddle in great confusion—

This was certainly a clear case of quick initiative—and snatching victory out of defeat. A fight without orders from higher up—

Capt. Snyder, who was in command of our Squadron—and the Men were very highly complimented by the Capt Commanding the Battery. Also Colonel J. K. Robison and by Genl J. I. Gregg—for our disinterested manifestation of true bravery in thus, when one would have been fully justifiable in evading the whole fracas, and breaking for the Regiment—to rush at once into a daring charge upon the enemy to the saving of 2 fine cannon & many soldiers, and a great stamped of the Boys in blue— . . .

The rear of our column occasionally charged the enemy rearward to prevent their coming too near and getting cross fire on the column at any point—Thus this was an eventful day, and yet with very little loss, and a steady advance towards Richmond—Evening! We did not stop, but kept up the little fight til dark and then lay on arms til 2 OCK A.M. [While Gregg's brigade protected the Federal rear and flanks in the fashion Cormany describes, the head of the Federal column crashed into (Gen J. E. B.) Stuart's roadblock. The roadblock was smashed and Stuart mortally wounded.]

May 12, 1864 Thursday. When we again advanced and at break of day found ourselves inside of the outer works—earth works—of Richmond. A severe fight followed—The enemy in front—on our right and in our rear—and no way of falling to the left—a rather precarious position 1 ½ miles from the Rebel Capital and thus attacked. There would seem to be considerable of a chance of being closed in on, overpowered and awfully whipped. We however fight them, mounted dis-mounted and with artillery for 5 or 6 hours—charging them frequently—

It was discovered that our only way out was laid with "mines"—another charge was ordered toward the right and front, our boys were in it—we took one small piece of artillery, and bunch of cav., supporters—By close questioning at Hd Qrs—it was brought out that this bunch, with their Lieut; were the very fellows who had put down the "Mines." Immediately—with open mouthed revolvers and carbines giving them a knowing wink, they were compelled to hastily take up the "mines" and so clear the way for our action and movement with safety (?)— . . .

During this engagement, at times, we could see immense crowds upon the Forts and embank to our right—near the City—we got it that the Rebel General was so certain of being able to take us in that he encouraged the Rebel Congress to adjourn and see him doing it, and of course the People wanted to see it also—

We were not taking Richmond either, anymore than Genl Steward [i.e., Stuart] was taking us. But we had made Genl Lees Army go hungry—and also solicitous for their rear—We had destroyed 3 trains they needed very much—We had attracted the Steward [Stuart] Cavalry to leave Lees army and look out for the safety of their capital—and we were not taking Richmond now. But we were not blown up yet, and so headed our column for the Chicohominy. . . .

Weary and exhausted, we cooked some coffee to regale ourselves. . . .

May 16, 1864 Monday. Pleasant Morning—News Papers came in—Also Rations and Forage—Glorious news from Armies all around—and now surely mail will soon come in—Yes! about sick—vomiting and purging—Ate too freely, and too rich, after so long a time of almost utter fasting—

Lots-o-the boys similarly affected. Fortunately we could just lie around all day and feed up gently and rest. . . .

May 20, 1864 Friday. We took up our line of march again at 5 OCK A.M. scoured the country and bivouaced at Coles Harbor [i.e., Cold Harbor] at 2 P.M.—In the evening our Regiment advanced to within ten miles of Richmond—drew up our Regiment in line, with sabers drawn for a charge. The skirmishers fire some and the enemy falls back—night being about upon us, we return to Coles Harbor and bivouac. . . .

May 22, 1864 Sunday. Cloudy—Roused at 3:30 A.M. took up the march at 4:30—Extremely hot—Very many of our Cavalry horses are playing out and being shot or abandoned on these raids—Cause? Hard marches—irregular rations—fearful strain on muscles & nerves—& lack of rest— . . .

May 24, 1864 Tuesday. . . . This is my 26th Birthday Anniversary—Thank the Good Lord that I am who—where, and what I am, and who's I am—How good is God to me, unworthy tho' I be—

May 25, 1864 Wednesday. We took up the march at 8 A.M. . . . Mail comes to us I had mailed my last to Pet May 1st and had received my last from her same day—all these 25 days we were in the enemys country—several times quite near Richmond—as noted heretofore—and entirely out of reach of Mail facilities. But today—thank the good Lord—Our mail comes up and I recieve five letters from Pet—. . . So we had a quiet day of reading letters from Home. Writing some—and reading "war news." We know almost nothing of what was being accomplished, save what we—cavalrymen—were doing—and we knew but little of that save what our own Regiment was closely engaged in—

May 26, 1864 Thursday. Rainy—I received my commission as 2nd Lieutenant today. Made some effort to be mustered out as Serg't and in as 2nd Lieut At 1:30 P.M. we took up the march again via Chesterfield Station & Edensville. . . .

June 6, 1864 Monday. I started for the Regiment Got outside of our lines being mis-directed, but no harm comes from it—about noon I joined my Regiment and obtained my discharge as Sergt, and a very good letter from my Darling. . . .

June 7, 1864 Tuesday. . . . Made application to be mustered in as 2nd Lieutenant. Made out Rolls &c &c—

June 8, 1864 Wednesday. Up betimes—Routine—I was mustered as 2nd Lieutenant at 5 OCK A.M.—Donned my shoulder straps and took off my Sergt's stripes—

Sergt Flannagan and Corpl Coble assisted me gleefully! . . .

June 11, 1864 Saturday. I am suffering from a severely enflamed eye. . . . at 8 ock we were fronted by the enemy and were in line of battle with Genl. Custer on the right, and our 2nd Brigade on and in left of R.R. by 9:30 the fight rages furiously. . . . P.M. The whole line charges with splendid results—Capturing 750 prisoners—Our regiment lost 4 killed and 10 wounded. . . .

June 12, 1864 Sunday. A beautiful day. . . . P.M. all hands tearing up R.R. track, or turning it up-side-down—'The process is rather simple—A joint is first broken on one side. Mean stand shoulder to shoulder—say one thousand abreast along the rail—a few with fence rails, and chunks, pry the rail and ties up for 100 or more feet, underpinning the one side, for a short distance—the [i.e., to] height of several feet—Now, at the word of command, every man lifts harder and harder, and soon the men at the broken joint, have the ties in perpendicular position while those next are nearly so. Continuing the lift and tearing up, while now the ties and rail at the break are beyond the perpendicular and so bear down and at the same time remaining spiked to the ties—help in the overturning process—so when once fairly started the R. R. track is turned upsidedown with considerable speed and the extreme strain and twist, of the turning over mass, twists and otherwise damages nearly every rail. . . .

June 18, 1864 Saturday. . . . I was ordered in Command of "I" Company— "C" and "I" Cos constitute a squadron. Lieut Caughy com'ds squadron— I took them to water. . . .

June 24, 1864 Friday. Marched at 6 OCK A.M. . . . All rather quiet for a little while—our line intact—I had dismounted, and was sitting on a Stump—close in front of my Company "I"—and was writing—making notes of our doings—Whereupon a Reb Sharp Shooter was getting range of me—one of my men seeing an occasional puffing up of the ground rather close in front of me caused by the enemy's bullet—remarked "Lieut! That Johny has pretty close range of you" I replied I observe, just then a bullet struck the stump, between my feet, taking with it a bit of my boot and barely grazed my left ankle—inside—slightly removing a little cuticle—but doing me no harm save what a boot-mender can repair.

A little later both Infantry and Cavalry charged us—We are being flanked and greatly outnumbered—and a general falling back takes place—with some regiments amounting to almost a stampede and panic—through some woodland—Our old 16th in good order—holds the extreme rear, firing as they fall back, thus keeping the enemy from coming too close—Lieut Caughy receives a wound—and I take command of the squadron—We are under awful firing—As we came out of a wood, The Col J. K. R with the 1st squadron faces the charging enemy and they pour volleys into them—thus retarding them—and the while I rallied my squadron some distance in the rear or rearward on the opposite side of the road—on an elevation. And we lustily sang the song "We'll rally round the flag Boys" Others, who had fallen back without orders rallied to us, and soon order was restored, and we presented a solid front—I warned the squadron that the Colonel would very soon be coming back to our right on the opposite side of the road—Every man to be at aready but not to fire a shot until I gave command Fire!—Then to pour it in with precission—and continuously, until the Reg't had time to form further back on our right and rear.

Soon our Boys came. The Col calling Steady! Steady Men! as they passed us. . . . the dense dust and firing of the enemy revealed to us their approach while we were invisible to them—When they came to about 100 yds of us, upon order "FIRE!" Such a volley greeted them as checked them all and dismounted many—and the same was repeated several times, when an effort to flank us made it necessary for us to "By fours, right about face" and move to the rear steadily, firing occasionally to the rear or "rear-right-oblique"—Soon we were opposite to the Regiment again—and then was their turn to greet any who rallied and drove (?) us. Thus by "eschelon" we held the enemy back—until night relieved us from further pressure and we bivouaced at Charles City Court House. . . .

June 26, 1864 Sunday. Hotest of the year—Lay in reserve all day. Did some fine sleeping—P.M. Recd a good letter from Pet—Quiet along the picket line all day—Eve. 8th Pa Cav relieved us. . . .

June 27, 1864 Monday. Cooler—Wrote all A.M. for Pet. . . . Thank the Lord I am kept so well and happy.

[*The Cormany Diaries: A Northern Family in the Civil War*, pp. 417–429, 432–439.]

While Samuel Cormany and the 16th Pennsylvania Cavalry were almost steadily on the move in Virginia, Rachel Cormany was rooted most of the time in Chambersburg, Pennsylvania, with Cora, the couple's daughter. Rachel Cormany's diary entries tell of her continuing health problems, her shortage of money, the frustrations of living as renters in the homes of other people, and a general weariness with life under wartime conditions: "O! when will my troubles cease." She described vividly one of the most controversial acts of the war: the deliberate burning of Chambersburg by Confederate forces on July 30, 1864.

March 21, 1864 Feel better than I have for some time. Last week I really though I was——. [Rachel thought she might be pregnant after Samuel had been home on leave.] but it was something else. I am sure I am well satisfied as it is. I tried to be cheerful under it but could not. . . . as soon as a change came I felt like another person. my appetite returned. I could sleep again & feel cheerful. Indeed—I did not think that I would be affected as I was about such a thing. . . . This morning my stovepipe caught fire. Mrs Merklein nearly went off the handle about it. she flew & flurried about like an old cluck when the hawk is after her yound ones. It almost made me fidgety to see her performing—She had the chimney all in ablaze when only the sparks were flying. O! deliver me from such people. . . .

April 4, 1864 Moved from Mrs Merkleins to Mrs McGowans—Had quite a time getting my things hauled—. . . .

April 12, 1864 My 28th Birthday—Wrote a letter to Mr C. also one to Mr McG—for Mrs Mc. Prepared supper for my sisters but they did not come. re'd 2 letters from My Samuel verry good ones too—Am so tired that I can scarcely get along—I went to the depot & took Cora along—which was too much after having been on my feet all day—

April 13, 1864 . . . Evening Sisters Mollie & Susie came to stay with me awhil. I am so glad they are once here—I have been looking for them so long. Maggie Hamilton & Miss Mahler came to Mrs McGowans. I do not know where to store all to sleep—. . .

April 25, 1864 Have not been well for several days. took cold—& I feel so worried about my husband—I feel like sitting & weeping all the time. . . . Another reason that I feel depressed for is that I am just out of money—flour—wood—potatoes—& in fact out of nearly everthing—Just now I am tired of living—God speed our release . . . from war & the troubles of war—If I only know that my husbands life would be spared I could rest easy—but if should he be taken—all would be gone—. A few days after the above was written I received a letter from my husband. . . . I also received letters with money. Truly the Lord provides for me. Sister Mollie remarked that it seemed as if an unseen hand was providing for me—

May 22, 1864 Last Thursday Sisters Mollie & Sue left for home. . . . I felt so lonely & had not been well for a week or more & since the 2nd inst had received no tidings from my husband. when I returned from the depot—I was almost ready to declare myself sick enough to go to bed. . . . Mr[s] McGowan (the lady of whom I rented) is sick too & has been since I live here. The lady living with her M. Hamilton was sick too & went home next morning. Well Thursday P.M. was spent rather uncomfortably all round—Evening came & with it a letter from my Precious—O! the light that letter brought with it. I was so glad I scarcely knew what to do with myself. I kissed the little missives run all through the house proclaiming my fortune, hurried my few duties over then struck for Mrs Snyder to tell her but she having had the same good fortune was on her way to tell me & I met her a few doors from so we returned together. Our brave husbands have seen hard marching & hard fighting. My Precious bears the mark of a minnie ball on his forehead he writes me—Thank the Lord that they are still spared. This A.M. I attended class & preaching—I was happy in class—O! this glorious religion of Jesus Christ I am not well today—feel much out of fix My little girl has been very unwell—but she is quite over her spell & is as mischievous as she well can be—here she comes so goodbye My old Journal. . . .

June 2, 1864 . . .I received a letter from Mr Cormany—he is still safe & well—he writes that he received a Lieutenants commission shortly before. I told Mrs Mc— she did not seem to like it she said a good many things that were meant to cut—& were hard to take. I made no replys for I knew it would only make it worse. . . . She remarked so short—Yes—Some are favored & others are not—What her man got he got honestly & if they got what was due them they could live better too. . . .

June 7, 1864 I am still getting better—I cough very much by spell I weeded my garden this A.M. also Mrs Mc's little onions I want to show her that being a Lieut's wife does not change me. I also helped her to make soap so I got only a few stitches sewed. My cough bothers me much. Cora put very strong lie in her mouth this morning which took the cuticle right off—her lips were only touched with it they are much swollen & sore. A despatch came this P.M. that Capt Harmony was killed. They have had desperate fighting before Richmond last week O! How I long for if but a few words from my husband—to know he still lives. . . .

July 19, 1864 Just a month has passed since I last wrote in my journal. I have had frequent communication with my husband during this month. his health is good, he has been in some desperate battles of late, he sent me his commission last week, he seems in good spirits. I long so to see him I wish he were home to stay. Since I last wrote I was a week at Orrstown drying cherries and left Cora with Mrs McG. We have had wonderful excitement about the rebels coming again. . . . Cora is well & talks nearly every thing quite plainly.

July 26, 1864 Cool this morning. Rained Sunday night & nearly all day yesterday. a nice soaking rain. All has been quiet for a few weeks about the rebels coming—last evening the excitement broke out again & all night farmers were going North with horses &c. A thousand rumers are afloat. If the rebels intend coming I wish they would hurry so the fuss would be over once—

August 6, 1864 Just a week this morning the rebels turned up in our devoted town again. before they entered they roused us out of our slumbers by throwing to shells in. this was between 3 & 4 A.M. by 5—the grey back hordes came pouring in. They demanded 500,000 dollars in default of which the town would be burned—They were told that it was imposible to raise that amount—The reb's then came down to 100,000 in gold which was just as imposible. when they were informed of the imposibility they deliberately went from house to house & fired it. The whole heart of the town is burned. they gave no time for people to get any thing out. each

had to escape for life & took only what they could first grab. some saved considerable. others only the clothes on their backs—& even some of those were taken off as they escaped from their burning dwellings. O! the 30th July 1864 was a sad day to the people of Chambersburg. In most of cases where the building were left money was paid. They were here too but we talked them out of it. We told them we were widdows & that saved us here. About 3000 were made homeless in less than three hours. This whole week has been one of great excitement. We live in constant dread. I never spent such days as these few last I never spent—I feel as if I could not stay in this country longer. I feel quite sick of the dread & excitement. [The action against Chambersburg was conducted by one of (Confederate Gen.) Early's subordinates, Brg. Gen. John McCausland. The damage included the destruction of 537 buildings (266 of which were residences or businesses) along with roughly a million dollars worth of private property. Extensive looting and robbery by Confederate enlisted men accompanied the systematic burning of the buildings themselves.]
[*The Cormany Diaries*, pp. 440–446.]

In striking contrast to the dismay which marked Rachel Cormany's description of the burning of Chambersburg by Confederate soldiers was the satisfaction reflected in the words of a Confederate army officer, Edgeworth Bird. Bird was not part of the Confederate army unit that burned Chambersburg, but he had passed through the town a year earlier during the Gettysburg campaign. When he wrote his wife on August 4, 1864, about the burning, he characterized it as an act of "retribution:"

> The beautiful town of Chambersburg is a black, charred mass. There is retribution at last. We all recall the defiant and scornful faces of its ladies as we marched through a year ago. I then and still respect them for their spirit, but their scorn has been turned into wailing.
>
> [*The Granite Farm Letters: The Civil War Correspondence of Edgeworth & Sallie Bird*. Edited by John Rozier. Athens and London, University of Georgia Press. Copyright 1988 by University of Georgia Press, pp. 180–181. Permission to reprint this passage granted by University of Georgia Press.]

The burning of Chambersburg was a by-product of the months-long engagement between the massed armies of Grant and Lee that, as we have seen, began in Virginia in May, 1864. Those Virginia battles were mentioned in the farm journal of the Harris family of South Carolina. The journal entries during most of the year 1864 were written by Emily L. Harris, since her husband David was away from home serving in the Confederate army. Emily Harris sandwiched comments about the military situation between accounts of her frustrating efforts to manage the family and the family farm in the absence of her husband—with frequent mention of letters from or to him ("Mr. Harris"). Most of the battles in Virginia were perceived as Confederate victories by Emily Harris, as was the fighting

around Atlanta, but she grieved over the heavy casualties. By late August, 1864,
she heard that an armistice to stop the war was being discussed in the North.

Emily L. Harris:

May 11 [1864]. We have had a little rain this evening and I have had thousands of cabbage plants set. One of the sows has one small Pig and some one has stolen another which would have had pigs. We have had six fat shoats stolen since Christmas. Oh! If I could discover the rogue.

A bloody battle is now being fought in Virginia, so far our troops are victorious. Every Christian ought to be engaged in prayer for surely the crisis must be at hand. Every heart should bow in prayer for our success, and for the souls of those who give their lives for their country. . . .

May 13. . . . Our corn is nearly gone and I've tried in vain to buy. I don't know what to do next. In all the darkness which surrounds us we at last see a few gleams of light. Our army has been successful at every point. The shout of victory comes to us from all parts of the Confederacy, but alas! with it the wail of the widow and the orphan.

May 15. Sunday evening. . . . The battle still goes on in Virginia and the news of victories is coming on every breeze. How we pity the brave men who are engaged in these battles. How we sympathize with the anxious hearts which almost stand still with suspense as they turn and listen in every direction for the last scrap of news from the battle. These hearts are more to be pitied than those that lie cold and still on the bloody feild. They are "Where the wicked cease from troubling and the weary are at rest."

May 18. Plowing and replanting corn in the barley feild. Weather pleasant but not as warm as we desire. The sounds of bloody strife still comes with every train from Virginia. Every body is anxious and gloomy. Constantly we are hearing of some brave man who has fallen, and whether an acquaintance or not, he is somebody's son, somebody's friend. Some face will grow pale at news of his death, perchance some heart break, some soul pray, in its anguish, for death.

May 19. This evening we have had a nice warm shower. A fine swarm of bees came out today. The first good Swarm we have had. I have just had a very pleasant letter from Mr Harris. He is on the Carolina coast doing picket duty. I Miss him very much in all my undertakings but the privation may be of service to me in after life and if he is of service to his country, I ought to be reconciled, for truly our country needs help in her fearful struggle for life. . . .

May 26. To day I have attended the funeral of aunt Jane Wells. We had thunder lightning and rain during the service. I have had a letter from Mr. Harris telling me that he is quiet well. . . . Our troops in Virginia are still bravely and successfully fighting our foes. Truly the country is pouring out its blood freely to win our freedom. . . .

May 29. I have just returned from a visit to the village. I went up yester-

day morning. While there I made a return of our property and the asses-
sor tells me our tax (Confederate tax) will be $581.45. I have the means to
pay it, but if we continue to be taxed during the next year as we have last
I am afraid our means will utterly fail. I must comfort myself with
"Sufficient unto the day is the evil thereof." I gave $5.00 for a pound of
soda, $1.00 for a paper of needles, $4.00 for a spool of white cotton thread,
$4.00 for a quire of paper. . . .

May 31. I have been quite busy today, scouring and scalding. Our hands
are plowing over corn second time, and hoeing and thinning it out. Our
corn looks as well as other peoples, but not very well. I have just received
a letter from Mr Harris telling me that he had been in a small fight with
some Yankee boats. I have been trying to get a petition signed to have him
detailed as farmer, but he tells me that his officers are determined to disapprove it. Now of course there is no hope but for him to remain and fight
our foes. I feel just as much like fighting our men who, standing at the
head of affairs, are the cause of keeping such as him in the field, as I do the
Yankees.

June 5. Sunday morning. . . . As usual, I shall employ myself today in writing to Mr Harris. I shall be troubled some to find wherewith to fill a letter
but letters, he says he must have, and I must try to give him what comfort
I can. It is little that he can have at last. Oh! "When this cruel war is over."

June 6. My birthday, I am thirty seven years old. I can scarcely hope to live
as many more. . . .

June 22. Last Sunday I received a letter from Mr Harris telling me that he
had applied for a furlough and would probably be at home in a few days.
No one can guess how glad I was. Last evening I sent to the station to
bring him home but, Alas! I only got a letter telling me to look for him no
more at present. I tried to look the disappointment directly in the face but
it cost me a few tears nevertheless. I did so much hope that he could get
home to help me with a heavy harvest and various other perplexing matters. It is bad for the *house* to be deprived of its band. We hear that the
yankeys are making a desperate attempt to take Petersburg. We have been
very successful all this Spring. If we have a reverse now, The Lord save or
we perish. . . .

July 1. Finished cutting wheat and rye. . . . This morning I had a letter from
Mr Harris. He tells me that there is no chance for him to get a furlough.   I
did not know how much I had hoped for it until I found that hope   destroyed. I must flounder along without him. I may have to do without him
forever. He tells me that his mess includes himself and one other,   and
they two draw 1 1/2 gal meal, 1 qt flour, 3 qt rice, 1 1/2 lbs of meat and a
tea cup full of salt for five days. TO DAY I HAD SOME CORN PLANTED.
. . .

July 8. They have had a battle on James Island—are still fighting there. Mr.
Harris is there. I feel very anxious, but why should I? The decrees of fate
are unalterable. The weather is hot and we are needing rain. Cutting

Spring oats and fretting because I cannot hire help. Our oats are very fine and I do hate to lose them. . . .

July 23. Finished hauling up the oats. . . . I had a letter from Mr. Harris which tells me that he has been in great danger of being killed by the fire. He has at least discovered how it feels to be shot at and missed. The weather is really cold. I could have enjoyed a fire all day. . . .

July 27. Today and yesterday Mr Allen has been threshing our small grain. . . . We have news of a victory at Atlanta. The victory has been hoped for a long time. I suppose the battle still goes on. No letter for me tonight. . . .

July 30. To day I went to the village and carried a box filled with good things for Mr Harris to be sent to him tomorrow. When I came home I found a letter from him telling me that he was now getting plenty to eat, which has not been the case all the time. His mess includes himself and one other man. . . . Their horses are poorly fed generally. The day he wrote, six ears of corn were given to 24 horses. I think the government should take care of their Cavalry horses, for they seem to be very scarce and difficult to obtain. During the past week we have been eating a very nice fat mutton, the first I have allowed myself since the war commenced. Weather warm and cloudy. . . .

August 2. Hoeing and laying bye cotton. . . . We have some very bad laws and some that oppress the people very much and still dont answer the purpose. The tax in kind is a perfect torment to the people and is so managed as not to feed the army. Thousands of bushels of corn rotted at the depots where it was delivered to the Government. . . .

August 20. This morning I had my turnips sown. . . . This morning we heard of another battle, another victory and the fall of several young men of our acquaintance—promising young men—true and brave. Lemuel Moorman, the only brother of our esteemed young friend, and teacher Virginia, is among the slain. His father, mother and sister all looked to this young man for support and guidance. The pitious shrieks of his sister are now ringing through the house. "Oh! how can I live without my brother?" How few have escaped the bitterness of this cruel war. . . .

August 27. Today I have ridden many miles among the neighbors in search of soap. I found two pounds at $1.50 per lb. I am tired and thoroughly sick of trying to live and make and keep something for the children. Every thing I lay my hands on seems to fail. . . . There is no pleasure in life and yet we are not willing to die. I do not know how it might be but I feel like I should welcome the *Messenger* if it were not for those who need my services here awhile longer.

August 30. Today we have commenced Pulling fodder at Camp Place. The Mornings are quite cool and the days quite hot. . . . Peace conventions are being held at the North, an armistice is talked of, and peace flags have been raised in New York. I tremble for fear it is too good to be true, or may amount to nothing.

[*Journals of David . . . Harris,* pp. 330–340.]

11. SLAVES AND FREEDPEOPLE

While the Union armed forces had not been victorious in every campaign, they had advanced by the summer of 1864 far into the western portions of the Confederacy from Tennessee through Louisiana, as well as into Virginia and other eastern Confederate states. These advances offered the possibility that slaves could flee from their masters and seek to place themselves under the protection of the Union forces.

The Union States Census of 1860 had counted approximately four million slaves, between 10 and 15 percent of the entire population, shortly before the Civil War broke out. The Emancipation Proclamation, as we have seen, declared free the slaves in specified states and counties that were in rebellion against the United States government on January 1, 1863. In actual practice, though, most slaves who got their freedom during the war years probably achieved it by escaping from their masters to the protection of the Union armed forces.

Varied descriptions of slaves, or of newly freed blacks, or of both, appear in the writings by several of the individuals presented in this volume, including, among others, Mary Chesnut, the members of the Jones family, Charlotte Forten, Marcus Spiegel, James Gooding, and Dr. Esther Hawks. But not many accounts by slaves or freedpeople themselves, and written during the war years, have survived—just as is true for most of the whites at the bottom of the economic and social scale. Among the relatively few writings from the years 1861 to 1865 that have survived are a few personal letters, plus miscellaneous communications (applications, affidavits, depositions, for example) to U.S. army officers, to U.S. civilian officials, or to agents of charitable organizations. Some of these miscellaneous communications by slaves and freedpeople asked for protection, some described the location of Confederate forces in their neighborhood, some recounted mistreatment by present or former owners, and some expressed other concerns. Many of the communications were signed with an "X," his or her "mark," in lieu of a signature.

In the absence of diaries or collections of letters written from 1861 to 1865 by slaves or freedpeople, the single letters and fragmentary communications presented here provide brief vignettes of the lives of slaves and freedpeople in what are probably their own words, or a close approximation thereof. These writings are preserved in the National Archives of the United States, and are now being published under the title Freedom: A Documentary History of Emancipation, 1861–1867.

Maryland Fugitive Slave to His Wife:

Upton Hill [Va.] January the 12 1862

My Dear Wife it is with grate joy I take this time to let you know Whare I am i am now in Safety in the 14th Regiment of Brooklyn this Day i can Adress you thank god as a free man I had a little truble in gitting away But as the lord led the Children of Isrel to the land of Canon So he led me to a land Whare fredom Will rain in spite Of earth and hell Dear you must make your Self content i am free from al the Slavers Lash and as you have chose the Wise plan Of Serving the lord i hope you Will pray Much and i Will try by the help of god To Serv him With all my hart I am With a very nice man and have All that hart Can Wish But My Dear I Cant express my grate desire that i Have to See you i trust the time Will Come When We shal meet again And if We dont met on earth We Will Meet in heven Whare Jesas ranes Dear Elizabeth tell Mrs. Own[ees] That i trust that She Will Continue Her kindness to you and that god Will Bless her on earth and Save her In grate eternity My Acomplements to Mrs Owens and her Children may They Prosper through life I never Shall forgit her kindness to me Dear Wife i must Close rest yourself Contented i am free i Want you to rit To me Soon as you Can Without Delay Direct your letter to the 14th Reigment New york State malitia Uptons Hill Virginea In Care of Mr Cranford Comary Write my Dear Soon As you C Your Affectionate Husban Kiss Daniel For me

John Boston

Give my love to Father and Mother

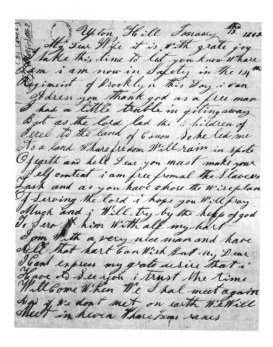

John Boston to Mrs. Elizabeth Boston, 12 Jan. 1862, enclosed in Maj Genl. Geo. B. McClellan to Hon Edwin Stanton, 21 Jan. 1862, A-587 1862, Letters Received, ser. 12, RG 94 [K-23]. The envelope is addressed, in a different handwriting, to "Mrs. Elizabeth Boston Care Mrs. Prescia Owen Ownesville Post Office Maryland."

[*Freedom: A Documentary History of Emancipation, 1861–1867*. Series I, Vol. I, *The Destruction of Slavery*. Edited by Ira Berlin, Barbara J. Fields, Thavolia Glymph, Joseph P. Reidy, and Leslie S. Rowland. Cambridge, Cambridge University Press. Copyright 1985 by Cambridge University Press, pp. 357–358. Permission to print this and other passages included in the present volume granted by Cambridge University Press.]

Louisiana Slave to the Commander of the Department of the Gulf

New Orleans March 4 [1863]

To Your Honour Major General Banks I earnestly request of your honour to grant a hearing in behalf of myself and husband, My mistress has hired me out at the rate of ten dollars a month and times are so dull that I proposed giving my madame eight dollars a month she would not accept of it and said I should come home and she would find a place for me in the work house or in the parish prison where she has my husband Charley Jones for five months I have a son who is home with my madame and I dont want to go home but I am willing to pay a liberal price until so times get better So I entreat of your honour to look and examine my case for I shall do whatever you advised me to do anything that is just and right I earnestly request of you to ansure this and lete me [*know*] what I should do for to releive my mind for I am afraid she may come and demand me and take me to prison any moment when I am willing to give my madam a liberal amount for my time Receive this and tele me what I shal do I remain your Obedent Servant

Edith Jones

Edith Jones to Your Honour Major General Banks, 4 Mar. [1863], J-21 1863, Letters Received, ser. 1920, Civil Affairs, Dept. of the Gulf, RG 393 Pt. 1 (C-705). No reply has been found in the letters-sent volumes of the Department of the Gulf.

[*Freedom: A Documentary History of Emancipation, 1861–1867*. Series I, Vol. III, *The Wartime Genesis of Free Labor: The Lower South*. Edited by Ira Berlin, Thavolia Glymph, Steven F. Miller, Joseph P. Reidy, Leslie S. Rowland, and Julie Saville. Cambridge, Cambridge University Press. Copyright 1990 by Cambridge University Press, p. 429. Permission to print this and other passages included in the present volume granted by Cambridge University Press.]

Statement by a Tennessee Fugitive Slave

Murfreesboro [Tenn.] Mar 12th 1863

Statement of Wiley Thompson (colored) I am a Servant of Newcome Thompson "the first" he lives on the Lewisburg Pike 2 1/4 miles beyon Shelbaville—I ran away from home on the night of the 2d "Inst" I learned from black persons who were in the camps around Shelbaville that the rebels claim to have about 100,000—troops at and between Shelbaville & Chattanoga–Fortified at Tullahoma—I was not in the encampments myself but heard that there were a good many troops at Shelbaville, heard there were some troops Encamped at Fall creek and along the road from there to Unionville—There was a Skirmish at Rover the day I came past (the 4th) I was in the woods there three days before I could get through the lines–was within hereing of the skirmish, I heard the Federals get the better of the Rebs & that they capd 50 prisoners—The Rebels say they are going to fight at Tulahoma, They have brought a good many troops from Mississippi. My master is a union man—told me to keep out of the way of the Rebels—but he has 2 sons in the rebel army—I know he tried to prevent one of them from going, My design is not to leave my master but want to go back when the Federals go—Understand their aim is to send a heavy force of cav in rear of Federal Army to neighborhood of Lavergne when Tulahoma is attacked in order to cut off reinforcements—They intend to Send Wheeler & I think Forrest—I got the information from the Servants of the officers—

his
Wiley X Thompson
mark

Statement of Wiley Thompson, 12 Mar. 1863, T 1863, Letters Received, ser. 925, Dept of the Cumberland, RG 393 Pt. 1 [C-24]. [*Freedom,* Series I, Vol. I, p. 302.]

Missouri Slave Woman to Her Soldier Husband

Mexico Mo Dec 30th 1863

My Dear Husband I have received your last kind letter a few days ago and was much pleased to hear from you once more. It seems like a long time since you left me. I have had nothing but trouble since you left. You recollect what I told you how they would do after you was gone. they abuse me because you went & say they will not take care of our children & do nothing but quarrel with me all the time and beat me scandalously the day before yesterday–Oh I never thought you would give me so much trouble as I have got to bear now. You ought not to left me in the fix I am in & all these little helpless children to take care of. I was invited to a party to night but I could not go I am in too much trouble to want to go to parties. the children talk about you all the time. I wish you could get a furlough & come to see us once more. We want to see you worse than we ever did before. Remember all I told you about how they would do me after you left–for they do worse than they ever did & I do not know what will become of me & my poor little children. Oh I wish you had staid with me & not gone till I could go with you for I do nothing but grieve all the time about you. write & tell me when you are coming.

Tell Isaac that his mother come & got his clothes she was so sorry he went. You need not tell me to beg any more married men to go. I see too much trouble to try to get any more into trouble too— Write to me & do not forget me & my children–farewell my dear husband from your wife

Martha

[Endorsement] Benton Bks Mo Jany 9th 1863 Lt Hussey is directed to send the man to whom this letter was sent, to me that I may get his Masters name &c in order to redress the wrongs complained of

Wm A Pile Brig Genl Comdg

[Endorsement] Geo—Cardwell Mexico—Mo has Seven Children—oldest 14 years of age Virginia Francis Richmond James Billy Joseph Benj—13 m Martha to My Dear Husband [Richard Glover], 30 Dec. 1863, enclosed in Brig. Genl. Wm. A. Pile to Maj. O. D. Greene, 11 Feb. 1864, P-91 1864, Letters Received, ser. 2593, Dept of the MO, RG 393, Pt. 1 [C-159]

Superintendent of the Organization of Missouri Black Troops to the Commander of the Department of the Missouri

Benton Barracks Mo Feb 23/64

Genl Richard Glover (a colored Soldier) Enlisted in Mexico Mo Dec 14th/63 and was mustered into Co. "A" 2nd Mo Vols A.D.—Some three weeks after his Enlistment I learned through Several Sources that his wife and Six children were being cruelly treated by Geo W Cardwell his former master

I directed my Adj Genl to write him a letter remonstrating against this treatment and Saying, unless it was desisted from the military authorities would have to interfere

One week ago to day Mr Cardwell brought Glovers wife and three youngest children to this city–kept them closely housed by the Scobee House–went with the woman to the Pro Mar Genls office to get a pass to take them to Kentucky–The woman at first refused to give her consent to go and was taken back to the Scobee House—and by threats of Selling her children and putting her in Jail unless she consented to go to Kentucky— She was so frightened and terrified that She consented to go and mr Cardwell obtained a pass issued Feby 19" for Martha and her children to be taken to Kentucky

I learned the facts of this case yesterday and that Cardwell would start on the five oclock train for Kentucky

I went in person immediately to the Scobee House took possession of the woman and children—procured a revocation of the permit and now hold the parties Subject to your order

I am informed by Capt Pollion and Dr Martin who are reliable Union men from Mexico that Cardwells family are openly and bitterly rebel— that Cardwell pretends to be Loyal but associates constantly with the worst rebels in the County—that a Box of goods for paynes rebel Co was secreted in Cardwells house in the early part of the war

Wm Smithey a man who attends to Cardwells matters in his absence, whipped Glovers wife most cruelly on monday Dec 28th with a leather Strap from Buggy Harness, and this when she is Pregnant and near confinement

The facts in regard to the threats used to induce the woman to consent to go to Kentucky can be proved by Mr Watson John Baldwin and others

This is not an isolated case, but only a sample of many Similar ones that have occurred during the last two months and I most respectfully and yet most earnestly protest against this infamy in the name of God Justice and humanity

Believing that you will do all that you have power to do, to correct these infamous evils, I most respectfully and earnestly request

1st That instructions be given the Pro Marshals of the Dept to grant no passes, to any man, to take the wife child or parent of a colored Soldier out of this State and they be held responsible for granting improper passes.

2nd That the Pro Mar Dept be required to furnish a report of all passes given for Slaves, to be taken out of the State during the last three months— giving name of the Slave, and owner, with their Residence date of permit and person to whom granted in order that I may ascertain, how many of the wives and children of colored Soldiers have been taken from the State, by Government authority and also from their former masters learn where they were taken—If this can be done, I will send reliable persons to ascertain their present where abouts and condition,—

I claim that it is due these men and the Loyal heart of the people of this State, that they know what has become of their families

3d That orders be sent out for the arrest of all persons, prowling over the state for the purpose of buying and smuggling to Kentucky the wives and children of these, Sable "Patriots" and true Heroes" And that all persons aiding or assisting them be arrested and Summarily punished I have the honor to be Very Respectfully Your obt Servt

Wm A Pile

Brig Genl. Wm. A. Pile to Maj. Genl. Rosecrans, 23 Feb. 1864, enclosed in Brig. Genl. Wm. A. Pile to Maj. O. D. Greene, 17 Mar. 1864, P-197 1864, Letters Received, ser. 2593, Dept. of the MO, RG 393 Pt. 1 [C-160].

[*Freedom: A Documentary History of Emancipation, 1861–1867*. Series II, *The Black Military Experience*. Edited by Ira Berlin, Joseph P. Reidy, and Leslie S. Rowland. Cambridge, Cambridge University Press. Copyright 1982 by Cambridge University Press, pp. 244–246. Permission to print this passage granted by Cambridge University Press.]

Two Applications by Mississippi Freedmen to the Commissioners of Plantations in the Department of the Tennessee

Vicksburg [Miss.] Jany 11th 1864

To the commissioners of Plantations. I the undersigned Josua Culverson, for Willis Culverson Lee Whaley, James Houston, Manuel Johns and

Nathan Buckner, (Colored) represent that we have belonged to the plantation owned by Levi Culverson, that said Culverson Abandoned his said place taking most of his negroes to Texas. over one year ago that we together with some twenty others have remained & wish to cultivate as much as we are able the Coming season Say About one hundred and fifty acres there are twelve double log cabins on the place and about eight hundred acres of Cultivable land.

his
Josua X Culverson
mark

Vicksburg Miss, Jan 19" 1864

To the U.S. Com of Plantations, The undersigned a Colored Loyal Citizen of the United States hereby makes application to lease of the Government the present Year upon the prescribed termes. The Hunt Place on the Miss River near Tallula Conting About One hundred & fifty acres tillable land

his
Major X Whiteing
mark

[Endorsement] I Know the old man who makes the above application. he has resided on the above place for years, and has had full Control of the same. Col Eaton has given him permission to take some of his relations from the Contraband Camp to his home. I Know he has the means to support them. I will endorse the old Mans Honesty and Industry and think him fully Competant to manage the small place he applies for Theodore Fitler a Citizen of Issaquena Co Miss Vicksburg Jany 18. 1864

Josua Culverson to the Commissioners of Plantations, 11 Jan. 1864, and Major Whiteing to the U.S. Com's of Plantations 19 Jan. 1864, Applications to Lease Plantations, Vicksburg District, 2nd Agency, RG 366 [Q-55]. George B. Field, a commissioner of plantations, witnessed Culverson's application; Fitler witnessed that of Whiteing. A notation on the wrapper of Culverson's application reads "Aworded conditionally"; there is no indication whether Whiteing's application was successful.
[*Freedom*, Series I, Vol. III, pp. 781–782.]

Contract between an Arkansas Farmer and Eight Arkansas Freedpeople

[Jackson Co., Ark., January 26, 1864]

This article of agreement entered into this 26th day of January A.D. 1864 between William R. Steen a white citizen aged 34 Years of the first part– and Carolina a colored woman age 40 Years, Charity a colered woman aged 40 years–Harriet a colered woman age 20 Years, Milly a colered girl aged 14 Years, Jake a colored man aged 55 Years, Frank a colored man aged 40 Years, Juliet a colored woman aged 45 Years, Emeline a colored woman aged 25 Years of the Second part. all of Jackson County State of Arkansas: Witnesseth That said Wm R. Steen agrees to hire said above named colored women and men to work upon a farm cultivated by Steen for the Year 1864, agreeing to give said women and men one third part of the crop raised upon the farm by their labor or the proceeds thereof to be divided between themselves as they may deem best in proportion to the labor performed by each, said Steen agreeing to subsist and clothe them and their children–and said colored women and men agreeing on their part to work and labor upon said farm for said Steen for the above stipulated price or part of the crop raised and further agreeing to work diligently and industriously to raise said crop and to behave themselves in an orderly manner, and obey all the laws that may be in force in the Land–Witness our hands the day and Year first above written

W R Steen
Caroline X Steen
Charity X Steen
Harriet X Steen
Milly X Steen
Jake X Steen
Frank X Steen

[In the margin] (Duplicate)
Contract between W. R. Steen and Caroline Steen et al., 26 Jan. 1864, Letters Sent, Reports, Affidavits, & Court Papers, ser. 348, Jacksonport AR Supt., RG 105 [A-2502]. Witnessed. All the "signatures" on this copy are in the same handwriting; neither Juliet nor Emeline, both of whom were listed in the contract, are among the signers.
[*Freedom*, Series I, Vol. III, p. 785.]

Testimony by a Corporal in a Louisiana Black Regiment before the American Freedmen's Inquiry Commission

[New Orleans February ? 1864]

Deposition of Octave Johnson, Corporal Co. C, 15th Regt. Corps d'Afrique.

I was born in New Orleans; I am 23 years of age; I was raised by Arthur Thiboux of New Orleans; I am by trade a cooper; I was treated pretty well at home; in 1855 master sold my mother, and in 1861 he sold me to S. Contrell of St. James Parish for $2,400; here I worked by task at my trade; one morning the bell was rung for us to go to work so early that I could not see, and I lay still, because I was working by task; for this the overseer was going to have me whipped, and I ran away to the woods, where I remained for a year and a half; I had to steal my food; took turkeys, chickens and pigs; before I left our number had increased to thirty, of whom ten were women; we were four miles in the rear of the plantation house; sometimes we would rope beef cattle and drag them out to our hiding place; we obtained matches from our friends on the plantation; we slept on logs and burned cypress leaves to make a smoke and keep away mosquitoes; Eugene Jardeau, master of hounds, hunted for us for three months; often those at work would betray those in the swamp, for fear of being implicated in their escape; we furnished meat to our fellow-servants in the field, who would return corn meal; one day twenty hounds came after me; I called the party to my assistance and we killed eight of the bloodhounds; then we all jumped into Bayou Faupron; the dogs followed us and the alligators caught six of them; "the alligators preferred dog flesh to personal flesh;" we escaped and came to Camp Parapet, where I was first employed in the Commissary's office, then as a servant to Col. Hanks; then I joined his regiment.

Testimony of Corporal Octave Johnson before the American Freedmen's Inquiry Commission, [Feb ? 1864], filed with O-328 1863, Letters Received, ser. 12, RG 94 [K-219].
[*Freedom*, Series I, Vol. I, p. 217.]

Affidavit of a Mississippi or Louisiana Freedman

Natchez Miss March 3 1864

Sam Goff, a Freedman formally belonging to James Brabston owner of the Gilliard Plantation, Appeared in this Office, And made the following statement. The said Goff was employed by Dewitt C. Brown on or about the First day of December 1863 at the rate of Seven Dollars per Month with board and Clothing. Said Brown being Leasee of said Plan: Said Goff has continued upon said plantation up to this time, And has lost no time through his own neglect And has received no money or Clothing from said Brown except one pair of Boots charged at seven Dollars,　Worth about Three Dollars and fifty cents. The said Goff further states that there are Thirty four Other Grown Laborers employed on the Plantation, being Fourteen Men and Twenty Women, And Twenty three Children, About Eight of which have assisted in picking of Cotton. These hands have been moved to the Johnson and Carr Plantations by said Brown and have worked on each place under his orders. The said Brown agreed to pay to each hand 1/4 [cents] per pound in addition to their Monthly wages, All Goods and Groceries furnished to the hands by Brown were paid for in Cash by the hands at the time. said Goff bought One hundred and sixty pounds of Flour for Ten Dollars Cash, Four pounds of Coffee for Three Dollars Cash and Three pounds of sugar for Seventy five cents Cash.

The said Goff for himself and as agent for the Other hands requests that the said Brown be required to pay the wages due to them in to the hands of the Ast spc Agt for Plantations of this District. To be held by him for distrburstion

In Testimony where of the said Saml Goff has hereunto set his hand and Seal this 3d day of March 1864

his

Samuel X Goff

mark

Affidavit of Samuel Goff, 3 Mar. 1864, Letters Received by Assistant Special Agents, Natchez District, 2nd Agency, RG 366 [Q-44]. The affidavit is headed "Office of Ast Sp Agt for Plantations Natchez District," and was sworn before William Burnet, the assistant special agent. The previous day, Burnet had asked the provost marshal general of the Department of the Gulf to arrest Brown, who was reportedly in New Orleans selling cotton gathered by freedpeople whose wages he "has not paid and utterly refuses to pay." Brown was soon arrested and returned to the Natchez area, remaining in detention until March 10, when he "closed his a/c satisfactorily with the hands." (Wm. Burnet to Genl Bowen, 2 Mar. 1864, Wm. Burnet to Capt. Grier, [early Mar. 1864], and Wm. Burnet to Capt. Walker, 10 Mar. [186]4, vol. 237 1/2, pp. 44–45, 47, 75, Press Copies of Letter Sent Relating to Abandoned and/or Confiscated Property, ser. 2295, Natchez MS Treasury Agent, RG 105 [A-9548].)

Contract between an Arkansas Planter and an Arkansas Freedman

Little Rock Ark. March 1,/64

Copy of Lease to Wash Keats,

I have this day rented of Mrs. Maris Thibault of Pulaski county, State of Arkansas, that portion of her plantation upon which her dwelling house, and gin are situate and known as Walnut ridge. The said land is supposed to contain One Hundred acres of tillable land: for which I am to pay the sum of four dollars per acre and furnish vegetables and fruit for family use—the buildings, orchards &c to be kept in good condition while in my possession—The Lease to expire on the last day of December 1864—

The Gin house to be used by the different lessees of Mrs. Thibault farm in ginning their respective crops,

The rent money to be paid after the crop is made, and before it is removed from said land—

his

Washington X Keats

mark

Contract between Mrs. Maria Thibault and Washington Keats, 1 Mar. 1864, Retained Copies of Reports, Reports Received, & Miscellaneous Papers, ser. 379, Little Rock AR Supt. of Freedmen, RG 105 [A-2533]. Witnessed. In the same file is a copy of a similar contract, also dated March 1, between Thibault and another freedman, Thomas Bass, who was to rent 150 acres of her plantation at $5 per acre and to have use of both the gin house and "half the buildings on the land leased by Washington Keats.

The dwelling house included."
[*Freedom*, Series I, Vol. III, pp. 790–791.]

Affidavit of a Tennessee Fugitive Slave

[Knoxville, Tenn. March 30, 1864]

Statement of "Jim" Heiskell

My name is Jim; I have been living on Bull run, with a man by the name of Pierce; they called him Cromwll Pierce. I run off from him nearly two months ago, because he treated me so mean: he half starved and whipped me. I was whipped three or four times a week, sometimes with a cowhide, and sometimes with a hickory. He put so much work on me, I could not do it; chopping & hauling wood and lumber logs. I am about thirteen years old. I got a pretty good meal at dinner, but he only gave us a half pint of milk for breakfast and supper, with cornbread. I ran away to town; I had a brother "Bob" living in Knoxville, and other boys I knew. I would have staid on the plantation if I had been well used. I wanted also to see some pleasure in town. I hired myself to Capt. Smith as a servant, and went to work as a waiter in Quarter Master Winslow's office as a waiter for the mess. After Capt. Winslow went home, I went to live with Bob, helping him.

Last Friday just after dinner, I saw Pierce Mr. Heiskell's overseer. He caught me on Gay street, he ran after me, and carried me down Cumberland street to Mr. Heiskell's house. Mr. Heiskell, his wife and two sons, and a daughter were in the house. Mr. Heiskell asked me what made me run away; he grabbed me by the back of the ears, and jerked me down on the floor on my face; Mr. Pierce held me & Mr. Heiskell put irons on my legs. Mr. Heiskell took me by the hair of my head, and Mr. Pierce took me around my body, they carried me upstairs, and then Mr. Heiskell dagged me into a room by my hair. They made me stand up, and then they laid me down on my belly & pulled off my breeches as far as they could, and turned my shirt and jacket up on my head. (I heard Mr Heiskell ask for the cowhide before he started with me upstairs.) Mr. Pierce held my legs, and Mr. Heiskell got a straddle of me, and whipped me with the rawhide on my back & legs. Mr. Pierce is a large man, and very strong. Mr. Heiskell rested two or three times, and begun again. I hollowed—"O, Lord" all the time. They whipped me, it seemed to me, half an hour. They then told me to get up and dress, and said if I did'nt behave myself up there they would come up again and whip me again at night. The irons were left on my legs. Mr. Heiskell came up at dark and asked me what that "yallow nigger was talking to me about." He meant my brother Bob, who had been talking to me opposite the house. I was standing up and then he (Mr. Heiskell) asked me about the "yaller nigger", he kicked me with his right foot on my hip and knocked me over on the floor, as the irons were on my feet, I could not catch myself. I knew my brother Bob was around the house trying to get me out. About one hour by sun two soldiers came to the house, one staid & the other went away. I saw them through the window. They had sabres. I thought they had come to guard me to keep Bob from getting me. I heard Bob whisling, and I went to the window and looked through the curtain. Bob told me to hoist the window, put something under it and swing out of the window. I did as my brother told me, and hung by my hands. Bob said "Drop," but I said I was afraid I would hurt myself. Bob said "Wait a minute and I will get a ladder." He brought a ladder and put it against the house, under the window. I got halfway down before they hoisted the window; I fell & Bob caught me and run off with me in his arms. I saw Mr. Pierce sitting at the window, he had a double-barreled gun in his hands. By the time I could count three I heard a gun fired two or three times, quick, I heard Mr. Pierce call "Jim" "Jim" and the guards hollered "halt; halt!" I had no hat or shoes on. We both hid, and laid flat on the ground. I saw the guard, running around there hunting for us. After lying there until the guards had gone away, we got up and Bob carried me to a friend's house. I had the irons on my legs. I got some supper and staid there until next day. My irons were taken off by a colored man, who carried me to the hospital. I am now employed working in the hospital N° I.

his

—signed— Jim X Heiskell–

mark

Affidavit of Jim Heiskell, [30 Mar. 1864], Records of the general Agent, RG 366 [Q-135]. Sworn before the army post commander. In the same file are a report by the provost marshal general of east Tennessee regarding the arrest of Bob Heiskell for threatening the life of his former master, and a statement by a surgeon in a black regiment describing the nature and extent of Jim Heiskell's injuries. (B. G. S. P. Carter to Maj. J. A. Campbell, 26 Mar. 1864; statement of Surgeon Ralph W. Cummings, 30 Mar. 1864.) Another letter in the file, written by Treasury Department assistant special agent William G. Brownlow, described William Heiskell as "an Honorable man . . . a Slave holder all his days . . . notorious for his kind treatment of his Slaves." According to Brownlow, William Heiskell was worth approximately $100,000 at the beginning of the war "and now he is reduced to poverty and lives alone off of his office, or salary as Local Agent." Brownlow explained the slaveholder's actions thus: "The Boy 'Robert' was walking these Streets with a revolver in hand and threatening the life of Mr Heiskell as he would go to and from his meals. He also planted himself on the Street opposite to Mr Heiskells house, and cursed Mrs Heiskell for a d——d old freckled faced bitch. The community irrespective of parties would have sustained Mr Heiskell if he had put a load of buckshot into him!"
(W. G. Brownlow to W. P. Mellen, Esq., 20 May 1864.)
[*Freedom*, Series I, Vol. I, pp. 320–322.]

12. MILITARY STALEMATE BY AUGUST, 1864, AND REPERCUSSIONS IN POLITICS, UNION AND CONFEDERACY

Unionists

Emily Harris's mention of the holding of "peace conventions" in the North reflected the hope of many Confederates by the summer of 1864 that supporters of the Union would become disillusioned and seek peace when their troops, after years of war, had still not subdued the Confederacy. Emily Harris hoped that there was strong sentiment in the North for making peace, but Frederick Douglass feared that sentiment.

By 1864, Douglass was concerned that as the war dragged on, without conclusive military victory and with ever-mounting casualties, opponents of the war in the North ("Copperheads," antiwar Democrats) might persuade the Northern public to make some sort of compromise with the Confederacy that would end the fighting and might leave slavery intact. He noted that even though the ending of slavery was by 1864 a goal of the war, blacks were not receiving equal treatment with whites either in the Union military forces or in civilian life. Moreover, the President and other leaders were now beginning to put forth plans for the government of Confederate regions captured by the Union army, and thus ultimately for the entire Confederacy if the Union won the war. Douglass was dismayed that those plans did not include voting for blacks on equal terms with whites, and did not include provisions to prevent the planter class from continuing to rule the blacks after the war, just as before.

Douglass's writings in the first eight months of 1864 thus reflected criticism of the Lincoln administration to the point of (1) support (in May, 1864) for the calling of a convention designed to replace Lincoln as the presidential candidate of the Republican party in the 1864 election and (2) urging an English correspondent (in June, 1864) to "rebuke" Lincoln and his government in the strongest terms.

The Mission of the War. Address Sponsored by Women's Loyal League and Delivered in Cooper Institute, New York City, February 13, 1864:

Ladies and Gentlemen:

. . . We are now wading into the third year of conflict with a fierce and sanguinary rebellion, one which . . . has planted agony at a million hearth-stones, thronged our streets with the weeds of mourning, filled our land with mere stumps of men, ridged our soil with 200,000 rudely-formed graves, and mantled it all over with the shadow of death. . . .

I know that many are appalled and disappointed by the apparently interminable character of this war. . . . Gov. Seymour [of New York] charges us with prolonging the war, and I say the longer the better if it must be so—in order to put an end to the hell black cause out of which the Rebellion has risen.

Say not that I am indifferent to the horrors and hardships of the war. I am not indifferent. In common with the American people generally, I feel the prolongation of the war a heavy calamity—private as well as public. There are vacant spaces at my hearthstone which I shall rejoice to see filled again by the boys who once occupied them—but which cannot be thus filled while the war lasts—for they have enlisted—"during the war." . . .

Ladies and gentlemen, there was a time when I hoped that events unaided by discussions would couple this Rebellion and Slavery in a common grave. But . . . the facts do still fall short of our hopes. The question as to what shall be done with Slavery—and especially what shall be done with the Negro—threaten to remain open questions for some time yet. . . .

Our chief danger lies in the absence of all moral feeling in the utterances of our rulers. . . . The great misfortune is and has been during all the progress of this war, that the Government and loyal people have not understood and accepted its true mission. . . .

While our Government has the meanness to ask Northern colored men to give up the comfort of home, endure untold hardships, peril health, limbs and life itself, in its defense, and then degrades them in the eyes of other soldiers, by offering them the paltry sum of $7.00 per month, and refuses to reward their valor with even the hope of promotion—the Democratic party may well enough presume upon the strength of popular prejudice for support.

While our Republican Government at Washington makes color and not character the criterion of promotion in the army. . . . I think we are in danger of a compromise with Slavery.

Our hopeful Republican friends tell me this is impossible—that the day of compromise with Slavery is past. This may do for some men, but will not do for me. . . . while we have a Democratic party at the North trimming its sails to catch the Southern breeze in the next Presidential election, we are in danger of compromise. Tell me not of amnesties and oaths of allegiance. They are valueless in the presence of twenty hundred millions invested in human flesh. Let but the little finger of Slavery get back into this Union, and in one year you shall see its whole body again upon our backs.

While a respectable colored man or woman can be kicked out of the commonest street car in New York where any white ruffian may ride unquestioned—we are in danger of a compromise with Slavery. . . . Until we shall see the election of November next, and that it has resulted in the election of a sound Anti-Slavery man as President, we shall be in danger of a slaveholding compromise. Indeed, as long as Slavery has any life in it, anywhere in the country, we are in danger of such a compromise.

Then there is the danger arising from the impatience of the people on account of the prolongation of the war. I know the American people. They are an impulsive people, impatient of delay, clamorous for change—and often look for results out of all proportion to the means employed in attaining them. . . . Now, this is just the sort of people whose votes may turn the scale against us in the last event. . . .

The hour is one of hope as well as danger. But whatever may come to pass, one thing is clear: The principles involved in the contest, the necessities of both sections of the country, the obvious requirements of the age, and every suggestion of enlightened policy demand the utter extirpation of Slavery from every foot of American soil, and the enfranchisement of the entire colored population of the country. Elsewhere we may find peace, but it will be a hollow and deceitful peace. Elsewhere we may find prosperity, but it will be a transient prosperity. Elsewhere we may find greatness and renown, but if these are based upon anything less substantial than justice they will vanish, for righteousness alone can permanently exalt a nation.

I end where I began—no war but an Abolition war; no peace but an Abolition peace; liberty for all, chains for none; the black man a soldier in war, a laborer in peace; a voter at the South as well as at the North; America his permanent home, and all Americans his fellow-countrymen. Such, fellow-citizens, is my idea of the mission of the war. If accomplished, our glory as a nation will be complete, our peace will flow like a river, and our foundations will be the everlasting rocks.

[*New York Tribune,* January (February?) 14, 1864]

To E. Gilbert, ESQ.

Rochester, May 23, 1864

Sir:

I mean the complete abolition of every vestige, form and modification of Slavery in every part of the United States, perfect equality for the black man in every State before the law, in the jury box, at the ballot-box and on the battle-field: ample and salutary retaliation for every instance of enslavement or slaughter of prisoners of color. I mean that in the distribution of offices and honors under this Government no discrimination shall be made in favor of or against any class of citizens, whether black or white, of native or foreign birth. And supposing that the Convention which is to meet at Cleveland means the same thing, I cheerfully give my name as one of the signers of the call. [The Convention, which met in Cleveland, May 31, 1864, was called by Republicans who were opposed to the re-election of Lincoln in 1864. Douglass, while supporting the calling of the Convention, was not one of the several hundred delegates who attended the Convention and who nominated John C. Fremont for President in place of Lincoln.]

Yours, respectfully,
Frederick Douglass

[*New York Times*, May 27, 1864]

To an English Correspondent

[June, 1864]

[Dear Sir:]

. . . The more you can say of *the swindle* by which our Government claims the respect of mankind for abolishing slavery—at the same time that it is practically reestablishing that hateful system in Louisiana, under General Banks—*the better.* I have not readily consented to the claims set up in the name of anti-slavery for our Government, but I have tried to believe all for the best. My patience and faith are not very strong now. The treatment of our poor black soldiers—the refusal to pay them anything like equal compensation, though it was promised them when they enlisted; the refusal to insist upon the exchange of colored prisoners when colored prisoners have been slaughtered in cold blood, although the President has repeatedly promised thus to protect the lives of his colored soldiers—have worn my patience threadbare. The President has virtually laid down this as the rule of his statesmen: *Do evil by choice, right from necessity.* You will see that he does not sign the bill adopted by Congress, restricting the organization of State Governments only to those States where there is a loyal majority. His plan is to organize such Government wherever there is one-tenth of the people loyal! —an entire contradiction of the constitutional idea of the Republican Government. I see no purpose on the part of Lincoln and his friends to extend the elective franchise to the colored people of the South, but the contrary. This is extremely dishonorable. *No rebuke of it can be too strong from your side of the water.* The Negro is deemed good enough to fight for the Government, but not good enough to enjoy the right to vote for the Government. We invest with the elective franchise those who with bloody blades and bloody hands have sought the life of the nation, but sternly refuse to invest those who have done what they could to save the nation's life. This discrimination becomes more dishonorable when the circumstances are fully considered. Our Government asks the Negro to espouse its cause; it asks him to turn against his master, and thus fires his master's hate against him. Well, when it has attained peace, what does it propose? Why this, to hand the Negro back to the political power of his master, without a single element of strength to shield himself from the vindictive spirit sure to be roused against the whole colored race.

[Frederick Douglass]

The Liberator, September 16, 1864
[*The Life and Writings of Frederick Douglass*, Vol. 3, pp. 386–389, 394–395, 400–404.]

Douglass's criticisms of Lincoln were not shared by George Templeton Strong, but Strong did note, as early as June, 1864, that people were "blue": "They have found out somehow that Grant will never get into Richmond after all." Northerners who were skeptical that Grant would capture Richmond may have remembered McClellan's experience in 1862, when his troops reached the outskirts of Richmond but could not take the city itself. Moreover, Grant's army had suffered an enormous number of casualties in approaching no closer to Richmond than had McClellan two years earlier. By August of 1864, Grant seemed stalled before Richmond and Sherman seemed stalled before Atlanta; casualties were high and new conscription calls were needed. The high hopes for a speedy and decisive victory that had been common in the United States in the spring of 1864 had turned, by the late summer, to war weariness, providing the basis for a movement to stop the war.

This movement to stop the war found its political home in the pro-peace faction of the Democratic party. In contrast to Douglass's criticism that the Lincoln administration was not vigorously shaping the war effort toward greater equality for blacks, the peace movement, at the opposite end of the political spectrum, criticized the Lincoln administration for the war effort itself, urging that the war be ended. The peace movement seemed to be growing, and toward the end of August, 1864, Lincoln was being told by some of his most prominent supporters that he could not win the upcoming election. Letters from two of those supporters are presented here: Thurlow Weed was a leading Republican politician from New York State, while Henry J. Raymond was both the influential editor of the New York Times *and also the chairman of the Republican National Committee.*

Thurlow Weed to Secretary of State William H. Seward, August 22, 1864:

When, ten or eleven days since, I told Mr. Lincoln that his re-election was an impossibility, I also told him that the information would soon come to him through other channels. It has doubtless, ere this, reached him. At any rate, nobody here doubts it; nor do I see any body from other States who authorises the slightest hope of success.

Mr. Raymond, who has just left me, says that unless some prompt and bold step be now taken, all is lost.

The People are wild for Peace. They are told that the President will only listen to terms of Peace on condition Slavery be "abandoned."

Mr. Swett is well informed in relation to the public sentiment. He has seen and heard much. Mr. Raymond thinks commissioners should be immediately sent, to Richmond, offering to treat for Peace on the basis of Union. That *something* should be done and promptly done, to give the Administration a chance for its life, is certain.

[*The Collected Works of Abraham Lincoln.* Edited by Roy P. Basler. 9 vols. New Brunswick, NJ, Rutgers University Press. Vol. VII, copyright 1953 by

The Abraham Lincoln Association, Springfield, Ill., pp. 514–515n1. Permission to print this and other passages included in the present volume granted by The Abraham Lincoln Association and Rutgers University Press.]

Henry J. Raymond to Abraham Lincoln, August 22, 1864:

I feel compelled to drop you a line concerning the political condition of the country as it strikes me. I am in active correspondence with your staunchest friends in every state and from them all I hear but one report. The tide is setting strongly against us. Hon. E. B. Washburne writes that "were an election to be held now in Illinois we should be beaten." Mr. Cameron writes that Pennsylvania is against us. Gov. Morton writes that nothing but the most strenuous efforts can carry Indiana. This state, according to the best information I can get, would go 50,000 against us tomorrow. And so of the rest. Nothing but the most resolute and decided action on the part of the government and its friends, can save the country from falling into hostile hands.

Two special causes are assigned to this great reaction in public sentiment,—the want of military successes, and the impression in some minds, the fear and suspicion in others, that we are not to have peace *in any event* under this administration until Slavery is abandoned. In some way or other the suspicion is widely diffused that we *can* have peace with Union if we would. It is idle to reason with this belief—still more idle to denounce it. It can only be expelled by some authoritative act, at once bold enough to fix attention and distinct enough to defy incredulity & challenge respect.

Why would it not be wise, under these circumstances, to appoint a Commissioner, in due form, *to make distinct proffers of peace to Davis, as the head of the rebel armies, on the sole condition of acknowledging the supremacy of the constitution,*—all other questions to be settled in a convention of the people of all the States? The making of such an offer would require no armistice, no suspension of active war, no abandonment of positions, no sacrifice of consistency.

If the proffer were *accepted* (which I presume it would not be,) the country would never consent to place the practical execution of its details in any but loyal hands, and in those we should be safe.

If it should be *rejected,* (as it would be,) it would plant seeds of disaffection in the south, dispel all the delusions about peace that prevail in the North, silence the clamors & damaging falsehoods of the opposition, take the wind completely out of the sails of the Chicago craft, reconcile public sentiment to the War, the draft, & the tax as inevitable *necessities,* and unite the North as nothing since firing on Fort Sumter has hitherto done.

I cannot conceive of any answer which Davis could give to such a proposition which would not strengthen you & the Union cause *everywhere.* Even your radical friends could not fail to applaud it when they should see the practical strength it would bring to the common cause.

I beg you to excuse the earnestness with which I have pressed this matter upon your attention. It seems to me calculated to do good—& incapable of doing harm. It will turn the tide of public sentiment & avert pending evils of the gravest character. It will rouse & concentrate the loyalty of the country &, unless I am greatly mistaken, give us an early & a fruitful victory.

Permit me to add that if done at all I think this should be done at once,—as your own spontaneous act. In advance of the Chicago Convention it might render the action of that body, of very little consequence.

I have canvassed this subject very fully with Mr. Swett of Illinois who first suggested it to me & who will seek an opportunity to converse with you upon it. . . .

[*The Collected Works of Abraham Lincoln*, Vol. VII, pp. 517–518n1.]

At the time in August when Lincoln was being told by supporters that he could not be reelected, he apparently agreed with that assessment of his political prospects. When his Cabinet met on August 23, Lincoln asked the Cabinet members to sign their names on the back of a paper which was folded in such a way that they could not see what was written inside. What the Cabinet members could not see was a statement written by Lincoln which read as follows:

Executive Mansion
Washington, Aug. 23, 1864.

This morning, as for some days past, it seems exceedingly probable that this Administration will not be re-elected. Then it will be my duty to so co-operate with the President elect, as to save the Union between the election and the inauguration; as he will have secured his election on such ground that he can not possibly save it afterwards.

A. Lincoln

[*The Collected Works of Abraham Lincoln*, Vol. VII, p. 514.]

The meeting at which Lincoln asked his Cabinet members to sign a folded piece of paper took place before the Democratic party held its national convention. At that national convention, in Chicago, August 29 to 31, the pro-peace faction of the party succeeded in having adopted as part of the national platform the statement it desired concerning the war:

> After four years of failure to restore the Union by the experiment of war . . . [we] demand that immediate efforts be made for a cessation of hostilities, with a view to an ultimate convention of the states, or other peaceable means, to the end that, at the earliest practicable moment, peace may be restored on the basis of the Federal Union.

The pro-peace faction was able also to secure the vice-presidential nomination for one of its supporters, George Pendleton, congressman from Ohio, who had op-

posed the war from its beginning. The nomination for President went to General George B. McClellan. Everything now seemed in place for the Democratic party to tap the "war weariness" and "longing for peace" sentiment and gain victory in the upcoming elections in the Union States.

Confederates

The sentiments of "war weariness" and "longing for peace" can certainly be found in the writings by Confederates in August, 1864, but those sentiments seem not to have been accompanied often with the view that the war was a failure that should be stopped. The checking of Grant before Richmond and of Sherman before Atlanta were disillusioning and disappointing to individuals in the Union states when measured against the high hopes in early 1864 for a speedy victory over the Confederates. But when measured against Confederate hopes of winning their independence, the fact that both Richmond and Atlanta were still in Confederate hands in August, 1864, despite all the Union troops hurled against them, could seem hopeful (or, at least, not a cause for despair) to many Confederates. And if large Confederate armies had not in the summer of 1864 duplicated their 1862 and 1863 invasions of Maryland and Pennsylvania, at least General Early's Confederate raiders had reached the outskirts of Washington, D.C., and had penetrated as far north as Chambersburg in Pennsylvania. Finally, there were no major elections in the autumn of 1864 in the Confederacy to focus attention on whether alternative military and political policies might be preferable to those of Jefferson Davis's administration.

Thus, Emily L. Harris's perception that the battles in Virginia and those around Atlanta were victories for the Confederates was comparable to what John Cotton was writing his wife in the summer of 1864 about the fighting in Georgia. Cotton, in the Confederate cavalry opposing Sherman's army in Georgia, reported to his wife on June 9 that:

> the yankeys charged our men nite before last . . . and we killed and captured fifteen hundred of them that is about the way they get done every time they attact us I think if they would come up and fite us a fare fite that we would give them the worst whipping they ever got it is reported by deserters and citizens comeing in to our lines that they are suffering very much for the want of rashons and that there horses and mules are starving for want to forage from all accounts there armey is in a very bad condition [p. 112]

Cotton wrote in a similar vein on June 27, and then noted in a letter of August 10 that

> there has been two very hard fites here at Atlanta . . . and reports says our men whiped them badly we still hold Atlanta and I hope we will bee able to still hold it [p. 117]

Mary Chesnut was not as optimistic as either John Cotton or Emily L. Harris, perhaps because she had spent most of the war, so far, around the center of

the government and had received a more complete view of the overall picture of
Confederate difficulties by 1864. Yet even Mary Chesnut's diary for the last ten
days of August contains as much optimism as pessimism when it mentions mili-
tary events (by August, 1864, Mary Chesnut's husband had been promoted to
brigadier general and sent to Columbia, South Carolina, where Jefferson Davis
was soon to be their house guest):

August 19, 1864. . . . . Letters from the army. Grant's dogged stay about
Richmond very disgusting and depressing to the spirits.

Perriman DePass's letter says they hope to stop Sherman.

Wade Hampton put in command of Southern cavalry. . . .
August 22, 1864. . . . Mobile half-taken.

The RR between us and Richmond tapped

Heavy fight in Florida. A company of South Carolinians surprised
and taken prisoners. Captain Smart—alas, not a smart captain. No one has
failed to make that too-evident comment.

So hardened are we to war and war's alarms. . . .
August 23, 1864. All in muddle, and yet the news, confused as it is, seems
good from all quarters.

Row in New Orleans—Memphis retaken [Nathan Forrest's Confederates seized Memphis on Aug. 21 but abandoned the city the same
day.]—2,000 prisoners captured at Petersburg—Yankee raid on Macon,
come to grief.

John Taylor Wood, fine fellow, in his fine ship *Tallahassee*. He is all
right. . . .

"How I wish General Lee had been sent west to stop Sherman."

Grant can hold his own as well as Sherman. Lee has a heavy handful
in the new Suwarrow. He has worse odds than anyone else, for when
Grant has ten thousand slain, he has only to order up another ten thousand and they are there—ready to step out to the front.
[*Mary Chesnut's Civil War*, pp. 637–640.]

Such Confederates as Mary Chesnut, John Cotton, and Emily L. Harris did
not express sentiments of despair in their writings in August, 1864. But the
events of the next few months were to present severe challenges to their hopes and
expectations.

13. THE END OF THE MILITARY STALEMATE, AND
MORE REPERCUSSIONS IN POLITICS,
SEPTEMBER–NOVEMBER, 1864

Unionists

It had been the military situation (stalemate and numerous casualties) that
had provided the base for the peace movement in the Union States in the late sum-

mer of 1864, and it was a dramatic change in the military situation that took away much of the support for the peace movement in the autumn of 1864.

The major change in the military situation came with great suddenness when the stalemate before Atlanta ended on September 1 and 2. The Confederate forces gave up Atlanta on September 1, and the Union army took over on the next day. It is difficult to exaggerate the effect of the capture of Atlanta on public opinion in the Union States, and that effect was magnified when Atlanta's capture was combined with two other victories by the Union armed forces. In a series of battles from mid-September to mid-October, the Union cavalry commander, General Philip Sheridan, led his troops to crushing victories over the Confederate forces of General Jubal Early, in the Shenandoah Valley of Virginia. Meanwhile, in a series of actions during the month of August, Union naval forces under the command of Admiral David G. Farragut had captured the fortifications in Mobile Bay and thus closed that seaport to Confederate shipping. Once Atlanta was captured, these Union victories in Mobile Bay assumed a new and greater importance in the public mind.

The military victories gave a great boost to morale in the Union states, reviving the conviction held by many Union supporters early in 1864 that victory for their forces in the war was certain and would not be long delayed. This boost in morale translated quickly into support for Lincoln and the Republican party in the upcoming elections. Already by September 13, Lincoln, who on August 23 had written that "it seems exceedingly probable that this Administration will not be reelected," now recorded his prediction that he would receive 172 electoral votes to McClellan's 66 votes.

The perception of change in the public mood after the capture of Atlanta may also have affected the response of General George B. McClellan to his nomination for President by the Democratic party Convention. McClellan had been nominated at the convention meeting on August 29, 30, and 31 after the convention had adopted its platform with its pro-peace plank. McClellan's letter of acceptance of the nomination was released on September 8, and in that letter McClellan, while accepting the nomination, rejected the portion of the party platform which began "After four years of failure," writing that he

> could not look in the faces of gallant comrades of the army and navy . . .
> and tell them that their labor and the sacrifice of our slain and wounded
> brethren had been in vain.

Rather than the party platform's "four years of failure" statement, McClellan wrote that when "our present adversaries are ready for peace, on the basis of the Union," peace negotiations could begin. McClellan emphasized that the restoration of the Union was "the one condition of peace—we ask no more." By making no mention of the abolition of slavery as a condition for peace, McClellan distinguished his position from that of the Republican party, whose platform called for the full and final abolition of slavery by amendment to the Constitution.

Whether or not the public reaction to the capture of Atlanta influenced McClellan's letter of acceptance, the public reaction did lead Lincoln to revise

*quickly his prediction of the outcome of the Presidential election. So, too, the plat-
form and candidates chosen by the Democratic National Convention led Frederick
Douglass quickly to revise, or reinterpret, or refocus, his statements about the
Lincoln administration and the approaching election. Writing on September 17,
Douglass expressed his strong preference for Lincoln and the Republicans over
McClellan and the Democrats. Faced with those alternatives, Douglass's choice
was clear, and he, like the Republican platform, urged the ending of slavery
throughout the restored Union. But Douglass also reported his suspicion that
Republican committees did not want him to campaign actively, for fear that they
would be branded the "N——r" party, and he continued to advocate suffrage for
black men, North and South, on equal terms with whites—a proposal that did not
have the support of many Republicans, nor was it favored, as Douglass had noted,
by all abolitionists.*

To William Lloyd Garrison, Esq.

Rochester, N.Y., Sept. 17, 1864

Dear Sir:

You were pleased to remark in the last number of *The Liberator* (head-
ing it with "Frederick Douglass on President Lincoln") that the secessionist newspapers in Great Britain are publishing with exultation a letter recently addressed by Mr. Douglass to an English correspondent, and you
further favor your readers with an extract from the same letter, which crit-
icizes in plain terms the policy of the present administration towards the
colored people of the country. I am sure you will allow me space in the
columns of the *Liberator* (not to qualify, not to take back any charge, statement, or argument contained in that letter, not even to find fault with its
publication, here or elsewhere, . . . but for the eyes of the esteemed friend
to whom it was addressed) to remove an inference respecting my present
political course, which may possibly and will probably be drawn from the
extract in question. In the first place, it is proper to state that that letter was
not written recently, as you mistakenly allege, but three months ago, and
was in no wise intended to be used against the present administration in
the canvass and issues as now made up between the great parties and especially by the disloyal and slavery perpetuating nominations placed before the country by the Chicago convention. Since the date of those nominations, we are met by a new state of facts, and new considerations have
arisen to guide and control the political action of all those who are ani-
mated by a sincere desire to see justice, liberty and peace permanently established in this rebellion and slavery cursed land. While there was, or
seemed to be, the slightest possibility of securing the nomination and election of a man to the Presidency of more decided anti-slavery convictions
and a firmer faith in the immediate necessity and practicability of justice
and equality for all men, than have been exhibited in the policy of the pre-

sent administration, I, like many other radical men, freely criticized, in private and in public, the actions and utterances of Mr. Lincoln, and withheld from him my support. That possibility is now no longer conceivable; it is now plain that this country is to be governed or misgoverned during the next four years, either by the Republican Party represented in the person of Abraham Lincoln, or by the (miscalled) Democratic Party, represented by George B. McClellan. With this alternative clearly before us, all hesitation ought to cease, and every man who wishes well to the slave and to the country should at once rally with all the warmth and earnestness of his nature to the support of Abraham Lincoln and Andrew Johnson, and to the utter defeat and political annihilation of McClellan and Pendleton; for the election of the latter, with their well known antecedents, declared sentiments, and the policy avowed in the Chicago platform, would be the heaviest calamity of these years of war and blood, since it would upon the instant sacrifice and wantonly cast away everything valuable, purchased so dearly by the precious blood of our brave sons and brothers on the battlefield for the perfect liberty and permanent peace of a common country. . . . nothing strange has happened to me in the said exultation over my words by the secessionist newspapers in Great Britain or elsewhere. The common example of those who do not go at all, playing off those who go farthest against those who go, but do not go fast and far enough, is but repeated in this exultation; and if I mistake not, in other days, there were often utterances of *The Liberator* itself, both on the eve and in the middle of the Presidential campaigns, which caused even greater exultation among the known enemies of liberty against timid, short-sighted and trimming anti-slavery men in the high places of the country, than anything I ever wrote concerning Mr. Lincoln and his administration could produce.

> Yours for freedom and the equal rights of all men,
>
> Frederick Douglass

The Liberator, September 23, 1864. . . .

The Cause of the Negro People
Address of the Colored National Convention
to the People of the United States, October 4–7, 1864

Fellow-Citizens:

The members of the colored National Convention, assembled in Syracuse, State of New York, October the 4th, 1864 . . . warmly embrace the occasion to congratulate you upon the success of your arms, and upon the prospect of the speedy suppression of the slaveholders' rebellion. . . . Having shared with you, in some measure, the hardships, perils, and sacrifices of this war for the maintenance of the Union and Government, we rejoice with you also in every sign which gives promise of its approaching termination. . . .

In view of the general cheerfulness of the national situation, . . . we venture to hope that the present is a favorable moment to commend to your consideration the subject of our wrongs, and to obtain your earnest and hearty co-operation in all wise and just measures for their full redress. . . .

Do you, then, ask us to state, in plain terms, just what we want of you, and just what we think we ought to receive at your hands? We answer: First of all, the complete abolition of the slavery of our race in the United States. . . .

Do you answer, that you have no longer anything to fear? that slavery has already received its death-blow? that it can only have a transient existence, even if permitted to live after the termination of the war? We answer, So thought your Revolutionary fathers when they framed the Federal Constitution; and to-day, the bloody fruits of their mistake are all around us. . . .

There is still one other subject, fellow-citizens,—one other want,—looking to the peace and welfare of our common country, as well as to the interests of our race; and that is, political equality. We want the elective franchise in all the States now in the Union, and the same in all such States as may come into the Union hereafter. We believe that the highest welfare of this great country will be found in erasing from its statute-books all enactments discriminating in favor or against any class of its people, and by establishing one law for the white and colored people alike. . . .

We are asked, even by some Abolitionists, why we cannot be satisfied, for the present at least, with personal freedom; the right to testify in courts of law; the right to own, buy, and sell real estate; the right to sue and be sued. We answer, Because in a republican country, where general suffrage is the rule, personal liberty, the right to testify in courts of law, the right to hold, buy, and sell property, and all other rights, become mere privileges, held at the option of others, where we are excepted from the general political liberty. What gives to the newly arrived emigrants, fresh from lands governed by kingcraft and priestcraft, special consequence in the eyes of the American people? It is not their virtue, for they are often depraved; it is not their knowledge, for they are often ignorant; it is not their wealth, for they are often very poor; why, then, are they courted by the leaders of all parties? The answer is, that our institutions clothe them with the elective franchise, and they have a voice in making the laws of the country. Give the colored men of this country the elective franchise, and you will see no violent mobs driving the black laborer from the wharves of large cities, and from toil elsewhere by which he honestly gains his bread. . . .

A special reason may be urged in favor of granting colored men the right [to vote] in all the rebellious States. . . .

Now, whoever lives to see this rebellion suppressed at the South, as we believe we all shall, will also see the South characterized by a sullen hatred towards the National Government. . . . and for a long time that country is to be governed with difficulty. We may conquer Southern armies by the sword; but it is another thing to conquer Southern hate. Now what is the natural counterpoise against this Southern malign hostility? This it is: give the elective franchise to every colored man of the South who is of sane mind, and has arrived at the age of twenty-one years, and you have at once four millions of friends who will guard with their vigilance, and, if need be, defend with their arms, the ark of Federal Liberty from the treason and pollution of her enemies. You are sure of the enmity of the masters,—make sure of the friendship of the slaves; for, depend upon it, your Government cannot afford to encounter the enmity of both. . . .

[*Proceedings of the National Convention of Colored Men Held in Syracuse,* New York, October 4–7, 1864, pp. 44–62.]

To Theodore Tilton

Rochester, October 15, 1864

My Dear Mr. Tilton:

I am obliged by your favor containing a copy of your recent speech in Latimer hall. . . .

I am not doing much in this Presidential canvass for the reason that Republican committees do not wish to expose themselves to the charge of being the "N——r" party. The Negro is the deformed child, which is put out of the room when company comes. I hope to speak some after the election—though not much before—and I am inclined to think I shall be able to speak all the more usefully because I have had so little to say during the present canvass. I now look upon the election of Mr. Lincoln as settled. When there was any shadow of a hope that a man of a more decided anti-slavery conviction and policy could be elected, I was not for Mr. Lincoln. But as soon as the Chicago convention, my mind was made up, and it is made still. All dates changed with the nomination of Mr. McClellan. . . .

Truly yours always,
Frederick Douglass

Frederick Douglass MSS, Buffalo Public Library [*The Life and Writings of Frederick Douglass, Vol. III,* pp. 406–409, 416–422, 424.]

Frederick Douglass and Abraham Lincoln may have responded in a more rapid and more dramatic fashion to the political and military events of late August and early September, 1864, than did other supporters of the Union, but those events figured, with varying degrees of prominence, in the writings of other Unionists. Samuel Cormany and Thomas M. Chester, for example, noted the reactions of Union soldiers to the capture of Atlanta and to the victories of Union General Philip Sheridan's troops in the Shenandoah Valley of Virginia.

Samuel Cormany's regiment continued in September and October, 1864, as in the preceding months, to be engaged in skirmishing, this time in the area around Petersburg, Virginia. Cormany and his fellow cavalrymen may have envied the cavalry units winning victories with General Sheridan in the Shenandoah Valley, but he noted philosophically that his regiment was following orders and doing its duty in serving in the Petersburg region. On one occasion he had a chance to observe General Grant and his staff from close range.

Samuel Cormany:

September 4, 1864 Sunday. Routine—Received Order No 53, assigning me to "Acting Adjutant 16th Penna Cavalry" I took up the duties at once—Wrote and worked in the office all day—. . . .

September 6, 1864 Tuesday. . . . Hitherto our Command has used Sharps Carbine—a breach loding—single-shooting gun—Today I make Requisition for the famous Spencer Carbine—a seven-shooter—carrying a thousand yards—I hope we get them soon—as our efficiency would be increaced approximately seven fold in a dismounted fight—

News comes "Atlanta has fallen"—great jollification—. . . .

September 20, 1864 Tuesday. . . . P.M. News of big victory of Genl. Sheridan Eve Marching orders! To be ready to break Camp on short notice—. . . .

September 23, 1864 Friday. News confirmed of Genl Sheridans great victory. . . .

October 13, 1864 Thursday. . . . After dark our Spencer Carbines arrive—with ammunition—We have a great time issuing them by night—Our men pleased we realize greatly increaced power and efficiency—. . . .

October 21, 1864 Friday. . . . Genl Sheridan is having glorious victories and we are "not in it" with him and our Cavalry Boys. But here is our post of duty, and we are obeying orders—I am pretty well, and keep thinking so much of my Rachel and our Cora. Oh! to see them, love and caress them. The good Lord bless and keep them happy—

October 22, 1864 Saturday. I have quite an experience clearing the camp of bummers and sending them out to the Reg't on Picket—. . . .

October 27, 1864 Thursday. . . . Some hard fighting sets in—Our Regiment is ordered to the Front—and we charge them out on Boynton Plank Road to within six miles of Petersburg—

Here—several hundred yards to our right, I observe "Genl Grants Head Qrs Flag" There is a lull in our fighting—awaiting orders—

The Col allows me to dash over to see the General and his staff—I ride up to within 150 to 200 feet of the flag. Genl Grant sits upon a rock at the foot of a huge old oak—His orderly and Horse near him—and about him stood Generals Meade, Hancock, Gregg & Mott, and others, holding a consultation—There was high tension easily to be seen—Genl. Grant was smoking—deliberately raising his cigar to his lips, taking a puff or several, then lowering it while he said something I could not understand—While thus engaged, once, as the hand & cigar were rising and were 1/2 way to his face—A Rebl shell exploded in the tree top, but the Generals hand never faltered, but reached his face and he took his puff leisurely—Then— with a word to his Generals—Grant mounted his horse, and the group moved to the right and rear, and in a minute another shell landed where the group had just been—and exploding played havoc with the big tree—

I dash back to the Col, and soon—about 3 P.M.—hard fighting opens up—Our regiment becomes very hotly engaged and keeps at it— [*The Cormany Diaries*, pp. 475, 478–479, 483–486.]

(Rachel Cormany, busy in taking care of herself and the Cormany's daughter in Harrisburg, Pennsylvania, did not mention in her diary the capture of Atlanta or the victories of Sheridan.)

Also, like Samuel Cormany, in the vicinity of Petersburg in the Union Army of the James were many regiments of black infantrymen. Reporting on those troops was a black civilian employed by the Philadelphia Press, *Thomas M. Chester, who has been described by his biographer as "the first and only black correspondent of a major daily during the [Civil] war." Chester's dispatches to his newspaper mentioned, among other topics, the reactions of black troops in the Army of the James to the military victories of the forces commanded by Generals Sherman and Sheridan.*

Headquarters 2d Brigade, 3d Division, 18th Army Corps

[Before Petersburg] September 4, 1864.

How the News from Atlanta Was Received

Day before yesterday this part of the army was officially informed that Atlanta was captured and a great victory had been gained. The cheers of the colored defenders about division headquarters (it should be remembered that the 3d Division is entirely composed of negro troops) were loud and prolonged. The different regiments in camp were soon electrified with the news, and caught up the subsiding cheers from headquarters and made the welkin ring with rejoicings and congratulations, until the spirit of enthusiasm reached the outermost pickets, who joined in the shout of exultation. The rebels in the woods opposite to our pickets rushed out inquiring what was the matter with the Yankees, and when informed that it was owing to the fall of Atlanta they forgot to return thanks for a courteous reply to their question. . . .

Desertion of Colored Soldiers

Joseph Haskins and Robert Beasely, members of the 5th U.S.C.T., deserted to the enemy on the morning the 2d inst. The 5th was recruited in Ohio, and to the credit of the loyal colored population of that State, it should be understood that these deserters did not come from that State, but were enlisted at City Point, together with several other contrabands, while the regiment was located at that place. These two, with Spencer Brown, whom I announced in a former despatch, the first desertions which have occurred among the colored troops to the enemy, have very naturally suggested many conjectures as to the cause, but as they are all speculation, I will mention but two, in no way holding myself responsible for their correctness: Some say it was the bad treatment of company commanders, while others affirm that it is the result of placing contrabands in a regiment of free colored men. There are regiments in this division, the men of which are so firmly attached to their officers that not the slightest fear is entertained that they will desert. There must be a cause, though by no means a justification, for such a vile act, which the authorities will learn, if they deem the matter worthy of an investigation. . . .

North of the James River, Sept. 7, 1864.
Intelligence from Richmond of yesterday and the day before acknowledges the capture of Atlanta by General Sherman, and ascribes it to the removal of General Johnston from command of the Army of Tennessee. . . .

One of the best evidences of confidence in the valor of colored troops is manifest in the fact that they are entrusted with holding the right of our line, which is the nearest point we possess to Richmond. Their character for fighting and discipline is established, and henceforth they may be expected to take a part in all the grand engagements along this line. They are anxiously waiting for the opportunity to meet the enemy, as, independent of the affair of Government, many of them have a private account which they are determined to settle at the first opportunity. . . .

Deep Bottom, Va., Sept. 24, 1864.
Late last night, the welcome intelligence that General Sheridan had attacked and gained another victory in the Shenandoah Valley reached acting Brigadier General Draper's headquarters, exciting mingled feelings of rejoicing and gratitude. When the good tidings were received by General Grant, he ordered a shotted-salute to be fired at daylight this morning along the entire line, but Gen. Butler requested that the Army of the James delay its firing until 8 o'clock, which was granted, with the view of making it more effectual. . . .

It seems that the disposition to treat colored persons as if they were human is hard for even some loyal men to acquire. The wrongs which they have suffered in this department would, if ventilated, exhibit a disgraceful depth of depravity, practiced by dishonest men, in the name of the Government. These poor people are not only plundered and robbed, but are kicked and cuffed by those who have robbed them of their hard earnings and then sent them to other parts of the department, confident that their ignorance would be a guard against discovery. At Dutch Gap

[Virginia] there is an occasional specimen of inhumanity exhibited towards the freedmen which is worthy of mention. It appears that Major Ludlow has charge of the grand operation of cutting the canal through on the James river, where the working parties are continually exposed to shot and shell. Among the colored troops are many laborers who are employed by the Government, and because they cannot continue their work like their soldier brethren, when shells are falling and exploding among them, this gallant Kentucky major amuses himself by tying up these redeemed freedmen. It is generally believed that his success in this great canal enterprise will be a brigadier general's commission of colored troops. This, to be as mild as possible, would be exceedingly unfortunate, and unjust to those who are making so many willing sacrifices for the perpetuation of the Union. Gen. Butler by no means justifies or allows any man, black or white, to be treated in an unwarrantable manner.

[*Thomas Morris Chester, Black Civil War Correspondent. His Dispatches from the Virginia Front.* Edited by R. J. M. Blackett. Baton Rouge and London, Louisiana State University Press. Copyright by Louisiana State University Press, pp. 117–119, 122–123, 136–138. Permission to print these and other passages included in the present volume granted by Louisiana State University Press.]

After the capture of Atlanta, both President Lincoln and Frederick Douglass predicted that Lincoln would be reelected in the election of 1864. Of all the Unionist writers, George Templeton Strong provided the most complete account of the election and its meaning and significance. Strong wrote from a decidedly pro-Lincoln perspective, and with a focus on New York City and State.

The focus was also on New York City and State in Maria Daly's diary, but her perspective on the election was almost directly opposite to that of Strong. She and her husband were ardent supporters of General McClellan and the Democrats, and she made bitter criticisms of Lincoln, Mrs. Lincoln, and any supporters of Lincoln, including those War Democrats who, from motives that were despicable (in Maria Daly's estimate), favored Lincoln.

George Templeton Strong:

October 13. . . . Results of the October [State] elections are not yet quite clear. Ohio and Indiana are all right, but the "home vote" in Pennsylvania is very close, and both sides claim it. The army vote will carry the state for the Administration, however, for the army is Republican ten to one. . . .

The Hon. old Roger B. Taney [Chief Justice of the United States Supreme Court] has earned the gratitude of his country by dying at last. Better late than never. . . . Even should Lincoln be defeated, he will have time to appoint a new Chief Justice, and he cannot appoint anybody worse than Taney. Chase may very possibly be the man. Curious coincidence that the judge whose opinion in the Dred Scott case proved him the most faithful of slaves to the South should have been dying while his own state, Maryland, was solemnly extinguishing slavery within her borders by voting on her new anti-slavery constitution. . . .

October 14. . . . What political issues have arisen for centuries more momentous than those dependent on this election? They are to determine the destinies—the daily life—of the millions and millions who are to live on this continent for many generations to come. They will decide the relations of the laboring man toward the capitalist in 1900 A.D., from Maine to Mexico.

October 15. Walk tonight and look in at the Club, seeking news and finding none. Mr. Ruggles looked in before dinner. Just returned from Washington. Abraham, the Venerable, says to him, "It does look as if the people wanted me to stay here a little longer, and I suppose I shall have to, if they do." . . .

October 20, THURSDAY. *Laus Deo.* Another victory by Sheridan. News came at noon today. Early's successor, the redoubtable Longstreet, attacked our Shenandoah Army at daybreak yesterday, between Strasburg and Winchester, with alarming vigor. He had probably been reinforced from Richmond. By twelve o'clock we had been driven four miles down the valley, with loss of guns and prospect of disastrous defeat, which might have cost the campaign and the election. At this stage of the transaction, Sheridan appeared on the field from Winchester on his way back after a visit to Washington. Then the tide of battle turned. The retreating lines were halted and formed again: the rebels were repulsed, and at three o'clock Sheridan became the assailant, and drove them back through Strasburg with loss of forty-three guns! He seems a brilliant practitioner, and our best fighting general. There are few cases in history of battle lost, and suddenly restored and converted into complete victory within six hours by the advent of a commander *sicut deus ex machina.* Of course, the affair may look otherwise when we learn more about it, but our intelligence is official, and this looms up *now* as the most splendid battle of the war. Either we fight better of late, or the rebels fight worse. . . .

Every symptom now apparent is unfavorable to the aspirations of G. B. ("Gun Boat") McClellan, and of "Peace and surrender at any price" Pendleton, but the damnable traitors who support them may be keeping some revolutionary movement in reserve for the day of election. . . .

October 22. . . . Heard the Eroica rehearsed at the Academy of Music, with Ellie. A slovenly performance, but the strength and beauty of the symphony was apparent nevertheless. I suppose it excelled by no extant orchestral work but the peerless C Minor. From beginning to end, it is an intense manifestation of that highest art which cannot be embodied in rules or canons of art. . . .

October 23. . . . Sheridan reports himself pursuing the routed rebels up the valley, and that they are throwing away their arms, and that considerable bodies of them are breaking up and taking to the mountains. This looks as if the character of the war were changing. . . . In July, 1861, a Northern mob and a Southern mob came into collision at Bull Run, and the North was routed. In 1864, Northern veterans are meeting Southern veterans in Georgia and on the Shenandoah, and the case is altered. . . .

November 3. Have just returned from the Broadway Theatre after a pleasant evening with Ellie and George Anthon. How long is it since I have taken her to the theatre? . . .

Seward telegraphs Gunther the Mayor to beware of a conspiracy to burn this and other Northern cities on or about November 8th. The community is infested by rebel refugees and sympathizers. There are doubtless rebel agents among them, eagerly watching their opportunity to do mischief. . . . But I predict no serious breach of the peace next week, though Rebeldom and Copperheadism are cornered and desperate and none too good to bring fire and knife into the streets of New York and Philadelphia. . . . It looks as if the Administration would be sustained by next Tuesday's election. God grant it! . . .

November 5. . . . The city is full of noises tonight. There is a grand McClellan demonstration in progress. Little "Mac" was to "review" his hordes of Celts and rebel sympathizers in person from the balcony of the Fifth Avenue Hotel. I have still respect enough for him left to believe that he must feel himself in a horribly false position. A general who commanded at Malvern Hill and Antietam in 1862 must be tempted to doubt his own identity when he hears Governor Seymour's "friends" hurrahing for him in 1864. . . .

November 8, TUESDAY. So this momentous day is over, and the battle lost and won. We shall know more of the result tomorrow. Present signs are not unfavorable. Wet weather, which did not prevent a very heavy vote. I stood in queue nearly two hours waiting my turn. . . .

This election has been quiet beyond precedent. Few arrests, if any, have been made for disorderly conduct. There has been no military force visible. It is said that portions of the city militia regiments were on guard at their armories, and that some 6,000 United States troops were at Governor's Island and other points outside the city, but no one could have guessed from the appearance of the streets that so momentous an issue was *sub judice*. . . .

November 9. Laus Deo! The crisis has been past, and the most momentous popular election ever held since ballots were invented has decided against treason and disunion. My contempt for democracy and extended suffrage is mitigated. The American people can be trusted to take care of the national honor. Lincoln is reëlected by an overwhelming vote. The only states that seem to have McClellanized are Missouri, Kentucky, Delaware, and New Jersey. New York, about which we have been uneasy all day, is reported safe at the Club tonight. The Copperheads are routed—

Subversi sunt quasi plumbum in aequis vehementibus. Poor "little Mac" will never be heard of any more, I think. No man of his moderate calibre ever had such an opportunity of becoming illustrious and threw it away so rapidly. Notwithstanding a certain lukewarmness in the national cause, his instincts and impulses were, on the whole, right and loyal. Had he acted on them honestly and manfully, he would have been elected. But his friends insisted on his being *politic,* and he had not the strength to resist them. He allowed Belmont and Barlow to strike out of his letter of acceptance a vigorous sentence declaring an armistice with armed rebels out of the question, and to append to it its unmeaning finale (which imposed on no man) stating that he assumed the views he had expressed to be what the Chicago Convention really meant to say in its treasonous resolutions. . . .

A very wet, warm day. Copperheads talk meekly and well. "It's a terrible mistake, but we have got to make the best of it and support the government." The serene impudence of this morning's *World* can hardly be matched. It says the mission of the Democratic Party for the next four years will be to keep A. Lincoln from making a dishonorable disunion peace with the South. . . .

November 10. Election returns improve. New York seems secure by from 5,000 to 7,500, Seymour running a little behind his ticket, and Missouri is claimed for the Administration, leaving poor McClellan only three states. If his wife and her mother, Mrs. Marcy, had not allowed themselves to be talked over by Belmont and Barlow, and brought household influence to bear upon him, he would not be in this plight. They prevailed on him to disregard General Dix's earnest advice and to try to ride two horses, Peace and War, at once. . . .

November 11. No material news, except that it is positively asserted that "Little Mac" has resigned his commission in a pet, and by way of spiting an unappreciative people. . . .

This election, peacefully conducted in a time of such bitter excitement, and with a result quietly recognized and acquiesced in by a furious malcontent minority, is the strongest testimonial in favor of popular institutions to be found in history.

[*The Diary of George Templeton Strong,* abridged edition, 1988, pp. 250–251, 253–255, 257–264.]

Maria Daly:

September 11, 1864. . . .

The great event of this last week is the nomination of General McClellan to the Chicago platform and the General's letter. The Judge [Maria Daly's husband] was president of the ratification meeting. It is difficult to determine who will be more successful, Lincoln or McClellan. . . .

McClellan's letter made a great commotion, frightening the Republicans, dissatisfying the peace men, but contenting the moderate people.
September 19, 1864

I went on Saturday evening, the 17th, to look at the Democratic ratification meeting in Union Square. . . . The Judge presided at stand No. 4. The Republican press say there were 25,000 persons present. The Democratic papers say 100,000. Their slogans were amusing. One was, "God forgive them, for they know not what they do." Another was a picture of Lincoln splitting rails, reading "Abe at home, March 3rd." Another was entitled "A Jester," and the Judge brought home a clever caricature of McClellan in the character of Hamlet, the gravedigger a jolly Irish soldier. Hamlet holds Lincoln's head in his hand and says, "A fellow of infinite jests, where be thy jibes now?" It is very uncertain who will conquer, but the Judge knew who he thought should conquer and took his part before it was a settled question. Many of our friends are waiting to see the outcome.

I left Father a McClellan man yesterday. I found him uncertain. . . .
September 25, 1864

I have forgotten to chronicle Farragut's exploit before Mobile. He had himself lashed in the rigging of his vessel with his trumpet in hand and his lieutenant below. He fired directly into the portholes of the forts, killing the gunners. This, however, was a month ago, but Mobile is not yet ours. Sheridan, too, has gained two victories over Early which are a great gain to the country. They will stop the raids into Pennsylvania which have been so successful for two summers. These events seem to have much lessened the chances of McClellan's success, although it is not fair that it should be so, for he is as much for the preservation of the Union in its integrity as anyone of the nation. . . .

Today I have been writing out all the bad things I have heard of Lincoln and his wife, hoping to get them into the papers. They [the Lincolns] so falsely and abominably abuse the Democrats and McClellan that I would like them to have what they deserve.

Mr. Sermon, a friend of the Judge . . . has been all through Illinois and tells us that Lincoln's partner has made three million dollars, having had permits for buying cotton, sugar, tobacco, etc., and that it is well understood that Lincoln goes shares. [Lincoln's partners were John T. Stuart, a business partner in 1837, Stephen T. Logan in 1841, and William H. Herndon, law partner from 1841 until 1865. Mrs. Daly's reference is undoubtedly to Herndon, and Mr. Sermon's story is typical of those being circulated about the President and his associates during this campaign.] . . . The set of china bought for the White House from a china merchant in the city, for one thousand five hundred dollars, appeared in the bill as costing three thousand dollars, Mrs. Lincoln pocketing one thousand five hundred dollars.

It is humiliating to all American women who have to economize and struggle and part with their husbands, sons, and brothers in these sad times, to see this creature sitting in the highest place as a specimen of American womanhood, and "Uncle Ape," as he should be called, the specimen of man. People seem to think boorishness and ignorance an evidence of honesty and sincerity. . . . Lincoln is a *clever* hypocrite under the mask of honest boorishness, else he would not stay in a position for which he is so eminently disqualified. . . .

All articles of consumption except fruit are double the usual price. A five-cent loaf of bread 10c, milk 10c per quart, potatoes $5.26 per barrel, beef 28c and 30c per pound, butter 65c per pound. We have almost discontinued the use of the latter article, as the dealers are holding back for high prices. The only means to lower their demands is non-consumption. . . .

October 30, 1864

The times seem to me so out of joint that I can scarcely bear to write. It seems to me that the country is mad. Lincoln is cheating as hard as he can, and good Democrats are helping him. . . .

We are at present ruled by New England, which was never a gentle or tolerant mistress, and my Dutch or German obstinate blood begins to feel heated to see how arrogantly she dictates and would force her ideas down our throats, even with the bayonet. And such a boor to represent our great nation! I would rather have a bull set up, like the Egyptians worship; he would do little mischief; he would not pretend to brains. *Illiterateness* is the fashion. Lincoln, a rail-splitter, and his wife, two ignorant and vulgar boors, are king and queen for now and candidates for election. Andy Johnson, who boasts that he was taught to read by his wife, is to be Vice President. It seems that statesmanship is much less of a trade than rail-splitting, shoemaking, or tailoring. . . .

November 6, 1864

Last evening we went to the Century Club, which gave a festival in honor of [William Cullen] Bryant's seventieth birthday. . . . Emerson gave a discourse which we arrived just in time to hear. . . . Emerson disappointed me. I never had much respect for him, but his face irresistibly reminds you of the figure of *Punch*—the long inquisitive nose, peaked chin, small intense eyes and meager lank frame. I had no desire to be presented to him. He looks like a man of no convictions. After a long, disjointed, wearisome, hesitating utterance, he said something about Bryant's writing his name on the ridges and mountains and engraving it on nature's shield like Phidias, who wrote his upon that of Pallas Athene. The idea was a good one when you at last got at it. . . .

November 7, 1864

. . . Tomorrow is election day and all good citizens must wish it over. To the great discontent of the public, especially the Democrats, General

[Benjamin F.] Butler has been put in command here and no one can tell what may not be done to secure Lincoln's election. Republicans are now most unscrupulous. I shall order my doors shut and open to no one after ten o'clock on any pretense of business, as the Judge is one of the electors of the electoral college and for McClellan. They may try to get him out of the way *pro tem*. . . .

A pious Republican told me a few days since a fabrication concerning the last hour of Judge [Roger B.] Taney, whom he says confessed at the last that the Dred Scott Decision had been forced upon him by his party. I exclaimed, "What a shame to attack an honest man's character when he is no longer here to defend himself!" He was a good Catholic, and had he had anything to confess would have done it long ago to his confessor. He is said to have died in the arms of a favorite slave, to have given them all their freedom and to have ordered his body to be laid out and watched by his house servants only. Judge Taney decided according to the laws of the United States. I suppose they [the laws] were in the wrong, perhaps, but not the Judge. . . .

November 15, 1864

The election has taken place. Lincoln has been reelected. *Vox Populi, vox Dei.* So it must be for the best. All now left us is to put the shoulder to the wheel and do our best to draw the governmental machine out of the slough. There was some ill feeling about General Butler's being sent here to overawe the election. However, there seems to be little ill feeling on either side—a hopeful sign for the country. It is well that Lincoln has so large a majority, as now there will be no one to lay the blame upon. . . .

Poor McClellan! What a lesson he has had of the instability of popular favor and of fair-weather friends. None of his old companions-in-arms, hardly, have voted for him, and the reason is clear—it would not be the way to promotion. A lady said to me a few days since, "What, your husband votes for McClellan and you have a brother in the army?"

Yesterday, Mr. Theodore Fay from Bremen, our former minister to Prussia, came in. He is for Lincoln and quoted what he called "Mr. Lincoln's very appropriate though homely saying that a countryman in crossing a dangerous stream or ford would not willingly change horses." I answered very mildly that Mr. Lincoln was very happy in these little sayings, that like in Scripture, you could always find a story or text to suit the occasion. Now those who, like my husband, voted for McClellan, could quote another of his aphorisms as their excuse. When removing some General (Rosecrans, I believe), he said, "They that made the mess are not exactly the ones to finish it." . . .

November 17, 1864

. . . The Republicans may deny it as they may, but the soldiers were not allowed to vote for McClellan.

[*Diary of a Union Lady,* pp. 302–308, 310–313, 315.]

Confederates

After the capture of Atlanta and the other Union victories in the early autumn of 1864, it was increasingly difficult for Confederates to remain optimistic about the success of their cause.

Henceforth, John Cotton, Emily L. and David G. Harris, and Mary Chesnut all reflected in their writings increasing pessimism about the possibility of the Confederacy's winning its independence. The degree of pessimism expressed by the particular individual seemed to vary directly in proportion to the extent of that person's information and awareness concerning the overall situation of the Confederacy. John Cotton's world was apparently confined primarily to the situation of his military unit and to his local surroundings. He expressed less pessimism than did the Harrises or Mary Chesnut. Although Mary Chesnut and her husband had moved from Richmond to Columbia, South Carolina, by September of 1864, the Chesnuts were still in touch with the Jefferson Davises and other Confederate leaders and thus were more aware than either Cotton or the Harrises of the Confederacy's total situation—and Mary Chesnut, after the fall of Atlanta, expressed in her writings virtually no optimism about the Confederacy's prospects.

John Cotton's unit was sent with Confederate General Wheeler's cavalry on a raid into east Tennessee with the goal of luring Union General Sherman back from the attack on Atlanta. That goal was not achieved, and, by November of 1864, Cotton and his comrades were back in Georgia to pursue Sherman's forces as they marched from Atlanta to the sea:

East tennessee Camp 4 miles from Jonesborough 100 miles north east of noxville September 24th 64

My dear beloved wife it is with uncertainly that I rite you a few lines you may get this and you may not but I hope you will these lines leave me well this is the 45 day we have been on this rade and I have been well all the time dont bee uneasy about me we hant had but little fiting to do but I have been in it all and hant been hurt yet I think we are out of danger now we are incide of our own lines. . . . how come us here we act behind [Confederate] general wheeler and got cut off from him there is a 2 briggades of us and part of another our men were very uneasy while we were in the yankey lines for fear we would bee captured but we got out safe we whiped the yankeys where ever we come in contact with them we have tore up a great deal of railroad on our rout but I am afraid it hant done much good we here that the yankeys has got atlanta but I here that our men has taken it back it ant worth while to say how bad I want to see you I hant here a word from you since I left home and this is only the three letter I have rote to you if I could see you I could tell you a heap I will rite more as soon as I get the chance nothing mor I remain your true lover til death

John W. Cotton . . .

Camped near thomaston Ga November 24 1864

Dear beloved wife I now take my pen in hand to rite you a few lines to let you no that I am well and all the rest of the boys we are ordered to macon ga what forces that are not with [Confederate General] hood in tennessee are all reporting at macon I recon you will here before you get this that the yankeys have burnt atlanta and all left there they are not far from macon some where but I cant tell you where it is thought they are trying to go to charleston where or savannah. . . .it will take us two more days to go to macon I hant anything to rite at present I will rite you again in a few days if I have the chance I hope these few lines may find you all well direct your letters to macon georgia nothing more but remain your best friend til death

John W Cotton

Camps Macon Ga November 26th 1864

Most Dear beloved wife I again take my pen in hand to try to let you no that I am well and all of our boys are too we have got to macon but the yankeys are gone they come near enough to throw shell in macon but the malish [militia] kept them of they only sent there cavalry here while there infantry passed on they are at miledgville or have been for several days old [Union General] shermans headquarters has been at miledgville it is thought they are making for savannar they are followed clostly by wheelers cavalry we will go on after them as soon as we can get arms and equip ment there is a talk of our drawing money but that is uncertain the man I sold my horse to told me this morning that he was ready to take up his note I have got my saddlebags and all my close but my pants some damd theaf took them out of my saddle bags if I ketch him with them on I will raise him out of his boots one time I hant got anything worth riting nothing more at present only I remain your true devoted husband til death

John W Cotton

Direct your letters to John W Cotton Co (C) 10 Confederate regt Macon Ga they say we will draw close today and I will try to draw some pants. . . . nothing more I will rite again when I get the chance
[*Yours Till Death*, pp. 118–120.]

Emily L. Harris wrote most of the entries in the family Journal *during the months of September, October, and November, 1864, since her husband David was away from home in the Confederate army in most of that period. Both Emily and David described worsening conditions on the home front and on the battlefields.*

Emily L. Harris:

September 6. . . . When I reached home I found the negroes skinning two of my finest milk cows. A tree fell across the fence of Dr. Dean's cane patch. They walked in and killed themselves eating cane. . . . Time has been that if we needed a milk cow we could go and buy one. Now we cannot. We have not the means and besides, we could scarcely find the cow if we had. Milk cows are selling at $500.00.

The propect for Peace is not so bright as it has been, or as we thought it was. Atlanta has fallen into the hands of the enemy and McClellan a man favoring a continuation of the war has been nominated for next Yankee President. . . .

September 7. I am boiling my dead cows and skinning off the grease to make soap. . . .

September 17. Saturday night. Nothing of importance has taken place in our family during the week. . . . The news from the army is anything but cheering. The Confederacy seems ready to cry out "Lord save or we perish." Letters from Mr. Harris are not che[e]rful. A sadness seems to have enveloped him. They are half fed and half paid. Their horses are not fed at all. Flour is selling at $1.00 per lb. Sweet Potatoes $2.00 per qt. Irish $1.50 and other things in proportion. The infantry privates are paid $12.00 per month, the calvalry $24.00. How many months wages will it take to buy a bushel of sweet potatoes? May a merciful God send wisdom to the men who stand at the helm of the nation.

The yellow fever is in Charleston. . . .

September 30. MOLASSES. I am so busy that I can hardly spare a moment for my journal. . . .

October 1. To day I have made twenty gallons of molasses. It was a very hard days work. A hard shower fell on me while I was dipping up the last. I do not feel in the mood to journalize. I labor under many difficulties and get on slowly with all I undertake. I surely am a bad manager. The great trouble is, there is no one on the place that has the welfare and prosperity of the family at heart but me. No one helps me to care and to think. . . . Losses, crosses and disappointments assail me on every hand. Is it because I am so wicked?

My Husband and children are well. Let me be thankful.

October 8. FINISHED MAKING MOLASSES. Saturday night. . . .

The yellow fever is still in Charleston, too close to James' Island to make me feel comfortable. My husband is on James Island. We have had another battle, another victory and have as usual paid dearly for it. Numerous brave, promising young men of Spartanburg are reported dangerously wounded. Where are the ones to fill the places of the gifted who have yeilded up their breath in this awful struggle? . . .

October 13. . . . The weather is extremely cold for the time of year. The Peace question is agitating the public mind. . . .

October 17. Finished first picking over cotton. The weather is cold. The family are sick. I am well myself. If I was sick what would become of the rest? I think I am of use to the family.

October 18. . . . Mr. Harris tells me that the troops on James island are not starving but next to it. Sprouted peas boiled without meat and cold rice was their bill of fare when he wrote last. He had given a woman $2.00 for a quart of sweet potatoes. . . .

October 29. HUSBAND AT HOME. Last night at the hour of midnight I heard a familiar step on the threshold of our home. The joyful news quickly brought the children out of their beds. After we all had hugged and kissed our best friend, we raised a light to gaze upon and scrutinize the beloved features which had begun to be something belonging to the past. Six months in camp has changed him but little in my eyes. Some of his freinds say he looks haggard and worn. I dont think so but I wonder that he is not. A man who loves his home as Mr Harris does, suffers heavily when seperated from it. His arrival has dispelled all gloom for the present.

October 30. Sunday night. Today we had freinds to dine with us. Dr Dean and his family, Gwin Harris and his, and Billy Ray and his. . . . Mr. Harris and Billy Ray have been in camp together and have been almost starved for a few months. I have never seen men eat like they do. . . .

November 8. The weather is warm as May and very cloudy and damp. Yesterday was quite rainy. . . . This is the day of the Northern Presidential election. The last one brought about a horrible war. Let us hope this will bring us peace.

David G. Harris:

November 8. On the 28 of October 1864 I came home after an absence of about six months on & near James Island in the confederate servise "of said servise." I am quite tired. There is no pleasure in being from home so long & at the same time being half fed doing hard duty getting but little grain and no thanks. I am a member of the Cavalry (1st S.C.C. Company C., Capt. Whatley). I have not yet been in a hard battle, but several small ones. And have heard the roar of cannon almost constantly for the last half year. The batteries in & about the City of Charleston are constantly shelling each other with not a days interruption. I have heard the whizzing of shell until I am tired of the sound. I am on a furlough of 15 days & will soon return again. I left home before the crop was planted & returned to find it being gathered. My wife, children and negroes have done well in my absence & have made enough to live upon if they are permitted to use it. But with the high prices we have to give, and pay the tenth of all the family can make, at the same time paying such an exorbitant tax, we find that our burden is about as much as we can well stand up to &c & at the same time make the two ends meet. . . .

We are gathering in our crop, and trying to make arangement to live another year. Provided we can escape the clutches of the yankeys. The war has been in progress nearly four years, & as far as I can see, we are as far from the end as we were at the begining. On the 8th the North elected a President, Lincoln & McClellan being the canidates. Perhaps this election may have some influence on our destany, & maybe it may have an effect to end the war. If it is not ended now, the Lord only knows what will. Our party is sending on its last men. We are putting forth our utmost strength, & I much fear that we will not be able to hold out much longer. But if our army can get supplies of provisions, we will fight them to the last rather than be subjugated.

The theives about me are troubling me as much as the war. It seems that they will steal all we have got and leave us but little for my family. November 13. For some days, I have been very busy prepairing to return to my command on James's Island. It is a bitter pill but must be swallowed with as much grace as possible.

This is Sunday & we are busy packing my box of provision to take to the coast with me. This visit has been one of pleasure to me, both day & night. . . . Yesterday, I bought 13 lbs of butter, paying four dollars per lb. We in the army have been hard up for something to eat, & I am going to try to take something to eat with me. To night I will bid farewell to my family—My wife, teacher & children & hunt my home in the tented feild. I hope we will meet again.

Emily L. Harris:

November 15. There are days of glad meetings and sadder partings. Yesterday morning at five o'clock I started my husband once more to do battle for his country. . . .

November 18. DONE PICKING COTTON. I went to town today. . . . Every body seems to be distressed about the war. The dark days have surely come. The Confederacy! I almost hate the word. May the Lord have mercy and incline our hearts to do his will. . . .

November 26. Saturday. . . . During the day Dr Dean and George captured Sam, a runaway negro that once belonged to him. The event saddened us all for the remainder of the day. The weather is pleasant and we are getting our wheat in very fast with five plows.

November 28. . . . The weather is pleasant. The family have colds. I have been trying to get some shoes made but have not succeeded. Every ones attention is now strained Yankeeward. Surely the end is near. God humble us and help us. . . .

November 30. After supper. The family are all sitting in the piazza. . . . Some say the war will continue four years more. If it does we will be nowhere and nobody.

[*Piedmont Farmer*, pp. 341–345, 347–351.]

The visit of Jefferson Davis as a house guest in the Chesnut home at Columbia, South Carolina, in October, 1864, was a pleasant and exciting interlude for Mary Chesnut. With that exception, however, her diary entries after the loss of Atlanta reflected gloom and dismay over the prospects for the Confederacy: "Since Atlanta I have felt as if all were dead within me, for ever." The letter from Mrs. Jefferson (Varina) Davis that Mary Chesnut included in her diary would presumably have done nothing to dispel fear and apprehension.

September 1, 1864. . . . Atlanta gone. Well—that agony is over. Like David when the child was dead, I will get up from my knees, will wash my face and comb my hair. No hope. We will try to have no fear.

*   *   *

Isabella to the rescue.

"Be magnanimous. Now I daresay you never tried the affectionate dodge."

"Never to mortal man."

"Then try it now. If my fiancé had lost a battle, I would—"

"What would you—eh?"

"I'd make love to him—straight out!" . . .

September 19, 1864. . . . My pink silk dress I have sold for six hundred dollars, to be paid in installments, two hundred a month for three months. And I sell my eggs and butter from home for two hundred dollars a month. Does it not sound well—four hundred dollars a month, regularly? In what?

"In Confederate money." Hélas! . . .

September 21, 1864. The president has gone west. Sent for J.C.

Went with Mrs. Rhett to hear Dr. Palmer. I did not know before how utterly hopeless was our situation. This man is so eloquent. It was hard to listen and not give way. Despair was his word—and martyrdom. He offered us nothing more in this world than the martyr's crown. He is not for slavery, he says. He is for freedom—and the freedom to govern our own country as we see fit. He is against foreign interference in our state matters. That is what Mr. Palmer went to war for, it appears. Every day shows that slavery is doomed the world over. For that he thanked God. He spoke of these times of our agony. And then came the cry:

"Help us, oh God. Vain is the help of man." And so we came away—shaken to the depths. . . .

The end has come. No doubt of the fact. Our army has so moved as to uncover Macon and Augusta.

We are going to be wiped off the face of the earth.

What is there to prevent Sherman taking General Lee in the rear? We have but two armies. And Sherman is between them now.

September 22, 1864. . . . J.C. and I had a most uncalled-for row. . . .

This morning at seven the president sent for J.C. to the [railroad] cars, and as he has not been at home since, I fancy he has gone to Kingsville. . . .

September 26, 1864. . . .

Mr. C. came home to dinner. He went as far as Kingsville with the president. Said Custis Lee was urging the president to relieve Hood and put Beauregard in his place, but the president was undecided. . . .

Saturday I remained home all day and arranged my house for the president's proposed visit. . . .

Yesterday . . . I walked home [from church] and the deep blue sky without a cloud. No Italian sky could ever have been more glorious. . . . All saddened, this world so beautiful, so sweet as nature shows it to us, and man so mean, so vile, so unworthy of his home. I said all this as I entered the piazza to J. C. And he meekly remarked, *women* are mean also. And then, with *dramatic* power of loathing and shame, he told that the day before he saw a poor negro woman in the last stages of pregnancy, sitting by the roadside in bitter wailing, her eyes smashed up, and frightfully punished in the face. He rode up and said: "Poor soul what can I do for you? How have you hurt yourself so?" She answered: "Ride on, Massa. You can do no good. My Missis has been beating me." He asked the brute's name and was answered "Mrs. Fergusson," some woman we did not know, thank Heaven. . . .

September 29, 1864. These stories of our defeats in the [Shenandoah] Valley fall like blows upon a dead body. Since Atlanta I have felt as if all were dead within me, forever. . . .

October 7, 1864. The president will be with us here in Columbia next Tuesday—so Colonel McLean brings us word.

I began at once to prepare to receive him in my small house. His apartments were decorated as well as Confederate stringency would permit. . . .

I went out to the gate to meet the president—who met me most cordially, kissed me, in fact. . . .

Immediately after breakfast General Chesnut drove off with the president's aides, and Mr. Davis sat out in our piazza. There was nobody there but myself, and some little boys strolling by called out: "Come here and look! There is a man in Mrs. Chesnut's porch who looks just like Jeff Davis on a postage stamp."

And people began to gather at once on the street. Mr. Davis then went in. . . .

The president was watching me prepare a mint julep for Custis Lee when Colonel McLean came in to inform us that a great crowd had gathered and that they were coming to ask the president to speak to them at one o'clock.

*   *   *

An immense crowd assembled—men, women, and children. . . . He [Mr. Davis] was thoroughly exhausted [after his speech], but we had a mint julep ready for him as he finished. . . .

I left the crowd overflowing the house and the president's hand nearly shaken off. And my head was then intent on the dinner to be prepared for them—with only Confederate commissariat. So the patriotic public had come to the rescue. I had been gathering what I could of eatables for a month, and now I found everybody in Columbia, nearly, sent me whatever they had that they thought nice enough for the president's dinner. . . . Then they had to go, and we bade them an affectionate farewell. Custis Lee and I had spent much time gossiping on the back porch. I was concocting dainties for dessert, and he sat on the bannister with a cigar in his mouth. But he spoke very candidly and told me many a hard truth for the Confederacy and the bad time which was at hand. What he said was not so impressive as the unbroken silence he maintained as to that extraordinary move by which Hood expects to entice Sherman back from us. Mrs. Preston says they do things that our woman's common sense regards as madness—no less—and then they talk so well, and we listen until almost they fool us into believing they have some reason for the wild work. But say what you will (none of us had said anything), this movement of the western army is against common sense. . . .

November 6, 1864. . . . A letter which was long coming and then misplaced—but I will copy it here—

October 8, 1864

My dear friend,

I should have written to you long since but have been in such a state of anxiety, and so unsettled, that I could not summon my mind (never great) to its duty. . . .

Thank you a thousand times, my dear friend, for your more than maternal kindness to my dear child. As to Mr. Davis, he thinks the best ham, the best Madeira, the best coffee, the best hostess in the world, rendered Columbia delightful to him when he passed through. . . .

We are in a sad, an anxious, state here now. The dead come in—the living do not go out so fast. However, we hope all things, and trust in God as the only one able to resolve the opposite states of feeling into a triumphant happy whole. . . .

I had a surprise of an unusually gratifying nature a few days since. I found I could not keep my horses—so I sold them. The next day they were returned to me, with a handsome anonymous note to the effect that they had been bought by a few friends for me. But I fear I cannot feed them. So my attention is now turned upon the green satin [dress] as a source of revenue. Can you make a suggestion about it? I think it will spoil if laid up and also go out of fashion. I shall probably never go into colors again and therefore can never want it. . . .

Strictly between us, *things look* very anxious *here*—. . . .

I am so constantly depressed that I dread writing—even four lines betray the feeling. . . .

Do write as often as you can, for added to my very sincere love for you, I have an enjoyment in your letters quite independent of friendly feeling. They are so charming in style. . . .

I cannot bear to think we shall grow further apart until you forget me.

As ever your devoted friend

V[arina] D[avis]

Love to Mr. Chesnut.

. . . A thousand dollars has slipped through my fingers already this week. At the commissaries I spent five hundred today for sugar, candles, a lamp, &c. . . . If you could see the pitiful little bundles this five hundred dollars bought. . . .

A letter from the western army signed Western Man—out and out for peace—peace at any price. «I call this treason.»

Sherman in Atlanta has left Thomas to take care of Hood. Hood has 30,000 men—Thomas 40,000 now—and as many more as he wants—he has only to ring the bell and call for more. Grant can get all that he wants, both for himself and for Thomas. All the world open to them. We shut up in a Bastille.

We are at sea. Our boat has sprung a leak.

[*Mary Chesnut's Civil War,* pp. 642–652, 662–664, 668–669.]

14. *UNION VICTORIES AND CONFEDERATE DEFEATS, NOVEMBER, 1864–APRIL, 1865*

Shortly after the elections of 1864 in the Union States ratified and solidified support for the war policies of the Lincoln administration, General Sherman began, on November 15, the march of his army from Atlanta across Georgia toward the Atlantic Ocean. This was the beginning of what turned out to be the final military phase of the war, marked by a series of virtually unchecked Union victories and Confederate defeats.

Sherman's Army in Georgia, November–December, 1864

Some members of the Jones family were in the path of Sherman's troops and suffered great damage to their property and serious threats to their personal safety. After Rev. Charles Colcock Jones died in 1863, his son, Colonel Charles C. Jones, Jr., was stationed in Savannah, Georgia, in the Confederate army. But Mary Jones, the wife of Rev. Jones, was at one of the family plantations, Montevideo, when Sherman's soldiers arrived in the vicinity on December 13, 1864. With her were her daughter (Mary S. Mallard), her daughter's husband (Rev. Robert Q. Mallard), the three small Mallard children, and a number of slaves. Rev. Mallard went to the Mallard home at Walthourville early in the morning of December 14 and was captured there by Union troops a few hours later. This left the two women, the three small children, and the slaves to face the Union soldiers who came to the plantation during the next three weeks. (Before long, a woman neighbor and her two small children took refuge in the Jones house.) In those weeks, Mary S. Mallard was in advanced pregnancy, and she gave birth in the plantation house to a daughter on January 4, 1865. Mary Jones and Mary Mallard both kept journals of their ordeal; the last entry in Mary Mallard's journal was dated January 2, two days before the birth of her daughter. Portions of the two journals are reprinted here.

Mrs. Mary S. Mallard in her Journal:

Montevideo, *Tuesday,* December 13, 1864

Mother rode to Arcadia this morning to superintend the removal of household articles and the remainder of library, etc., . . . and lingered about the place until late in the afternoon, when she started to return to Montevideo. It was almost sunset, and she was quietly knitting in the carriage, fearing no evil. Jack was driving, and as they came opposite the Girardeau place . . . a Yankee on horseback sprang from the woods and brought his carbine to bear upon Jack, ordering him to halt. Then, lowering the carbine, . . . he demanded of Mother what she had in the carriage.

She replied: "Nothing but my family effects." . . .

"Where are you going?"

"To my home." . . .

"I am a defenseless woman—a widow—with only one motherless child with me. Have you done with me, sir? Drive on, Jack!"

Bringing his carbine to bear on Jack, he called out: "No! Halt!" He then asked: "Where are the rebels?"

"We have had a post at No. 3."

Looking into the carriage, he said: "I would not like to disturb a lady; and if you will take my advice you will turn immediately back, for the men are just ahead. They will take your horses and search your carriage, and I cannot say what they will do."

Mother replied: "I thank you for that," and ordered Jack to turn. Jack saw a number of men ahead, and Mother would doubtless have been in their midst had she proceeded but a few hundred yards. (This must have been an officer; he was a hale, hearty man, well dressed, with a new blue overcoat, and well appointed in every respect.) Jack then drove through. . . .

It was now quite dark. When she came to the junction with the Walthourville road, there she met a company of cavalry commanded by Captain Little. She informed them of the position of the Yankees, and entreated that he would give her an escort if but for a few miles. . . . He replied they were ordered to that point, and if she would stay with them or go with them they would protect her, but they could not send anyone with her. . . .

"Then I will trust in God and go forward!" . . .

Every moment she expected to meet the Yankees. . . . At the avenue our picket was stationed, who informed her that the bridges on the causeway had been taken up, and her carriage could not cross over. Mother replied: "Then I must get out and walk, for I must reach home tonight if my life is spared!" She rode up to the dwelling house; Dr. and Mrs. Way came to the carriage and pressed her very kindly to remain all night. She had resolved to walk home when Mr. William Winn, one of the picket guard, rode up and informed Mother the bridges had been fixed so as to allow the carriage to pass over. . . .

Turning up the Darien road, she made her way through an obscure and very rough road through the woods which had been used as a wood road, just back of our encampment. Jack was unacquainted with the way. The old horses completely tired out, so that with difficulty she passed into the old field back of the Boro into the road leading to our enclosure, reaching home after nine o'clock.

I was rejoiced to hear the sound of the carriage wheels, for I had been several hours in the greatest suspense, not knowing how Mother would hear of the presence of the enemy, and fearing she would unexpectedly find herself in their midst at the Boro.

Late in the evening Milton came running in to say a boy had met the oxcarts going to Arcadia and told them they could not pass, for the Yankees were in the Boro. . . .Fearing a raiding party might come up, immediately I had some trunks of clothing and other things carried into the woods, and the carts and horses taken away and the oxen driven away, and prepared to pass the night alone with the little children, as I had no idea Mother could reach home.

After ten o'clock Mr. Mallard [Mary S. Mallard's husband] came in to see us, having come from No. 3, where a portion of Colonel Hood's command was stationed. . . . Mr. Mallard stayed with us until two o'clock A.M. and, fearing to remain longer, left to join the soldiers at No. 4 1/2 (Johnston Station), where they were to rendezvous. . . . he lingered as long as possible, reading a part of the 8th Chapter of Romans and engaging in prayer before leaving. . . . Before parting he went up and kissed his children, charging me to tell them "Papa has kissed them when asleep." I had a fearful foreboding that he would be captured. . . .

Wednesday, December 14th. Although it had been much past midnight when we retired, Mother and I rose early, truly thankful no enemy had come near us during the night. We passed the day in fearful anxiety. Late in the afternoon Charles came into the parlor, just from Walthourville, and burst into tears.

I asked what was the matter.

"Oh," he said, "very bad news! Master is captured by the Yankees, and says I must tell you keep a good heart."

This was a dreadful blow to us and to the poor little children. Mamie especially realized it, and cried all the evening; it was heartrending to see the agony of her little face when told her papa was taken prisoner. . . .

Thursday, December 15th. About ten o'clock Mother walked out upon the lawn, leaving me in the dining room. In a few moments Elsie came running in to say the Yankees were coming. I went to the front door and saw three dismounting at the stable, where they found Mother and rudely demanded of her: "Where are your horses and mules? Bring them out!"— at the same instant rushing by her as she stood in the door. I debated whether to go to her or remain in the house. The question was soon settled, for in a moment a stalwart Kentucky Irishman stood before me, having come through the pantry door. I scarcely knew what to do. His salutation was: "Have you any whiskey in the house?"

I replied: "None that I know of."

"You ought to know," he said in a very rough voice.

I replied: "This is not my house, so I do not know what is in it."

Said he: "I mean to search this house for arms, but I'll not hurt you." . . .

He then opened the side door and discovered the door leading into the old parlor. "I want to get into that room."

"If you will come around, I will get the key for you."

As we passed through the parlor into the entry he ran upstairs and commenced searching my bedroom. "Where have you hid your arms?"

"There are none in the house. You can search for yourself." . . .

While he was searching my bureau he turned to me and asked: "Where is your watch?"

I told him my husband had worn my watch, and he had been captured the day before at Walthourville.

Shaking his fist at me, he said: "Don't you lie to me! You have got a watch!"

I felt he could have struck me to the floor; but looking steadily at him, I replied: "I have a watch and chain, and my husband has them with him."

"Well, were they taken from him when he was captured?"

"That I do not know, for I was not present."

Just at this moment I heard another Yankee coming up the stair steps and saw a young Tennessean going into Mother's room, where he commenced his search. Mother came in soon after and got her keys; and there we were, following these two men around the house, handing them keys (as they would order us to do in the most insolent manner), and seeing almost everything opened and searched and tumbled about. . . .

Mother asked him if he would like to see his mother and wife treated in this way—their house invaded and searched.

"Oh," said he, "none of us have wives!"

Whilst Mother walked from the stable with one of the Yankees from Kentucky he had a great deal to say about the South bringing on the war. On more than one occasion they were anxious to argue political questions with her. Knowing it was perfectly useless, she would reply: "This is neither the time nor place for these subjects. My countrymen have decided that it was just and right to withdraw from the Union. We wished to do it peaceably; you would not allow it. We have now appealed to arms; and I have nothing more to say with you upon the subject."

Mother asked him if he would like to see his mother and sisters treated as they were doing us.

"No," said he, "I would not. And I never do enter houses, and shall not enter yours."

And he remained without while the other two men searched. They took none of the horses or mules, as they were too old.

A little before dinner we were again alarmed by the presence of five Yankees dressed as marines. One came into the house—a very mild sort of a man. We told him the house had already been searched. He asked if the soldiers had torn up anything. One of the marines (as they called themselves) came into the pantry and asked if they could get anything to eat. Mother told them she had only what was prepared for our own dinner, and if they chose they could take it where it was—in the kitchen. . . .

We hoped they would not intrude upon the dwelling; but as soon as they finished eating, the four came in, and one commenced a thorough search, ordering us to get him all the keys. He found some difficulty in fitting the keys, and I told him I would show them to him if he would hand me the bunch.

He replied: "I will give them to you when I am ready to leave the house."

He went into the attic and instituted a thorough search into every hole and corner. He opened a large trunk containing the private papers of my dear father. . . .

After spending a long time in the search, they prepared to leave with all the horses. Mother told them they were over seventeen years old and would do them no service. They took away one mule, but in a short time we saw it at the gate: they had turned it back. . . .

Mother felt so anxious about Kate King that she sent Charles and Niger in the afternoon to urge her coming over to us, and told them if she was too unwell to walk or ride, they must take her up in their arms and let someone help to bring the little children. . . .

Friday, December 16th. . . . [Kate did come] in great fear and trembling, not knowing but that she would meet the enemy on the road. We all felt truly grateful she had been preserved by the way.

About four in the afternoon we heard the clash of arms and noise of horsemen, and by the time Mother and I could get downstairs we saw forty or fifty men in the pantry, flying hither and thither, ripping open the safe with their swords and breaking open the crockery cupboards. Fearing we might not have a chance to cook, Mother had some chickens and ducks roasted and put in the safe for our family. These the men seized whole, tearing them to pieces with their teeth like ravenous beasts. They were clamorous for whiskey, and ordered us to get our keys. One came to Mother to know where her meal and flour were, insisted upon opening her locked pantry, and took every particle. They threw the sacks across their horses. Mother remonstrated and pointed to her helpless family; their only reply was: "We'll take it!" . . .

A number of them went into the attic into a little storeroom and carried off twelve bushels of meal Mother had stored there for our necessities. She told them they were taking all she had to support herself and daughter, a friend, and five little children. Scarcely one regarded even the sound of her voice; those who did laughed and said they would leave one sack to keep us from starving. But they only left some rice which they did not want, and poured out a quart or so of meal upon the floor. At other times they said they meant to starve us to death. They searched trunks and bureaus and wardrobes, calling for shirts and men's clothes.

We asked for their officer, hoping to make some appeal to him; they said they were all officers and would do as they pleased. We finally found one man who seemed to make a little show of authority, which was indicated by a whip which he carried. Mother appealed to him, and he came up and ordered the men out. They instantly commenced cursing him, and we thought they would fight one another. They brought a wagon and took another from the place to carry off their plunder.

It is impossible to imagine the horrible uproar and stampede through the house, every room of which was occupied by them, all yelling, cursing, quarreling, and running from one room to another in wild confusion. Such was their blasphemous language, their horrible countenances and appearance, that we realized what must be the association of the lost in the world of eternal woe. Their throats were open sepulchres, their mouths filled with cursing and bitterness and lies. These men belonged to

Kilpatrick's cavalry. We look back upon their conduct in the house as a horrible nightmare, too terrible to be true. . . .

Mrs. Mary Jones in her Journal:

Montevideo, *Saturday*, December 17th, 1864

About four o'clock this morning we were roused by the sound of horses; and Sue, our faithful woman, came upstairs breathless with dismay and told us they had come upon the most dreadful intent, and had sent her in to tell me what it was, and had inquired if there were any young women in my family. Oh, the agony—the agony of that awful hour no language can describe! No heart can conceive it. We were alone, friendless, and knew not what might befall us. Feeling our utter weakness and peril, we all knelt down around the bed and went to prayer; and we continued in silent prayer a long time. Kate prayed, Daughter prayed, and I prayed; and the dear little children, too, hearing our voices, got up and knelt down beside us. And there we were, alone and unprotected, imploring protection from a fate worse than death, and that our Almighty God and Saviour would not permit our cruel and wicked enemies to come nigh our persons or our dwelling. . . .

New squads were arriving. In the gray twilight of morning we looked out of the window and saw one man pacing before the courtyard gate between the house and the kitchen; and we afterwards found he had voluntarily undertaken to guard the house. In this we felt that our prayers had been signally answered.

Mrs. Mary S. Mallard in her Journal:

Montevideo, *Saturday*, December 17th, 1864

As soon as it was light Kate discovered an officer near the house, which was a great relief to our feelings. Mother and I went down immediately, when she said to him: "Sir, I see that you are an officer; and I come to entreat your protection for my family, and that you will not allow your soldiers to enter my dwelling, as it has been already three times searched and every particle of food and whatever they wanted taken." He replied it was contrary to orders for the men to be found in houses, and the penalty was death; and so far as his authority extended with his own men, none of them should enter the house. He said he and his squad (there were many others present) had come on a foraging expedition, and intended to take only provisions. . . .

The Yankees made the Negroes bring up the oxen and carts, and took off all the chickens and turkeys they could find. They carried off all the syrup from the smokehouse. We had one small pig, which was all the meat we had left; they took the whole of it. Mother saw everything like food stripped from her premises, without the power of uttering one word.

Finally they rolled out the carriage and took that to carry off a load of chickens. They took everything they possibly could.

The soldier who acted as our volunteer guard was from Ohio, and older than anyone we had seen; for generally they were young men and so active that Mother called them "fiery flying serpents." As he was going Mother went out of the house and said to him: "I cannot allow you to leave without thanking you for your kindness to myself and family; and if I had anything to offer I would gladly make you some return."

He replied: "I would not receive anything, and only wish I was here to guard you always." . . .

Immediately we went to work moving some salt and the little remaining sugar into the house; and while we were doing it a Missourian came up and advised us to get everything into the house as quickly as possible, and he would protect us while doing so. . . . He said he had enlisted to fight for the *Constitution;* but since then the war had been turned into another thing, and he did not approve this abolitionism, for his wife's people all owned slaves. . . .

Soon after this some twenty rode up and caught me having a barrel rolled toward the house. They were gentlemanly. A few only dismounted; said they were from various of our Confederate States. They said the war would soon be over, for they would have Savannah in a few days.

I replied: "Savannah is not the Confederacy."

They spoke of the number of places they had taken.

I said: "Yes, and do you hold them?"

One of them replied: "Well, I do admire your spunk." . . .

Sabbath, December 18th. We passed this day with many fears, but no Yankees came to the lot; . . .

In the afternoon, while we were engaged in religious services, reading and seeking protection of our Heavenly Father, Captain Winn's Isaiah came bringing a note from Mr. Mallard to me and one from Mr. John Stevens to Mother, sending my watch. This was our first intelligence from Mr. Mallard, and oh, how welcome to us all; though the note brought no hope of his release. . . . We were all in such distress that Mother wrote begging Mr. Stevens to come to us. We felt so utterly alone that it would be a comfort to have him with us.

Monday, December 19th. Squads of Yankees came all day, so that the servants scarcely had a moment to do anything for us out of the house. The women, finding it entirely unsafe for them to be out of the house at all, would run in and conceal themselves in our dwelling. The few remaining chickens and some sheep were killed. These men were so outrageous at the Negro houses that the Negro men were obliged to stay at their houses for the protection of their wives; and in some instances they rescued them from the hands of these infamous creatures.

Tuesday, December 20th. A squad of Yankees came soon after break-fast. . . . Needing a chain . . . they went to the well and took it from the well bucket. Mother went out and entreated them not to take it from the well, as it was our means of getting water. They replied: "You have no right to have even wood or water," and immediately took it away.

Wednesday, December 21st. 10 A.M. Six of Kilpatrick's cavalry rode up, one of them mounted on Mr. Mallard's valuable gray named Jim. They looked into the dairy and empty smokehouse, every lock having been broken and doors wide open day and night. . . .

She told them her house had been four times searched in every part, and everything taken from it. And recognizing one who had been of the party that had robbed us, she said: "You know my meal and everything has been taken." . . .

She then entreated them, on account of the health of her daughter, not to enter the house. With horrible oaths they rode off, shooting two ducks in the yard.

About half an hour later, three came. One knocked in the piazza and asked if Mother always kept her doors locked. . . . Asked if we knew Mrs. S—— of Dorchester, for he had turned some men out of her house who were ransacking it. He demeaned himself with respect, and did not insist upon coming in. . . .

One hour after, five came. Mother and Kate trembled from head to feet. It appeared as if this day's trials were more than they could bear. They knelt and asked strength from God; went down and found that three had already entered the pantry with false keys brought for the purpose. They immediately proceeded to cut open the wires of the safe and took all they wanted, amongst other things a tin kettle of eggs we had managed to get. . . .

She remonstrated against their coming over the house, and told them of the order of the officers. They replied none of their officers prohibited them from coming in, and they would be damned if they would mind any such orders, and would be damned if they did not go where they pleased, and would be damned if they did not take what they pleased. Mother remonstrated, and in her earnest entreaty placed her hand upon the shoulder of one of them, saying: "You must not go over my house." Strange to say, they did not go beyond the pantry, and appeared restrained, as we afterwards believed, by the hand of God. . . .

At dinner time twelve more came—six or seven to the door asking for flour and meal. Mother told them she was a defenseless widow with an only daughter on the eve of again becoming a mother, a young friend, and five little children dependent on her for food and protection. They laughed and said: "Oh, we have heard just such tales before!" . . . Twelve sheep were found shot and left in the pasture—an act of wanton wickedness.

Late in the afternoon more came and carried off the few remaining ducks. Going to the Negro houses, they called Cato, the driver, and told him they knew he was feeding "that damned old heifer in the house," and they would "blow out his damned brains" if he gave her another morsel to eat, for they meant to starve her to death. Pointing to the chapel, they asked what house that was. Cato answered: "A church which my master had built for the colored people on the place to hold prayers in the week and preach in on Sunday." They said: "Yes, there he told all his damned lies and called it preaching." And with dreadful oaths they cursed him. . . .

Mrs. Mary Jones in her Journal:

Montevideo, *Thursday,* December 22nd, 1864
Several squads of Yankees came today, but none insisted upon coming into the house. . . . One attempted forcibly to drag Sue by the collar of her dress into her room. Another soldier coming up told him to "let that old woman alone"; and while they were speaking together she made her escape to the dwelling, dreadfully frightened and thoroughly enraged. . . . Sue's running into the house sent a thrill of terror into Kate and myself, for we were momentarily expecting them to enter the house. My heart palpitates with such violence against my side that with pain I bear the pressure of my dress.

If it was not for the supporting hand of God we must give up and die. . . . Besides our morning and evening devotions Kate, Daughter, and I observe a special season every afternoon to implore protection for our beloved ones and ourselves and deliverance for our suffering country. . . .

Mrs. Mary S. Mallard in her Journal:

Montevideo, *Thursday,* December 22nd, 1864
About midday the two little boys Mac and Pulaski made their appearance, having escaped from the Yankees at Midway. One of the officers told Pulaski Mr. Mallard was at the Ogeechee bridge, and had been preaching for them and walking at large. They had put no handcuffs on him, and he was walking at large, and they gave him plenty to eat. We are all thankful to hear from him.

Pulaski says he asked for the well chain. They cursed him and said his mistress should do without it.

One squad who came to the house asked Mother when she had seen any rebels, and if there were any around here. She told them her son-in-law had been captured more than a week before, and he was the only gentleman belonging to our household.

Looking fiercely at her, he said: "If you lie to me I will—" The rest of the sentence Mother did not quite understand; it was either "I'll kill you" or "I'll blow your brains out."

She immediately stepped out upon the little porch, near which he was sitting on his horse as he spoke to her, and said to him: "In the beginning of this war one passage of Scripture was impressed upon my mind; and it now abides with me: 'Fear not them which kill the body and after that have no more that they can do. But fear Him who, after He hath killed, hath power to cast into hell.' I have spoken the truth, and do you remember that you will stand with me at the Judgment Bar of God!"

There were quite a number around. One man said: "Madam, if that is your faith, it is a good one."

She replied: "It is my faith, and I feel that it has power to sustain me." . . .

Early in the afternoon the same officer called who had previously been in the house. He immediately inquired if the men had done any injury within since he was here last. Whilst he conversed with Kate and Mother his men were firing and killing the geese in the lot and loading their horses with them.

Before leaving he asked for a glass of water. Mother handed him a glass, saying: "I regret that I cannot offer a glass of fresh water, for you have taken even the chain from my well bucket."

He replied very quickly: "I did not do it. Neither did my men do it." . . .

Friday, December 23rd. A day of perfect freedom from the enemy at our dwelling. Five or six rode through the pasture, but none came to the house or Negro houses.

Mrs. Mary Jones in her Journal:

Montevideo, *Saturday,* December 24th, 1864

As we were finishing our breakfast, which we always had to take in the most hurried manner with every window tightly closed upstairs in my chamber, five Yankees made their appearance from different approaches to the house. Kate and I went down, as usual, with beating hearts and knees that smote together, yet trusting in our God for protection.

One knocked at the door next the river. I requested him to go around to the front door, and—most amazing—he answered "Yes, ma'am" and went around. When the door was unlocked he said: "We have come to search for arms."

I told him the house had again and again under that plea been thoroughly searched; not the minutest drawer or trunk but had been searched.

He replied: "I would not like to do anything unpleasant to you."

A Dutchman said: "I have come to search your house, mistress, and I mean to do it. If you have two or three thousand dollars I would not touch it; but I am coming into your house to search it from top to bottom."

I told him the officers had said the soldiers must not enter private dwellings.

He replied: "There is no officer; we are independent scouts and do as we please." He looked up at the windows, and went around the front of the house, remarking in the most cruel manner: "This house will make a beautiful fire and a great smoke."

I said: "Surely you would not burn a house that was occupied!"

He replied: "Your soldiers would do it. I came here to fight, and I mean to do it." Then he insisted upon coming in.

I told him of my daughter's situation and entreated him not to come in, for she was daily expecting to be confined.

"Tell her to go to her room; we will not disturb her. We have not come to insult ladies."

I said: "If you are determined to search, begin your work at once." For they were pushing into the rooms, and with them an insolent little mulatto boy, who commenced running about the parlor. I called to the Dutchman and said: "Order that boy out of my house!"

He immediately stamped his foot and said: "Get out of this house and stay by the horses!"

They searched from the attic down. One of the party wanted to take a comforter, but the Dutchman said: "Let it alone." . . .

Again they surveyed the house, asked if I knew North and South Hampton, said they had just burnt both places, that my house would be a beautiful flame, and that night they would return and burn it down. . . .

My mind is made up not to leave my house until the torch is put to it. . . .

Our agony and distress are so great I sent Cato to Captain Winn and Mr. Stevens this afternoon to tell them our situation. We received a note signed "S," saying they did not think the threat would be executed, and that it was reported by the enemy that Savannah was evacuated two days ago, our forces going into Carolina and the Yankees capturing two hundred cars and thirty thousand bales of cotton and nine hundred prisoners.

We have all spent a miserable day, but have committed ourselves to Him who never slumbers nor sleeps. We are completely cut off from all creature helps, from all human sympathy. Helpless—oh, how utterly helpless! And yet blessed be God! We feel that we are in the hollow of His almighty hand. It is a precious, precious feeling that the omnipotent, omnipresent Jehovah is with us, and that Jesus, our Divine Redeemer and Advocate, will be touched with our sorrows.

The darkness of night is around our dwelling. We are all upstairs in one room with closed windows and a dim light. Our poor little children have eaten their supper. We have dressed them warmly, and they have been put to bed with their clothes on, that they may be ready to move at an instant's warning. My poor delicate suffering, heart-weary child I have forced to lie down, and persuaded Kate to do so also.

Kept watch alone until two o'clock, and then called Kate, who took my place, and I threw myself on the bed for an hour.

May God keep us safe this night! To Him alone do we look for protection from our cruel enemies.

Mrs. Mary S. Mallard in her Journal:

Montevideo, *Sunday*, December 25th, 1864

With great gratitude we hailed the light this morning, having passed the night. And no enemy has come nigh our persons or our dwelling; although there are appearances of horse tracks. . . .

At breakfast two Yankees rode around the lot, but seeing nothing to take went away; and we were not further interrupted. . . .

Monday, December 26th. Saw no one all day. Towards evening we ventured out with the poor little children, and as we were returning saw one at a distance.

Tuesday, December 27th. No enemy today. Bless the Lord for this mercy!

Wednesday, December 28th. Another day without the appearance of the Yankees. Could we but know we should be spared one day we would breathe freely, but we are in constant apprehension and terror. . . .

Thursday, December 29th. Free from intrusion until afternoon, when three Yankees and one Negro came up. Lucy ran into the house and locked the door after her, which seemed to provoke them. Three came to the door, and after knocking violently several times one broke open the door. Mother and Kate went down as soon as they could, and when he saw them he cursed awfully. They insisted upon coming in, and asked for that "damned wench" that had locked the door, threatening to "shoot her damned brains out," using the Saviour's name in awful blasphemy. . . .

The cook, seeing the party, locked herself into the cooking room; but they thundered at the door in such a manner I had to call to her to open it, which when she did I could scarce keep from smiling at the metamorphosis. From being a young girl she had assumed the attitude and appearance of a sick old woman, with a blanket thrown over her head and shoulders, and scarcely able to move. Their devices are various and amusing. Gilbert keeps a sling under his coat and slips his arm into it as soon as they appear; Charles walks with a stick and limps dreadfully; Niger a few days since kept them from stealing everything they wanted in his house by covering up in bed and saying he had *"yellow fever"*; Mary Ann kept them from taking the wardrobe of her deceased daughter by calling out: "Them dead people clothes!"

Friday, Saturday, Sabbath, and Monday. No enemy came to the dwelling . . . .

Mrs. Mary Jones in her Journal:

Montevideo, *Tuesday*, January 3rd, 1865

Soon after breakfast three Yankees rode up and wanted to search for rebels and arms. They dismounted and sat upon the front porch. With much entreaty, and reminding them of the orders of their commander and the feeble condition of my daughter, they refrained from coming in. . . .

Four others rode up and proceeded to search the outhouses. In the loft to the washroom they found some ear corn that we had concealed there to sustain our lives. They immediately commenced knocking off the shingles, and soon broke a large hole in the roof, those within hallooing and screaming and cursing to those without to come and see what they had found.

The one who had been speaking to us assured us they would do us personally no harm. I asked him to prevent their breaking down the house.

He called out: "Stop, boys!"

They replied: "We have found a lot of corn!"

"Well, you must let it alone." (I had told them we put it there to keep ourselves and the servants from starving.)

After this they ceased knocking off the shingles.

Seeing there was some trace of humanity in him, I related Mr. Mallard's capture, and that he was a minister of the gospel. . . .

He was a Methodist, but had many friends who were Presbyterians; his parents Baptist. I asked him to stay and protect us while this lawless squad remained; but he said they must go, and rode off, while the others proceeded to gather all they wanted from the people's houses, making the Negroes fill the bags and take them out. . . .

Wednesday, January 4th. At daylight my daughter informed me she was sick. She has been in daily expectation of her confinement for two weeks. I sent immediately for the servants. . . . Prepared a yellow flag for Charles (in case he met the Yankees) and wrote to Dr. Raymond Harris, three miles off and the only physician I know of in the county: "I entreat you to come to the help of my suffering child." Charles started before sunrise, going through the woods.

My heart was filled with intense anxiety and distress, especially as my child had an impression something was wrong with her unborn infant— the consequence of injuries received from a severe fall from a wagon, breaking her collarbone and bruising her severely, as they were making their retreat from Atlanta on the approach of General Sherman.

Dr. Harris, with a kindness and courage never to be forgotten, came without delay and in the face of danger; for the enemy was everywhere over the county. He looked very feeble, having been recently ill with pneumonia. Soon after being in her room he requested a private interview, informing me that my child was in a most critical condition, and I must be prepared for the worst. For if he did not succeed in relieving the difficulty, her infant at least must die.

I replied: "Doctor, the mother first."

"Certainly," was his answer.

He returned to her room and with great difficulty and skill succeeded in effecting what he desired. God, our compassionate Saviour, heard the voice of faith and prayer; and she was saved in childbearing, and at eleven o'clock gave birth to a well-formed infant—a daughter.

During these hours of agony the yard was filled with Yankees. It is supposed one hundred visited the place during the day. They were all around the house; my poor child, calm and collected amid her agony of body, could hear their conversation and wild halloos and cursing beneath her windows. Our dear friend Kate King had to meet them alone. She entreated that they would not come in or make a noise, for there was sickness in the house.

They replied: "We are not as bad as you think us. We will take off our spurs and come in." And one actually pushed by her and came in.

She stepped upon the porch and implored if there was one spark of humanity or honor about them that they would not come in, saying: "You compel me to speak plain. There is a child being born this very instant in this house, and if there is an officer or a gentleman amongst you I entreat you to protect the house from intrusion."

After a while they left, screaming and yelling in a most fiendish way as they rode from the house.

Dr. Harris returned with Charles as a guide and reached his home safely, having met only one of the enemy. . . .

Thursday, January 5th. Three Yankees rode up in the forenoon and asked for me. I met them at the front porch. They wished to know if there were sick soldiers in the house.

"No, my daughter is sick."

They propounded the usual questions. I told them of the capture of my daughter's husband, and as they were Kilpatrick's men, asked if they would take a letter to him. They said they would; and I wrote telling him of the birth of the baby; and Daughter sent him her Greek Testament, Kate sent a letter North, and Mrs. King one to Clarence.

This man told me he was from Indiana; was a Virginian by birth. Said there was great dissatisfaction in the army on account of the present object of the war, which now was to free Negroes. . . .

This man said his name was James Y. Clark, and was the only one of all we saw whose name we heard. A mere youth with him said he had a brother who had been a prisoner in Georgia, and when sick had been taken into a family and nursed; and whenever he met a Georgian he would treat him as well as his own men. They spoke more kindly than any we have conversed with. . . .

Saturday, January 7th. . . . No enemy thus far. God be praised for His goodness and mercy! Our nights have been free from intrusion. . . .

As I stand and look at the desolating changes wrought by the hand of an inhuman foe in a few days, I can enter into the feelings of Job when he

exclaimed: "Naked came I out of my mother's womb, and naked shall I return thither; the Lord gave, and the Lord hath taken away: blessed be the name of the Lord." All our pleasant things are laid low. Lover and friend is put far from us, and our acquaintance into darkness. We are prisoners in our own home; we dare not open windows or doors. Sometimes our little children are allowed under a strict watch and guard to run a little in the sunshine, but it is always under constant apprehension. The poor little creatures at a moment's warning—just let them hear "Yankee coming"—rush in and remain almost breathless, huddled together in one of the upper rooms like a bevy of frightened partridges. To obtain a mouthful of food we have been obliged to cook in what was formerly our drawing room; and I have to rise every morning by candlelight, before the dawn of day, that we may have it before the enemy arrives to take it from us. And then sometimes we and the dear little ones have not a chance to eat again before dark. The poor servants are harassed to death, going rapidly for wood or water and hurrying in to lock the doors, fearing insults and abuse at every turn. Do the annals of civilized—and I may add savage—warfare afford any record of brutality equaled in extent and duration to that which we have suffered, and which has been inflicted on us by the Yankees?
[*The Children of Pride*, pp. 1220–1242.]

Mrs. Mary Jones's graphic description of the "brutality inflicted on us by the Yankees" serves as an extended counterpart to Rachel Cormany's account, quoted above, of the burning of Chambersburg, Pennsylvania (July, 1864), by Confederate forces: "They [the Confederate soldiers] deliberately went from house to house and fired" the town.

When we quoted Rachel Cormany's description, we presented a contrasting reaction to the burning of Chambersburg by an officer in the Confederate army. In a similar fashion, a version of events in Georgia from a perspective different from that of Mary Jones was provided in an entry in the diary of a Union officer, Major Henry Hitchcock, who was a member of General Sherman's staff. Hitchcock dated an entry in his diary on December 10, 1864 (within a few days of Mary Jones's first encounter with Union soldiers), and listed his location as "about 5-1/2 miles from Savannah" (probably within thirty miles of the Jones plantation):

Camp on "Millen (Dirt) Road" (or "Louisville Road"), About
5-1/2 miles from Savannah. Sat. December 10/64
 . . . I may well thank God for the health and safety which has thus far been my own lot, as well as for the safety of this magnificent army. . . . I do not forget, and God knows I am sorry for the people of the regions we have traversed. . . . Their losses, their terrors (many of which they find and acknowledge to be groundless) their sufferings, all are implied in and inevitable with war—and for this war, not we but *their* "leaders" and their

own moral and physical cowardice three years ago are responsible. This Union and its Government must be sustained, at any and every cost; to sustain it, we must war upon and destroy the organized rebel forces,—must cut off their supplies, destroy their communications, and show their white *slaves* (these people say themselves that they are so) their utter inability to resist the power of the U.S. To do this implies and requires these very sufferings, and having thus only the choice of evils—war now so terrible and successful that none can dream of rebellion hereafter, or everlasting war with all these evils magnified a hundred fold hereafter,—we have no other course to take. At least I am glad to remember that I have not only not abused nor insulted a single person, but have repeatedly stopped the depredations of soldiers.

[*Marching with Sherman: Passages From the Letters and Campaign Diaries of Henry Hitchcock*. Edited by M. A. DeWolfe Howe. New Haven, Yale University Press. Copyright 1927 by Yale University Press, pp. 166–168. Permission to print this passage granted by Yale University Press.]

The Army of Sherman in South Carolina and North Carolina, January–April, 1865

By the time in early January, 1865, when the members of the Jones family had seen what they hoped was the last of Sherman's army, that army had pressed on to Savannah. The Confederate defenders of Savannah evacuated the city on December 21, 1864, and the Union forces moved in. Most of the Confederate units that had defended Savannah were now moved north and west of the city, across the Savannah River and into South Carolina, to obstruct the further movement of Sherman's army. Among the Confederate troops in South Carolina in the general vicinity north of Savannah were John Cotton and David Harris.

Cotton, in his letters to his wife in January and February, 1865, summarized the desperate Confederate military situation succinctly: "Here is shermans hole armey and nobody to fite them only a few cavalry and a few miltia." Cotton's letters made clear his view that the Confederate military forces were defeated beyond repair and that the fighting should stop:

South Carolina Camps near Lortonsville
[Lawtonville?]
January 20th 1865

Most dear beloved wife I again take my pen in hand to rite you a few more lines to try to let you no that I am well. . . . we have not drawn our money yet but I have plenty I would like to send you some for I am afraid you hant got money enought to pay your war tax but this ant what bothers me most I ant herd from you since I left home but I hope you have herd from me if I cant from you you cant no how bad I want to here from home.

. . . I will start this by hand as there is no regular mail from here I hant any nuse we here the general hood is whiped out of tennessee and is in Mississippi and we here that a part of lees armey is at branchville southcarolina it looks like the yankeys has got the upperhand of us I would like to here of some terms of peace before the runn clear over us I think they will take charlestan without a fite our soldiers are very much dishartened and the most of them say we are whiped it is said the georgia is holding conventions to no whether to go back in the union or not if she goes back it will look like rest will have to go two I hate the thoughts of going back but if we have to do it the sooner the better I have suffered two much in this war to ever go back to the union willingly I would give a heap of see you and the children and see you all well and have one frolick with them there is nothing in this world that can gratify my feelings like beeing with a kind and affectionate wife I dont think that if I were at home to stay clere of this war I would ever want to leave home again hothing more at present only I remain affectionate husband til death

John W Cotton. . .

Camp Southcarolina January 27th 1865
    Most dear beloved wife and hyly esteemed wife I once more take my pen in hand to rite you a few more lines to try to let you no that I am well and in hopes these few lines may find you all enjoying the same blessing and I want to let you no that I hant herd from you yet I want to hear from you very bad I dont see much satisfaction now nor want until I here from home all thoe I am doing very well you all mite get sick and die and me not here anything about it I hant got any thing hardly We here that there is some proposals for peace but I fear that ould jef daves wont come to them it dont look to me like there any use of fiting any longer I think they had better make peace now then to wate til we are subjugated it looks like we cant whip no where they whip us at every point here is shermans hole armey and nobody to fite them only a few cavalry and a few militia. . . . I cant rite but little but I think if I could get a letter from you I think I would rite a heap more I would love to see you and no how you all are getting on and I would love to no what people think about the war we here that tennessee has gone back in the union and georgia is trying to go back two. . . . nothing more only I remain your affectionate husband and friend til death

John W Cotton

Southcarolina Camps near Cartonville [Lawtonville?] February 1st 1865
    dear wife again I take my pen in hand to rite you a few more lines to try to let you no that I am well. . . . I dont no what to rite without I would get a letter from you I hant got nary one yet there was fore come to our regiment last nite but nary a one from our settlement home sweet home

how I long to here from home but would rather bee at home. . . . the yankeys are advancing there scouts were in 7 or 8 miles of here last nite we are falling back as they advance. . . . I here that general wheeler said we would have armistis in less than ten days but I dont no whether he said it or not we here a heap about peace but we dont no whether to believe it or not but I would be glad if it was true nothing would do me more good than anything else for themto make peace for I want to come home very bad for I dont want to spend all of the best of my life here in this cruel and unholy war but I hope to outlive it so I can once more enjoy freedom again I daont no what else to rite now I must stop riting for the man that is going home is hollowing for the letters nothing more your affectionate husband til death

John W Cotton

[*Yours Till Death*, pp. 124–128.]

Whether Cotton participated in any battles against Sherman's army in South Carolina or North Carolina is not known; his letter of February 1 to his wife is the last that has been found. What is known is that he survived the war and was paroled as a prisoner of war at Talladega, Alabama, on May 25, 1865.

David G. Harris apparently did not take part in any sizable engagements against Sherman's army in South Carolina and North Carolina, although he was frequently near that army. In mid-December, 1864, he had been detached from his cavalry command on James Island, in Charleston harbor, and sent with other dismounted cavalrymen to serve on foot in the South Carolina region north of Savannah, where it was assumed that Sherman's forces would advance. From that part of South Carolina, Harris was eventually marched into North Carolina and then to Cheraw, South Carolina. There, he and other dismounted Confederate cavalrymen were told to secure horses for themselves as best they could. Harris took this opportunity to go home in search of a horse for himself, arriving home by March 14, 1865, after having walked (by his estimate) some 300 miles. He never returned to the army, and saw the war wind down from the relative comfort and safety of his home.

The entries made by Emily L. Harris in the family journal during the months when her husband was on the move in front of Sherman's army reveal the continuing difficulties she faced and her growing despair over the Confederate military situation. Typical were her comments at the end of the old year and the beginning of the new year:

December 31. [1864] . . . What an eventful year it has been. . . . Few have been made to rejoice and many to mourn. The Nation mourns and bleeds. Wounded from crown to sole it now is gasping almost at the mercy of its foes! Without a miraculous intervention of the God of battles our once proud Confederacy must sink to rise no more. This is not alone the opinion of an illjudging woman but of the greater part of the Solomons of the land. . . .

During this year I have had trials only known to myself and in which no one did or could sympathize. My Husband has been at home but two weeks since the middle of April and I have struggled faithfully, if not successfully to some, from diminishing our little property. I have had some losses and many crosses and disappointments to contend with. Many times I should utterly fail to continue the struggle if I had no children. I sometimes feel very lonely and sad. I'm without father mother brother or sister. No one seems to think that I ever sigh for love and kind words.

There has been no death and but one birth in the family during the year. All seem well and contented. We have felt but little of the horrors of the war in our circle. . . .

January 1. [1865] New year. Sunday morning. It is a cold bright day. The children are all engaged with some book and we are all as happy as the gloomy aspects of the times and the dangerous and critical state of our country will admit. Our best freind, the King of the household, the Head of the family is exposed to the inclemency of the winter and the shells of the enemy, . . . cold shivering and hungry, struggling almost without hope for the independence of the Confederacy. The war goes on with unabated fury. Many are crying out for peace. Many are willing to unite again with the hated Yankees rather than continue the hard and seemingly hopeless struggle. Our state, which has until recently stood like the land of Goshen amid the plagues of Egypt is now threatened with the dreadful ravages of the foe. I do say fervently—Let God's will be done.

[*Piedmont Farmer*, pp. 355–357.]

Whether or not David G. Harris and John Cotton took part in a major military action against Sherman's army in South Carolina, the northward movement of that army from Savannah, beginning in January, 1865, affected directly the lives of both men. So, too, that northward movement was to affect directly the life of Mary Chesnut, since Columbia, South Carolina, the home of the Chesnuts from July, 1864, lay squarely in the path of Sherman's troops. Not far from Columbia was Mulberry, the plantation that belonged to Mary Chesnut's father-in-law, who was now elderly and enfeebled, and Mulberry was also on the route that some Union troops would take. Mary Chesnut and her husband were to flee Columbia to escape the oncoming troops, and the Chesnut plantation was to be severely damaged. Symbolism and irony were combined in the fact that the town in which Mary Chesnut took refuge when she escaped from Columbia was named "Lincolnton" (North Carolina), and the owner of a wagon in which she rode while there was named "Sherman" ("the name was the last drop in my cup"). After the capture and burning of Columbia in mid-February, one disaster after another came quickly to the Confederacy—and Mary Chesnut, like Mary Jones, sought solace in the Book of Job: "Job is my comforter now."

January 7, 1865. . . . Not by one word or look do these slaves show that they know Sherman and freedom is at hand. They are more obedient and more considerate than ever—to me. . . .

January—. Yesterday I broke down—gave way to abject terror. The news of Sherman's advance—and no news of my husband. Today—wrapped up on the sofa—too dismal for moaning, even. There was a loud knock. Shawls and all, I rushed to the door. Telegram from my husband.

"All well—be at home on Tuesday." . . .

I felt as lighthearted as if the war were over. . . .

January 16, 1865. My husband is at home once more—for how long, I do not know. . . .

A month ago my husband wrote me a letter which I promptly suppressed after showing it to Mrs. McCord. He warned us to make ready—for the end had come. Our resources were exhausted—and the means of resistance could not be found. . . .

February 8, 1865. . . . Our commissioners the Laodicean Stephens, Campbell, &c were received by Lincoln with taunts and derision. [At the Hampton Roads Conference on Feb. 3, Lincoln offered the Confederates some concessions, but not the independence that Jefferson Davis demanded for the South. "Laodicean," from Revelation 3:15–16, signifies one who is lukewarm in politics or religion.] Why not? He has it all his own way now. . . .

February 16, 1865. Lincolnton, North Carolina. A change came o'er the spirit of my dream—dear old quire of yellow, coarse, Confederate homemade paper! Here you are again—and an age of anxiety and suffering has passed over my head since I wrote and wept over your forlorn pages.

My ideas of those last days are confused.

The Martins left Columbia the Friday before I did. And their mammy, the negro woman who had nursed them, refused to go with them. That daunted me. . . .

Then I met Mr. Christopher Hampton arranging to take off his sisters. They were flitting—but only as far as Yorkville. He said it was time to move on; Sherman at Orangeburg was barely a day's journey from Columbia, and that he left a track as bare and blackened as a fire in the prairies.

So my time had come, too. My husband urged me to go home. He said Camden would be safe enough. They had no spite to that old town—as they have to Charleston and Columbia. Molly, weeping and wailing, came in while we were at table, wiping her red-hot face with her cook's grimy apron. She said I ought to go among our own black people on the plantation. They would take care of me better than anyone else. So I agreed to go to Mulberry or the Hermitage plantation and sent Laurence with a wagon load of my valuables.

Then a Miss Patterson called—a refugee from Tennessee. She had been in a country overrun by Yankee invaders—and she described so graphically all the horrors to be endured by those subjected to fire and sword and rapine and plunder that I was fairly scared and determined to come here. This is a thoroughly out-of-all-routes place. And yet I can go to

Charlotte. I am half way to Kate at Flat Rock. And there is no Federal army between me and Richmond. . . .

I took French leave of Columbia, slipped away without a word to anybody. Isaac Hayne and Mr. Chesnut came down to the Charlotte depot with me. Ellen, my maid, left husband and only child—but she was willing to come—very cheerful in her way of looking at it.

"Who guine trouble my William—dey don't dares to. Claiborne (her husband) kin take good care of William. I never traveled 'round with Missis before—and I wants to go this time." . . .

Here I am brokenhearted—an exile.

Such a place. Bare floors. For a feather bed, a pine table, and two chairs I pay 30 dollars a day. Such sheets!—but I have some of my own. . . .

February 23, 1865. Isabella has been reading my diaries. How we laugh. My sage ratiocinations—all come to naught. My famous insight into character—utter folly. They were lying on the hearth, ready to be burned, but she told me to hold on—think of it awhile. *"Don't be rash."* . . . the 10 volumes of memoirs of the times I have written . . . still I write on, for if I have to burn—and here lie my treasures, ready for the blazing hearth—still they have served already to while away four days of agony. . . .

Letter from my husband—he is at Charlotte. He came near being taken prisoner in Columbia, for he was asleep the morning of the 17th, when the Yankees blew up the RR depot. That woke him, of course. He found everybody had left Columbia and the town surrendered by the mayor, Colonel Goodwyn. Hampton and his command had been gone several hours. Isaac Hayne came away with General Chesnut. There was no fire in the town when they came away. They overtook Hampton's command at Meeks Mill. That night, from the hills where they encamped they saw the fire and knew the Yankees were burning the town—as we had every right to expect they would. . . .

Charleston and Wilmington—surrendered. I have no further use for a newspaper. I never want to see another one as long as I live. . . .

Shame, disgrace, beggary—all at once. Hard to bear.

Grand smash—

Rain—rain outside—inside naught but drowning floods of tears. . . .

February 25, 1865. . . . General and Mrs. Johnston stay at the Phifers.

Mrs. Johnston said she would never own slaves.

"I might say the same thing, I never would. Mr. Chesnut does, but he hates all slavery, especially African slavery."

"What do you mean by African?"

"To distinguish that form from the inevitable slavery of the world. All married women, all children, and girls who live on in their father's houses are slaves."

"Oh! Oh!" . . .

My days are past—my purposes broken off—even the thoughts of my heart (Job). [Job 17:11]

> Be fair, or foul—or rain, or shine,
> The joys I have possessed *in spite of fate* are mine,
> Not Jove himself upon the past has power,
> What has been-has been—and I have had my hour.
>   [Horace, *Odes*, book 3, ode 29.] . . .

Yesterday the wagon in which I was to go to Flat Rock drove up to the door. . . .

The man who owned the wagon was standing in the door. . . . I asked the man his name. . . . He showed great hesitation in giving it. At last:

"My name is Sherman—and now I see by your face that you won't go with me. My name is against me these times." Here he grinned: "But you leave *Lincoln*ton."

The name was the last drop in my cup. . . .

February 26, 1865. Mrs. Munro offered me religious books which I declined, being already provided with the Lamentations of Jeremiah, the Penitential Psalms of David, the denunciations of Isaiah, and above all the patient wail of Job. Job is my comforter now.

And yet I would be so thankful to know it never would be any worse with me. My husband is well and ordered to join the Great Retreater. I am bodily comfortable, if somewhat dingily lodged, and I daily part with my raiment for food. We find no one who will exchange eatables for Confederate money. So we are devouring our clothes. . . .

In a later entry in her diary [May 7, 1865], Mary Chesnut described what happened to the Chesnut plantation at Mulberry when Sherman's army passed that way in February, followed in April by a Union army force commanded by General Edward E. Potter that destroyed Confederate supplies and railroad lines in South Carolina:

Mrs. Bartow drove with me to our house at Mulberry. On one side of the house every window was broken, every bell torn down, every piece of furniture destroyed, every door smashed in. The other side intact.

Maria Whitaker and her mother, who had been left in charge, explained this odd state of things.

"They were busy as beavers. They were working like regular carpenters, destroying everything, when the general came in. He said it was shame, and he stopped them. Said it was a sin to destroy a fine old house like that whose owner was over ninety years old. He would not have had it done for the world. It was wanton mischief." He told Maria soldiers at such times were so excited, so wild and unruly.

They carried off sacks of our books. Unfortunately there were a pile of empty sacks lying in the garret. Our books, our papers, our letters, were strewed along the Charleston road. Somebody said they found some of them as far away as Vance's Ferry.

This was Potter's raid. Sherman only took our horses. Potter's raid, which was after Johnston's surrender, ruined us finally, burning our mills and gins and a hundred bales of cotton. Indeed nothing is left now but the bare land and *debts* made for the support of these hundreds of negroes during the war. . . .

A hired man is far cheaper than a man whose father and mother, his wife and his twelve children have to be fed, clothed, housed, nursed, taxes paid and doctors' bills—all for his half-done, slovenly, lazy work. So for years we have thought—negroes a nuisance that did not pay.

They pretend exuberant loyalty to us now. Only one man of Mr. C's left his plantation with the Yankees. . . . we were quickly ruined after the surrender!

Cotton at a dollar a pound—that cotton saved, and we would be comparatively in easy circumstances. Now it is the devil to pay—and no pitch hot.

Well—it was to be.

[*Mary Chesnut's Civil War,* pp. 698–699, 702, 704, 710, 715–717, 724–725, 729–731, 733, 802–803.]

The Armies of Grant and Lee in Virginia, March–April, 1865

The spectacular successes of Sherman's army in Georgia and South Carolina were a prelude to what turned out to be the final showdown between the opposing armies of Grant and Lee. Confederate troops made an assault near Petersburg in the early morning of March 25, 1865, but that assault was soon repulsed and Union counterattacks were started, leading to the capture of both Richmond and Petersburg by April 3. Thomas M. Chester, the reporter for the Philadelphia Press, *was with the first Union troops who entered Richmond and described in his dispatches the earliest days of the Union occupation of the city.*

Hall of Congress:

Richmond, April 4, 1865

Seated in the Speaker's chair, so long dedicated to treason, but in the future to be consecrated to loyalty, I hasten to give a rapid sketch of the incidents which have occurred since my last despatch.

To Major General Godfrey Weitzel was assigned the duty of capturing Richmond. . . .

Every regiment tried to be first. All cheerfully moved off with accelerated speed. The pickets which were on the line during the night were in the advance.

Brevet Brigadier General Draper's brigade of colored troops,

Brevet Major General Kautz's division, were the first infantry to enter Richmond. . . .

In passing over the rebel works, we moved very cautiously in single file, for fear of exploding the innumerable torpedoes which were planted in front. . . .

Along the road which the troops marched, or rather double quicked, batches of negroes were gathered together testifying by unmistakable signs their delight at our coming. Rebel soldiers who had hid themselves when their army moved came out of the bushes, and gave themselves up as disgusted with the service. The haste of the rebels was evident in guns, camp equipage, telegraph wires, and other army property which they did not have time to burn. . . .

There were many persons in the better-class houses who were peeping out of the windows, and whose movements indicated that they would need watching in the future. There was no mistaking the curl of their lips and the flash of their eyes. . . .

The citizens stood gaping in wonder at the splendidly-equipped army marching along under the graceful folds of the old flag. Some waved their hats and women their hands in token of gladness. The pious old negroes, male and female, indulged in such expressions: "You've come at last"; "We've been looking for you these many days"; "Jesus has opened the way"; "God bless you"; "I've not seen that old flag for four year"; "It does my eyes good"; "Have you come to stay?"; "Thank God", and similar expressions of exultation. . . .

As we entered all the Government buildings were in flames, having been fired by order of the rebel General Ewell. The flames soon communicated themselves to the business part of the city; and continued to rage furiously throughout the day. All efforts to arrest this destructive element seemed for the best part of the day of no avail. . . .

The flames, in spreading, soon communicated to poor and rich houses alike. All classes were soon rushing, into the streets with their goods, to save them. They hardly laid them down before they were picked up by those who openly were plundering everyplace where anything of value was to be obtained. It was retributive justice upon the aiders and abettors of treason to see their property fired by the rebel chiefs and plundered by the people whom they meant to forever enslave. As soon as the torch was applied to the rebel storehouses, the negroes and poor whites began to appropriate all property, without respect to locks or bolts. About the time our advance entered the city the tide of this inadmissible confiscation was at its highest ebb. . . .

As soon as Gen. Ripley was assigned to provost duty, all plundering immediately ceased, the flames were arrested, and an appearance of recognized authority fully sustained. Order once more reigns in Richmond. . . .

The F.F.V.'s have not ventured out of their houses yet, except in a few cases, to apply for a guard to protect their property. In some cases negroes have been sent to protect the interest of these would-be man sellers. . . .

When the army occupied the city there were innumerable inquiries for Jeff Davis, but to all of which the answer was made that he went off in great haste night before last, with all the bag and baggage which he could carry. . . . Jeff's mansion, where he lived in state, is now the headquarters of Gen. Weitzel. . . .

Hall of Congress:

Richmond, April 6, 1865

The exultation of the loyal people of this city . . . is still being expressed by the most extravagant demonstrations of joy. The Union element in this city consists of negroes and poor whites, including all that have deserted from the army, or have survived the terrible exigencies which brought starvation to so many homes. As to the negroes, one thing is certain, that amid every disaster to our arms, amid the wrongs which they daily suffered for their known love for the Union, and amid the scourging which they received for trying to reach our army and enlist under our flag, they have ever prayed for the right cause, and testified their devotion to it in ten thousand instances, and especially in aiding our escaped prisoners to find our lines when to do so placed their own lives in peril.

The great event after the capture of the city was the arrival of President Lincoln in it. He came up to Rocket's wharf in one of Admiral Porter's vessels of war, and, with a file of sailors for a guard of honor, he walked up to Jeff Davis' house, the headquarters of General Weitzel. As soon as he landed the news sped, as if upon the wings of lightning, that "Old Abe," for it was treason in this city to give him a more respectful address, had come. Some of the negroes, feeling themselves free to act like men, shouted that the President had arrived. . . . when they learned that it was President Lincoln their joy knew no bounds. By the time he reached General Weitzel's headquarters, thousands of persons had followed him to catch a sight of the Chief Magistrate of the United States. When he ascended the steps he faced the crowd and bowed his thanks for the prolonged exultation which was going up from that great concourse. The people seemed inspired by this acknowledgment, and with renewed vigor shouted louder and louder. . . .

The President and party entered the mansion, where they remained for half an hour, the crowd still accumulating around it, when a headquarters' carriage was brought in front, drawn by four horses, and Mr. Lincoln, with his youngest son, Admiral Porter, General Kautz, and General Devin entered. The carriage drove through the principal streets, followed by General Weitzel and staff on horseback, and a cavalry guard.

There is no describing the scene along the route. The colored population was wild with enthusiasm. Old men thanked God in a very boisterous manner, and old women shouted upon the pavement as high as they had ever done at a religious revival. But when the President passed through the Capitol yard it was filled with people. Washington's monument and the Capitol steps were one mass of humanity to catch a glimpse of him. . . .

It must be confessed that those who participated in this informal reception of the President were mainly negroes. There were many whites in the crowd, but they were lost in the great concourse of American citizens of African descent. Those who lived in the finest houses either stood motionless upon their steps or merely peeped through the window-blinds, with a very few exceptions. The Secesh-inhabitants still have some hope for their tumbling cause. . . .

The people of Richmond, white and black, had been led to believe that when the Yankee army came its mission was one of plunder. But the orderly manner in which the soldiers have acted has undeceived them. The excitement is great, but nothing could be more orderly and decorous than the united crowds of soldiers and citizens. . . .

When the President returned to the flag-ship of Admiral Porter, in the evening, he was taken from the wharf in a cutter. Just as he pushed off, amid the cheering of the crowd, another good old colored female shouted out, "Don't drown, Massa Abe, for God's sake!"

The fire, which was nearly extinguished when I closed my last despatch, is entirely so now. Thousands of persons are gazing hourly with indignation upon the ruins. Gen. Lee ordered the evacuation of the city at an hour known to the remaining leaders of the rebellion, when Gens. Ewell and Breckinridge, and others, absconded, leaving orders with menials, robbers, and plunderers, kept together during the war by the "cohesive power of public plunder," to apply the torch to the different tobacco warehouses, public buildings, arsenals, stores, flour mills, powder magazines, and every important place of deposit. A south wind prevailed, and the flames spread with devastating effect. . . . In short, Secession was burnt out, and the city purified as far as fire could accomplish it. . . .

Lieut. Gen. Grant will arrive in this city tomorrow, and will doubtless receive an ovation equal to President Lincoln's.

[*Thomas Morris Chester . . . His Dispatches from the Virginia Front*, pp. 288–297, 299.]

Lee's army was not trapped in either Richmond or Petersburg, but fled westward from both cities with the ultimate goal of joining the one other Confederate army still in existence—that of General Joseph Johnston. Grant immediately ordered the Union cavalry and infantry units into action to pursue, and ultimately to surround, the fleeing Confederate troops. Samuel Cormany's regiment was part of the pursuing cavalry forces. He returned from leave and joined his regi-

ment on April 3, just as the chase was beginning, the chase that ended with Lee's surrender on April 9. Cormany vividly described what he called "this wild adventurous work of crushing the Southern Cause."

April 3, 1865 Monday. Morning News—Petersburg fell into our hands at 5 A.M.—at 8 ock Captain Robins—Lieut Dunn and I start for Petersburg— Pass over some of the recently hotly contested works and lines. We enter the city. . . .

My! What a warm greeting from Officers and Men on a/c of their Adjutants return—

It was surely delightful—But I was so fatigued by this time I could hardly dismount or mount—But to be again well enough to take my place—with the Colonel at the head of The Column . . . was decidedly refreshing.

P.M. we started out on the march—were on the move til 10-11 OCK, and encamped on the Vamoose road—near V-creek—a great day— Everything everywhere on the move—and everybody wild with excitement over the recent victories, and the brilliant prospects before us, now that the old lines of battle are broken up—Petersburg is taken, and we have the Rebels on the run, And we are in good trim to keep it up.

April 4, 1865 Tuesday. Marched via Manburg. . . where we found General Phil Sheridan and lots of Cavelry at about 3 A.M.—in the night—The march has been very wearing. O how sleepy and tired I am. . . . We bivouaced a while and slept—a nap—til 4 A.M.

April 5, 1865 Wednesday. . . . I am still weak, but strange to say, there is such exileration in these events, and my connection with and relation to them—that I am strengthening up manifestly, daily—At 8 A.M. we took up the march via Amelia Springs. . . .

We soon became engaged, and . . . made 5 or 6 charges against vastly superior numbers . . . and we went into bivouac Camp at Gedersville—

April 6, 1865 Thursday. Up and in line by 8 A.M.—See Reb Trains, moving paralell with our road for several hours—Our Reg't was ordered to move towards it. Soon we found ourselves engaged, and supported, but met with too much force, so we withdrew some, and, moved on paralell. . . .

Next we flanked some Rebel works—But here mounted men came up, gained the line on us, and Captured Genl Ewell—and his staff & c— &c—and we divided the glory amongst us any old way [Lt. Gen. Richard S. Ewell, one of Lee's corps commanders, surrendered himself, his staff, and what was left of his two divisions near Sailor's (sometimes Saylor's or Sayler's) Creek.]. . . .

No time to cook—eat—sleep or anything but "go in on them." . . .

April 7, 1865 Friday. Cloudy—Rained Some—We moved on at 6 ock A.M. across the Appoxmattox—

Rebels burned the long R.R. Bridge and set fire to the Road Bridge—
We move on to Farmville— . . . once fairly out of town we were apprised
of a large wagon train which was moving across our road at right angles
going south or S.W. This train we were instructed to charge, and seek to
capture, or destroy. . . . we advanced—on almost a charge—and soon were
fired upon by the train escort, which we ignored, moving right on—
to make a charge, which The Colonel and I were discussing—when a bullet hit the Col in the leg, and another hit our Chief Bugler, when the Col
said "Go on in Adjutant—I'm hit," and he rode off to the right, and I led
on. . . .

The road was narrow—so it was difficult for the Captain and myself
to pass the men in column. . . . I "jumped the fence" and rode in the field
and so was making good time towards reaching my point, when suddenly
a huge ditch—or washout—8 or 10 feet wide, and 6 or 8 feet deep confronted me—it was bridged on the road—but there was a high fence to my
left, and a squad of rebel infantry coming out of the brush 100 yds to my
right—demanding my surrender—I gave my horse the rein, and my two
spurs and he cleared the gully—only his hind feet did not go quite far
enough, but by throwing myself forward after a little moments awful
struggle—he recovered himself and we went on—

I can't see why those 30 or 40 rebs didn't shoot me—Guess they were
too cock sure I'd land in the gully—and be their game—or else too star-
tled looking at the awful venture to remember they had guns. A minute
later, they fired a volley after me, and the bullets buzzed like bees over
head—but not one touched me or my horse—. . . . We remained on the line
til dusk—Then moved back through town. . . . we had no time to cook or
eat all day—save eating raw pork and hard tack—"On horse" and "to
horse" til 2:30 A.M.—O my! I am awfully weak and weary & sleepy. . . .
April 8, 1865 Saturday. Clear—fine . . . massed at Poplin Station where we
captured 3 Engines and some rolling stock. did some reconnitering and in
P.M. marched around via Evergreen Station to Appomattox Station and
went into camp about 10 P.M. weary—sleepy—and hungry—The day has
been beautiful—General Sheridan—by a yankee trick—captured three
trains of cars from the Johnies—The Trains had come up from the
Southern department, not well posted as to latest doings &c.
April 9, 1865 Sunday. We had a late supper about midnight—good fresh
mutton, and potatoes—biscuit—milk & Coffee—Slept til about 6AM and
had a dandy breakfast akin to supper—and at 8 A.M. mounted and
moved out, and soon met the Enemy in force—A general engagement
seemed pending—The rebel Cavalry fell back before us, and on our right,
our Infantry and Artillery seemed to be forming into line. . . . The enemy
cavalry disappeared from our front, and our regiment was ordered to dismount. . . . so our dismounted men—with our 7 shooting Carbines, and 6
shooting revolvers, and abundance of ammunition . . . and formed in line

of battle our right connecting with the Infantry line—our men lying on the open ground about 4 or 5 feet apart—each one capable to shoot 13 times without re-loading—and instructed to hold his place at all hazzards—we were to hold our line by all means. . . .

I heard the enemys coming—one could see their double line—with steady tread, but they saw us not—lying on the ground—but a quick Attention! Fire at Will! rang out, and our line opened—with deadly aim— and volley after volley was poured into the approaching lines with terrible effect—

In vain their Officers tried to hold their men—and keep advancing— Too many fell, and too many others wounded fell back—and then too, the lay of the ground would occasion all but well taught & drilled shooters to shoot too high—overshoot. This was their failure—But they came on—in some fashion—til some were quite close—The cloud of smoke was blinding—our men knew no faltering—but with a yell, as if to Charge—many arose—using their revolvers, and now the scattering enemy broke to the rear, across the little rise of ground—leaving many dead wounded and dying I ran along our line ordering "Men! Load up quickly—Carbines first—Bully! Boys! you never flinched a bit. You may have to do it again, but you Cant do it better—I returned to the Captain—reported what I had done and he fairly flooded us all with praise "Bully!" was his word—We could now hear the enemy on the job of rallying—and could easily understand how difficult was their task. Again, I ran along the line with "They'll come again—Do as before. Dont fire til you have the command, but remember the lay of the land—and just exactly where the chests of the bodies are and aim there &c" and soon, on they came—steadily—over the rise—and into view—next again the Command—and the boys poured in as before, and the enemy overshot as before—and their retreat again was as much or more of a skedaddle and our boys fairly followed them but were commanded to re-load to the limit—as they may obtain reinforcements—and try us harder—"But Boys we must hold at all hazzards" . . . now our Regiment is soon mounted again, and in Column of fours, moving towards the left. . . .

The Command now given to our Brigade was "Prepare to Charge!" "Draw Saber." Every Sabre was bare. Just then! away! far! off! to our right our ears caught the sound of Cheering—But the command came "Forward—Guide Right—March!" and the brigade—en masse moves steadily—slowly—men clasp the hilt of the sword tensly—awaiting the final "CHARGE!" to be given But a moment and it was given a great line of the enemy cavalry now appeared out from the woods—a few shots were being fired by 1st Maine—The cheering on our right became plainer The Brigade Charge started—Now a Staff officer, on a black Horse—came dashing up towards the Brigade Head Qrs Flag exclaiming "For Gods sake Stop that Charge!"—an occasional shot still goes off—The Rebels show the white flag, and Their Bugle blows "Cease firing" and Ours blows the HALT! and all is quiet an instant—

O what a lull! What a wondering Why?—Flags of Truce meet—Whats' up? The News! "Generals Grant and Lee are counselling"—Next Comes the Cry, "LEE SURRENDERS!"

"Ye Gods!" What cheering comes along in waves from far off to the right, becoming more intense as taken up by those commands nearer to us. Now our Brigade lets loose more fully as the news is confirmed. Hats and caps uplifted on the points of Sabers are whirled and waved overhead—and with tearful voices—Scores of overjoyed men exclaim "Now I can go home to Wife Babies Mother Sister Sweetheart, and our Country is forever safe—

The tension, and nerve of Our Regiment has been on tremendous strain all day, and for five days now—In fact day and night. . . .

At night fall—we simply bivouac—on nearly the same ground—and rest for the night—Captain Snyder & I have our Fly up as shelter—

April 10, 1865 Monday. Slept finely, All in Joy that Lee has surrendered—. . . .

We ate early breakfast and at 7:30 we took up the march via Appomattox Court House—

Saw the Site where Genl Lee Surrendered to our General Grant, and hosts and hordes of surrendered Rebs all about the place and surrounding country—. . . .

We moved on to Prospect Station and encamped at 3 P.M. rained at times all day—making matters a little disagreeably joyful—But with it all, we closed the day "After the surrender" with a sumptuous Ham—eggs—and Slap-Jack supper, and other good things Our Mess Wagon and our Head Quarters darkies brought up—

[*The Cormany Diaries*, pp. 531, 533, 535–541.]

15. THE FIGHTING STOPS AND TRAGEDY STRIKES, APRIL, 1865

Lee surrendered his army to Grant, as Samuel Cormany described in his diary, on Sunday, April 9. That surrender, followed soon by the surrender of General Joseph Johnston's Confederate army in North Carolina, marked both the failure of the Confederate quest for independence and also the success of Unionist attempts to preserve the Union and to abolish the institution of slavery.

Before either Unionists or Confederates had much of a chance to digest the news of the ending of armed hostilities, however, President Lincoln, on Friday, April 14, was shot at Ford's Theater, and died the next morning, Saturday, April 15. Thus, within less than a week, individuals North and South were confronted with two remarkable occurrences, the ultimate ramifications of which were not easy to foresee.

Most of the cast of characters presented in this volume, whether Unionist or Confederate, reflected (in their comments upon Lee's surrender, Lincoln's assassination, and related happenings) the deep impact of those momentous events upon their consciousness.

Unionists

Among the Unionists, George Templeton Strong, as usual, presented one of the most detailed accounts of the eventful April days—from the victories of the Union forces before Richmond and Petersburg to his attendance at the memorial service in the East Room of the White House where Lincoln's body lay in state.

April 3. Petersburg and Richmond! *Gloria in excelsis Deo.*

New York has seen no such day in our time nor in the old time before us. . . .

Walking down Wall Street, I saw something on the *Commercial Advertiser* bulletin board at the corner of Pine and William Streets and turned off to investigate. I read the announcement "Petersburg is taken" and went into the office in quest of particulars. The man behind the counter was slowly painting in large letters on a large sheet of brown paper another annunciation for the board outside: "Richmond is"— "What's that about Richmond?" said I. "Anything more?" He was too busy for speech, but he went on with a capital C, and a capital A, and so on, till I read the word CAPTURED!!! . . .

An enormous crowd soon blocked that part of Wall Street, and speeches began. . . . the meeting, organized at about twelve, did not break up, I hear, till four P.M. Never before did I hear cheering that came straight from the heart, that was given because people felt relieved by cheering and hallooing. . . .

I walked about on the outskirts of the crowd, shaking hands with everybody, congratulating and being congratulated by scores of men I hardly know even by sight. Men embraced and hugged each other, *kissed* each other, retreated into doorways to dry their eyes and came out again to flourish their hats and hurrah. There will be many sore throats in New York tomorrow. . . .

After dinner to the Union League Club. Vast crowd, enthusiasm, and excitement. . . .

It seems like a Fourth of July night—such a fusillade and cannonade is going on. Thus ends a day *sui generis* in my life. We shall long remember that the first troops to enter Richmond were niggers of Weitzel's corps. It is a most suggestive fact. It's said there were abundant signs of Union feeling in the city. Lee, Davis, & Co. are supposed to be making for Burke's

Junction. Lynchburg or Danville is doubtless their proposed harbor of refuge. . . .

April 4. Ellie set off for City Point on the steamer *George Leary* with a large pleasant party. . . . I fear she and her party will be disappointed after all and unable to visit Richmond. . . .

No news from the front up to half-past one. . . . At last came announcements on bulletin boards and an extra with despatches. They indicate that Lee is damaged and demoralized. The country is full of stragglers. We bag prisoners in large handfuls. Lee's course is marked by abandoned artillery and by burned or charred wagons and caissons. Great store of war material found at Richmond, including railroad rolling stock. . . .

Guns popping off in every direction tonight. A salute of one hundred guns fired at the foot of Wall Street this morning, and another in front of the Union League Club tonight. . . .

April 6. . . . Today's news is good and full of promise. Lee is retreating perforce toward Lynchburg. . . . Jeff Davis made a moonlight flitting Sunday night and is believed to have taken a special train for Danville. . . .

April 7. . . . At noon came more good news. Lee's army again routed yesterday. More guns and wagon trains captured. . . .

April 8, Saturday. . . . For the first time in my life, I think, I have heard two of Beethoven's symphonies within twenty-four hours. The Ninth was rehearsed by the Philharmonic corps at the Academy of Music at three o'-clock, and this evening I heard the Seventh at Irving Hall. . . .

April 9. Not a word from the army. This naturally makes one a little anxious. Nor have I yet any news from Ellie and her party. I rather infer from her silence that they have penetrated to Richmond. . . .

*   *   *

LEE AND HIS ARMY HAVE SURRENDERED! *Gloria in Excelsis Deo. Et in Terra, Pax hominibus bonae voluntatis.*

April 10, Monday. A series of vehement pulls at the front door bell slowly roused me to consciousness soon after I hurried in last night and routed me out of bed at last. I made my way downstairs in my dressing gown, half awake, and expecting to find Ellie returned from her James River trip. But it was George C. Anthon come to announce The Surrender and that the rebel army of the Peninsula, Antietam, Fredericksburg, Chancellorsville, The Wilderness, Spotsylvania Court House, and other battles, has ceased to exist. . . . God be praised!

To bed again, but sleep was difficult. . . . Find the correspondence between Grant and Lee in the morning papers at the breakfast table. It is creditable to Grant, who opened it, and not discreditable to Lee. . . .

It has rained hard all day; too hard for jubilant demonstrations out of doors. We should have made this Monday something like the 3rd of April, 1865, I think, had the sun shone, and could we have congregated in the streets without umbrellas. Guns have been firing all day in spite of foul weather. . . .

April 11. . . . To Trinity Church at half-past twelve. . . . Vinton made a very short and a very judicious little address from the pulpit, enforcing the duty of forgiveness and charity. In alluding to the President, he used terms that do his insight credit: "Wise, merciful, resolute, Christian," or their equivalent. Many loyal men hold Lincoln a sensible, commonplace man, without special talent, except for story telling, and it must be admitted that he sometimes tells stories of the class that is "not convenient" and does not become a gentleman and the holder of the exalted place. But his weaknesses are on the surface, and his name will be of high account fifty years hence, and for many generations thereafter. . . .

April 15, Saturday. Nine o'clock in the morning. LINCOLN AND SEWARD ASSASSINATED LAST NIGHT! ! ! !

The South has nearly filled up the measure of her iniquities at last! Lincoln's death not yet certainly announced, but the one o'clock despatch states that he was then dying. Seward's side room was entered by the same or another assassin, and his throat cut. It is unlikely he will survive, for he was suffering from a broken arm and other injuries, the consequence of a fall, and is advanced in life. . . . *Eheu* A. Lincoln! . . .

Poor Ellie is heartbroken, though never an admirer of Lincoln's. We shall appreciate him at last.

Up with the Black Flag now!

Ten P.M. What a day it has been! Excitement and suspension of business even more general than on the 3rd instant. Tone of feeling very like that of four years ago when the news came of Sumter. This atrocity has invigorated national feeling in the same way, almost in the same degree. People who pitied our misguided brethren yesterday, and thought they had been punished enough already, and hoped there would be a general amnesty, including J. Davis himself, talk approvingly today of vindictive justice and favor the introduction of judges, juries, gaolers, and hangmen among the dramatis personae. . . . Tonight the case stands thus:

Abraham Lincoln died at twenty-two minutes after seven this morning. He never regained consciousness after the pistol ball fired at him from behind, over his wife's shoulder, entered his brain. Seward is living and may recover. The gentleman assigned to the duty of murdering him did his butchery badly. The throat is severely lacerated by his knife, but it's believed that no arteries are injured. Fred Seward's situation is less hopeful, his skull being fractured by a bludgeon or sling shot used by the same gentleman. . . .

The temper of the great meeting I found assembled in front of the Custom House (the old Exchange) was grim. . . . It was the first great patriotic meeting since the war began at which there was no talk of concession and conciliation. . . .

[Washington, D.C.] *Wednesday the 19th* was a bright cloudless day. All places of business closed, of course. Learned that members and officers of the Sanitary Commission . . . had places on the official programme and were expected to attend the ceremonial in the East Room, a privilege eagerly sought by all sorts of people but not solicited or invited by any of us. We went in a body to the office of the Secretary of the Treasury in the Treasury building. . . . A little before twelve we marched to the White House through the grounds that separate it from the Treasury, were shewn into the East Room and took our appointed place on the raised steps that occupied three of its sides—the catafalque with its black canopy and open coffin occupying the centre. I had a last glimpse of the honest face of our great and good President as we passed by. It was darker than in life, otherwise little changed. Personages and delegations were severally marshalled to their places quietly and in good order; the diplomatic corps in fullest glory of buttons and gold lace; Johnson and the Cabinet, Chief Justice Chase, many senators and notables, generals and admirals, Grant, Farragut, Burnside (in plain clothes), Davis, Porter, Goldsborough, and others. About 650 in all.

The appearance of the assemblage was most distinguished. . . . Of the religious service, the less that is said the better, for it was vile and vulgar; Bishop Simpson's whining, oratorical prayer most nauseous. When this was finished, the coffin was lifted and the assemblage followed it silently, reverently, and in perfect order. . . . So ended the most memorable ceremonial this continent has ever seen. I count it a great privilege to have been present. There will be thousands of people ten years hence who would pay any money to have been in my place.
[*The Diary of George Templeton Strong*, abridged edition, 1988, pp. 285–292, 294–295, 298–299.]

Maria Daly, as would be expected, saw events in New York in a perspective different from Strong's, but she too was caught up in the excitement of the April military victories for the Union. The assassination softened her estimate of Lincoln but did not completely erase her previous reservations about him and his administration.

April 5, 1865

Richmond is ours! Lee is retreating! . . . The streets are brilliant with flags. On Saturday when the news came, there was an impromptu meeting in Wall Street. All business adjourned, a few speeches, and then the multitude sang the Doxology and the 100th Psalm in Wall Street, the seat of the money-changers; it was a good augury. When I got the extra containing the great news, the tears rushed to my eyes, my heart to my throat. I could not speak. . . . May God's blessing come with it [peace] and make us less a money-loving, selfish, and self-sufficient people, purified by this great trial. . . .

April 8, 1865

Captures and victories every day! Lee is so surrounded that he must either disband his army or surrender. Grant at last reaps the reward of his long, patient waiting. . . .

April 9, 1865

The Judge is busy upon some important law business which will take him to Washington. Mr. Evarts told him that no man could go to Washington that would have more confidence with the President, for that he [the President] had not only a high opinion of his [the Judge's] abilities . . . but likewise the greatest confidence in his integrity. . . .

April 10, 1865

Last night at midnight we heard an extra called. The Judge rushed to the door, "Surrender of Lee's army, ten cents and no mistake," said the boy all in one breath (a true young American). It was Palm Sunday, and hosanna may we well cry! Glory be to God on high; the rebellion is ended! Phil, my brother, is uninjured, and peace soon to descend to bless the land again. . . .

April 15, 1865

What dreadful news! President Lincoln assassinated; Secretary Seward's throat cut! Just as we were rejoicing over the return of peace, everything once again in confusion. Poor Lincoln! The Judge is in Washington. He left on the twelfth, and fortunately dined out yesterday in company with Sir Frederick Bruce, the new English minister, and Senator Sumner. He was not, therefore in the theater. . . . The assassin is supposed to have been J. Wilkes Booth. . . . God save us all. What may not a day bring forth!

April 19, 1865

Had letters from the Judge. The last thing the poor President did was to write on a card an order to admit him and Mr. Ashburne on Saturday morning. . . .

Booth is not yet caught, but it is said it will be impossible for him to escape. Several arrests of men in female attire have been made. It would seem that it is a plot in which many are inculpated. It will make a martyr of Abraham Lincoln, whose death will make all the shortcomings of his life and Presidential career forgotten. . . .

Easter morning, instead of the Resurrection and Christ has Arisen, the clergymen began with Abraham Lincoln, mentioning that he was sacrificed on Good Friday, and it seemed to me that they gave Our Lord only the second place in his own house. . . . I must feel that all the glory of our success must be ascribed to God alone, who makes use of the foolish things of this world to confound the wise and the weak things of the world to bring to naught those who are mighty. The poor rail-splitter, who in these four years of severe schooling had at last learned that only a military man could carry on military operations; whose vanity and self-sufficiency lost us Chancellorsville and Fredericksburg; whose political jealousy kept one of our ablest generals unemployed for two years and at last sent him to Europe because nothing could be given him to do on this continent; whose indecent speeches and stories made him and the nation a byword; whose weakness allowed unlimited plunder by those around him, even members of his own family; whose undignified haste in going to Richmond in the rear of a conquering army and placing himself in the seat, still warm, of Jefferson Davis, sending for Mrs. Lincoln and receiving the visits of his rebellious subjects, was the regret of all noble-minded people! All this will be forgotten in this shameful, cowardly act of his assassination, whilst his heart was full of forgiveness of his enemies, and whilst he was planning for the good of all, having only now just begun to understand the work which four years ago the *South,* by their rebellion, by their desertion of the Democrats of the North, thrust upon him. For it was the rejection of Douglas by the Charleston Convention four years ago that elected Abraham Lincoln and Jefferson Davis, and it was not any fault in Abraham Lincoln. Nor can we blame him that when elected by a legal majority, he accepted the Presidency. . . . as President of the United States, his government as that of right and law was the one to be sustained by all lovers of their country.

[Daly, *Diary of a Union Lady,* pp. 348–355.]

Before the final battles for Richmond and Petersburg began, Charleston, South Carolina, was captured by Union forces in mid-February, 1865. Several weeks later, Dr. Esther Hawks was in captured Charleston present at a mammoth celebration at Fort Sumter, four years after its surrender in April, 1861—with General (Major in 1861) Robert Anderson, Henry Ward Beecher, William Lloyd Garrison, and other notables on hand. She was in Charleston when she learned of Lee's surrender and of Lincoln's assassination—and she noted that at least one teacher (white Southerner) expressed approval of the assassination.

[Charleston, South Carolina April, 1865]

April 10th   Went into the Normal School this morning and assumed command. . . . .

Great preparations are being made to commemorate the event of raising the old flag over Ft. Sumpter [Sumter]—by Gen. Anderson—none but invited guests will attend—a great company of illustrious names are expected from the north—and the occasion will be one long remembered.

Thurs. [Wednesday] 12th. . . . The news of the evacuation of Richmond, and its occupancy by our troops today confirmed and the still more joyful intelligence of the surrender of Lee's entire army to Gen. Grant. The victory is complete—the surrender unconditional! The army disbanded—soldiers to return home, and all the officers paroled! The city is wild with rejoicing. The colored people go about singing "Glory to God! all our trials seem o'er!"—There is great rejoicing in the city. . . .

Friday 14th   We were astir bright and early. At 9.A.M. a carriage came to take us—(Mr & Mrs. M. [Morse] Miss B. [Buttrick] Dr. Bennett and myself) to the wharf, where we, with a large company of citizens, visitors and offices went on board the *Canonacus* for the Ft. . . . The beautiful and novel appearance of the Fort was sufficient to engage our attention until the arrival of the distinguished visitors. . . . Gen. Anderson was the hero of the occasion and headed the procession—he is a tall thin white-haired man, but every inch a soldier—next came Henry Ward Beecher who is the orator of the day, and with him Mrs. Beecher, then Senetor Wilson—Geo. Thompson of Eng. Wm. L. Garrison—Theodore Tilton, Judge Kelly & Kellogg of Penn.—and a great many other distinguished visitors and military and navy offices. . . . Beecher was the orator for the occasion. An attempt to give an idea of his speach would be worse than useless—suffice it, that he held the vast audience by the spell of his eloquence, bound for more than an hour. . . . Then the same old flag went up, raised by the hands of Gen. Anderson, amidst the shouts and tears of the audience. Maj. Gen. Anderson was very much affected during the ceremonies—as indeed was everyone. . . . It was a scene never to be forgotten!—and we all hope, never to be repeated The glorious old flag floats once more over the spot where it was for the first time humbled! . . .

19th   School was hardly open this morning before Mr. Hurley came in and told me that President Lincoln had been assassinated—and that Sect. Seward was just alive, an attempt haveing been made to murder him at the same time. It seemed too horrible to believe! When he made the announcement to the school—many of the older children cried aloud. It seemed impossible to go on with school exercises. Soon after Mr. H. [Hurley] had gone several of the large girls who are in classes taught by the white southern teachers, came to me, weeping bitterly and begged to be taken out of their classes. I let them go home at the time and must watch my teachers for any *expression* of disloyalty. The greatest gloom pervades the city. Every native is looked at suspiciously—and I have no doubt but the least expression of gratification at this national calamity will be dealt roughly with. . . . There are constant complaints of teachers expressing disloyal sentiment in hearing of the children and I have been obliged to dissmiss one of them for speaking with disrespect of the murdered President. . . .

26th   Went to school in good season to day. . . . My teachers are not the most efficient. I have but two northern ones. Had to turn one out of school last week for expressing disloyal sentiments before the school children. Miss Peoples—she denies the charge but I have no reason to doubt the girls who say they heard her say that "Lincoln ought to have been murdered four years ago." . . .

May 1st . . . just heard the good news that Johnson and Beauregard have surrendered with their entire army! So the "rebellion" is over! Four long years of the most terrible and bloody warfare any nation every [sic.]

endured, and the old flag floats triumphant over us again—with its glory undimmed and every star brighter than before; "Glory to God! who hath given us the victory!!" . . .

May 2nd   The official announcement of the death of the President only reached us to-day and all business has been suspended by order of the Sect. of War so no schools for today. The public buildings, Military Hd. Qtrs., schoolhouses and a few other places are draped with black.—The colored people are frightened and apprehensive. They feel a personal loss, and fear the result of it to themselves!

[*A Woman Doctor's Civil War*, pp. 128–131, 133–137, 139.]

At the time of Lincoln's assassination, Frederick Douglass was at his home in Rochester, New York. The last time Douglass had visited Lincoln in the White House was on March 4, 1865, in the evening after Lincoln had delivered his Second Inaugural Address. Douglass had been in the crowd that heard the address (as was John Wilkes Booth), and had been seen in the crowd by Lincoln. That night, Douglass attended the Inaugural Ball at the White House, despite the efforts of some guards to prevent his entrance. Douglass described the events of that Inauguration Day in an edition of his autobiography published in 1881:

It was my good fortune to be present at [Lincoln's] inauguration in March, and to hear on that occasion his remarkable inaugural address . . . .

The inauguration, like the election, was a most important event. . . . Reaching the Capitol, I took my place in the crowd where I could see the Presidential procession as it came upon the east portico, and where I could hear and see all that took place. . . . [the] solemn words of [The Second Inaugural Address by] our martyred president . . . struck me at the time, and have seemed to me ever since to contain more vital substance than I have ever seen compressed in a space so narrow; yet on this memorable occasion when I clapped my hands in gladness and thanksgiving at their utterance, I saw in the faces of many about me expressions of widely different emotion.

On this inauguration day, while waiting for the opening of the ceremonies, I made a discovery in regard to the Vice President—Andrew Johnson. There are moments in the lives of most men, when the doors of their souls are open, and unconsciously to themselves, their true characters may be read by the observant eye. It was at such an instant I caught a glimpse of the real nature of this man, which all subsequent developments proved true. I was standing in the crowd by the side of Mrs. Thomas J. Dorsey, when Mr. Lincoln touched Mr. Johnson, and pointed me out to him. The first expression which came to his face, and which I think was the true index of his heart, was one of bitter contempt and aversion. Seeing that I observed him, he tried to assume a more friendly appearance; but it was too late; it was useless to close the door when all within had been seen. His first glance was the frown of the man, the second was the bland and sickly smile of the demagogue. I turned to Mrs. Dorsey and said, "Whatever Andrew Johnson may be, he certainly is no friend of our race." ...

In the evening of the day of the inauguration, another new experience awaited me. The usual reception was given at the executive mansion, and though no colored persons had ever ventured to present themselves on such occasions, it seemed now that freedom had become the law of the republic, now that colored men were on the battle-field mingling their blood with that of white men in one common effort to save the country, it was not too great an assumption for a colored man to offer his congratulations to the President with those of other citizens. I decided to go. . . . It was finally arranged that Mrs. Dorsey should bear me company, so together we joined in the grand procession of citizens from all parts of the country, and moved slowly towards the executive mansion. I had for some time looked upon myself as a man, but now in this multitude of the èlite of the land, I felt myself a man among men. I regret to be obliged to say, however, that this comfortable assurance was not of long duration, for on reaching the door, two policemen stationed there took me rudely by the arm and ordered me to stand back, for their directions were to admit no persons of my color. The reader need not be told that this was a disagreeable setback. But once in the battle, I did not think it well to submit to repulse. I told the officers I was quite sure there must be some mistake, for no such order could have emanated from President Lincoln; and if he knew I was at the door he would desire my admission. . . . a gentleman who was passing in, recognized me, and I said to him: "Be so kind as to say to Mr. Lincoln that Frederick Douglass is detained by officers at the door." It was not long before Mrs. Dorsey and I walked into the spacious East Room, amid a scene of elegance such as in this country I had never witnessed before. Like a mountain pine high above all others, Mr. Lincoln stood, in his grand simplicity, and *home-like beauty*. Recognizing me, even before I reached him, he exclaimed, so that all around could hear him, "Here comes my friend Douglass." Taking me by the hand, he said, "I am glad to see you. I saw you in the crowd to-day, listening to my inaugural address; how did you like it?" I said, "Mr. Lincoln, I must not detain you with my poor opinion, when there are thousands waiting to shake hands with you." "No, no," he said, "you must stop a little, Douglass; there is no man in the country whose opinion I value more than yours. I want to know what you think of it?" I replied, "Mr. Lincoln, that was a sacred effort." "I am glad you liked it!" he said, and I passed on, feeling that any man, however distinguished, might well regard himself honored by such expressions, from such a man.

It came out that the officers at the White House had received no orders from Mr. Lincoln, or from any one else. They were simply complying with an old custom, the outgrowth of slavery.

[*Life and Times of Frederick Douglass, Written By Himself* (1881). Facsimile

Douglass attended a hastily called public memorial meeting in Rochester, New York, on the day of Lincoln's death, April 15, 1865. Not having been invited to speak at the gathering, Douglass was seated in the audience, but from that audience there arose a cry that Douglass address the crowd. His remarks were printed in a Rochester newspaper and are reprinted here from a present-day collection of Douglass's writings.

Our Martyred President: An Address Delivered in Rochester, New York, on 15 April 1865 . . .

Mayor Moore and Fellow Citizens: This call to address you on this occasion was quite unexpected to me, and one to which I find it almost impossible to respond. If you have deep grief in the death of Abraham Lincoln, and feel in it a severe stab at Republican institutions, I feel it on all these accounts and more. I feel it as a personal as well as national calamity; on account of the race to which I belong and the deep interest which that good man ever took in its elevation. . . . A dreadful disaster has befallen the nation. It is a day for silence and meditation; for grief and tears. Yet I feel that though Abraham Lincoln dies, the Republic lives; (cheers;) though that great and good man, one of the noblest men [to] trod God's earth, (applause,) is struck down by the hand of the assassin, yet I know that the nation is saved and liberty established forever. (Loud applause.) . . .

Only the other day, it seemed as if this nation were in danger of losing a just appreciation of the awful crimes of this rebellion. We were manifesting almost as much gratitude to Gen. Lee for surrendering as to Gen. Grant for compelling him to surrender! (Cheers.) It seemed to me that Gen. Lee was about the most popular man in America. (Applause and laughter.) . . . I was afraid the American people were growing weak. It may be in the inscrutable wisdom of Him who controls the destinies of Nations, that this drawing of the Nation's most precious heart's blood was necessary to bring us back to that equilibrium which we must maintain if the Republic was to be permanently redeemed. (Applause.) . . . if treason expects to gain anything by this hell-black assassination, it will be awfully disappointed. To-day, to-day as never before this North is a unit! (Great applause.) To-day, to-day as never before, the American people . . . resolve . . . that they will exact ample security for the future! (Cheers.) And if it teaches us this lesson, it may be that the blood of our beloved martyred President will be the salvation of our country. . . .

This new demonstration of the guilt of slavery, teaches another lesson. Hereafter we must not despise any hand or any arm that has been uplifted in defence of the Nation's life. Let us not be in too much haste in the work of restoration. Let us not be in a hurry to clasp to our bosom that spirit

which gave birth to Booth. When we take to our arms again, as brethren, our Southern foes, let us see to it that we take also our Southern friends. (Cheers.) Let us not forget that justice to the negro is safety to the Nation. . . . Let us not remember our enemies and disenfranchise our friends. The black man will not only run everywhere to bring us information and to warn us of dangerous plots, through marsh and fen and forest, will not only bear exposure and privation, and lead and feed our fugitive prisoners . . . will not only build for you ramparts of earth and solid stone, but they offer you ramparts of flesh, and fight the battles of the nation amid contumely and persecution. (Cheers.) For the safety of all, let justice be done to each. I thank you, gentlemen, for the privilege of mingling my sorrows and hopes with yours on this memorable occasion.
[*The Frederick Douglass Papers: Series One.* Vol. 4. Edited by John W. Blassingame and John R. McKivigan. New Haven and London, Yale University Press. Copyright 1991 by Yale University, pp. 74–79. Permission to print this passage granted by Yale University Press.]

Ten days after Samuel Cormany had recorded in his diary the surrender of Lee's army, he (still with his regiment in Virginia) noted briefly his shock and sorrow at the assassination of Lincoln:

April 19, 1865 Wednesday. . . . Spring is here—Trees are leafing and blooming . . . and every thing seems gay and happy, and yet We all mourn, aye! more. For the Great Man—Great above all others in the U.S. is Dead! by an Assassin—and Who can Fill the vacancy?

Rachel Cormany in April and May, 1865, was living with her aunt and uncle on their Pennsylvania farm. Her diary entries during those months mention her dismay at the assassination of Lincoln ("My God what does it all mean—Is anarchy & destruction coming upon us?"), but that dismay seems to have been matched by her despair and weariness with the conditions of her own life:

April 4, 1865 Rainy day. daughter had Croup last night for first time, seemed almost strangled, sat up a long time to watch her . . . feel tired. News has reached us that Richmond & Petersburg have fallen—Salutes were fired. . . .
April 12, 1865 This is my 29th Birthday. Not a very gay day for me. Uncle & Aunt are both sick. Still they are not bedfast. I do the milking & in fact all the work. . . .
April 15, 1865 Baked bread pies & cake—every thing got very nice, did the cleaning &c—Well I nearly gave out before I got done. . . . This P.M. a neighbour came in & told us a dispatch had come that President Lincoln was assassinated. The report is that the President was going to a theatre & was shot just as he stepped on the platform to go in, & that he died this morning. Also that Sec. Seward had been indisposed and an attempt was made to assassinate him—O! how dreadful it seems. The one that shot the

Pres. was caught—I feel like weeping over the nations loss. My God what does it all mean—Is anarchy & destruction coming upon us? When will the end be—My God hasten the time when peace shall reign again. O! for a word from my dear husband. Hope he is safe & well—. . . I am very tired head aches considerable. . . .

May 10, 1865   It has been cloudy all week & rained every day—. . . I feel so lonely—Cora is so full of her fun & pranks—that she annoys the old people. I whip & punish her often but it is no sooner over than forgotten & the same thing done again I feel this evening as if it would be a blessing to the world in general & myself in particular if Cora & I could just shut my (our) eyes never to open in this world—It is not right to feel thus. Hence I pray for Grace to live right & to overcome evil. In seven weeks I have received but three letters from my husband which is so unusual that I do not know what to make of it. He has always been so punctual in writing. O! how wretched I am.

[*The Cormany Diaries*, pp. 542–543, 546.]

Thomas M. Chester was still in Richmond when he learned of Lincoln's assassination. He noted that "loyal people" there were stricken with sadness, but he suggested (as had Dr. Esther Hawks in Charleston) that some Southern whites expressed satisfaction over Lincoln's death:

Richmond, April 17, 1865.

The dreadful intelligence from Washington was received in this city yesterday about noon. The first report came that he [President Lincoln] was dead, which smote the hearts of the loyal people with deep sadness, but they resolved not to credit it. But soon the official confirmation removed all doubts, and the people were overwhelmed with profound grief. The effect of this sad news has filled the heart of loyalty with mourning, and caused the rebels to quake with apprehension. . . . Persons who were prominently connected with the rebellion have signified their intention, and will soon move in public meetings, to denounce the act in fitting language, and adopt such expressions of condolence as the circumstances require. This may serve a purpose, and may for a time pass for genuine sincerity, but to every reflecting mind there can be but one conclusion—that the death of the President of the United States is another one of the infamous crimes which logically followed the efforts of treason to dismember the Union. It was, no doubt, committed at the instigation of traitors, with the object of affording them the consolation of making good their boast that Abraham Lincoln should never be acknowledged as their President. This class of persons need a little looking after, or we shall soon learn that some other idol of the loyal North has been murdered by those whose opportunities for slaying Union patriots in the field have so greatly diminished, but who do not hesitate to avail themselves of the services of the assassin. . . .

Petersburg, April 19, 1865

Jubilant Traitors

It matters not where I may go, whether stopping in towns or cities, or passing through the country, the unfeigned grief of an afflicted people, caused by the assassination of President Lincoln, is everywhere manifested by loyal hearts. There is no disguising the fact that the paroled rebel officers and soldiers, strutting about in their red sashes, swords, and pistols, evince the most jubilant manifestations of satisfaction. Such exhibitions were always offensive to the soldiers of the Union, but since the murder of the fountain head of loyalty, by the conspiracy of treason, they have become an outrage upon the feelings of our patriot troops. Every consideration of right, as well as justice to the memory of the venerated dead and respect for the feelings of living heroes, demands that these arrogant rebels, who are hourly declaring that, as soon as they are exchanged, they are resolved to enter the field in behalf of Jeff Davis, should be stripped of the villainous gray in which they delighted to murder soldiers of the Union, and the color stamped with infamy.
[Chester, *Dispatches*, pp. 310–313.]

The reactions to the events of April, 1865, by four Unionists of the Cast of Characters are not available. We have no record of the views of Cyrus Pringle, and no entries in Charlotte Forten's journal from May 15, 1864, to November, 1885, have survived. Long before April, 1865, the war, as we have seen, had taken the lives of James Gooding and Marcus Spiegel.

Confederates

Just as Lee's surrender brought unbounded joy to most Unionists, it brought deep gloom to most Confederates. Lincoln's assassination elicited overwhelming grief and outrage from many Unionists, but individual Confederates differed one from another in their response to Lincoln's death.

Mary Chesnut viewed the events of April, 1865, without hope and without illusion, from the home of the Chesnuts at Chester, South Carolina. There they were visited by Mrs. Jefferson (Varina) Davis on her journey away from Richmond, but even the momentary pleasure of that visit was tinged with sadness and gloom. Mary Chesnut continued to speculate about what the slaves were thinking beneath the "shining black mask they wear." "This foul murder" was her own description of Lincoln's assassination, but she quoted an acquaintance who called the death of Lincoln "a warning to tyrants."

[Chester, South Carolina] *April 7, 1865.* Richmond has fallen—and I have no heart to write about it. Grant broke through our lines. Sherman cut through them. . . .

They are too many for us.

Everything lost in Richmond, even our archives.

Blue-black is our horizon. . . .

With this storm of woe impending, we snatched a moment of reckless gaiety—Major and Mrs. Hamilton, Captain Barnwell, and Ogden—patriots supposed to be sunk in gloomy despondency. We played cards. Then the stories told were so amusing I confess I laughed to the point of tears.

I knew the trouble was all out there, but we put it off, kept it out one evening—let it bang at the door as it would. . . .

April 15, 1865. . . . Mrs. Davis came. We went down to the cars at daylight to receive her. She dined with me. Lovely little Piecake, the baby, came, too. . . .

In fact, it was a luncheon or breakfast she stayed for here. Mrs. Brown prepared a dinner for her at the station. I went down with her. She left here at five o'clock.

My heart was like lead, but we did not give way. She was as calm and smiling as ever. . . .

April 19, 1865. . . .

[Charlotte, N.C.] April 7th, 1865

My very dear Friend,

. . . Out of the depths of wretchedness and uncertainty, the *worst* has raised and buoyed me a little. I, at least, expect nothing more just now of a public nature. . . .

So I am sitting down, taking account of my dead hopes. There is one effect of this stifling pressure upon us which is not altogether undesirable—we are benumbed. . . .

I hear horrid reports about Richmond. It is said that all below 9th Street to the Rocketts has been burned by the beggars who mobbed the town. The Yankee performances have not been chronicled.

May God take our cause into His own hands. . . .

With love to your dear husband from Maggie and myself.

Believe me very affectionately and sincerely your friend.

[Varina Davis] . . .

April 22, 1865. This yellow Confederate quire of paper blotted by my journal has been buried three days with the silver sugar dish, teapot, milk jug, and a few spoons and forks that follow my fortunes as I wander. . . .

It has been a wild three days. Aides galloping around with messages. Yankees hanging over us like the sword of Damocles. We have been in queer straits. We sat up at Mrs. Bedon's, dressed, without once going to bed for forty-eight hours. And we were aweary. . . .

Colonel Cad Jones came with a dispatch, a sealed secret dispatch. It was for General Chesnut. I opened it.

Lincoln—old Abe Lincoln—killed—murdered—Seward wounded!

Why? By whom? It is simply maddening, all this.

I sent off messenger after messenger for General Chesnut. I have not the faintest idea where he is, but I know this foul murder will bring down worse miseries on us.

Mary Darby says: "But they murdered him themselves. No Confederates in Washington."

"But if they see fit to accuse us of instigating it?"

"Who murdered him?"

"Who knows!"

"See if they don't take vengeance on us, now that we are ruined and cannot repel them any longer."

Met Mr. Heyward. He said: . . . See, our army are deserting Joe Johnston. That is the people's vote against a continuance of the war. And the death of Lincoln—I call that a warning to tyrants. He will not be the last president put to death in the capital, though he is the first." . . .

April 23, 1865. My silver wedding day—and, I am sure, the unhappiest day of my life. . . .

Buck wrote the epitaph of the Southern Confederacy. I forget all but the rhymes.

Lee's tears—outsiders sneers—Yankees' jeers. Did we lose by imbecility or because one man cannot fight ten for more than four years? We waited and hoped. They organized and worked like moles with the riches of all the world at their backs. They have made their private fortunes by their country's war. We talked of negro recruits. The Yankees used them— 18 million against six. The odds too great. . . .

Someone asked coolly, "Will General Chesnut be shot as a soldier—or hung as a senator?"

"I am not of sufficient consequence," answered he. "They will stop short of brigadiers—and then, I resigned my seat in the Senate months before there was any secession."

"But after all, it is only a choice between drumhead court-martial, short shrift, and a lingering death at home from starvation—&c&c."

And these negroes—unchanged. The shining black mask they wear does not show a ripple of change—sphinxes. Ellen has had my diamonds to keep for a week or so. When the danger was over she handed them back to me, with as little apparent interest in the matter as if they were garden peas. . . .

Joe Johnston has made his last retreat—as Stonewall and Lee have gained their last victory.

[*Mary Chesnut's Civil War*, pp. 782–783, 785–787, 791–795.]

Mrs. Mary Jones, by the end of March, 1865, concluded that the Jones plantations in southeast Georgia were unsafe from possible further attacks by Union soldiers and by marauding bands, and she undertook a difficult and hazardous two-week journey to her brother's plantation, "Refuge," in southwest Georgia

(Baker County). Mrs. Jones's correspondence with her children, and with various other relatives, reveals both how long it took for the news of Lee's surrender and of Lincoln's assassination to reach south Georgia, and also how disrupted were the conditions of everyday life there. Caroline, the daughter of Mrs. Jones, makes the only mention of Lincoln's assassination—"the righteous retribution upon Lincoln."

Mrs. Mary Jones to Mrs. Susan M. Cumming

Montevideo, *Saturday*, March 25th, 1865

My dear Sister, . . . we have concluded to leave this place on Wednesday of the coming week, stay Wednesday night with Julia on Taylor's Creek, *D.V.* We hope most fervently you will be able to move at the same time, and that we may be permitted to go together. We will have only our buggies, *and a one-horse cart* to help us with our baggage, provisions, etc., and *six* servants, one of them an infant. This is a very short notice and very limited conveyance, but we can do no better. I cannot even take Mr. Jones's papers that I value above all things. My heart is very sad. But God reigns!

Do let me know your plans. . . .

Ever your affectionate sister,
Mary Jones.

Mrs. Susan M. Cumming to Mrs. Mary Jones

Flemington, *Saturday*, April 15th, 1865

My dear Sister,

You can scarce imagine the pleasure your letter gave us. . . . I feel most thankful that amid the perils and dangers of the way you had progressed so far, and trust you are safely lodged in Cousin John's hospitable mansion ere this. . . .

A Mr. Smith has just come here from Savannah, and says Richmond has fallen on the 5th after heavy loss on both sides. Mr. Rahn's son William was killed in North Carolina on the 8th of March. Mr. Grest's Swiss nephew and Mrs. Spencer's son Captain Spencer are dead. Oh, that these days of suffering affliction may be shortened for the elect's sake! . . .

Your affectionate sister,
S. M. Cumming.

Mrs. Mary Jones to Col. William Maxwell

Refuge, *Saturday*, April 22nd, 1865

My dear Brother,

We left Liberty on the 31st of March and reached the home of my dear brother on the 13th of April, where we received the warmest welcome. . . .

Much as I regretted your not coming with us at this time, I often rejoiced that you were spared the fatigue and exposure of the journey. We had to camp out several nights, and traveled often from daylight to dark, not making over sixteen or twenty miles. . . .

On Wednesday of this week we were all thrown into great distress. The Yankees were reported within ten miles of us and advancing with cannon. . . . We have every reason to apprehend their raid through this country now that Columbus is in their hands. And God alone knows what will become of this land if they should desolate it as they did ours. . . .

My dear brother, I am deeply concerned for my poor servants, and for the fate of my home, containing everything of value that I have in the world. Do if possible send an occasional message to my people. . . . *This is a far-off* land; I think a whole continent lies between Liberty and Baker. . . .

Ever your affectionate sister,
Mary Jones.

Mrs. Mary Jones to Col. Charles C. Jones, Jr.

Refuge, *Tuesday,* April 25th, 1865

My dear Son,

. . . We reached my brother's home on Thursday the 13th, where we received the warmest welcome. It was my intention so soon as I was rested from the fatigues of the journey to take your dear child with Susan your servant and proceed immediately on to Augusta, hoping that I would find uninterrupted communication by railroad from Albany to Augusta. The recent developments of the enemy have disappointed these plans. . . . *The report* of an armistice for ninety days has reached us; but in this *far-off land* it seems very difficult to obtain any reliable information of the state of the country. We have been in great fear of an inroad upon this section. God in mercy grant us protection and deliverance from such suffering! . . .

Your affectionate mother,
Mary Jones.

Mrs. Caroline S. Jones to Mrs. Mary Jones

Augusta, *Sunday,* April 30th, 1865

My dearest Mother,

. . . How my heart sank within me when I heard of the successive capture of Selma, Montgomery, and Columbus, fearing it was but a prelude to the devastation of the rich and coveted acres of Southwest Georgia, and that my dear mother and sister might again be called to pass through the trying scenes they have just passed! . . .

We are almost paralyzed here by the rapid succession of strange and melancholy incidents that have marked the last few weeks—the sudden collapse of our tried and trusted General Lee and his army, about which, sad as it is, I can feel no mortification, for I know he did all that mortal man could do; then the rumors of peace, so different from the rapturous delight of a *conquered peace* we all looked forward to; then the righteous retribution upon Lincoln. One sweet drop among so much that is painful is that he at least cannot raise his howl of diabolical triumph over us. . . .

You will be grieved to hear that our storeroom was broken into and one-third of our flour and every vestige of bacon we owned in the world stolen from us a few nights ago. . . . I have taken the hint and moved what little I had left upstairs into the garret. . . .

Most affectionately your daughter,
Caroline Jones

[*The Children of Pride*, pp. 1260–1262, 1265–1269.]

No records have survived that indicate how John Cotton responded to the military collapse of the Confederacy and to the assassination of Lincoln.

The entries by David G. Harris in his journal in April and May, 1865, indicate that the news of the last days of the Confederacy took almost as long to reach his farm in upland South Carolina as it did to reach members of the Jones family in south Georgia. As late as April 18, Harris wrote of his imminent return to the Confederate army, and only on April 21 did he learn of Lee's surrender. Harris's response to military defeat differed from that of Mary Chesnut and the members of the Jones family: They mourned the collapse of their entire way of life, whereas Harris noted with relief that he could stay with his family and his farm, rather than returning to the army. He did not mention the assassination of Lincoln.

April 11. The day is cool & damp, & for a long time I have been oppressed with terible bad cold. In the night I can scarcely sleep. Em & the girls are raising a fine lot of poultry. Richmond & Petersburg has been given up to the yankeys &c. . . .

April 16. . . . I did expect to have gone back to my Regiment long before this, but have been putting if off from day to day. Now I think that I am sure to go in a few days. . . .

April 18. In the fore noon, four hands busy planting corn in the Long Bottom. . . . Spring is upon us in all its glory & pleasure. I have become interested in my farm again & am lo[a]th to leave it and return to the army. I had much rather be at home than in the army & had much rather face my family than Yankeys. But so it is, and love it or not love it, my country claims my services & they will have it. Many men has come home from the army. Some to stay if they can, while others are willing to return after staying a few days with their family. . . .

April 21. *Went to the village to hear the news. Lee has surrendered. Johnstone is about to surrender.* The soldiers are coming home in gangs & we have gone up the Spout. Perhaps it is all for the best. At least, I am releived from the army at present. . . . I am now going to work insted of to the war. I think I will like it the best. . . .

May 1.   The first of May is generally looked forward to as a day of pleasure & beauty on account of the mildness of the weather & the flowry season. But this has not been a day of pleasure to many in Spartanburg
village because *The Yankey are in the village* to day. But they have done no
injury to private propperty, with the exception of taking every good horse
& mule they could find. They took three good mules and one good horse
from father. They left the village this evening, having entered it
yesterday. . . .

May 2.   Went to the village to hear the news. The inhabitants had been
badly frightened but not much hurt. The yankeys have all departed and
gone their way rejoiceing. We certainly are badly whipped. Georgia,
Florida, South Carolina, North Carolina & Virginia have . . . surrendered.
[*Piedmont Farmer*, pp. 370–373.]

16. AFTER FOUR LONG YEARS OF WAR: PERSONAL EXPERIENCES IN PERSPECTIVE

*"Did we lose by imbecility," Mary Chesnut asked in her diary entry of April
23, 1865, "or because one man cannot fight ten for more than four years?" In posing this question, Mary Chesnut reflected an urge to come to terms with her personal experiences since 1861, to understand what her wartime experience meant
from the vantage point of 1865. Such comments in the last few months of the
fighting by several of the Confederates and Unionists presented in this volume
provide some indication of how they viewed their personal experience as the war
wound down. Some of those 1865 comments, just as comments made earlier in the
war, mentioned the will of God, or the actions of God.*

*Mary Chesnut's question about how the Confederates lost the war expressed
an attitude common among individuals on the losing side, whether in wars or in
other types of conflicts, whether in the Southern United States in the 1860s or in
other places at other times. "Losers" usually seem to feel a greater psychological
pressure than do "winners" to explain to themselves and to others the outcome of
the conflict in which they have been engaged. Since our cause was morally (or cul-
turally or intellectually) superior, so runs the thought that gnaws at the consciousness of losers, why did it not triumph as it should have?*

*There was little question by April, 1865, that such Confederates as Mary
Chesnut or the members of the Jones family were losers. After accompanying
Mary Chesnut and Mary Jones from the hopeful and exciting days of 1861 to the
gloom and defeat of 1865, it is understandable that they both came to look to Job
for solace. Like Job, Mary Chesnut and Mary Jones had seen their possessions dis-
appear and their lives permanently changed. The society that had sustained the
two Confederate women at its apex seemed to them to be collapsing and engulf-
ing them in its ruins. Both women had fallen from their lofty positions of social
prestige and personal well-being to an uncertain future, each reduced to flight*

from the armed forces of their enemy. Mary Jones, in effect, spoke for both of them when she wrote in her journal under the date of January 7, 1865:

> As I stand and look at the desolating changes . . . I can enter into the feelings of Job when he exclaimed: 'Naked came I out of my mother's womb, and naked shall I return thither; the Lord gave, and the Lord hath taken away.'

The words of Job could now in 1865 seem to both Mary Jones and Mary Chesnut a realistic description of their lives, a terse summary of the meaning of their personal experience in the Civil War.

Unlike Mary Jones and Mary Chesnut, the members of the Cotton and Harris families had never occupied an elevated place in the social, economic, or political life of the Confederacy. Thus, neither John and Mariah Cotton nor David and Emily Harris had as much to lose, in a material sense, as did the Chesnut and Jones families when the Confederacy was defeated. Moreover, armed enemy soldiers had not come to the very doorsteps of the Harris and (so far as is known) the Cotton families, had not directly threatened the homes and personal security of family members who were not in uniform. The writings of members of the Cotton and Harris families in the last few months of the fighting did not suggest that the military defeat of the Confederacy meant the doom of their way of life. While they were loyal Confederates to the end of the war, and were dismayed by the military defeat of the Confederate armed forces, their writings seem to indicate that they accepted military defeat as reality and wished to get on with their lives.

In the last few surviving letters by John Cotton, for example, letters dated in late January and early February, 1865, he made it clear that he did not want to rejoin the Union—but that no other choice for Confederates seemed possible. Given that situation, rejoining the Union would be better done sooner than later. Cotton, not wanting to spend the remainder of his life in the army, wrote that he hoped to outlive the war "so I can once more enjoy freedom."

In a similar vein, both Emily and David Harris faced the prospect of military defeat with seeming equanimity. Emily, after noting on January 1, 1865, that South Carolina was "threatened with the dreadful ravages of the foe," stated, much as if she were in another part of the world, "Let God's will be done." She commented without criticism that "many [of her acquaintances, presumably] are willing to unite again with the hated Yankees rather than continue the hard and seemingly hopeless struggle." (Emily Harris's attitude here was in contrast to that of Mary Chesnut, who had remarked on November 6, 1864, concerning a letter from the western army that advocated peace at any price, "I call this treason.") David Harris took the news of Lee's surrender calmly:

> We have gone up the Spout. Perhaps it is all for the best. At least, I am releived from the army at present. . . . I am now going to work instead of to war. I think I will like it the best. [April 21, 1865]

Compared with the deep despair and gloomy forebodings expressed by Mary Chesnut and Mary Jones, the Harrises and John Cotton reflected a feeling almost of relief at the prospect of peace. The personal experience of civil war expressed by John Cotton and the Harrises might be summarized as a long, arduous, exhausting struggle that left them on the losing side, but able at long last in 1865 to resume their prewar, nonmilitary lives.

If "losers" in wars and other contests (such as Mary Chesnut) can feel psychological pressure to account for their side's defeat, so too "victors" in contests can feel psychological promptings. Those promptings often predispose "victors" to consider their triumph as proof positive of the superior merit of their cause in the contest, and, by extension, proof of the superior merit of themselves as individuals. From the perspective of victors, there is usually no great mystery as to why the contest turned out as it did—virtue triumphed, as it should have done, the best side (and presumably the ablest individuals) won the victory.

With that outlook, we would not expect such victors as George Templeton Strong, or Maria Daly, or Frederick Douglass, or other Unionists to worry, in the spring of 1865, about why the Union triumphed—and they did not leave a record of such worry. Rather, they described the glorious nature of the Union victory. "Four long years," wrote Dr. Esther Hawks on May 1, 1865, "of the most terrible and bloody warfare any nation every endured, and the old flag floats triumphant over us again—with its glory undimmed and every star brighter than before." In like manner, Frederick Douglass had declared on April 15, "I know that the nation is saved and liberty established forever." The Civil War experience for the Union victors was personal participation in a mighty struggle, in which, after great adversity, right and justice had triumphed.

But the assassination of President Lincoln, in the very moment of Union victory, while it served to strengthen one aspect of the victors' version of their personal experience of the war, served also to place a question mark concerning that experience. The assassination reinforced the views of the victorious Unionists in the rightness of their cause by revealing the opposite side of the coin, i.e., by demonstrating the wickedness of the Confederacy and of its ideas and actions. "The South," wrote George Templeton Strong on April 15, "has nearly filled up the measure of her iniquities at last. . . . Up with the Black Flag now!" From Richmond on April 17, Thomas M. Chester declared that there could be "but one conclusion—that the death of the President of the United States is another one of the infamous crimes which logically followed the efforts of treason to dismember the Union."

The tragic assassination, in addition to confirming for the victors their superior morality, also raised troubling questions. One question was whether the murder of Lincoln was a portent of further evils to come. "My God," wrote Rachel Cormany on April 15, "what does it all mean—is anarchy and destruction coming upon us?" A second and related question was whether the former Confederate foes had really been vanquished, or did they still possess the potential and the desire to obstruct and thwart the Union as in the years before 1861? Was the meaning of the personal experience of Unionists, in short, actually participation in a glorious triumph, or would that turn out to be an illusion? Perhaps the death of

Lincoln, Frederick Douglass suggested in his public remarks on April 15, was, "in the inscrutable wisdom of Him who controls the destinies of Nations," necessary for the redemption of the Republic. Because of the assassination, it could seem that the Republic must again be redeemed from the threat of its foes, just as in the days of wartime.

Answers to the questions posed to the victorious Unionists by the slaying of Lincoln could not be known in April, 1865. But it was noticeable that in the comments upon the assassination, just as in comments upon other events from 1861 to 1865, some Unionists and some Confederates made reference to the hand of God. Those references at times indicated a belief that God was supporting in the war the side of the person who made the reference. As early as April, 1861, for example, Mary Chesnut reported from Charleston that some Confederate women said that "God is on our side. . . . Of course He hates the Yankees." Among Unionists, both Maria Daly and Dr. Esther Hawks suggested Divine support for their side when they wrote in 1865 that God was responsible for the victory of the Union military forces. This anomaly, as it might seem to present-day observers, of Unionists and Confederates, each thinking that God aided their own cause, was apparently not discussed by any of the Confederates or Unionists in this book's Cast of Characters. That situation did, however, draw comment and analysis from President Abraham Lincoln in March, 1865.

Both sides in the war, Lincoln noted in his Second Inaugural address, "read the same Bible, and pray to the same God; and each invokes His aid against the other." Many of his fellow Unionists, as Lincoln acknowledged, would consider it preposterous that Confederate slaveowners should expect God's help for their cause, but Lincoln expressed that Unionist view in the mildest of words, and without self-righteousness: "It may seem strange that any men should dare to ask a just God's assistance in wringing their bread from the sweat of other men's faces." Immediately countering whatever partisan sting might have attached even to his mild language, Lincoln warned himself and his fellow Unionists: "but let us judge not that we be not judged."

As Lincoln concluded his analysis, he rose above his own position as victorious Unionist: "The prayers of both [Confederates and Unionists] could not be answered; that of neither has been answered fully. The Almighty has His own purposes." In raising the possibility that God might not have supported either side in the Civil War, Lincoln transcended the views of both Unionist victors and Confederate losers. He set forth a caution of universal applicability, not only for 1865, but for victors and losers in all contests and in all eras: However virtuous, noble, and praiseworthy one considers one's own personal experience, and however despicable one considers the personal experience of one's foe, one must be forever wary of assuming that those opinions are in accord with the purposes of the Almighty.

From the perspective of Lincoln's words, the appropriate sentiment for both Unionist victors and Confederate losers concerning their own personal experience in the Civil War was: "With malice toward none, with charity for all." That

standard enunciated by Lincoln was to be difficult for ordinary mortals, whether Unionists or Confederates, to live up to in the years following 1865.
[*Collected Works of Abraham Lincoln*, Vol. VIII, p. 333.]

17. THE CAST OF CHARACTERS AFTER 1865 (IN ORDER OF APPEARANCE)

MARY BOYKIN (MILLER) CHESNUT did not continue her diary after July 1865. "I do not write often now," she explained, in beginning the entry for the last day in her diary, "—not for want of something to say, but from a loathing of all I see and hear. Why dwell upon it?" She did make attempts after 1865 to prepare her wartime diary for publication, but the diary was not published until almost two decades after her death. Her life after 1865 was marked by economic hardship and, at times, by poor health. She and her husband did manage to build a new house in Camden, South Carolina, to which they moved in 1873, and Mary lived there until her death in 1886, aged sixty-three. (Her husband and her mother had both died in 1885.)

DAVID GOLIGHTLY HARRIS did continue his farm journal for a few years after 1865, but those years were not good for him. He lost his slaves, and his farm did not prosper, despite his hard work; he had to sell land in 1872 and again in 1873 to pay taxes. Added to his economic difficulties was his bitterness over the policies of Radical Reconstruction. Perhaps due to these factors, he stopped keeping his journal in 1870—the last sentence of the last entry in the journal was: "Taxes has come again & as usual, little or no money." He died in 1875, at the age of fifty-one. EMILY LILES HARRIS did not write in the journal after 1865. Presumably she shared the difficult times faced by her husband, but she survived him by twenty-four years, dying at the age of seventy-two, in 1899.

GEORGE TEMPLETON STRONG, unlike both David G. Harris and Mary Chesnut, did continue his diary until his death, commenting there on the same wide range of topics as in the years before 1865. He remained an active observer of political and economic events, continued to attend music concerts and plays, continued his interests in Columbia University and Trinity church—until he was slowed by ill health. His ill health was the subject of the last entry in his diary, and less than a month after that last entry he died, in July, 1875, aged fifty-five.

FREDERICK DOUGLASS after 1865 continued to urge that blacks, North and South, be given the vote on the same basis as whites. To secure the vote and other goals for blacks, Douglass supported the Republican party, and loyalty to the party was a central theme in his life after the war—even though the party was falling under the control of economic special interest groups. Douglass moved to Washington, D.C., in 1872, and held a series of (relatively minor) governmental positions, including: secretary of the Santo Domingo Commission (1871); marshal (1877–1881) and recorder of deeds (1881–1886) of the District of Columbia; minister to Haiti (1889–1891). He published new and updated editions of his autobiography in 1881 and 1893. When he died in 1895 he had reached the age of seventy-eight.

THE JONES FAMILY. MARY JONES returned from her brother's plantation in Baker County (Georgia), to which she had fled in the closing days of the war, and was back at the Jones plantation, Montevideo, by October, 1865. She tried, unsuccessfully, for two years to run Montevideo on a paying basis, and then in January, 1868, moved to New Orleans to live with her daughter and her daughter's family. In December, 1868, she returned briefly to Liberty County and visited her husband's tomb, returning to New Orleans the following month. Her health declined, and she died in April, 1869, at the age of sixty-one.

CHARLES COLCOCK JONES, JR. continued to live in Savannah after the war, and attempted to manage a cotton plantation. That attempt had little success, and economic conditions in Savannah were not promising; to make matters worse, his wife's health was poor. Thus, when he received an offer in November, 1865, to be a partner in a New York law firm, he accepted, and practiced law in New York City for the next eleven years. In the spring of 1877, he returned to Georgia with his family, bought an antebellum mansion near Augusta, and practiced law there. Over the years he published some ten volumes on various aspects of Georgia history. He died in 1893, aged sixty-one.

MARIA LYDIG DALY lived after 1865 much as she had lived before. She, like George Templeton Strong, continued after 1865 to keep a diary, making entries up to within one year of her death. She and her husband continued to live in New York City and to take a prominent part in many social, educational, and political activities. They were received at the White House by President Andrew Johnson, and numbered among their friends and acquaintances the U.S. Grants and Grover Clevelands. Their personal fortunes were increased by inheritances, and they traveled to Europe and built a vacation home on Long Island. They had no children, but both of them were active supporters of the Union Home and School, an organization to care for motherless children of Union veterans. Maria Daly had been one of the founders of the Union Home and School in 1861, and she served as its president from 1865 until it was disbanded in 1884, after caring for and educating more than 5,000 children. Ill health incapacitated her in the 1890s, and she died in 1894, aged seventy-one.

Even less is known about what happened to *JOHN WEAVER COTTON* and *MARIAH HINDSMAN COTTON* after 1865 than during the Civil War years. It is known that John died not long after the war ended, in December, 1866, when he was thirty-five. The editor of the wartime Cotton letters has written concerning John Cotton: "Family tradition says he came home [from the war] in the rain with measles, from which he never recovered." [p. viii] Apparently no information is available about Mariah Cotton after 1865. "The short and simple annals of the poor."

CHARLOTTE FORTEN GRIMKÉ continued to suffer from ill health after 1865, and continued her interest in teaching the freed slaves. Whether she continued to keep a journal is not known, but if she did keep a journal after 1865, the sole portion that has survived covers only the years from 1885 to 1892. She lived in Massachusetts until 1871, then spent a year teaching in Charleston, South Carolina. In 1872, she moved to Washington, D.C., and lived there for most of the remainder of her life. While in Washington, she met and married a mulatto graduate student, Francis Grimké, who had been born a slave, an illegitimate child of a wealthy Charleston planter, Henry Grimké, and his slave mistress, Nancy Weston. Francis Grimké, twelve years younger than Charlotte, graduated from the Princeton Theological Seminary in 1878 and became pastor of a Presbyterian church in Washington, D.C. He and Charlotte had one child, a girl who died as an infant in 1880. Except for four years, 1885 to 1889, when Francis was pastor of a Presbyterian church in Jacksonville, Florida, Francis and Charlotte resided in Washington, D.C., an apparently happy and devoted couple. Charlotte became increasingly ill in the second decade of the twentieth century, and after an illness that kept her in bed for thirteen months, she died in July, 1914, aged seventy-six.

SAMUEL CORMANY and *RACHEL BOWMAN CORMANY* continued to make entries in their diaries after they were reunited in the summer of 1865, but most of the entries after 1865 have not survived. They left Chambersburg, Pennsylvania, in 1865 and lived in various locations for the next two decades—Missouri, Kansas, Canada, and Michigan. Samuel was a farmer for a time, but then became a minister of the United Brethren Church. Rachel helped with the farm and looked after the children—Cora had been born in 1862, and three more children were born after 1865, two of the three dying as infants. By 1880, Rachel was active in the Women's Christian Temperance Union and in the national kindergarten movement. The Cormanys moved back to Pennsylvania in 1886 and lived there for the rest of their lives. Both Rachel and Samuel were bothered increasingly by ill health, and Rachel died of cancer in 1899 at the age of sixty-two. Samuel remarried in 1904, but his second wife died in 1915. Samuel lived until 1921 and was almost eighty-three when he died.

CYRUS GUERNSEY PRINGLE after 1865 became a collector of botanical specimens, receiving the encouragement and aid of Professor Asa Gray of Harvard. Pringle's wife separated from him, and they were divorced in 1877. A few years later, he began botanical explorations, first of the Pacific Coast regions and then of Mexico. The later years of his life were spent at the University of Vermont, where his herbarium was located, and he supplied botanical specimens to collectors in the United States and abroad. He died in 1911, aged seventy-three.

ESTHER HILL HAWKS remained in Florida for approximately five years after the war ended, serving for a brief period in 1866 as acting assistant commissioner, Freedmen's Bureau and Abandoned Lands. She returned to Lynn, Massachusetts, in 1870, and practiced medicine there in the town where both Lydia E. Pinkham and Mary Baker Eddy lived. Quite successful in her medical practice, she became a highly respected public figure, a member of the Woman's Rights or Suffrage Club, and an elected member of the Lynn School Board. Her Civil War medical service was recognized in her unanimous election in 1899 to the New Hampshire Association of Military Surgeons at the formation of that group. She died in 1906, at the age of seventy-three.

THOMAS MORRIS CHESTER went to England in 1866, and then on to Russia for a brief visit there. When he returned from Russia to England, he studied for three years at the Middle Temple, and in 1870 he became the first black American to be called to the English bar. He returned to the United States in 1870, moved to New Orleans in 1871, and lived there for most of the next two decades, with frequent trips back to Pennsylvania. He practiced law in Louisiana and was the first black to be admitted to the Louisiana bar (1873). Taking an active part in the Reconstruction government of Louisiana, he held several state and federal offices there. In 1879 he married a black schoolteacher in New Orleans, twenty-one years younger than himself. He returned to Harrisburg, Pennsylvania, in 1892, and died there later that year from an apparent heart attack at the age of fifty-eight. By that time, most of the high hopes for black equality that had flourished in the days of emancipation had come to seem impossible in the changed spirit that had come over the nation.